ESSENTIAL INTEROPERABILITY STANDARDS

A new international instrument is needed to address access to interoperability standards and standards-essential intellectual property, which are critical to maintaining technological advancement and promoting cost-effective solutions for consumers. Applying law and economics methodologies, Simon Brinsmead systematically explores how international and domestic law deals with these matters. This important book includes an examination of the technical and economic nature of interoperability standards; a detailed analysis of the issues arising under intellectual property and competition law; an analysis of whether liability or exclusive property rules should apply with respect to interoperability standards and SEIP; and consideration of feasible international approaches. Finally, Brinsmead includes a draft of his proposed international soft law instrument as a starting point for future discussions in the field. Of interest to lawyers, regulators and scholars, this work offers a meaningful contribution to international governance, harmonization of laws and technological advancement.

SIMON BRINSMEAD is Principal Legal Officer with the Office of International Law, Attorney-General's Department (Australia), where he practises public international law. He leads teams advising on international trade and investment law and jurisdiction, immunities and international organizations law. He is experienced in WTO and investor–state dispute settlement and the negotiation of trade and investment agreements.

CAMBRIDGE INTERNATIONAL TRADE AND ECONOMIC LAW

Series editors

Dr Lorand Bartels, *University of Cambridge*
Professor Thomas Cottier, *University of Berne*
Professor Tomer Broude, *Hebrew University of Jerusalem*
Professor Andrea K. Bjorklund, *McGill University, Montréal*

Processes of economic regionalisation and globalisation have intensified over the last decades, accompanied by increases in the regulation of international trade and economics at the levels of international, regional and national laws. At the same time, significant challenges have arisen with respect to economic liberalisation, rule-based systems of trade and investment, and their political and social impacts. The subject matter of this series is international economic law, in this contemporary context. Its core is the regulation of international trade, investment, finance and cognate areas such as intellectual property and competition policy. The series publishes books on related regulatory areas, in particular human rights, labour, environment and culture, as well as sustainable development. These areas are horizontally interconnected and vertically linked at the international, regional and national levels. The series also includes works on governance, dealing with the structure and operation of international organisations related to the field of international economic law, and the way they interact with other subjects of international and national law. The series aims to include excellent legal doctrinal treatises, as well as cutting-edge interdisciplinary works that engage law and the social sciences and humanities.

Books in the series

Essential Interoperability Standards
Simon Brinsmead

Shareholders' Claims for Reflective Loss in International Investment Law
Lukas Vanhonnaeker

Transparency in the WTO SPS and TBT Agreements: The Real Jewel in the Crown
Marianna B. Karttunen

Emerging Powers in International Economic Law
Sonia E. Rolland and David M. Trubek

Commitments and Flexibilities in the WTO Agreement on Subsidies and Countervailing Measures
Jose Guilherme Moreno Caiado

The Return of the Home State to Investor-State Disputes: Bringing Back Diplomatic Protection?
Rodrigo Polanco

The Public International Law of Trade in Legal Services
David Collins

Industrial Policy and the World Trade Organization: Between Legal Constraints and Flexibilities
Sherzod Shadikhodjaev

The Prudential Carve-Out for Financial Services: Rationale and Practice in the GATS and Preferential Trade Agreements
Carlo Maria Cantore

Judicial Acts and Investment Treaty Arbitration
Berk Demirkol

Distributive Justice and World Trade Law: A Political Theory of International Trade Regulation
Oisin Suttle

Freedom of Transit and Access to Gas Pipeline Networks under WTO Law
Vitalily Pogoretskyy

Reclaiming Development in the World Trading System, 2nd edition
Yong-Shik Lee

Developing Countries and Preferential Services Trade
Charlotte Sieber-Gasser

WTO Dispute Settlement and the TRIPS Agreement: Applying Intellectual Property Standards in a Trade Law Framework
Matthew Kennedy

Establishing Judicial Authority in International Economic Law
Edited by Joanna Jemielniak, Laura Nielsen and Henrik Palmer Olsen

Trade, Investment, Innovation and Their Impact on Access to Medicines: An Asian Perspective
Locknie Hsu

The Law, Economics and Politics of International Standardisation
Panagiotis Delimatsis

The WTO and International Investment Law: Converging Systems
Jürgen Kurtz

Export Restrictions on Critical Minerals and Metals: Testing the Adequacy of WTO Disciplines
Ilaria Espa

Optimal Regulation and the Law of International Trade: The Interface between the Right to Regulate and WTO Law
Boris Rigod

The Social Foundations of World Trade: Norms, Community and Constitution
Sungjoon Cho

Public Participation and Legitimacy in the WTO
Yves Bonzon

The Challenge of Safeguards in the WTO
Fernando Piérola

General Interests of Host States in International Investment Law
Edited by Giorgio Sacerdoti, with Pia Acconci, Mara Valenti and Anna De Luca

The Law of Development Cooperation: A Comparative Analysis of the World Bank, the EU and Germany
Philipp Dann

WTO Disciplines on Subsidies and Countervailing Measures: Balancing Policy Space and Legal Constraints
Dominic Coppens

Domestic Judicial Review of Trade Remedies: Experiences of the Most Active WTO Members
Edited by Müslüm Yilmaz

The Relevant Market in International Economic Law: A Comparative Antitrust and GATT Analysis
Christian A. Melischek

International Organizations in WTO Dispute Settlement: How Much Institutional Sensitivity?
Marina Foltea

Public Services and International Trade Liberalization: Human Rights and Gender Implications
Barnali Choudhury

The Law and Politics of WTO Waivers: Stability and Flexibility in Public International Law
Isabel Feichtner

African Regional Trade Agreements as Legal Regimes
James Thuo Gathii

Liberalizing International Trade after Doha: Multilateral, Plurilateral, Regional, and Unilateral Initiatives
David A. Gantz

Processes and Production Methods (PPMs) in WTO Law: Interfacing Trade and Social Goals
Christiane R. Conrad

Non-Discrimination in International Trade in Services: 'Likeness' in WTO/GATS
Nicolas F. Diebold

The Law, Economics and Politics of Retaliation in WTO Dispute Settlement
Edited by Chad P. Bown and Joost Pauwelyn

The Multilateralization of International Investment Law
Stephan W. Schill

Trade Policy Flexibility and Enforcement in the WTO: A Law and Economics Analysis
Simon A. B. Schropp

ESSENTIAL INTEROPERABILITY STANDARDS

Interfacing Intellectual Property and Competition
in International Economic Law

SIMON BRINSMEAD

Office of International Law, Attorney-General's Department (Australia)

Shaftesbury Road, Cambridge CB2 8EA, United Kingdom

One Liberty Plaza, 20th Floor, New York, NY 10006, USA

477 Williamstown Road, Port Melbourne, VIC 3207, Australia

314–321, 3rd Floor, Plot 3, Splendor Forum, Jasola District Centre, New Delhi – 110025, India

103 Penang Road, #05–06/07, Visioncrest Commercial, Singapore 238467

Cambridge University Press is part of Cambridge University Press & Assessment, a department of the University of Cambridge.

We share the University's mission to contribute to society through the pursuit of education, learning and research at the highest international levels of excellence.

www.cambridge.org
Information on this title: www.cambridge.org/9781108823227

DOI: 10.1017/9781108913706

© Simon Brinsmead 2021

This publication is in copyright. Subject to statutory exception and to the provisions of relevant collective licensing agreements, no reproduction of any part may take place without the written permission of Cambridge University Press & Assessment.

First published 2021
First paperback edition 2023

A catalogue record for this publication is available from the British Library

Library of Congress Cataloging-in-Publication data
Names: Brinsmead, Simon, 1975– author.
Title: Essential interoperability standards : interfacing intellectual property and competition in international economic law / Simon Brinsmead, Office of International Law, Attorney-General's Department (Australia).
Description: Cambridge, United Kingdom ; New York, NY : Cambridge University Press, 2021. | Series: Cambridge international trade and economic law | Based on author's thesis (doctoral – Universität Bern, 2018). | Includes bibliographical references and index.
Identifiers: LCCN 2021000452 (print) | LCCN 2021000453 (ebook) | ISBN 9781108843010 (hardback) | ISBN 9781108913706 (ebook)
Subjects: LCSH: Internetworking (Telecommunication) – Law and legislation | Intellectual property. | Antitrust law.
Classification: LCC K564.C6 B75 2021 (print) | LCC K564.C6 (ebook) | DDC 346.04/8–dc23
LC record available at https://lccn.loc.gov/2021000452
LC ebook record available at https://lccn.loc.gov/2021000453

ISBN   978-1-108-84301-0   Hardback
ISBN   978-1-108-82322-7   Paperback

Cambridge University Press & Assessment has no responsibility for the persistence or accuracy of URLs for external or third-party internet websites referred to in this publication and does not guarantee that any content on such websites is, or will remain, accurate or appropriate.

For Penny, Esther and Jay

CONTENTS

Foreword *page* xvii
THOMAS COTTIER
Preface xix
List of Abbreviations xxi

PART I **Foundations and Problems**

1 Introduction 3

  1.1 Interoperability Standards, Network Externalities and Market Dominance 3

  1.2 Balancing the Interests of Creators and Users of Essential Interoperability Standards through Intellectual Property and Competition Law 4

  1.3 Interfacing Intellectual Property and Competition in International Economic Law 8

  1.4 Methodology 10

  1.5 Structure of This Work 14

2 Standards and Interoperability Standards 16

  2.1 The Fundamental Importance of Standards and Interoperability 16

  2.2 Defining the Concept of an Interoperability Standard 17
    2.2.1 Some Basic Definitions 17
    2.2.2 Typologies of Standards 19
    2.2.3 Interoperability Standards: Definitions 21

  2.3 Notable Interoperability Standards: from QWERTY towards an Internet of Things 25

2.3.1 Keyboard Configurations: QWERTY and Its Discontents   26
2.3.2 Video Recording Formats: the Standards War between VHS and BETAMAX   27
2.3.3 The 802.11 Family of Wireless Area Network Standards   28
2.3.4 Internet Standards: Transmission Control Protocol/Internet Protocol   29
2.3.5 Mobile Wireless Standards: from 1G to 4G and beyond   32
2.3.6 Near Field Communications Standards   33
2.3.7 Mobile Payment Standards: Cash Goes Wireless   34
2.3.8 Towards an Internet of Things   35

2.4 Who Makes Interoperability Standards?   36
2.4.1 International Organizations: the International Telecommunication Union   37
2.4.2 International Bodies: ISO, IEEE and IETF   39
2.4.3 Regional and National Standard-Setting Organizations   42
2.4.4 Private Standard-Setting Organizations and Consortia   43
2.4.5 Single-Firm Standard-Setting   44

2.5 The Creation of Interoperability Standards   44
2.5.1 Overview of the Standard-Setting Process   44
2.5.2 'Best Practice': ISO and Others   46

2.6 Economic Characteristics of Interoperability Standards: Network Effects, and How Standards Become Standard   48
2.6.1 Standardization through Force of Law   48
2.6.2 Standardization through Widespread Marketplace Acceptance   49

3 Interoperability Standards and International Economic Law   54

3.1 The Provisions of the TRIPS Agreement   54
3.1.1 The Minimum Standards of Protection Articulated in the Provisions of the TRIPS Agreement   54
3.1.2 Certain Provisions of the TRIPS Agreement Exhibiting the Character of Maximum Standards   57

3.1.3 Significance of the TRIPS Flexibilities   62

3.2 The WTO Agreement on Technical Barriers to Trade   69

3.3 The WTO Telecommunications Agreement   72

3.4 The WTO Information Technology Agreement   74

3.5 International Competition Law   75

3.6 Concluding Observations   77

PART II   **The Impact of Intellectual Property and Competition Laws**

4 Interoperability Standards and Intellectual Property   81

4.1 The Concept of Standards-Essential Intellectual Property   81

4.2 The Law and Economics of Intellectual Property Protection   81

4.3 Patents   84
    4.3.1 Standards-Essential Patents   84
    4.3.2 Standards-Essential Patents, Hold-Up and Royalty Stacking   90
    4.3.3 Defences to SEP Infringement   97
    4.3.4 Remedies for Patent Infringement   100
    4.3.5 SEPs in the Particular Context of Software Patenting   111

4.4 Copyrights   118
    4.4.1 Standards-Essential Copyright   118
    4.4.2 Remedies for Infringement of Standards-Essential Copyright   140

4.5 Protection for the Layout Topographies of Integrated Circuits   148

4.6 Trade Secrets   148

4.7 Compulsory Licensing of Intellectual Property Rights   150

4.7.1 Compulsory Licence for Established Contravention of Competition Law   150

4.8 Concluding Remarks about Standards-Essential Intellectual Property   154

5 Interoperability Standards and Competition Law   157

    5.1 Introductory Comments   157

    5.2 The Essential Facilities Doctrine   157
        5.2.1 Historical Development and Intellectual Foundations of the Essential Facilities Doctrine   158
        5.2.2 Development of the Essential Facilities Doctrine in European Cases   178
        5.2.3 The Doctrine in the Context of Intellectual Property and Interoperability Standards   182
        5.2.4 Application of the Doctrine to Interoperability Standards and Standards-Essential Intellectual Property   191
        5.2.5 The Law and Economics of the Essential Facilities Doctrine   193

    5.3 Request for Injunction in Relation to Standards-Essential Patents as a Competition Law Breach   201
        5.3.1 United States Law   202
        5.3.2 European Law   203
        5.3.3 Chinese Law   209
        5.3.4 Merits of Applying the Unilateral Disciplines to Address Injunctions for FRAND-Encumbered SEPs   209

    5.4 Excessive or Unfair Pricing   212
        5.4.1 European Law   213
        5.4.2 Chinese Law   214
        5.4.3 Excessive Pricing: Concluding Observations   215

    5.5 Misconduct or Fraud in the Creation of Standards   215
        5.5.1 United States Law   216
        5.5.2 European Law   219
        5.5.3 Chinese Law   220
        5.5.4 Conclusions Regarding Fraud and Misconduct in Standard-Setting   221

5.6 Tying   221

5.7 Horizontal Conduct   223
    5.7.1 United States Law   223
    5.7.2 Chinese Law   225
    5.7.3 European Law   225
    5.7.4 Concerted Practices and Interoperability Standards – Analysis   227

5.8 Competition Law Approaches to SEIP: Conclusions   228

PART III   **Towards Liability and Compensation**

6 Exclusive Property Rules or Liability Rules for Interoperability Standards and Standards Essential Intellectual Property?   233

  6.1 Exclusive Property Rules, Liability Rules and Inalienability Rules   233
    6.1.1 The Coase Theorem   233
    6.1.2 The Calabresi and Melamed Framework   234
    6.1.3 Extensions of the Calabresi and Melamed Framework   237

  6.2 Standards-Essential Intellectual Property: Exclusive Property Rules or Liability Rules?   239
    6.2.1 Existing Scholarship   239
    6.2.2 Analysis: Liability or Exclusive Property Rules for Standards-Essential Intellectual Property?   244
    6.2.3 The Choice between Exclusive Property Rules and Liability Rules for Standards-Essential Intellectual Property: Concluding Observations   257

  6.3 Exclusive Property Rules, Liability Rules and Refusals to Supply   258

  6.4 Implications for Injunctions and Compensation   261
    6.4.1 Implications for Injunctions   261
    6.4.2 Implications for Compensation   263
    6.4.3 Implications for Compulsory Licensing   276
    6.4.4 Broader Implications for Unilateral Competition Law Disciplines, Including the Essential Facilities Doctrine   278

7 Access to Interoperability Standards and
  Standards-Essential Intellectual Property   279
  International Dimensions

  7.1 Basis for an International Approach   279
  7.2 Binding Treaty Action or International Soft
      Law?   282
  7.3 Selecting the Appropriate Forum   288
      7.3.1 International Organization for Standardization   289
      7.3.2 International Telecommunication Union   290
      7.3.3 World Intellectual Property Organization   291
      7.3.4 World Trade Organization   292
      7.3.5 International Competition Network   293
      7.3.6 Organization for Economic Co-operation and
            Development   295
      7.3.7 Standalone Forum   296
      7.3.8 Analysis and Conclusions as to the Appropriate
            Forum   301
  7.4 The Appropriate Process to Be Followed in Developing
      an Expert Manual   305
      7.4.1 Expertise   306
      7.4.2 Adequately Representative Composition of an Expert
            Group   306
      7.4.3 Robust and Transparent Process   306
  7.5 The Appropriate Purpose and Structure of an Expert
      Manual   308
      7.5.1 General Observations   308
      7.5.2 Proposed Substantive Contents   309
  7.6 Consistency with International Law of the Proposed
      Approach   313
      7.6.1 Patents   313
      7.6.2 Copyrights   325
      7.6.3 Layout Circuits   329
      7.6.4 Trade Secrets   330
      7.6.5 Enforcement of Intellectual Property Rights   330
      7.6.6 Conclusion regarding Consistency of the Proposed Approach
            with Existing International Agreements   331

8 Concluding Observations   333

9 Draft Expert Manual   347

Bibliography   356
Index   395

FOREWORD

Value chains and trade in components presupposes a complex legal regime of interfacing and matching different products, both in domestic law and the realm of international law. It is part of an operating system in the background which often is not easy to understand. Technological standards securing the operability and interface of products, in particular in communications and information technology, show a variety of legal qualities. They may exist de facto, they may emanate from agreement in domestic or international law, or they qualify as intellectual property, either patents or copyright, or sui generis rights, thus granting monopoly and exclusive right to companies. As other companies and competitors equally depend upon such standards essential for the purpose of interface, right owners inherently enjoy a powerful position which may foster or harm technology development and competitors, and benefit or harm consumers.

The present book, based upon a doctoral thesis submitted to the University of Bern, Switzerland, carefully and extensively addresses the legal challenges encountered in the field of standards-essential intellectual property (SEIP), and in particular of standards-essential patents (SEP). Dr Brinsmead analyses different school of thought and approaches in case law, in particular in the EU, the USA and China. He carefully studies the background in international law and domestic law, in particular competition law. While the EU and China essentially rely upon competition law and in result on the essential facility doctrine containing the abuse of a dominant position, the US approach essentially relies upon restrictions inherent to intellectual property, in particular fair use and compulsory licensing. The book expounds the relevant case law in these jurisdictions and discusses pro and cons of different approaches, taking into account the literature on law and economics. It offers a wealth of information on the timely subject, from surveys of relevant international law to detailed accounts of the case law. It includes a pertinent history of the essential facility doctrine and thus of the relationship of intellectual property and competition law on both sides of the Atlantic. The author concludes by supporting an approach based upon inherent but limited restrictions of IP to liability and compensation, as opposed to property rights entitling full injunctions. He suggests developing an expert manual able to guide domestic courts within the framework of existing international law, in particular the TRIPs Agreement of the WTO. A very interesting draft proposal completes the work.

Dr Brinsmead was able to combine practical experience in the field and a deep academic interest in the subject. Readers, lawyers and policy-makers alike will greatly benefit from this combination and the clarity of a talented mind in understanding and further developing the operating system humming in the background of millions of transactions in cooperation and competition alike.

Thomas Cottier
March 2020

PREFACE

This work was drafted as a doctoral dissertation for the requirements of a Dr Iur. (PhD in Law) undertaken at the University of Bern, supervised by Professor Emeritus Thomas Cottier. The original manuscript has been revised to take account of recent developments with a view to publication. While drafting the dissertation between 2012 and 2018, I practised public international law with the Office of International Law, Attorney-General's Department in Canberra, Australia. During this time, I undertook numerous trips to Bern, to participate in doctoral seminars at the World Trade Institute and also to discuss progress with Professor Cottier and draft the dissertation. I have fond memories of the lively discussions that took place in the Silva Casa auditorium at the Institute, between Professor Cottier's many doctoral students who were undertaking their research in such a plethora of legal fields.

Between November 2017 and February 2018, I undertook a visiting fellowship with Xiamen University School of Law in Fujian Province, China. Academic staff at XMU Faculty of Law were generous with their time, and I engaged in numerous stimulating discussions and workshops there. I also made substantial progress towards the final submission draft without the competing demands of my professional work.

I must acknowledge the profound impact of Professor Cottier upon the published thesis. Many of the ideas contained within this work are his – but any remaining errors are of course mine. He was an encouraging, supportive and infinitely helpful supervisor. He brought the accumulated wisdom from his wealth of experience in supervising many previous doctoral candidates to our conversations. His grasp of the scope, breadth, structure and detail of this work have been far beyond what I could have expected from a doctoral supervisor.

I am also deeply grateful to my wife Penny and our two children Esther and Jay for help and support along the way. Doctoral research is immensely time-consuming. Their patience is greatly appreciated.

Likewise, I would like to thank my parents for their encouragement from the very outset of this project.

Thanks to many colleagues at the Australian Government with whom I held stimulating and insightful conversations about this work as it progressed. Last but not least, I must thank Finola O'Sullivan and Marianne Nield for guiding me through my introduction to the world of academic publishing.

ABBREVIATIONS

2G	Second generation
3G	Third generation
3GPP	Third Generation Partnership Project
4G	Fourth generation
5G	Fifth generation
ALAC	At-Large Community
AML	China Anti-Monopoly Law
AMPS	Advanced Mobile Phone Service
ANSI	American National Standards Institute
API	Application programming interface
ARPANET	Advanced Research Projects Network Administration
ASA	American Standards Association (predecessor to ANSI)
ASO	Address Supporting Organization
CCITT	Consultative Committee for International Telephony and Telegraphy
ccNSO	Country Code Names Supporting Organization
CD	Compact disc
CEPT	European Conference of Postal and Telecommunications Administrations
CDMA	Code Division Multiple Access
CONTU	United States Commission on the New Technological Uses of Copyrighted Works
Council for TRIPS	Council for Trade-Related Aspects of Intellectual Property Rights
CRO	Collective rights organization
CSIRO	Australia Commonwealth Scientific and Industrial Research Organization
DARPA	United States Defence Advanced Research Projects Agency
DDR-SDRAM	Double data rate synchronous dynamic random-access memory
DNS	Domain Name System
DRAM	Dynamic random-access memory
DVD	Digital versatile disc

EC	European Commission
ECJ	European Court of Justice
ECMA (now Ecma International)	European Computer Manufacturers Association
ECPR	Efficient Component Pricing Rule
EEA	European Economic Area
EEC	European Economic Community
EPC	European Patent Convention
EU	European Union
ETSI	European Telecommunications Standards Institute
FRAND	Fair, reasonable and non-discriminatory
FTC	United States Federal Trade Commission
FTC Act	United States Federal Trade Commission Act 1914
GAC	Governmental Advisory Committee
GATT 1994	General Agreement on Tariffs and Trade 1994
GATS	General Agreement on Trade in Services
GPRS	General Packet Radio Service
GNSO	Generic Names Supporting Organization
GSM	Global System for Mobile Communication
GUI	Graphical user interface
HTTP	Hypertext Transfer Protocol
IAB	Internet Architecture Board
ICANN	Internet Corporation for Assigned Names and Numbers
ICN	International Competition Network
IEEE	Institute of Electrical and Electronics Engineers
IEEE-SA	IEEE Standards Association
IEC	International Electrotechnical Commission
IETF	Internet Engineering Task Force
IMT-2000	International Mobile Telecommunications for the Year 2000
INWG	International Packet Networking Group
IP	Intellectual property
IPR	Intellectual property right
IoT	Internet of Things
IPHC	Japan Intellectual Property High Court
IPv4	Internet Protocol version 4
IPv6	Internet Protocol version 6
ISO	International Organization for Standardization
ISOC	Internet Society
ITA Committee	Committee of Participants on the Expansion of Trade in Information Technology Products
ITR	International Telecommunication Regulations
ITU	International Telecommunication Union

JEDEC	Joint Electron Device Engineering Council
JTC 1	Joint Technical Committee 1
Kbit/s	Kilobit per second
LAN	Local area network
LTE	Long-Term Evolution
Mbit/s	Megabit per second
MFN	Most-favoured-nation
MPEG	Moving Picture Experts Group
NATO	North Atlantic Treaty Organization
NDRC	China National Development and Reform Commission
NFC	Near-field communication
NTM	Non-tariff measure
OECD	Organization for Economic Cooperation and Development
OFDM	Orthogonal Frequency Division Multiplexing
OSI	Open Systems Interconnection
PAE	Patent assertion entity
PCT	Patent Cooperation Treaty
PLT	Patent Law Treaty
RAND	Reasonable and non-discriminatory
RFID	Radio Frequency Identification
SCPA	United States Semiconductor Chip Protection Act 1984
SDO	Standards development organization
SDRAM	Synchronous dynamic random-access memory
SEIP	Standards-essential intellectual property
SEP	Standards-essential patent
SPC	China Supreme People's Court
SPLT	Substantive Patent Law Treaty
SSO	Standard-setting organization
TBT Agreement	Agreement on Technical Barriers to Trade
TBT Committee	Committee on Technical Barriers to Trade
TCP/IP	Transmission Control Protocol/Internet Protocol
TDMA	Time Division Multiple Access
TFEU	Treaty on the Functioning of the European Union
TRIPS Agreement	Agreement on Trade-Related Aspects of Intellectual Property Rights
TSAG	Telecommunication Standardization Advisory Group
UK	United Kingdom
USA	United States of America
USITC	United States International Trade Commission
UTSA	United States Uniform Trade Secrets Act
VHS	Video Home System
W-CDMA	Wideband Code Division Multiple Access

W3C	World Wide Web Consortium
WG	Working group
WCT	WIPO Copyright Treaty
WPPT	WIPO Performances and Phonograms Treaty
WIPO	World Intellectual Property Organization
WLAN	Wireless local area network
WTO	World Trade Organization
WTSA	World Telecommunications Standards Assembly

PART I

Foundations and Problems

1

Introduction

This work examines the potential for international economic law to provide a harmonized approach to securing access to essential interoperability standards and standards-essential intellectual property (SEIP). In particular, it considers whether it would be both optimal and feasible to pursue the negotiation of an international instrument addressing issues arising in connection with access to essential interoperability standards and SEIP, and notably whether an essential facilities doctrine should form the primary basis for such an international initiative. While the essential facilities doctrine is ultimately found not to provide the basis for an optimal and feasible approach, this work nevertheless proposes a way forward, drawing on insights from the law and economics distinction between liability rules and exclusive property rules.

1.1 Interoperability Standards, Network Externalities and Market Dominance

Interoperability standards provide crucial information infrastructure that supports the growth of our increasingly digitized economies. In bygone eras, interoperability standards have provided the indispensable underpinnings for the development of railroads and international shipping, not to mention the keyboard layout of typewriters and keyboards. In more recent times interoperability standards have been equally critical to computing, telecommunications and the Internet. Standards will form the backbone of industries of the future such as mobile payments services and the Internet of Things (IoT). Given the fundamental importance of standards and interoperability, it is important to ensure that society is able to reap the full benefits associated with the creation, implementation and use of interoperability standards.

Many of the interoperability standards that have become essential information infrastructure were not drafted by governments. They have been drafted by groups of private actors, who came together in groupings exhibiting varying degrees of formality. Adequate incentives are needed for private actors to draft new, better standards for the future.

Yet, standardization and market dominance often go hand-in-hand. Information markets, including standardized markets, are often subject to strong network externalities, positive feedback loops and 'tipping' towards a single dominant actor; such markets frequently exhibit 'winner-take-all' or 'winner-take-most' characteristics, and can also be characterized by 'path-dependence', which in some cases might give rise to risks of an entire industry being 'locked in' to an inferior technology, owing to the pervasive effects of network externalities over time.

At the same time, the network externalities associated with interoperability standards are maximized when as many people as possible join a network – real or virtual. As such, incentives are also needed to ensure that the promoters of standards keep the standard sufficiently open, so as to obtain the widest possible dissemination and use of the standard. In many cases, optimizing these incentives involves a balancing exercise.

1.2 Balancing the Interests of Creators and Users of Essential Interoperability Standards through Intellectual Property and Competition Law

Traditionally the two most important levers for regulating interoperability standardization have been intellectual property and competition laws. Intellectual property laws provide inventors, creators of works and others a statutory, time-limited monopoly in exchange for the publication of the invention or work. Such a time-limited monopoly is generally manifested in a bundle of exclusive rights; the inventor or author is entitled to exclude others from using the invention or work.

Intellectual property rights are territorial in nature, and vary from jurisdiction to jurisdiction, with some international harmonization. There are many facets to an intellectual property right – the conditions governing its award, the scope of its exclusive rights, exceptions to it, remedies for its infringement and others. These 'facets' are levers which can be tweaked by legislators (and in common law jurisdictions, the courts) to ensure that intellectual property rights secure their underlying purpose, namely to promote innovation and thus maintain the speed of technological advance of society.

Competition laws also seek to promote innovation and growth, but they do so via a different modality – by disciplining the actions of private actors that are harmful to the competitive process. Whilst the paradigmatic competition rules concern coordinated conduct – the prohibition of price-fixing being a prime example – many jurisdictions' competition laws also address unilateral conduct, including refusals to supply goods or services and, in exceptional circumstances, refusals to licence intellectual property rights. Where harmonization of intellectual property law is partial and incomplete, international harmonization of competition law is largely absent.

Unsurprisingly, then, various jurisdictions are taking widely divergent approaches to addressing the concerns associated with access to interoperability standards and SEIP. What precisely are those concerns? First, where a de facto standard is the creation of a single, dominant firm, that firm may in some instances possess the power to control access to the standard. The European Commission's case against Microsoft Corporation (and in some ways the United States case against Microsoft also, as reflected in the remedies ultimately imposed on Microsoft) could be characterized as resulting from such a fact situation.

Microsoft, having effectively created a de facto standard in the form of its Windows operating system software, denied its competitors access to certain communication protocols indispensable to communications between the Windows operating system software and Microsoft's Active Directory server operating system software, as well as to certain 'server-server' communications protocols. For denying its competitors access to interoperability standards which were considered indispensable to competition in the market for supplying workgroup server operating systems software, Microsoft was accused by the European Commission of abusing its dominant market position pursuant to Article 82 of the Treaty of Rome (now Article 102 of the Treaty on the Functioning of the European Union). Such conduct could be characterized as the denial of access to an essential facility (namely to the relevant communications protocols).

Microsoft had succeeded in creating a de facto interoperability standard – its near-ubiquitous Windows personal computer operating system software – despite keeping certain of its interfaces secret. Moreover, Microsoft's competitors were unable to obtain details of those interfaces through reverse engineering, because of the cost and time of undertaking such a reverse-engineering exercise; in the meantime, Microsoft could easily defeat reverse-engineering attempts by updating the interfaces.[1]

---

[1] *Microsoft (Case COMP/C-3/37/792 – Microsoft)* (European Commission) [683–7]; *Microsoft v. Commission of the European Communities (Case T-201/04)* [2007] 2007 ECR II-03601 (European Court of First Instance) II–3708.

Thus, the core of the EU Microsoft case was the question of access to interoperability information. The question of intellectual property was, in a sense, incidental: Microsoft raised intellectual property as an objective justification for its refusal to provide the interoperability information to its competitors, rather than asserting its intellectual property rights in claims before the courts.

The nature of standards-essential intellectual property, in this instance standards-essential copyrights, played a larger role in the US case of *BellSouth* v. *Donnelley*, in which BellSouth Advertising and Publishing Corporation (BAPCO), a wholly-owned subsidiary of Florida's incumbent telecommunications network operator, refused to supply copyrighted telephone listings to Donnelley, who wished to create a competing directory.

Unlike in the EU Microsoft case, however, the information in question was already in the public domain, so Donnelley was able to copy it and create a rival telephone directory. BellSouth sued for copyright infringement; Donnelley counterclaimed for refusal to supply the listings, citing the essential facilities doctrine. The United States District Court for the Southern District of Florida upheld BellSouth's copyright claim and did not summarily dismiss the essential facilities counterclaim;[2] the United States Court of Appeals, Eleventh Circuit, hearing the matter on appeal, resolved the matter not through application of the essential facilities doctrine, but rather by careful application of the limiting doctrines in copyright law, notably the distinction between unprotectable ideas and protectable expressions, the need for copyrighted works to be original (little was original about BellSouth's directory, whose layout was rather commonplace), and merger doctrine.[3]

Quite similarly, in the Magill case in the EU, three broadcasters refused to supply copyrighted television guide listings to Magill, who wished to publish a weekly television guide. Magill (which does not involve any interoperability standard) was more like Donnelley than Microsoft, because the listings were already published and Mr Magill was readily able to copy them; the only impediment was the broadcasters' assertion of copyright. The European courts, including the Court of Justice,

---

[2] *BellSouth Adv & Pub* v. *Donnelley Inf Pub* [1988] 719 FSupp 1551 (United States District Court for the Southern District of Florida).

[3] *BellSouth Advertising & Pub Corp* v. *Donnelley Information Pub Inc* [1993] 999 F2d 1436 (United States Court of Appeals for the Eleventh Circuit).

1.2 BALANCING THE INTERESTS OF CREATORS

intervened to prevent the assertion of copyright, applying the doctrine of abuse of a dominant market position.[4]

Similar facts obtained in the IMS Health case, where IMS Health sought injunction to preclude its competitors from copying the format of its pharmaceutical sales data reports. Like in the Donnelley case, these facts gave rise to tension between, on the one hand, the protection of intellectual property, in this case copyright inhering in the structure of a database, and on the other hand, the need for competitors to access a reporting format which had clearly become standard in the marketplace and which was demanded by consumers (IMS Health's competitors tried to develop their own sales data formats, but customers asked for IMS Health's '1860 brick structure' instead). After complicated litigation involving both copyright claims before the German courts and rulings by the European Commission,[5] the Court of First Instance[6] and the Court of Justice[7] on a claim of abuse of a dominant market position, the case eventually settled after the German Higher Regional Court clarified that IMS Health's competitors could use the brick structure without infringing copyright, provided that sufficient modifications were made.[8]

Underlying all these cases is the notion that interoperability standards can become essential to competition in a market. In many cases this essentiality or dominance will be solidified by intellectual property protection, including copyright protection over certain expressions (such as database structures and software code), patent protection of inventions and trade secret protection for certain processes not within the public domain.

An intellectual property right is, in essence, a time-limited legal monopoly to exploit an intellectual property right or alternatively licence the

---

[4] *Magill TV Guide/ITP, BBC and RTE (89/205/EEC)* [1988] OJ 78 43 (European Commission); *Radio Telefis Eirann v. Commission of the European Communities* [1991] European Court of First Instance T-69/89, II-00485 ECR; *Radio Telefis Eirann (RTE) and Independent Television Publications (ITP) v. Commission of the European Communities (C-241/91 and C-242/91 P)* [1995] ECR -00743 (European Court of Justice).
[5] *NDC Health/IMS Health: Interim Measures (Case COMP D3/38044)* [2001] OJ 59 (European Commission).
[6] *IMS Health Inc v. Commission of the European Communities (Case T-184/01 R)* [2001] ECR II-03193 (European Court of First Instance).
[7] *IMS Health GMBH & Co and NDC Health GMBH & Co (Case C-418-01)* [2004] ECR -05039 (European Court of Justice).
[8] Alison Jones and Brenda Sufrin, *EU Competition Law* (5th ed., Oxford University Press 2014) 532.

right to someone else capable of exploiting it. Intellectual property rights generally confer exclusivity on their owner: the owner is entitled to exclude any other person from engaging in acts such as copying, using, making or importing the invention or work. Yet such exclusivity in a sense runs against the grain of standardization, whose underlying purpose is to enable the widest possible use of protocols, interfaces and information, since expanding implementation of an interoperability standard as broadly as possible maximizes the positive network externalities associated with the standard.

Where a standard has become essential to competition in a market, any undertaking or undertakings able to control access to the standard (including through the assertion of any standards-essential intellectual property rights) may have the means (if not the incentive; this is quite controversial)[9] to exclude competitors from using the standard, thus reserving for itself a monopoly in the market for the standardized commodity. Unsurprisingly, numerous lawyers and economists have contemplated whether concerns surrounding access to interoperability standards warrant regulatory intervention, for example in the form of the imposition of an essential facilities doctrine.[10]

1.3 Interfacing Intellectual Property and Competition in International Economic Law

Leading jurisdictions are developing bodies of jurisprudence to address such concerns. In the United States, the limiting doctrines in intellectual

---

[9] For the foundational works propounding the single monopoly profit theorem in the economics of industrial organization, see, e.g., Ward S. Bowman, 'Tying Arrangements and the Leverage Problem' (1957) 67 Yale Law Journal 19; Robert H. Bork, *The Antitrust Paradox: A Policy at War with Itself* (The Free Press 1993).

[10] Teague I. Donahey, 'Terminal Railroad Revisited: Using the Essential Facilities Doctrine to Ensure Accessibility to Internet Software Standards' (1997) 25 AIPLA Quarterly Journal 277; Marina Lao, 'Networks, Access and "Essential Facilities": From Terminal Railroad to Microsoft' (2009) 62 Southern Methodist University Law Review 557; Richard N. Langlois, 'Technological Standards, Innovation and Essential Facilities: Toward a Schumpeterian Post-Chicago Approach' in Jerry Ellig (ed.), *Dynamic Competition and Public Policy: Technology, Innovation and Antitrust Issues* (Cambridge University Press 2001); Nicholas Economides, 'The Microsoft Antitrust Case' (2001) 1 Journal of Industry, Competition and Trade 7; Francois Leveque, 'Innovation, Leveraging and Essential Facilities: Interoperability Licensing in the EU Microsoft Case' (2005) 28 World Competition 71; Christian Ahlborn, David S. Evans and A. Jorge Padilla, 'The Logic & Limits of the Exceptional Circumstances Test in Magill and IMS Health' (2004) 28 Fordham International Law Journal 1109.

property law have been the main avenue to address such concerns. The decision of the United States Supreme Court in *eBay* v. *MercExchange* was a notable watershed, opening the way for the lower courts to adopt a more flexible and case-by-case approach to the injunctive remedy as a means of addressing patent hold-up and royalty stacking claims. Nevertheless, these moves remain a work-in-progress. Injunctions still remain the norm in actions brought before the United States International Trade Commission (USITC). The question of how, precisely, a fair, reasonable and non-discriminatory (FRAND) royalty should be calculated remains far from settled, although some early attempts from the lower courts, notably the decision of Judge Robart in *Microsoft* v. *Motorola*, show particular promise. Finally, the decision in *Oracle* v. *Google* raises the spectre of parallel concerns concerning access to standards-essential copyrights.

The European Union provides a more variegated landscape. While European competition laws are enshrined in the EU's constituent treaty and present a high level of harmonization across the bloc, intellectual property laws are harmonized to a much lesser extent; the grant and enforcement of intellectual property rights is left primarily to the Member States. German courts, which tend to grant injunctions for patent infringement as a matter of course, have become the venue of choice for SEP holders. In the *Apple* v. *Motorola* litigation, this dynamic reached its logical conclusion: the courts issued injunction banning the sale of Apple's laptops and cell phones in Germany for infringing Samsung SEPs. At this point, the EU competition regulatory authorities intervened. Since then the EU has developed a more comprehensive regime for regulating access to SEPs, with the unilateral disciplines in competition law as the centrepiece. Chinese courts have also tended to rely on competition laws in the form of the essential facilities doctrine to ensure access to SEPs, but in cases such as the Qualcomm litigation, this has come to represent a doctrine of excessive pricing.

The well-known distinction in law and economics between exclusive property rules and liability rules can be useful in structuring these discussions, as well as identifying points of convergence between leading jurisdictions. Adopting this framework, both the United States approach (where injunctions are unavailable for certain infringements) and the EU/China approach (where competition law disciplines such as the essential facilities doctrine apply) both involve the substitution of an exclusive property rule (either patent injunction or per se legality for refusals to licence) with a liability rule (in the form of either no injunction plus reasonable royalties, or imposition of a compulsory licence for breach of the competition laws).

Although jurisdictions continue to develop domestic approaches, the divergent approaches and interests across jurisdictions raise concerns of a collective action problem. International economic law has to date provided little guidance on these matters. Moreover, in the current climate of rising economic nationalism, developing new disciplines in international economic law would seem unduly ambitious, at least for the moment.

As such, it is important, timely and feasible for an expert-led colloquium to convene to provide guidance in the form of a soft law manual for courts, regulators, standard setting organizations (SSOs) and other relevant parties regarding the proper 'rules of the road' for ensuring access to essential interoperability standards and SEIP. This can be accomplished in a manner which is faithful to the purposes and procedures of intellectual property and competition law, and which moreover is wholly consistent with the present obligations imposed by international economic law, notably international intellectual property law. A draft of such an instrument is provided in Chapter 9.

Harmonization of this hitherto controversial area of law would seem to offer considerable benefits, and merits careful consideration. This is unlikely to be the last word on this already much-debated subject. Standardized technologies continue to move forward at a remarkable pace; future readers of this work may well be familiar with technologies mentioned here as future prospects. Any expert manual will therefore require frequent upgrades.

Preserving the balance which has always been inherent in intellectual property law between the competing rights of creators and users of technological knowledge, between initial and follow-on innovation, between present, upgraded and future standardization initiatives, which at the margins is more of an art than a science, would seem to be the key to addressing these difficult issues on an ongoing basis.

1.4 Methodology

In terms of its methodological approach, this work borrows from the 'topical approach to law' pioneered by German jurist Theodor Viehweg. The topical approach to law, which may be characterized as a 'premodern systematization of reasoning (and argumentation)', and one opposed to the deductive reasoning attributed to Réné Descartes,[11] is fundamentally 'the art of problem-thinking';[12] the problem itself is 'previously given and continually guiding'.[13] 'Problem thinking' is to be contrasted with 'system thinking'.[14] Rather than constructing a 'system' in order to solve a given legal problem, we are urged instead to use the problem itself as our starting point, and to collect various topics (or *topoi*) which can then be applied in a more or less unstructured way so as to generate a solution which is apt to resolve the problem in question. Such *topoi* may be described as '*general propositions or concepts* that provide *premises of arguments* used in a certain discourse and are *collectively accepted* by the participants in the discourse as being plausible'.[15] The topical approach to problem-solving is thus described by Esser:

> Topical reasoning can and should afford to justify results not following logically and inevitably from established principles, but to present them intelligibly out of the matter (aus der Sache einsichtig darstellen). While, in dogmatic deduction, the reduction of complexity to logically relevant aspects becomes a technique, things are different here: The situation needs to be assessed in all of its complexity, in order to discuss all problems with a view to achieving an ideal solution (das Lösungsideal 'problematisieren'). Encompassing all the complexities of competing legal interests has to replace the depreciation of problems in deductive logical systems and all formal considerations in order to discover convincing reasons.[16]

Such an approach is not wholly opposed to deductive reasoning; rather, as Stoeckli states: 'problem and system cannot be separated completely from each other, because between them exist "essential entanglements"'.[17] Instead, the topical approach should be viewed as a type of rationality, albeit one better suited to practical problems such as those occurring in

---

[11] Guenther Kreuzbauer, 'Topics in Contemporary Legal Argumentation: Some Remarks on the Topical Nature of Legal Argumentation in the Continental Law Tradition' (2008) 28 Informal Logic 71, 73.
[12] Theodor Viehweg, *Topics and Law* (Peter Lang 1993) 19.
[13] Ibid. 20.
[14] Ibid.
[15] Kreuzbauer (n. 11) 79. Emphasis in original.
[16] Josef Esser, *Vorverständnis Und Methodenwahl* (Athenäum-Fischer- Taschenbuch-Verlag 1972) 157–8; see Thomas Cottier, *Equitable Principles of Maritime Boundary Delimitation: The Quest for Distributive Justice in International Law* (Cambridge University Press 2015) 606 for translation.
[17] Walter Stoeckli, 'Topic and Argumentation: The Contribution of Viehweg and Perelman in the Field of Methodology as Applied to Law' (1968) 54 Archives for Philosophy of Law and Social Philosophy 581, 586.

fields such as medicine, engineering, politics or law.[18] Problem-thinking generally avoids very long inferential chains: 'Problem thinking always shies away from being bound'.[19] Rather, 'Coherence of deduction is possible only in a restrictive way, if the original complexe [sic] connections are to be preserved'.[20] There is considerable congruence between the topical method of legal reasoning and the approach traditionally taken by the law of equity.[21]

Viehweg's treatise advanced both positive and normative claims about topical reasoning. Viehweg argued that all legal reasoning is in a sense topical, and moreover that topical reasoning is an appropriate methodological approach to legal problem solving.[22] Topical legal reasoning was introduced to the realm of public international law by way of German arguments presented to the International Court of Justice during the course of the 1969 North Sea cases,[23] and is evident in the approach of WTO panels and the Appellate Body.[24] Topical reasoning is also evident in the competition law analysis, where economic concepts such as the definition of markets or the establishment of a dominant market position are intertwined with legal analysis.[25] Given its capacity to integrate harmoniously insights from a variety of fields of scholarship, a topical jurisprudence is eminently well-suited not merely to a multidisciplinary approach to the interpretation of legal text, but also to a multidisciplinary approach to evaluating and proposing new disciplines in international economic law.

This work, rather than rigidly applying a particular methodology as its fulcrum, instead takes its orientation fundamentally from the problem at hand, namely concerns regarding access to interoperability standards and to SEIP. It is the problem which suggests the methodologies appropriate to developing a solution. To propose a solution to this problem, this work evaluates relevant *topoi* such as applicable competition intellectual property laws as well as considerations deriving from law and economics and the technical characteristics of standards, to develop a normative approach to

---

[18] Kreuzbauer (n. 11) 76.
[19] Viehweg (n. 12) 29.
[20] Stoeckli (n. 17) 586.
[21] Cottier (n. 16) 605–10.
[22] Kreuzbauer (n. 11) 72.
[23] Cottier (n. 16) 605.
[24] Ibid. 607.
[25] Ibid.

addressing concerns associated with access to interoperability standards and SEIP.

Within the prism of the topical approach, this work also applies a number of other recognized methodologies. First, existing international rules are assessed in order to ascertain the extent to which these rules presently address access to interoperability standards and the SEIP. Next, comparative analysis of the laws of leading jurisdictions, in particular the United States, the European Union and China,[26] is undertaken with a view to identifying commonalities and points of divergence between these jurisdictions. For any international instrument to be feasible and potentially impactful, it needs to align to a considerable degree with the laws of major jurisdictions: if it does not, any such initiative is likely to be marginalized. As such, while this exercise is comparative in nature, it is also informed by a dose of realism: any proposed international approach must take cognizance in large measure of the existing laws 'on the books' in the most significant jurisdictions.

Thirdly, this work applies analytical tools from law and economics. Economic analysis of law essentially involves using the analytical tools of the discipline of economics to provide insights either into: (i) how laws currently operate (i.e. positive analysis) and (ii) what the optimal laws would or should be (i.e. normative analysis).[27]

In this work, the normative branch of law and economics is applied. These tools are applied in furtherance of a number of distinct purposes. In particular, the Calabresi and Melamed matrix of liability rules, property rules and inalienability rules[28] is applied to identify a potential point of commonality between the laws of leading jurisdictions: namely that in all jurisdictions, in some circumstances, a property rule is substitutable for a liability rule in order to address concerns arising in relation to interoperability standards and SEIP.

---

[26] This approach makes intuitive sense, since the United States, the European Union and China are increasingly recognized as the world's three economic superpowers; see, e.g., Rafael Leal-Arcas, 'China's Attitude to Multilateralism in International Economic Law and Governance: Challenges for the World Trading System' (2010) 11 The Journal of World Investment & Trade 259, 260. In addition, much of the important technology and many of the key standardization initiatives take place within these jurisdictions.

[27] See Stephen Shavell, *Foundations of Economic Analysis of Law* (Belknap Press 2004) 1–5; A Mitchell Polinsky, *An Introduction to Law and Economics* (4th ed., Wolters Kluwer 2011) xix.

[28] See, generally, Guido R. Calabresi and A. Douglas Melamed, 'Property Rules, Liability Rules, and Inalienability: One View of the Cathedral' (1972) 85 Harvard Law Review 1089.

The tools of law and economics are further applied with a view to identifying those potential points of alignment among jurisdictions' laws that are not merely feasible but are also optimal from a welfare perspective. This is a reasonable policy matrix to apply, because the underlying rationale for both competition and intellectual property laws derives from economic theory. Having identified a point of potential compromise that is both feasible and optimal, this work proceeds to apply a theoretical analysis to address whether such an approach can translate into an international instrument, if so which kind of instrument, whether hard or soft law.

Finally, legal analysis is undertaken in order to assess whether the solution proposed is likely to remain consistent with existing international rules. Accordingly, based on the identification and evaluation of these diverse *topoi*, conclusions are reached and recommendations are made concerning pathways towards an international approach to addressing concerns associated with access to interoperability standards and to SEIP.

1.5 Structure of This Work

This work is structured as follows. Part I introduces core introductory concepts. Chapter 2 explains the nature of interoperability standards, and provides an introduction to the economics of interoperability standards. Chapter 3 also surveys existing provisions of international law that may potentially address the matters under discussion.

Part II then examines the core domestic law regimes of competition and intellectual property law, with a view to identifying issues of concern, differences of approach and also commonalities. Chapter 4 discusses the concept of 'standards-essential intellectual property', focussing on the most affected areas of intellectual property protection: patents, copyrights and trade secrets, with some discussion also of protection of the layout topographies of integrated circuits. Chapter 5 evaluates the applicable bodies of competition law, with a particular focus on the essential facilities doctrine as it is understood under United States and European law.

Part III considers more general questions of liability compensation, and evaluates possible international approaches. Chapter 6 introduces the distinction in law and economics between liability rules and exclusive property rules, and considers whether a liability rule or an exclusive property rule is preferable in regards to SEIP. Applying the matrix of liability rules, Chapter 6 offers some ways forward, focussing particularly on the particular circumstances in which the injunctive remedy should be made available to SEIP holders, and also some principles for the calculation of appropriate compensation, for example in the form of reasonable royalties. Chapter 7 considers possible international approaches to resolving issues associated with access to interoperability standards and SEIP. Both hard and soft law approaches are considered, and a range of possible fora for such discussions is evaluated. Chapter 8 offers some concluding views. Chapter 9 provides a draft soft law instrument, namely an expert manual, to address issues associated with access to interoperability standards and SEIP.

2

Standards and Interoperability Standards

2.1 The Fundamental Importance of Standards and Interoperability

Standards play a profoundly important role in the development of an information economy and an information society. In particular, standards play a crucial role in developing common platforms that facilitate the sharing of information. They provide the essential information infrastructure[1] underpinning numerous industries from computing to telecommunications. For example, an empirical study found that a single laptop computer implemented 251 technical interoperability standards, with many more likely being of relevance.[2] Wireless communications technologies generally require standardized solutions, usually a single standardized solution.[3] In previous eras standardized solutions were critical to the development of network industries such as railroads.[4] The development of standardized freight containers provided a tremendous impetus to global seaborne trade.[5] Interoperable standardized solutions are driving new frontiers of digital business such as mobile

---

[1] See D. Tilson, K. Lyytinen and C. Sorensen, 'Desperately Seeking the Infrastructure in IS Research: Conceptualization of "Digital Convergence" As Co-Evolution of Social and Technical Infrastructures', *2010 43rd Hawaii International Conference on System Sciences* (2010); Knut Blind, 'From Standards to Quality Infrastructure' in Panagiotis Delimatsis (ed.), *The Law, Economics and Politics of International Standardisation* (Cambridge University Press 2015) 71–2.

[2] Brad Biddle, Andrew White and Sean Woods, 'How Many Standards in a Laptop? (And Other Empirical Questions)', *2010 ITU-T Kaleidoscope: Beyond the Internet? – Innovations for Future Networks and Services* (2010).

[3] William Webb, 'The Role of Networking Standards in Building the Internet of Things' (2012) 1 Communications & Strategies 57, 59.

[4] Douglas J. Puffert, 'Path Dependence in Spatial Networks: The Standardization of Railway Track Gauge' (2002) 39 Explorations in Economic History 282.

[5] Marc Levinson, *The Box: How the Shipping Container Made the World Smaller and the World Economy Bigger* (2nd ed., Princeton University Press 2016).

payment systems.⁶ Standardized approaches offer many benefits including: enabling more competition among hardware suppliers; facilitating greater economies of scale for hardware suppliers, leading to lower costs for the industry as a whole, and therefore greater prospects for uptake of a technology; a higher degree of peer review in standards development, and the benefits resulting from higher levels of interoperability, including interoperability on a worldwide basis.⁷

The importance of interoperability standards has been enhanced by the ongoing convergence of the computing and telecommunications industries.⁸ Interoperability standards are likely to become more, not less, important in the future as technological developments such as the Internet of Things (IoT) deliver networked approaches to an increasing variety of ordinary consumer products.⁹ As such, it is desirable to develop adequate 'rules of the road' now, rather than later.

2.2 Defining the Concept of an Interoperability Standard

2.2.1 Some Basic Definitions

Meanings customarily given to the term 'standard' include: the authorized exemplar of a unit of measure or weight; a normal uniform size or amount; a prescribed minimum size or amount; an authoritative or recognized exemplar of correctness, perfection or some definite degree of any quality; and a commodity, the value of which is treated as invariable, in order that it may serve as a measure of value for all other commodities.¹⁰

The International Organization for Standardization (ISO) and the International Electrotechnical Commission (IEC) define 'standard' to mean: 'Document, established by consensus and approved by a recognized body, that provides, for common and repeated use, rules, guidelines or characteristics for activities or their results, aimed at the

---

[6] Andrew S. Lim, 'Inter-Consortia Battles in Mobile Payments Standardisation' (2008) 7 Electronic Commerce Research and Applications 202.
[7] Webb (n. 3) 60.
[8] Brad Biddle and others, 'The Expanding Role and Importance of Standards in the Information and Communications Technology Industry' (2012) 52 Jurimetrics 177, 179.
[9] Luigi Atzori, Antonio Iera and Giacomo Morabito, 'The Internet of Things: A Survey' (2010) 54 Computer Networks 2787; Lu Tan and Neng Wang, 'Future Internet: The Internet of Things', *2010 3rd International Conference on Advanced Computer Theory and Engineering (ICACTE)* (2010); Webb (n. 3).
[10] *Oxford English Dictionary* (2nd ed., Oxford University Press 1989).

achievement of the optimum degree of order in a given context'.[11] The ISO provides a more general definition on its website: 'a standard is a document that provides requirements, specifications, guidelines or characteristics that can be used consistently to ensure that materials, products, processes and services are fit for their purpose'.[12] The ISO's website definition notably excludes the element of establishment by consensus and by a recognized body, thereby extending the scope of the definition to potentially include de facto standards as well. This approach is therefore to be preferred.

A definition is also included in the WTO Agreement on Technical Barriers to Trade: 'Document approved by a recognized body that provides, for common and repeated use, rules, guidelines or characteristics for products or related processes and production methods, with which compliance is not mandatory. It may also include or deal exclusively with terminology, symbols, packaging, marking or labelling requirements as they apply to a product, process or production method'.[13] The WTO definition is closely based on superseded ISO/IEC definitions. It includes the element that the document is not mandatory. This is indeed generally the case with standards, although standards are sometimes given force of law, for example through statutes or regulations; this does not detract from their nature as standards. Three other notable definitions of standards are: (i) 'the means used in determining "the way things should be"';[14] (ii) 'a construct that results from reasoned, collective choice and enables agreement on solutions of recurrent problems';[15] and 'a package of information in which solutions for matching problems have been defined'.[16]

---

[11] 'ISO/IEC Guide 2:2004 Standardization and Related Activities – General Vocabulary' para. 3.2 www.iso.org/standard/39976.html accessed 30 November 2017.

[12] 'International Organization for Standardization Website' www.iso.org/standards.html accessed 30 November 2017.

[13] Agreement on Technical Barriers to Trade, 15 April 1994, Marrakesh Agreement Establishing the World Trade Organization, Annex 1A 1994 (1868 UNTS 120) para. 2 Annex 1.

[14] Paul A. David, 'Some New Standards for the Economics of Standardization in the Information Age' in Partha Dasgupta and Paul Stoneman (eds.), *Economic Policy and Technological Performance* (Cambridge University Press 1987) 211.

[15] Gregory Tassey, 'Standardization in Technology-Based Markets' (2000) 29 Research Policy 587, 588.

[16] Henk J. de Vries, 'Standardisation' in Panagiotis Delimatsis (ed.), *The Law, Economics and Politics of International Standardisation* (Cambridge University Press 2015) 24.

The *Elgar Encyclopaedia of International Economic Law* suggests the following definition: 'Standards may be described as non-binding rules that seek to promote order with respect to products, services or processes by encapsulating expert knowledge in the form of written requirements'.[17] This definition is also sufficiently broad to encompass de facto standards. It also makes particular reference to expert knowledge, and expresses the need for the standard to be written. As such, this definition provides a reasonable basis upon which to proceed.

2.2.2 Typologies of Standards

An initial distinction should be drawn between formal and de facto standards.[18] Formal standards are drafted and approved by a recognized standards development organization such as ISO, IEC or the Institute of Electrical and Electronics Engineers (IEEE). De facto standards might be developed in a less formal context (e.g. by a consortium or a firm), but attain the status of a standard through marketplace acceptance. Formal standards could be further classified based on the organization developing the standard (e.g. whether it is a public or private body).

The most useful typologies for present purposes are those based on the economic effects of standards.[19] David, for example, distinguishes between: (i) standards for reference (e.g. currencies, weights, measures); (ii) standards for minimal admissible attributes (e.g. minimum safety levels or product quality); and (iii) standards for interface compatibility (e.g. codes, screw threads, signal frequencies).[20] A similar taxonomy has been proposed by Krechmer.[21] Tassey includes a fourth category, variety reduction standards, which 'limit a product to a certain range or number of characteristics such as size or quality levels'.[22] Likewise, Blind suggests

---

[17] Simon Brinsmead, 'Delegated Regulation: Normalisation', *Elgar Encyclopaedia of International Economic Law* (Edward Elgar 2017).

[18] Tassey (n. 15) 587–8; Angsana A. Techatassanasoontorn and Shugang Suo, 'Influences on Standards Adoption in de Facto Standardization' (2011) 12 Information Technology Management 357, 357–8.

[19] Blind (n. 1) 58–9; Knut Blind, *The Economics of Standards: Theory, Evidence, Policy* (Edward Elgar 2004) 14.

[20] David (n. 14) 214.

[21] Ken Krechmer, 'The Fundamental Nature of Standards: Technical Perspective' (2000) 38 IEEE Communications Magazine 70.

[22] Tassey (n. 15) 590; Andrea Barrios Villarreal, *International Standardization and the Agreement on Technical Barriers to Trade* (Cambridge University Press 2018) 82–5.

four categories, namely compatibility/interface standards; minimum quality/safety standards; variety reduction standards; and information standards.[23]

Drawing on these various taxonomies, the following simplified taxonomy is proposed:

- Reference standards: standards for reference and definition, such as currencies, weights and measures;
- Quality standards: standards for minimal admissible attributes (e.g. quality and safety requirements);
- Interoperability standards: standards for interface compatibility; and
- Variety reduction standards: standards for reducing variety among goods, services or components.

These types are not mutually exclusive and a particular standard could exhibit the characteristics of more than one type of standard.[24] For example, the width of the rail gauge is an example of both a variety reduction standard (since the variety of gauge widths is reduced to one) and an interoperability standard (since the standardized gauge width facilitates the interoperability of rolling stock created for a given gauge width). Likewise, cargo container standards (notably those developed by ISO) both limited variety but also designed standardized interfaces to facilitate the movement of cargo from rail to road to ship to truck seamlessly. Hence, we categorize standards in order to study their economic effects, rather than to compartmentalize them within mutually exclusive categories.[25]

This work focuses on the third type of standard identified: standards for interface compatibility, which are often referred to as 'compatibility', 'interface' or 'interoperability' standards. We focus on this particular type of standard because the economic issues and legal concerns associated with this type of standard are distinct.

In particular, the phenomenon of network effects (discussed at Section 2.5.2.1) distinguishes interoperability standards from other types of standards, and invites questions as to whether interoperability standards should be conceptualized as infrastructure, public goods or, in the parlance of competition law, as essential facilities, or, put another way, whether traditional economic thinking about the effects of overwhelming

---

[23] Blind (n. 1) 59–61; Blind (n. 19) 14.
[24] Villarreal (n. 22) 82; Blind (n. 1) 59; Blind (n. 19) 14.
[25] See Blind (n. 1) 59.

supply-side economies of scale (in particular where such economies of scale give rise to subadditivity and thus natural monopoly) should apply with equal force in the context of demand-side economies of scale, or whether there are subtleties and nuances regarding interoperability standards, and also of network effects, which militate against such an extrapolation. In this work the term 'interoperability standard' is used throughout.

Interoperability standards are of particular importance in relation to the information, technology and communications sector, since these economic sectors tend to be characterized by networks that involve many discrete components, often supplied by different firms, which must interoperate seamlessly in order for the consumer to be able to enjoy the final product or service (e.g. a mobile telephony service).[26]

2.2.3 Interoperability Standards: Definitions

David describes interoperability standards as follows: 'The third functional class of standards provides information required to facilitate physical interactions and behavioural "transactions" at interfaces between objects, or between agents, and also between objects and agents (as in the layout of airplane cockpits, and the oft-cited case of typewriter keyboard layouts and touch-typists)'.[27] Tassey provides the following description of interoperability standards:

> Standards specify properties that a product must have in order to work physically or functionally with complementary products within a product or service system ... Compatibility or interoperability is typically manifested in the form of a standardized interface between components of a larger system. An effective interface standard does not affect the design of the components themselves, such as numerically controlled machine tools or the components of these tools, including controllers.[28]

Meddeb provides the following functional definition: 'The goal of a standard is typically to unify interfaces, protocols, and services so that various systems can be interconnected'.[29] Krechmer distinguishes

---

[26] Ibid. 60; Neil Gandal and Pierre Régibeau, 'Standard-Setting Organisations' in Panagiotis Delimatsis (ed.), *The Law, Economics and Politics of International Standardisation* (Cambridge University Press 2015) 394.
[27] David (n. 14) 216.
[28] Tassey (n. 15) 590.
[29] A. Meddeb, 'Internet of Things Standards: Who Stands out from the Crowd?' (2016) 54 IEEE Communications Magazine 40, 46.

between interface standards and protocol standards. Under this approach, interface standards 'are implemented by defining the transmitted signals that pass across the interface and using the minimum definition of the receiver functions necessary to ensure compatibility'; protocol standards, by contrast, are 'used to define both the transmitter and receiver function at the same time'.[30]

To comprehensively understand the nature of interoperability standards, we need to understand the related concepts of 'protocol' and 'interface'. A protocol may be defined as: 'An agreement that governs the procedures used to exchange information between cooperating entities. More specifically, a protocol is such an agreement operating between entities that have no direct means of exchanging information, but that do so by passing information across a local interface to so-called lower-level protocols, until the lowest, physical level is reached'.[31] Turning to the concept of an 'interface', the *Oxford Dictionary of Computing* defines 'interface' as: '1. A common boundary between two systems, devices or programs. 2. The signal connection and associated control circuits that are used to connect devices. 3. Specification of the communication between two program units'.[32] More philosophically, an interface is 'a boundary or zone of encounter that actively extends into and conditions that which it separates'.[33] Interfaces may exist: (i) between hardware and hardware (e.g. a USB port on a personal computer or laptop); (ii) between hardware and software (e.g. an operating system); (iii) between software and software (e.g. application programming interfaces for software interoperability); and (iv) between computers and humans (e.g. a graphical user interface). Interfaces may become standardized;[34] a standardized interface is an interoperability standard.

The related concepts of 'compatibility' and 'interoperability' are also of relevance. 'Compatibility' may be defined as: '1. of hardware, the ability of a subsystem (e.g. memory) or an external device (e.g. a terminal) to be substituted for the originally designated equipment . . . 2. Of software, the ability of a computer to execute directly program code that was compiled,

---

[30] Krechmer (n. 21) 70.
[31] *Oxford Dictionary of Computing* (6th ed., Oxford University Press 2008).
[32] Ibid.
[33] Branden Hookway, *Interface* (MIT Press 2014) 9.
[34] Pamela Samuelson, 'Are Patents on Interfaces Impeding Interoperability?' (2009) 93 Minnesota Law Review 1943, 1949–50.

2.2 CONCEPT OF AN INTEROPERABILITY STANDARD

assembled, or written in machine language for another computer'.[35] Another definition is: 'The ability of one device to accept data handled by another device without conversion of the data or modification of the code'.[36]

'Interoperability' may be defined as: 'The ability of systems to exchange and make useful information in a straightforward and useful way; this is enhanced by the use of standards in communication and data format'.[37] Another definition is: 'the ability to transfer and render useful data and other information across systems ... applications or components'.[38] Put another way: 'Interoperability doesn't require that two systems be identical in design or implementation, only that they can exchange information and use the information they exchange. Interoperability requires that the information being exchanged is conceptually equivalent; once this equivalence is established, transforming different implementations to a common exchange format is a necessary but often trivial thing to do'.[39] Drawing on these diverse definitions, it can be seen that interoperability standards generally specify either protocols or interfaces (which provide an agreed framework for exchanging information) in order to promote compatibility or interoperability between distinct elements (which may be products, services, programmes or some other type of module) which form part of a larger system.

Definitionally speaking, the boundary between the concepts of 'protocol' and 'interface' will not always be clear. Whilst it may in some particular contexts be feasible to subdivide interoperability standards into interface standards (e.g. mobile telephony standards such as the 4G LTE standard, or the Microsoft Windows operating system) and protocol standards (e.g. Transmission Control Protocol/Internet Protocol (TCP/IP) or Ethernet), the lack of clarity concerning this distinction suggests that it is preferable to focus at a higher level of abstraction, namely all such standards (whether they specify interfaces or protocols) that seek to promote interoperability or compatibility between distinct elements within a larger system. The definitions of 'compatibility' and 'interoperability' cited above suggest quite clearly that these two

---

[35] Oxford Dictionary of Computing (n. 31).
[36] *McGraw-Hill Dictionary of Scientific and Technical Terms* (6th ed., McGraw-Hill 2003).
[37] Oxford Dictionary of Computing (n. 31).
[38] Urs Gasser and John Palfrey, *Interoperability: The Promise and Perils of Highly Connected Systems* (Basic Books 2012) 5.
[39] Samuelson (n. 34) 1947.

words are synonyms and can be employed interchangeably. For clarity of expression, the term 'interoperability' is used throughout this work.

One of the key benefits of interoperability standards is that they are able to promote modular solutions to complex problems. 'Modularity' may be defined as: 'The property of functional flexibility built into a computer system by assembling discrete units which can be easily joined to or arranged with other parts or units'.[40] Langlois explains the concept of modularity as follows: 'Modularity refers both to the structure of the system's design and to its standards, that is, it refers to the degree to which the system is in fact decomposable into modules and to the degree to which the interfaces among the modules are fixed and invariant'.[41] Modularity implies a higher degree of simplicity for each module in the system, which needs to take cognizance only of: (i) the technical requirements pertaining to that particular module; and (ii) the specifications governing the interrelations between all parts in the system.

To explain this in more concrete terms, cargo liner shipping before the era of standardized cargo containers was much more complex and costly because each ship had to be loaded and unloaded taking cognizance of each of the uniquely different items to be loaded onto the ship. The relationships between each of these items gave rise to even greater uniqueness and complexity. By contrast, the development of standardized cargo containers allowed for a much more simplified solution. Customers could take responsibility for arranging the contents of each particular container. The shipping line could simply concern itself with loading, unloading, stacking and conveying the standardized containers. Such a modular system thus promotes simplicity and efficiency, and lends itself to the dynamic growth of systems.

The concept of an interoperability standard is also very similar to that of a 'platform', which can be described as: 'a set of stable components that supports variety and evolvability in a system by constraining the linkages among the other components'.[42] In many instances the concepts of 'platform' and 'standard' will overlap: a standardized solution will

---

[40] 'Modularity', *McGraw-Hill Dictionary of Scientific and Technical Terms* (6th ed., McGraw-Hill 2003).
[41] Richard N. Langlois, 'Technological Standards, Innovation and Essential Facilities: Toward a Schumpeterian Post-Chicago Approach' in Jerry Ellig (ed.), *Dynamic Competition and Public Policy: Technology, Innovation and Antitrust Issues* (Cambridge University Press 2001) 209–10.
[42] Carliss Y. Baldwin and C. Jason Woodard, 'The Architecture of Platforms: A Unified View' in Annabelle Gawer (ed.), *Platforms, Markets and Innovation* (Edward Elgar, 2009).

provide the basis for the establishment of a platform. Whilst the two terms are not necessarily perfect synonyms, many insights from the economic literature of platforms will also be relevant in the context of interoperability standards.

Perhaps the defining characteristic of interoperability standards is their association with network externalities or network effects.[43] This is of crucial importance to assessing interoperability standards, because these standards do not need to attain the force of law in order to become de facto mandatory in the marketplace. The operation of network effects in technology markets (and indeed in other markets) can give to a non-binding standard a status that, in a de facto sense, approaches the force of law. As we will see, this gives rise to critical intersections with the laws of intellectual property and competition. The crucial intersection with intellectual property law arises because standards very often incorporate technologies which are subject to intellectual property rights, especially patents. Regarding competition laws, where an interoperability standard has attained widespread marketplace acceptance, it is very difficult for market participants to avoid using the standard. As a result, the concept of 'standardization' can overlap very significantly with competition law concepts of dominance and, in some cases, monopoly, thus potentially calling for the application of competition laws.

2.3 Notable Interoperability Standards: from QWERTY towards an Internet of Things

Once the concept of an interoperability standard has been defined, it becomes apparent that real-world examples abound. David, for example, supplies a broad array of examples of interoperability standards which include the physical design of interfaces, screw threads, signal frequencies, contractual forms, diplomatic protocols and vernacular languages.[44] The breadth of this set of examples is useful because it illustrates that interoperability standards are by no means confined to the fields of information and communications technology; they arise in many other fields of endeavour.

Interestingly, language is one example cited. A language is effectively a common set of protocols that enables communication between people. If two people wish to communicate with each other but do not speak the

---

[43] Villarreal (n. 22) 82–3.
[44] David (n. 14) 214.

same language, there are a number of ways to overcome the problem. First, one of the people could learn the other's language. Second, they could both learn a third language. Third, they could use some kind of translation mechanism, for example dictionaries. These choices equally arise in many fields of technology.

Generally speaking, no person or group of people is able to control the contents of a language; usage is the final determinant of what is, or is not, part of any given language. Languages are (thankfully) not subject to intellectual property rights. As with many other interoperability standards, competition can arise between languages for predominance. Some languages (especially in the contemporary era English, but in older times French, Latin and Chinese) can attain the status of lingua franca and be employed widely in common usage, even by people whose native language is not the lingua franca. The competition between languages to attain the status of a lingua franca could be described as a 'standards war'.

Although it is equally possible to confine the field of study to standards within a particular field of technology (e.g. standards pertaining to the information and communications technology industries),[45] defining the field of study to interoperability standards has value because some of the most paradigmatic examples of interoperability standards predate the advent of the information and communications industries as we understand them today.

2.3.1 Keyboard Configurations: QWERTY and Its Discontents

One (de facto) standard much discussed in the economics literature is the QWERTY typewriter keyboard layout. The QWERTY configuration was included in a typewriter design patented by Christopher Latham Scholes in 1868, and sold to Remington in 1873.[46] QWERTY was designed to minimize the incidence of keys near to each other being struck in close succession, since this tended to jam early typewriters.[47] The QWERTY layout has survived and remains dominant to this day. Economic writers, notably David, have argued that QWERTY's persistence owes more to historical accident than superior quality, and that another keyboard

---

[45] See, e.g., Han-Wei Liu, 'International Standards in Flux: A Balkanized ICT Standard-Setting Paradigm and Its Implications for the WTO' (2014) 17 Journal of International Economic Law 551.

[46] Paul A. David, 'Clio and the Economics of QWERTY' (1985) 75 American Economic Review 332, 333.

[47] Ibid.

layout, patented by Dr August Dvorak in 1936, engenders such superior typing speeds that it would be efficient for existing QWERTY typists to be retrained in Dvorak instead.[48]

The theory of 'path dependence' presented by Farrell and Saloner[49] has been applied to the example of QWERTY to explain how a standard that is technically inferior can survive, even though superior alternatives exist, because of imperfect information leading to coordination problems. David's findings have been subject to considerable criticism, notably by Liebowitz and Margolis (1990), who contend that the case against QWERTY was based on inadequately designed studies that could have been biased in favour of the competing Dvorak design.[50] Liebowitz and Margolis also observed that the Dvorak design did not perform significantly (if at all) better than QWERTY in properly designed experiments, and that any advantage held by Dvorak would not justify switching from QWERTY.[51]

The debate is likely to continue; in any case, the QWERTY keyboard layout is now almost 150 years old, has survived at least one major technological change (namely the transition from typewriters to word-processing computers), and has long outlived the specific problem it was intended to solve. Therefore, irrespective of whether QWERTY is ultimately to be considered an inferior or superior solution to competing alternatives, it is instructive as an example of path-dependence and the potential for standardized solutions to persist over time.

2.3.2 *Video Recording Formats: the Standards War between VHS and BETAMAX*

Sony's Betamax and Matsushita/JVC's Video Home System (VHS) were the leading candidates to standardize consumer video recording formats. Betamax was commercially available from April 1975, roughly two years before VHS. Sony executives believed VHS used technology copied from Betamax.[52] Betamax and VHS were clearly the market-leading formats

---

[48] David (n. 46).
[49] Joseph Farrell and Garth Saloner, 'Standardization, Compatibility and Innovation' (1985) 16 The RAND Journal of Economics 70.
[50] Stan J. Liebowitz and Stephen E. Margolis, 'The Fable of the Keys' (1990) 33 Journal of Law & Economics 1, 6–17.
[51] Ibid. 6–16.
[52] Stan J. Liebowitz and Stephen E. Margolis, 'Path Dependence, Lock-In and History' (1995) 11 Journal of Law, Economics & Organization 205, 220.

and there were few differences between them. One significant difference, however, was the larger cassette used by VHS, which provided a better trade-off between picture quality and playing time.[53] Both Sony and Matsushita gained US and Japanese partners in their attempt to achieve dominance. Fierce competition (including on the key features of playing time and price) saw VHS draw ahead of Betamax. By mid-1979 VHS was outselling Betamax by two to one, and by 1984 all manufacturers except Sony had adopted VHS.[54] Betamax survived in small numbers, however, because a small group of aficionados considered its picture quality superior. This contention was not, however, borne out in surveys of picture quality by Consumer Reports.[55] It is noteworthy that the market dominance achieved by VHS lasted only as long as the VCR remained in consumer use, illustrating the time-limited nature of monopolies arising from network effects.

2.3.3 The 802.11 Family of Wireless Area Network Standards

Wireless Local Area Network (WLAN) protocols provide wireless data transmission. Today essentially all WLAN protocols in use form part of the 802.11 family of standards developed under the auspices of the IEEE. The Wi-Fi Alliance, established in 2003 to promote conformance with the 802.11 standards through certification, now has over 750 members, and the name 'Wi-Fi' has become synonymous with the 802.11 family of standards.[56] The origins of the 802.11 standard lay in a decision of the US Federal Communications Commission to open up several unlicensed frequency bands to use by new electronic applications.[57] Negotiation of a standard within the IEEE forum was approved by IEEE's Executive Committee in July 1990, with the first meeting of the 802.11 Working Group held in the same year.[58] The original IEEE 802.11 standard was released in

---

[53] Ibid.
[54] Ibid. 221.
[55] Ibid. 222.
[56] Ian Sherlock, 'Wi-Fi Alliance: Connecting Everyone and Everything, Everywhere' (2017) 1 IEEE Communications Standards Magazine 6.
[57] 'A Brief History of Wi-Fi' [2004] *The Economist* www.economist.com accessed 10 March 2018.
[58] Kai Jakobs, Wolter Lemstra and Victor Hayes, 'Creating a Wireless Standard: IEEE 802.11' in Wolter Lemstra, Victor Hayes and John Groenewegen (eds.), *The Innovation Journey of Wi-Fi: The Road to Global Success* (Cambridge University Press 2010).

1997.⁵⁹ This was revised in 1999, and received approval as an ISO/IEC standard in the same year.⁶⁰ Another standard, 802.11a, was released at almost the same time, using a different modulation technique (Orthogonal Frequency Division Modulation) to achieve higher speeds within the 5GHz frequency band.⁶¹ The 802.11g standard, released in 2003, provided much higher data rates (54Mbit/s) than the 802.11b standard, operating in the 2.4Ghz frequency range and using the OFDM modulation technique.⁶² A further version, 802.11n, released in 2009, can operate in either the 2.4GHz or 5GHz bands, and can achieve data rates as high as 600 Mbit/s.⁶³

2.3.4 Internet Standards: Transmission Control Protocol/Internet Protocol

Many examples of interoperability standards in the information and communications technology field concern communication protocols. A famous example is the TCP/IP, which has come to be the dominant communications protocol for the Internet (including for the World Wide Web). The Internet can be described as: 'The Internet is at once a worldwide broadcasting capability, a mechanism for information dissemination, and a medium for collaboration and interaction between individuals and their computers without regard for geographic location'.⁶⁴ At the heart of TCP/IP's architecture is the concept of packet-switching: messages are broken down into smaller 'packets' which are then conveyed across the Internet via separate channels, to be reassembled on arrival by the host, based on the instructions in the message header.⁶⁵ Packet switching was developed from theoretical work undertaken in the early 1960s by Leonard Kleinrock at the Massachusetts Institute of

---

[59] Guido R. Hiertz and others, 'The IEEE 802.11 Universe' [2010] IEEE Communications Magazine 62, 62.
[60] Ibid. 63.
[61] Joonsuk Kim and Inkyu Lee, '802.11 WLAN: History and New Enabling MIMO Techniques for next Generation Standards' (2015) 53 IEEE Communications Magazine 134, 134.
[62] Hiertz and others (n. 59) 63.
[63] Jerry D. Gibson (ed.), *Mobile Communications Handbook* (3rd ed., CRC Press 2013) 406–8.
[64] Barry M. Leiner and others, 'A Brief History of the Internet' (2009) 39 Computer Communication Review 22, 22.
[65] Andrew L. Russell, 'OSI: The Internet That Wasn't' [2013] *IEEE Spectrum* https://spectrum.ieee.org/tech-history/cyberspace/osi-the-internet-that-wasnt accessed 11 March 2018.

Technology, British researchers David Davies and Roger Scantlebury, and Paul Baran's research at the RAND Corporation.[66] Packet-switching represented a major change from 'circuit-switching' used in telecommunications networks, where a dedicated channel must be established in order to convey messages.[67]

TCP/IP was developed by engineers Robert Kahn and Vinton Cerf, under the auspices of the Defence Advanced Research Projects Agency (DARPA), a United States government-funded defence research project. Kahn and Cerf presented their proposal to a 1973 meeting of the International Packet Network Working Group (INWG) in Sussex, United Kingdom.[68]

TCP/IP was able to provide a common protocol for switching communications across multiple networks, including multiple networks of different types (e.g. fixed, wireless, satellite).[69] This is accomplished based on the principle of 'open architecture':

> In an open-architecture network, the individual networks may be separately designed and developed and each may have its own unique interface which it may offer to users and/or other providers. including other Internet providers. Each network can be designed in accordance with the specific environment and user requirements of that network. There are generally no constraints on the types of network that can be included or on their geographic scope, although certain pragmatic considerations will dictate what makes sense to offer.[70]

The specifications of TCP/IP have always been open and have been available to all prospective users at minimal cost, one of the main reasons why it became the dominant standard for the Internet.[71] The development of TCP/IP is primarily the responsibility of the Internet Engineering Task Force (IETF);[72] TCP/IP has been upgraded over time to enhance its functions, for example the move from IPv4 to IPv6 to

---

[66] Leiner and others (n. 64) 23.
[67] Russell (n. 65); Leiner and others (n. 64) 23.
[68] Leiner and others (n. 64) 25.
[69] David C. Mowery and Timothy Simcoe, 'Is the Internet a US Invention?—An Economic and Technological History of Computer Networking' (2002) 31 NELSON + WINTER + 20 1369, 1373; Andrew L. Russell, '"Rough Consensus and Running Code" and the Internet-OSI Standards War' (2006) 28 IEEE Annals of the History of Computing 48, 49.
[70] Leiner and others (n. 64) 24.
[71] Mowery and Simcoe (n. 69) 1373.
[72] Ibid. 1374; Oki Eijo and others, *Advanced Internet Protocols, Services and Innovations* (John Wiley & Sons 2012) 2.

accommodate much larger volumes of Internet traffic following the explosive growth of the World Wide Web.[73]

TCP/IP was not the only possible communications protocol available; in the early days of computing networks, competing (and mutually non-interoperable) network architectures were developed by IBM, DEC and Honeywell.[74] Another early alternative was the X.25 protocol developed by the International Telecommunication Union (ITU)'s Consultative Committee for International Telephony and Telegraphy (CCITT), which would have placed more responsibility on network nodes rather than the hosts at each end of the network, imposed uniform requirements on all participating networks (including private networks) and, most probably, would have given control over network access to telecommunications incumbents.[75]

Nevertheless, TCP/IP's main rival was the Open Systems Interconnection (OSI) protocol, originated in 1977[76] and developed by ISO in close collaboration with other SSOs including the European Computer Manufacturers Association (ECMA) (now Ecma International), the ITU's CCITT and IEEE.[77] The first version of OSI was published in 1984.[78] Various upgraded versions were subsequently released, including a connectionless model for data transmission in 1994.[79] TCP/IP and OSI were, at various times, championed by the US and European governments, respectively.[80] TCP/IP was first recognized as standard by the United States defence community, in 1980,[81] and in 1983 became standard for all communications on ARPANET, the forerunner to the Internet.[82]

By 1994, TCP/IP had been accepted by the United States' National Institute of Standards and Technology (NIST), and the advent of the World Wide Web, which took advantage of the distributed, end to end

---

[73] Amer Nizar Abu Ali, 'Comparison Study between IPV4 & IPV6' (2012) 9 International Journal of Computer Science Issues 314, 314–15.
[74] Ivo Maathuis and Wim A. Smit, 'The Battle between Standards: TCP/IP vs OSI Victory through Path Dependency or by Quality?', *Proceedings of the Third IEEE Conference on Standardization and Innovation in Information Technology* (IEEE 2003) 164.
[75] Janet Abbate, *Inventing the Internet* (MIT Press 1999) 152–67.
[76] Russell (n. 69) 52.
[77] Maathuis and Smit (n. 74) 164.
[78] Ibid.
[79] Ibid.
[80] Maathuis and Smit (n. 74).
[81] Leiner and others (n. 64) 26.
[82] Ibid.

character of the packet-switched Internet, had solidified its dominance; the market had 'tipped' in TCP/IP's favour.[83] TCP/IP ultimately prevailed, and has since achieved total market dominance.

Whilst OSI appears to have held certain technical advantages over TCP/IP (e.g. superior security), it also suffered from a number of drawbacks, including a committee-based process that was too slow[84] and some features included more for political than technical reasons,[85] and much higher licence fees for users.[86] Maathuis and Smit concluded that neither third-degree nor second-degree path dependency (adopting the framework of Liebowitz and Margolis) could be observed with respect to the choice of TCP/IP over OSI,[87] although clearly the importance of historical selection choices and network effects cannot be dismissed in this regard.

2.3.5 Mobile Wireless Standards: from 1G to 4G and beyond

The air interface is the central interface of every mobile system. An air interface is a radio-frequency translating interface for wireless communications. In cellular communications, the air interface is the radio-frequency-based connection between a Mobile End System and a Mobile Data Base System.[88] The first mobile standards were primarily analogue (e.g. Advanced Mobile Phone System (AMPS), developed in the United States). Different standards were used in Europe and the Scandinavian countries.[89]

AMPS was succeeded during the 1980s by digital cellular systems based on Time Division Multiple Access (TDMA) technology.[90] These included the GSM[91] standard developed initially within the European Conference of Postal and Telecommunications Administrations (CEPT)[92] and later the European Telecommunications Standards Institute (ETSI), and the

---

[83] Russell (n. 69) 56.
[84] Maathuis and Smit (n. 74).
[85] Ibid. 166–7.
[86] Ibid. 168–9.
[87] Ibid. 172–3.
[88] 'Mobile Air Interface', *Telecommunications Illustrated Dictionary* (2nd ed., CRC Press 2002).
[89] Erik Dahlmann, Stefan Parkvall and Johan Skold, *4G: LTE/LTE-Advanced for Mobile Broadband* (2nd ed., Academic Press 2014) 2.
[90] Gibson (n. 63) 429–30.
[91] GSM initially stood for *Groupe Spécial Mobile*, later renamed Global System for Mobile Communications.
[92] CEPT membership consists of 48 European postal and telecommunications administrations.

2.3 NOTABLE INTEROPERABILITY STANDARDS

US-TDMA standard. During the 1980s, systems based on Code Division Multiple Access (CDMA) were also developed.[93]

With the move towards third generation mobile technologies, more concerted attempts were made to create global cellular standards. A number of standards were developed which complied with the International Mobile Telecommunications for the year 2000 (IMT-2000) standard developed by ITU. ITU has developed overarching guidance for 3G and 4G mobile systems, without engaging in drafting detailed technical specifications.[94]

The Third Generation Partnership Project (3GPP), comprising telecommunications associations from Europe, the United States and Asian countries, developed the Universal Mobile Telecommunications System (UMTS), based on GSM 2G technology. UMTS uses Wideband Code Division Multiple Access (W-CDMA) technology and its standards were drafted by ETSI. The Third Generation Partnership Project 2 (3GPP2) (a collaboration between Japanese, US, Korean and Chinese telecommunications associations) developed the competing cdma2000 third-generation standard, based on 2G CDMA technology.[95]

The fourth generation (4G) standards for mobile telephony have since been developed, with the Long-Term Evolution (LTE) standard emerging as the leading standard worldwide. LTE was developed by 3GPP under the auspices of ETSI as the successor to W-CDMA, again took place under the umbrella of a coordinating ITU standard, termed IMT-Advanced.[96] Rapid progress is now seen towards 5G standards.[97]

2.3.6 Near Field Communications Standards

Near field communications (NFC) is a short-range wireless technology that enables communications between devices by bringing them close to

---

[93] Gibson (n. 63) 430.
[94] Dahlmann, Parkvall and Skold (n. 89) 4.
[95] Qi Bi, George I Zysman and Hank Menkes, 'Wireless Mobile Communications at the Start of the 21st Century' [2001] IEEE Communications Magazine 110, 112.
[96] Christopher Cox, *An Introduction to LTE: LTE, LTE-Advanced, SAE and 4G Mobile Communications* (1st ed., John Wiley & Sons 2012) 1.
[97] Panagiotis Demestichas and others, 'Emerging Air Interfaces and Management Technologies for the 5G Era' (2017) 2017 EURASIP Journal on Wireless Communications and Networking 184; Toni Levanen and others, 'Radio Interface Evolution towards 5G and Enhanced Local Area Communications' (2014) 2 IEEE Access 1005; see Jeffrey G. Andrews and others, 'What Will 5G Be?' (2014) 32 IEEE Journal on Selected Areas in Communications 1065.

each other.[98] Connection is initiated automatically when the devices are close to each other.[99] NFC evolved from Radio Frequency Identification (RFID) technology.[100] NFC operates at 13.56MHz, at rates ranging from 106 kbit/s to 424 kbit/s. NFC is standardized by ECMA-340 and ISO/IEC 18092. NFC standards have promise as the basis for mobile payment systems. Smartphones are increasingly sold with NFC capability embedded.[101]

2.3.7 Mobile Payment Standards: Cash Goes Wireless

Mobile payments involve 'the payment of products or services based on functionalities of mobile phones'.[102] Establishing a mobile payments network involves partnerships between financial institutions, goods and services suppliers, mobile operators, hardware vendors (e.g. suppliers of NFC chips), software providers and handset manufacturers,[103] with perhaps the critical alliance that between banks (who controlled access to customers' funds) and mobile network operators (who controlled access to mobile users' accounts).[104] Both groups sought to 'own' the customers for purposes of mobile transactions; these disagreements manifested in technical questions such as whether to place the NFC chip inside the subscriber identity module (SIM) card (which would give control of the transaction to mobile operators) or outside the SIM (which would enable financial services suppliers to exercise greater control).[105]

These technical and commercial issues have led to intense inter-consortium rivalry which has slowed down the development of agreed standards.[106] Uptake of mobile payment systems in the United States and Europe, where existing credit card payment systems are well established, has been noticeably slow; systems have emerged much more quickly in

---

[98] Tomi Aarnio, 'Near Field Communication: Using NFC to Unlock Doors' (Master's Thesis, Aalto University 2013) 7.
[99] Ibid.
[100] Ibid.
[101] Ibid.
[102] Pinar Ozcan and Filipe M Santos, 'The Market That Never Was: Turf Wars and Failed Alliances in Mobile Payments' (2015) 36 Strategic Management Journal 1486, 1493.
[103] Ibid. 1491.
[104] Ibid. 1494.
[105] Ibid. 1494–5.
[106] Ibid. 1495–7.

Japan, Korea and China, where the existing payment systems were not as well developed.[107]

2.3.8 Towards an Internet of Things

The coming Internet of Things may be described as follows: 'The concept of IoT is to enable real world objects with speech, vision, hearing, smell, and touch, so inanimate things can perform jobs more accurately and responsively collaboratively and with learning'.[108] In practical terms, this means that:

> many machines, sensors and other electronic devices could be connected back to a core database that could process and act upon the information that they transmit. For example, in a smart city sensors could measure traffic levels and cause the alteration of traffic light timing patterns. Or they could measure the level of rubbish in dustbins resulting in optimised rubbish collection schedules.[109]

The advent of the Internet of Things is expected to have a significant impact on the daily lives of consumers, with applications envisaged in the fields of assisted living, e-health, enhanced learning,[110] as well as significant industry applications in automation, logistics and intelligent transportation.[111] The Internet of Things will almost certainly require a standardized approach;[112] no currently available standard, however, can deliver the necessary capability.[113]

Established standard-setting organizations such as IETF, IEEE and ETSI are likely to play a critical role in developing the necessary standards;[114] ISO/IEC and ITU are also engaged on this issue.[115] Other promising initiatives include the 'Weightless' technology being pursued through

---

[107] Miao Miao and Krishna Jayakar, 'Mobile Payments in Japan, South Korea and China: Cross-Border Convergence or Divergence of Business Models?' (2016) 40 Telecommunications Policy 182, 183.
[108] Amy J. C. Trappey and others, 'A Review of Essential Standards and Patent Landscapes for the Internet of Things: A Key Enabler for Industry 4.0' (2017) 33 Advanced Engineering Informatics 208, 210.
[109] Webb (n. 3) 57.
[110] Atzori, Iera and Morabito (n. 9) 1.
[111] Ibid.
[112] Webb (n. 3) 60; Trappey and others (n. 108) 212.
[113] Webb (n. 3) 58.
[114] Trappey and others (n. 108) 212.
[115] Aref Meddeb, 'Internet of Things Standards: Who Stands Out from the Crowd?' [2016] IEEE Communications magazine – Communications Standards Supplement 41, 42–3.

a consortium modelled closely on the Bluetooth consortium, with a view to sidestepping the inevitable problems associated with the assertion of SEPs.[116] In view of the tremendous complexity involved in developing an Internet of Things, the definition of an agreed standardized approach still appears to be some way off. Meddeb concludes: 'Do we have a common and clear understanding of a standard IoT service? The answer is quite mitigated. In fact, to some extent, the overwhelming number of standards might have contributed in further exacerbating the ambiguity about service and may deepen the interoperability issues'.[117] Resolving such problems of definition and standardization represents an essential prerequisite to the development of this technology.

2.4 Who Makes Interoperability Standards?

There is no set requirement for a standard to be formulated under the auspices of some particular body or type of bodies. Rather, a standard can be established in an institutional setting that can range across the full spectrum in terms of degrees of formal organization, from longstanding international organizations (such as the ITU) to informal setting within consortia or single firms.

The international standard-setting landscape today is relatively fragmented, with standard-setting activities stretched across many competing organizations. Over the years there have been many shifts in forum, as industry players have perceived particular standard-setting organizations as being unresponsive to the needs of the particular standard-setting process at hand,[118] as the following anecdote (which provides for an example of forum shifting between IEEE and the ECMA) indicates:

> When, for example, the standardization of the Ethernet protocol for local area networks ran into difficulties in IEEE's Committee 802, the main sponsors of the project – DEC, Intel and Xerox – initiated a parallel procedure in ECMA. ECMA was much smaller than IEEE. Some of the actors, who had hampered progress in the IEEE, were not represented. The opposition was much more suave, and ECMA agreed fairly quickly on the standard, which had been blocked in IEEE. However, Ethernet's main opponent, IBM, was active in both IEEE and ECMA and had to be bought off with a package deal. IBM agreed to Ethernet. However, DEC,

---

[116] Webb (n. 3) 64–5.
[117] Meddeb (n. 115) 46.
[118] See Philipp Genschel, 'How Fragmentation Can Improve Co-Ordination: Setting Standards in International Telecommunications' (1997) 18 Organization Studies 603.

2.4 WHO MAKES INTEROPERABILITY STANDARDS?

Intel and Xerox had to let IBM's Token Ring standard pass in return. After having been passed by ECMA, the standard was reconsidered by IEEE and also passed as an IEEE standard.[119]

This excerpt illustrates the essentially footloose character of interoperability standard-setting: it is quite feasible for a given standard-setting initiative to shift from one forum to another; this could occur for reasons ranging from a broader (or narrower) selection of industry players, to the particular rules of the standard-setting forum in question (including the precise terms of its intellectual property policies). This has significant implications for the regulation of interoperability standard-setting activities.

The main players are sketched in the following section; nevertheless, it must be emphasized that standard-setting remains a rapidly changing and variegated field, and the emergence of new players, models and structures in the future is highly likely.

2.4.1 International Organizations: the International Telecommunication Union

The ITU, as the longest-established and one of the highest-profile standard-setting organizations, is, along with the ISO and the IEC, considered one of the 'big three' in international standard-setting.[120] Like the other two, its headquarters are in Geneva. Unlike the other two, the ITU is a genuine international organization – the only international organization with a major role in creating interoperability standards. The ITU traces its lineage to the foundation of the International Telegraph Union in 1865, making it one of the world's oldest international organizations.[121] The modern ITU is actually a fusion of two earlier organizations: the International Telegraph Union and the International Radio Union.[122]

Membership of the ITU can take two forms: State membership and Sector membership. Only sovereign States can be State Members. The rights of State Members include: to take part in all conferences; to be

---

[119] Ibid. 612.
[120] Liu (n. 45).
[121] George A. Codding Jr., 'Three Times Forty: The ITU in a Time of Change' in Lawrence S. Finkelstein (ed.), *Politics in the International System* (Duke University Press 1988) 324.
[122] George A. Codding Jr., 'The International Telecommunication Union: 130 Years of Telecommunications Regulation' (1994) 23 Denver Journal of International Law and Policy 501, 501.

eligible for election to the ITU Council; and to nominate nationals as candidates for election as officials of the ITU or as members of the Radio Regulations Board. Sector membership is also available in respect of one of the ITU's three sectors: the Radiocommunications Sector (ITU-R), the Telecommunications Standardisation Sector (ITU-T) and the Telecommunications Development Sector (ITU-D). A Sector Member may become either a full member (this is open to both state and non-state entities) or an Associate Sector Member. Sector membership comprises all State Members together with non-state entities that have been granted sector membership. Non-state entities wishing to become Sector Members must be authorized by an appropriate State Member. The rights of Sector Members include: to take part in the works of their sector; to provide chairmen and vice-chairmen of Sector assemblies, and world telecommunication development conferences; and (within limits) to formulate the questions and recommendations the Sector deals with.[123]

The ITU formulates standards through two of its three sectors: the ITU-R and the ITU-T. The ITU-T works through World Telecommunication Standardisation Assemblies (WTSA), study groups, a Telecommunication Standardisation Advisory Group (TSAG) and the Telecommunications Standardization Bureau.[124] ITU-T study groups take responsibility for standardization with respect to various issue areas such as: broadband cable and TV, protocols and test specifications, multimedia, and Internet of Things and applications. Recent accomplishments of the ITU in standard-setting include the H.350 standard for the storage and location of information relating to video and voice over Internet Protocol technologies, developed jointly with the IETF.[125] Important accomplishments of ITU-R include developing overarching frameworks for the development of advanced mobile telephony standards.[126]

ITU has traditionally been perceived to be slow and cumbersome in its standard-setting processes, and tied too closely to incumbent

---

[123] 'Membership Categories' (*International Telecommunication Union*) www.itu.int accessed 8 March 2018.

[124] 'The Framework of ITU-T' (*International Telecommunication Union*) www.itu.int/en/ITU-T/about/Pages/framework.aspx accessed 8 March 2018.

[125] Jon Saltzman, Samir Chatterjee and Murali Raman, 'A Framework for ICT Standards Creation: The Case of ITU-T Standard H.350' (2008) 33 Information Systems 285.

[126] 'About Mobile Technology and IMT-2000' (*International Telecommunication Union*) www.itu.int accessed 8 March 2018.

telecommunications monopolies.[127] Nevertheless by streamlining its standard-setting processes, ITU has been able to address at least the first perceived deficiency.[128] Today ITU remains an important part of the standard-setting landscape, particularly within its traditional field in telecommunications standard-setting, where its role is increasingly seen as complementary with the roles played by other standard-setting organizations.

2.4.2 *International Bodies: ISO, IEEE and IETF*

2.4.2.1 The International Organization for Standardization

Despite its name, ISO is not an international organization; rather, ISO describes itself as a network of national standards bodies. ISO is an independent, non-governmental organization made up of members from the national standards bodies of 164 countries. Founded in 1947, it is headquartered in Geneva, Switzerland. ISO is a network of national standards bodies, one per country.[129] Each member is the most representative body for standardization in its country.[130] Many ISO members are part of the government structure of their countries, or are mandated by government. Others are private sector organizations often set up by national partnerships of industry associations.[131]

There are three categories of ISO member: subscriber member; correspondent member; and full member. ISO members are free to decide their level of membership, based on their technical and financial capabilities. Full members have full voting rights and influence in ISO standards development, strategy and policy meetings. They can adopt ISO International Standards as national standards. They enjoy access to all ISO meetings – technical, strategy and policy – and can speak and vote to influence the agenda and direction that the ISO system takes, including

---

[127] Kai Jacobs, Rob N. Procter and Robin Alun Williams, 'The Making of Standards: Looking inside the Work Groups' (2001) 39 IEEE Communications Magazine 102, 104; Stanley Besen and Joseph Farrell, 'The Role of the ITU in Standardization: Pre-Eminence, Impotence or Rubber Stamp?' (1991) 15 Telecommunications Policy 311, 311–12.

[128] Besen and Farrell (n. 127) 312; Jacobs, Procter and Williams (n. 127) 104.

[129] Jonathan Koppell, 'International Organization for Standardization' in Thomas Hale and David Held (eds.), *Handbook of Transnational Governance: Institutions & Innovation* (Polity Press 2011) 289.

[130] 'ISO Membership Manual' (International Organization for Standardization 2015) 6 www.iso.org accessed 8 March 2018.

[131] Koppell (n. 129) 289–90.

the content of ISO International Standards. Correspondent members may be observers in ISO standards development, strategy and policy meetings. They have no voting rights. They can attend ISO meetings as observers; hence they cannot influence the agenda and direction that the ISO System takes, nor the content of ISO International Standards. Subscriber members have no participation in ISO Standards development, strategy or policy meetings. They have no voting rights.[132]

ISO works together with another international body, the IEC, and, occasionally, ITU through Joint Technical Committee 1 (JTC 1) to develop standards for the information and communications technology sectors.[133] Within JTC 1 there are approximately twenty working groups,[134] such as ISO/IEC JTC 1/SC7, which develops software and systems engineering standards.[135] Joint Technical Committee 1 has developed a number of important international standards in the software and systems engineering field, including Software Life Cycle Processes (ISO/IEC 12207), Systems Life Cycle Processes (ISO/IEC 15288) and Software Process Assessments (ISO/IEC 15504), which have gained widespread acceptance and use in these fields.[136] JTC1 has also collaborated with ITU-T to develop a number of important standards including video coding standards, such as the H.264/MPEG-4 Advanced Video Coding Standard,[137] and image coding standards, such as the JPEG XR (ITU-T T.832, ISO/IEC 29199-2) standard.[138]

ISO has approved a number of other significant interoperability standards, including: the 802.11 family of standards (which was developed by IEEE) (ISO/IEC/IEEE 8802-11), shipping container standards (ISO 668:2013 and ISO 1496-1:2013); electronic identification cards, such as smart cards (ISO/IEC 7816); and open systems interconnection (ISO/IEC 9834 family of standards).[139]

[132] 'ISO Membership Manual' (n. 130) 16–17.
[133] Koppell (n. 129) 293.
[134] Ibid.
[135] Claudia Y. Laporte, Alain April and Alain Renault, 'Applying ISO/IEC Software Engineering Standards in Small Settings: Historical Perspectives and Initial Achievements', *Proceedings of the SPICE 2006 Conference, May 4–5, 2006, Luxembourg* (Curran Associates, Inc).
[136] Ibid. 32.
[137] Thomas Wiegand and Gary J. Sullivan, 'The H.264/AVC Video Coding Standard [Standards in a Nutshell]' (2007) 24 IEEE Signal Processing Magazine 148.
[138] Frederic Dufaux, Gary J. Sullivan and Touradj Ebrahimi, 'The JPEG XR Image Coding Standard [Standards in a Nutshell]' (2009) 26 IEEE Signal Processing Magazine 195.
[139] 'Popular Standards' (*International Organization for Standardization*) www.iso.org/popular-standards.html accessed 8 March 2018.

2.4.2.2 Institute of Electrical and Electronics Engineers

Founded in 1884,[140] the IEEE is a technical professional society with over 423,000 members, mostly engineers, scientists and other like professionals.[141] IEEE has been incorporated in the State of New York, in the United States, as a not-for-profit corporation since 1896.[142] IEEE undertakes standard-setting activities through the IEEE Standards Association (IEEE-SA), which has already developed over 1,300 standards, with a further 600 in development.[143] Well-known standards developed by IEEE include Wi-Fi (a product of the 802.11 working group) and the Ethernet standard for local area network technology (a product of the 802.3 working group).[144]

2.4.2.3 Internet Engineering Task Force

The IETF describes itself as: 'a loosely self-organized group of people who contribute to the engineering and evolution of Internet technologies. It is the principal body engaged in the development of new Internet standard specifications'.[145] The IETF describes its mission as: 'to produce high quality, relevant technical and engineering documents that influence the way people design, use, and manage the Internet in such a way as to make the Internet work better. These documents include protocol standards, best current practices, and informational documents of various kinds'.[146] This mission is pursued through the guiding principles of: open process; technical competence; volunteer core; rough consensus and running code; and protocol ownership.[147]

The slogan of 'rough consensus and running code' has become something of a catchcry for the IETF, and for the Internet community more generally. It is embodied in an early quote about the IETF from David Clark: 'We reject kings, presidents and voting. We believe in rough

---

[140] Marc Rysman and Timothy Simcoe, 'Patents and the Performance of Voluntary Standard-Setting Organizations' (2008) 54 Management Science 1920, 1922.
[141] 'History of IEEE' (*IEEE*) www.ieee.org accessed 9 March 2018.
[142] 'Tax and Corporate Information' (*IEEE*) www.ieee.org/about/help/business_policies/tax_corp_info.html accessed 8 March 2018.
[143] 'IEEE at a Glance' (*IEEE*) www.ieee.org accessed 8 March 2018.
[144] Biddle and others (n. 8) 183; Charles Spurgeon, *Ethernet: The Definitive Guide* (O'Reilly Media Inc 2000) 6–7.
[145] 'The Tao of the IETF: A Novice's Guide to the Internet Engineering Task Force' www.ietf.org/tao.html accessed 30 November 2017.
[146] Harald Alvestrand, 'A Mission Statement for the IETF' (29 April 2004) https://tools.ietf.org accessed 30 November 2017.
[147] Ibid.

consensus and running code'.[148] Alvestrand defines the concept as: 'We make standards based on the combined engineering judgement of our participants and our real-world experience in implementing and deploying our specifications'.[149] The IETF does not have a formal corporate structure, and does not provide for membership.[150] However, the IETF works in close collaboration with a number of other organizations that do maintain a formal structure, including the Internet Architecture Board (IAB) and the Internet Society (ISOC).[151]

IETF is responsible for producing many of the standards that underpin the Internet, including the TCI/IP protocol suite and the HTTP protocol.[152] These protocols have been upgraded regularly within the IETF forum, including IPv6, the latest version.[153] IETF has developed numerous other standards such as: Multipurpose Internet Mail Extensions (MIME); Simple Network Management Protocol (SNMP); Open Shortest Path First (OSPF); Internet Protocol Security (IPSEC); and Resource Reservation Protocol (RSVP).[154]

2.4.3 Regional and National Standard-Setting Organizations

Standards can be created by regional or national standard-setting bodies, or by governments. For example, the ETSI is a not-for-profit organization based in France. ETSI is recognized by the EU as a European Standards Organization and has approximately 800 member organizations.[155] ETSI is perhaps best known for sponsoring the creation of the GSM family of wireless telecommunications standards, which includes the highly successful 3G W-CDMA[156] and 4G LTE wireless interface standards.[157]

---

[148] 'The Tao of the IETF: A Novice's Guide to the Internet Engineering Task Force' (n. 145); Russell (n. 69) 49.
[149] Alvestrand (n. 146).
[150] Russell (n. 69) 54–5.
[151] 'The Tao of the IETF: A Novice's Guide to the Internet Engineering Task Force' (n. 145).
[152] Janet Wilson, 'The IETF: Laying the Net's Asphalt' (1998) 31 Computer 116, 116.
[153] Shane Kerr, 'IETF Support for IPv6 Deployment' (*IETF Journal*, 7 October 2007) www.ietfjournal.org/ietf-support-for-ipv6-deployment/ accessed 8 March 2018.
[154] Masataka Ohta, 'IETF and Internet Standards' [1998] IEEE Communications Magazine 126, 128.
[155] 'About ETSI' (*ETSI*) www.etsi.org/about accessed 9 March 2018.
[156] Jeffrey L. Funk, 'The Co-Evolution of Technology and Methods of Standard Setting: The Case of the Mobile Phone Industry' (2008) 19 Journal of Evolutionary Economics 73, 84–6.
[157] Dahlmann, Parkvall and Skold (n. 89) 1–17.

2.4.4 Private Standard-Setting Organizations and Consortia

Many standards are drafted by private SSOs with no links to government. One example is the JEDEC Solid State Technology Association, which develops standards for the microelectronics industry.[158] JEDEC is particularly well-known for developing semiconductor memory standards including DRAM and DDR synchronous DRAM.[159] There are many other such organizations: Baron and Spulber have compiled a database of 670 active SSOs, and suggest there are approximately 1,000 in operation.[160] Moreover, standards need not necessarily be set by a formal standard-setting body. Consortia standardization may be characterized as 'hybrid' standardization that sits somewhere between formal and de facto standard setting.[161]

A good example of consortium standard setting is the Bluetooth Alliance. Its origins lay in the development by Ericsson and Nokia of certain short-range radio communication technologies.[162] Both firms realized that a purely proprietary approach would not work and that alliances were necessary. An alliance was formed to promote a standardized approach. A structure was created that differentiated between promoters (who drafted standards documents) and adopters (who were granted full access to relevant intellectual rights but did not have a say in standards-setting).[163] The Bluetooth Special Interest Group (SIG) was formally established in 1998.[164] The standard has proven highly successful and Bluetooth capability is now included as standard in many laptops. Other notable examples include the Mobile Payment Forum and the Blu-Ray Disc Association. The Mobile Payment Forum is a consortium launched in November 2001 to create a standardized approach to mobile payments, using payment card accounts.[165] The Blu-Ray Disc Association is another consortium

---

[158] 'About JEDEC' (*JEDEC*) www.jedec.org/about-jedec accessed 9 March 2018.
[159] 'Why JEDEC Standards Matter' (*JEDEC*) www.jedec.org accessed 9 March 2018.
[160] Justis Baron and Daniel Spulber, 'Technology Standards and Standard Setting Organizations: Introduction to the Searle Center Database' (2018) 27 Journal of Economics & Management Strategy 462, 464–72.
[161] Thomas Keil, 'De Facto Standardization through Alliances – Lessons from Bluetooth' (2002) 26 Telecommunications Policy 205, 206.
[162] Ibid. 208.
[163] Ibid.
[164] 'Our History' (*Bluetooth*) www.bluetooth.com/about-us/our-history accessed 9 March 2018.
[165] Lim (n. 6) 211.

which focusses on developing standards for the Blu-Ray audiovisual technology.[166]

2.4.5 Single-Firm Standard-Setting

De facto standards can arise from competition in the marketplace between incompatible alternatives, based on user choices of technology.[167] Paradigmatic examples include computer operating systems such as Microsoft Windows and Google Android. Another classic example noted above was the 'standards war' between Sony and Matsushita to standardize videocassette technology, with Matsushita's VCR standard ultimately achieving dominance. In this situation, consumers place a high value on compatibility but vendors are unwilling to offer compatible solutions, leading to a 'standards war' between incompatible solutions. Where network effects, positive feedback loops and tipping are evident, the end result of the standards war may be the dominance of one particular technology over all others, in some cases resulting in monopoly or near-monopoly.[168]

2.5 The Creation of Interoperability Standards

Just as there is no particular requirement as to where standards are drafted, or by whom, there is also no single standardized procedure or formula for creating a standard. Rather, standards are created in diverse settings using a variety of approaches that vary substantially in terms of their degrees of formality. In many ways the degree of formality of the approach pursued in creating the standard reflects the degree of formality of the standard-setting body.

2.5.1 Overview of the Standard-Setting Process

Whilst modalities of standards creation will vary across organizations, creating a standard within a formally established SSO usually includes the following steps, as seen in Table 2.1.

---

[166] 'General Info' (*Blu-ray Disc*) www.blu-raydisc.com accessed 10 March 2018.
[167] Techatassanasoontorn and Suo (n. 18) 357.
[168] Philip Anderson and Michael L. Tushman, 'Technological Discontinuities and Dominant Designs: A Cyclical Model of Technological Change' (1990) 35 Administrative Science Quarterly 604, 613–16.

2.5 THE CREATION OF INTEROPERABILITY STANDARDS 45

Table 2.1 *Overview of steps involved in the standard-setting process*

Step	Description	Example
Idea	Every standardization begins with an idea	
Approval to begin the standards drafting process	Many SSOs include an initial approval requirement before a working group is established and drafting begins	In IEEE, a Project Authorization Request must be submitted, setting out the reason for the project and what the proposed standard will do. The PAR is reviewed by the New Standards Committee, which considers the PAR and makes recommendations to the IEEE-SA Standards Board. Once a PAR is approved by the Board, the standards project begins.[169]
Establishment of a working group	Standards are generally drafted by groups of experts in a working group. The WG may meet at intervals or remotely (e.g. through teleconference or email)	ITU-T standardization is carried out by technical Study Groups. There are currently 20 SGs covering various fields.[170]
Drafting the standard	The WG drafts the standard	ISO standards are generally drafted by an Advisory Group responsible to the relevant technical management board[171]
Submission of standard for approval	Once the WG has drafted the standard, it is generally forwarded to the SSO's plenary body for approval	In ISO, a Final Draft International Standard is submitted to ISO/Central Secretariat by the committee secretary. The FDIS is then circulated to ISO Members for a two-month vote.[172]

[169] 'Submitting a Project Request' (*IEEE Standards Association – Developing Standards*) https://standards.ieee.org/develop/par.html accessed 21 July 2016.
[170] 'ITU-T Study Groups (Study Period 2017–2020)' (*International Telecommunication Union*) www.itu.int accessed 12 March 2018.
[171] 'ISO/IEC Directives Part 1: Procedures for the Technical Work' (2016) 8–9 www.iec.ch accessed 30 November 2017.
[172] 'Developing ISO Standards' (*International Organization for Standardization*) www.iso.org accessed 22 July 2016.

Table 2.1 (cont.)

Step	Description	Example
Approval by the SDO	Within SSOs, standards are normally approved by consensus. Different SSOs will have different conceptions of consensus, which often involves voting, with a high minimum threshold of approving votes required.	The IETF favours 'rough consensus and running code'. 'Rough consensus' may be defined as: strongly held objections must be debated until most people are satisfied that such objections are wrong.
Appeals	Many SSOs include an appeals process	In ISO, national bodies can appeal a variety of decisions taken in relation to standard-setting, within 12 weeks of the decision.[173]
Publication	The standard is made publicly available. Generally, the standard is subject to copyright and often a fee is charged for access.	Specifications adopted by the Bluetooth Alliance are made available from Bluetooth Alliance website[174]

2.5.2 'Best Practice': ISO and Others

One way to evaluate the standard-setting processes of various SSOs is to examine them against the various good practice guides promulgated by ISO, the WTO and other bodies. The classic document outlining best practice in standard-setting is itself a standard, created by ISO: the ISO/IEC Guide 59: 1994 Code of Good Practice for Standardization.[175]

The key elements of 'best practice' as outlined in this document are: use of written procedures based on the consensus principle;[176]

---

[173] 'ISO/IEC Directives Part 1: Procedures for the Technical Work' (n. 171) 39.
[174] 'Specifications' (*Bluetooth*) www.bluetooth.com/specifications accessed 25 January 2018.
[175] 'ISO/IEC Guide 59: 1994 Code of Good Practice for Standardization' www.iso.org/standard/23390.html accessed 20 May 2019.
[176] Ibid. 4.1.

2.5 THE CREATION OF INTEROPERABILITY STANDARDS   47

availability of an appeals mechanism for the impartial handling of any procedural or substantive complaints;[177] timely public notification of standard-setting activity;[178] provision on request of a copy of a draft standard;[179] provision of a reasonable opportunity to review and comment on draft standards;[180] approval based on evidence of consensus;[181] prompt publication of approved standards;[182] maintenance of proper records;[183] standards should be expressed in terms of performance rather than design or descriptive characteristics;[184] standards should not include a patented item unless this is justifiable for technical reasons and the right holder agrees to negotiate licences with interested applicants, wherever located, on reasonable terms and conditions;[185] and participation in the standards development process should be available to materially and directly interested persons and organizations within a coherent process.[186]

The WTO has also become an active participant in recent decades, notably with the inclusion of a Code of Good Practice for the Preparation, Adoption and Application of Standards in the final texts of the Uruguay Round of negotiations, annexed to the Agreement on Technical Barriers to Trade (TBT).[187] The TBT Code of Good Practice appears to be based on the ISO Code, and many of its provisions are very similar. Notably, however, the provisions of the ISO Code dealing with intellectual property were omitted in their entirety.

The WTO's Technical Barriers to Trade Committee (TBT Committee) has also produced a document entitled Principles for the Development of International Standards, which sets out a number of recommendations for standard-setting that include transparency, openness, impartiality and consensus, effectiveness and relevance and the development

---

[177] Ibid. 4.2.
[178] Ibid. 4.3.
[179] Ibid. 4.4.
[180] Ibid.
[181] Ibid. 4.5.
[182] Ibid. 4.7.
[183] Ibid. 4.8.
[184] Ibid. 5.6.
[185] Ibid. 5.8.
[186] Ibid. 6.1.
[187] Agreement on Technical Barriers to Trade, Annex 1A to the Marrakesh Agreement Establishing the World Trade Organization (adopted 15 April 1994, entry into force 1 January 1995) (1868 UNTS 120).

dimension.[188] This document, whilst insightful, is conspicuously silent on issues concerning intellectual property.

2.6 Economic Characteristics of Interoperability Standards: Network Effects, and How Standards Become Standard

Standards need to obtain widespread usage in order to be relevant. This can be obtained in one of two basic ways. First, the promoters of the standard could lobby a government to have the standard given the force of law, or for the government to provide incentives for people to use the standard. Second, the standard could become widely accepted by participants in the marketplace.

2.6.1 Standardization through Force of Law

Governments may choose to make standards mandatory for a number of reasons. In some cases, governments may mandate standards for reasons of quality or safety. For example, motor vehicles must generally comply with many mandatory standards relating to safety, emissions etc. In some cases, governments may mandate compliance interoperability standards. For example, China has mandated interoperability with China UnionPay's payment card network,[189] including mandatory compliance with certain associated technical standards.[190] In at least some cases, mandating interoperability may be done simply to promote consumer convenience: private players may insist in non-interoperable approaches for commercial reasons or simply due to a lack of coordination. For example, the lack of a universal standard in relation to mobile phone chargers causes constant frustration to consumers.[191]

In some cases, the government might consider that until a standard is mandated, the market will be unable to coalesce around any interoperable solution. States may also mandate conformity with interoperability standards for reasons of industrial policy – to favour local technologies or

---

[188] 'Decisions and Recommendations Adopted by the WTO Committee on Technical Barriers to Trade since 1 January 1995' (World Trade Organization, Committee on Technical Barriers to Trade 2011) WTO Doc G/TBT/1/Rev.13, 46 https://docs.wto.org accessed 8 October 2020.

[189] WTO, *China – Certain Measures Affecting Electronic Payment Services – Report of the Panel* (16 July 2012) WT/DS413/R [7.720], [7.731].

[190] Ibid. 7.737.

[191] See E. Waffenschmidt, 'Wireless Power for Mobile Devices', *2011 IEEE 33rd International Telecommunications Energy Conference (INTELEC)* (2011).

2.6 ECONOMIC CHARACTERISTICS OF INTEROPERABILITY 49

intellectual property holders. For example, it has been reported that a number of European governments mandated colour television standards in order to protect their domestic producers,[192] and US Government policy favoured 2G and 3G mobile telephony standards developed by IEEE, a US-based SSO.[193] It is worth noting that when States mandate interoperability standards, they will be subject to international trade law (e.g. the WTO Agreement obligations concerning non-discrimination).

For example in *China – Electronic Payment Services*, China's mandating of local interoperability standards was found to have accorded less favourable treatment under Article XVII (National Treatment) of the WTO General Agreement on Trade in Services (GATS) to United States suppliers.[194] The panel found that China had required all issuers of payment cards in China to comply with certain technical standards which, in effect, required them to acquire services from China UnionPay, China's 'national champion' payment card supplier. However Chinese law did not mandate compliance with technical standards established by rival payment card suppliers. As such, China was found to have accorded less favourable treatment to foreign payment card issuers.[195]

Therefore, whilst the tendencies of States to favour producers in establishing mandatory standards is unquestionably an issue that warrants careful study, international rules exist which are either tailored expressly towards addressing the issue (such as the WTO TBT Agreement), or which are drafted sufficiently broadly as to provide a means of addressing such issues as an when they arise (which occurred, for example, in the case of *China – Electronic Payment Services*, where the general non-discrimination obligation outlined in Article XVII of the GATS was applied).

2.6.2 Standardization through Widespread Marketplace Acceptance

If a proposed standard is not mandated or supported by a government, it can only become a 'standard' if it achieves the requisite degree of

---

[192] Neil Gandal and Oz Shy, 'Standardization Policy and International Trade' (2001) 53 Journal of International Economics 363, 364; Rhonda Crane, *The Politics of International Standards: France and the Color TV War (Communication and Information Science)* (Ablex Publishing 1979); Liu (n. 45) 563–4.
[193] Webb (n. 3) 61.
[194] *WTO, China – Certain Measures Affecting Electronic Payment Services – Report of the Panel (16 July 2012) WT/DS413/R* (n. 189) [7.687]–[7.733].
[195] Ibid. [7.737].

acceptance in the marketplace. This is true regardless of whether the standard has been prepared under the auspices of a highly regarded SSO (such as ISO), a consortium or a single firm. To achieve acceptance in the marketplace the standard must be attractive to potential users. In practice this is likely to preclude any proposed standard that is prohibitively expensive or available only subject to highly restrictive licensing terms. Standardization, therefore, necessitates a degree of openness.

In many cases there will be multiple standards competing to standardize the market. For example, the mobile payments market currently sees many different proposals striving to attain the status of a market standard.[196] In some cases (particularly where consumers do not place a high valuation on interoperability, i.e. network effects are not especially strong), the market may tolerate multiple, non-interoperable solutions. However, in situations where consumers place a high value on interoperability, there is likely to be a 'standards war' or 'standards race', where proposed standards compete in a 'winner-take-all' contest to achieve standardization for the entire market.[197]

The contest between VHS and Betamax (discussed above) is perhaps the paradigmatic example. Having lost the standards war, Betamax quickly became irrelevant and VHS dominant.

2.6.2.1 Network Effects

Since the 1980s a considerable economic literature has appeared examining in depth the dynamics of 'standards wars', and explaining why such winner-take-all contests arise.[198] The key insight was that interoperability standards are often characterized by demand-side economies of scale, also known as network externalities or 'network effects'.

A distinction is generally drawn between direct network effects (where consumers are interlinked via a physical network) and indirect network effects (where consumers are effectively linked through a 'virtual network').[199] Telecommunications networks are an example of the

---

[196] Lim (n. 6).
[197] See Anderson and Tushman (n. 168).
[198] David (n. 14); Carl Shapiro and Hal Varian, *Information Rules* (Harvard Business Press 1998); David (n. 46); Farrell and Saloner (n. 49); Michael L. Katz and Carl Shapiro, 'Systems Competition and Network Effects' (1994) 8 The Journal of Economic Perspectives 93; Neil Gandal, 'Compatibility, Standardization and Network Effects: Some Policy Implications' (2002) 18 Oxford Review of Economic Policy 80; Jeffrey Church and Neil Gandal, 'Network Effects, Software Provision, and Standardization' (1992) 40 The Journal of Industrial Economics 85.
[199] Katz and Shapiro (n. 198) 96–100.

2.6 ECONOMIC CHARACTERISTICS OF INTEROPERABILITY

former, the network of computer hardware and software users being an example of the latter. Direct or indirect network effects arise because of a positive externality: as each incremental user joins the network, every existing member benefits because the network is now larger.

Consider a telephone network: each person who joins the network gets the benefit of being able to call everybody else connected to the network. But each member of the network is now better off because they have more people to call. Because of these network externalities, larger networks have a competitive advantage over smaller networks. The market may coalesce around a small number of such networks, or even a single network, leading to monopoly. Information markets frequently display a 'winner-take-all', or 'winner-take-most' character,[200] because of the high premium placed on interoperability and standardization in these markets.

Moreover, once a network has become established, network effects can become a formidable barrier to new entry into the market, because of collecting switching costs.[201] If one supplier has achieved a monopoly and a new entrant tries to enter the market with a better product, the new network can only obtain customers if all the existing market participants switch at once – otherwise those who do switch will suffer from the lack of network effects associated with the new product. There are considerable coordination problems entailed in a whole market making such a switch.[202] Nevertheless such network effects should not be seen as insurmountable and superior products can still enter the market.[203]

It should be emphasized that the 'winner-take-all' or 'winner-take-most' character of many information markets is not necessarily problematic and does not necessarily presage a large role for competition authorities. Network effects confer benefits on society and society as a whole benefits from the market coalescing around a given standard. Economides observes:

> In industries with significant network externalities, under conditions of incompatibility between competing platforms, monopoly may maximize social surplus. When strong network effects are present, a very large market share of one platform creates significant network benefits for this platform which contribute to large consumers' and producers' surplus. It is possible to have situations where a breakup of a monopoly into two competing firms of incompatible standards reduces rather than

---

[200] Nicholas Economides, 'The Microsoft Antitrust Case' (2001) 1 Journal of Industry, Competition and Trade 7, 12.
[201] Blind (n. 19) 15.
[202] Shapiro and Varian (n. 198).
[203] Economides (n. 200) 14.

increases social surplus because network externalities benefits are reduced. This is another way of saying that de facto monopolization is valuable, even if it is done by a monopolist.[204]

From a regulatory perspective, the core question will often be how to preserve the societal benefits of network effects, whilst at the same time addressing the most egregious acts of monopolistic practices in connection with highly dominant standards. This can often lead to questions of how the competing incentives for initial and follow-on innovation can best be balanced.

2.6.2.2 Two-Sided Markets

Many information markets are two-sided: it is possible to charge both producers and consumers for use of the standard. In such markets, it is the interaction between suppliers and consumers in a virtual network relationship that leads to the emergence of a dominant standard. A simple example is users of video games and gaming consoles: buyers will choose the console for which the most games are available. Dominant firms can take advantage of this dynamic by supplying both sides of the market. Network effects come into play on both sides of the market. Buyers of gaming consoles want to buy the console that has the most games available for it. Creators of games want to write games for the largest installed base of consoles. The market may 'tip' towards a single dominant gaming platform. This dynamic is present in many information markets: computer hardware and software; computer operating software and applications software; and mobile telephony handsets and base station networks.

A number of points can be made about such two-sided markets. First, in many cases there will be strong incentives for firms to engage in cross-subsidies. As Rochet and Tirole put it, 'monopoly and competitive platforms price to get both sides on board'.[205] For example, a supplier of gaming consoles might offer consoles at reduced prices in order to sell more games. In its early days, Microsoft gave away its operating system software to companies in order to develop a larger installed base of users. Second, competing platforms are likely to choose their compatibility strategy carefully to maximize the chance of becoming dominant. In some cases, the would-be platform may restrict compatibility to

---

[204] Ibid. 13–14.
[205] Jean-Charles Rochet and Jean Tirole, 'Platform Competition in Two-Sided Markets' (2003) 1(4) Journal of the European Economic Association 990, 1013.

discourage customers from purchasing from its competitors. In other cases, a more complex strategy may be followed: maintaining a high degree of compatibility in the beginning to attract more users to the network, but restricting compatibility later on to drive competitors out of the market. This was detailed by the European Commission in its case against Microsoft, which was seeking to dominate the market for server operating software.

2.6.2.3 Implications for Standards Development

If the standard has been created, and is controlled, by a single dominant firm or by a small consortium, achieving the status of a market 'standard' may provide the prospect for charging at least some of the above-market rents associated with monopoly.[206] If, by contrast, the standard is created by a recognized SSO (e.g. ISO, IETF, ETSI), then the policy of the SSO will likely require that the standard be made available publicly and be available for use to any person or organization, perhaps subject to a one-off fee to obtain a copy of the standard (which is generally subject to copyright). Monopolistic exploitation by the SSO is thereby precluded. However, exploitation may still be possible by IP holders who have contributed essential technologies to the standard. In this case the IP policy of the SSO may well assume considerable importance.

---

[206] But see Economides (n. 200) 20–1. Microsoft was found to be charging far below the monopoly price despite its overwhelming market power.

3

Interoperability Standards and International Economic Law

International economic law (notably, international intellectual property law and international trade law) has not to date addressed in any depth concerns associated with access to interoperability standards and to SEIP. The core agreement with the potential to address such issues is the WTO Agreement on Trade-Related Aspects of Intellectual Property Law (TRIPS Agreement), Annex 1C to the Marrakesh Agreement Establishing the World Trade Organization.[1]

3.1 The Provisions of the TRIPS Agreement

Although the TRIPS Agreement acknowledges the potential for the protection and enforcement of intellectual property rights to constitute barriers to legitimate trade, for the most part it does not mandate measures by Members to address such matters. While certain provisions of international intellectual property may be said to impose ad hoc disciplines, the TRIPS Agreement, together with the various World Intellectual Property Organization (WIPO) treaties incorporated, falls far short of articulating a concrete agenda for ensuring access to interoperability standards and SEIP.

3.1.1 The Minimum Standards of Protection Articulated in the Provisions of the TRIPS Agreement

International intellectual property laws, notably the provisions of the TRIPS Agreement, together with a number of intellectual property conventions established under the auspices of WIPO, impose minimum standards of protection with respect to the relevant rights, including

---

[1] Agreement on Trade-Related Aspects of Intellectual Property Rights, Annex 1C to the Marrakesh Agreement Establishing the World Trade Organization (adopted 15 April 1994, entered into force 1 January 1995) (1869 UNTS 299).

3.1 THE PROVISIONS OF THE TRIPS AGREEMENT

patents, copyrights and layout circuits, with some international protection of trade secrets as well. Article 1(1) of TRIPS articulate how the minimum standards relate to more extensive protection levels: 'Members may, but shall not be obliged to, implement in their law more extensive protection than is required by this Agreement, provided that such protection does not contravene the provisions of this Agreement'. Thus, higher levels of protection are permitted than the TRIPS minimum, subject to the important proviso that such high levels of protection must themselves remain consistent with the TRIPS standards.

The requirement that TRIPS-plus measures remain consistent with the requirements of the Agreement may also give rise to certain maximum standards of protection, particularly in light of the objectives and principles of the Agreement as articulated in Articles 7 and 8. Thus, Hilty articulates the 'minimum standard' in the following terms:

> These attempts of the TRIPS negotiators to bestow somewhat more balance on this youngest overarching IP agreement lead to the result that the freedom of providing protection beyond the required level is not infinite. Exceeding a certain degree of protection could conflict with the mentioned balancing provisions: the more the protection covers, the more likely it is that public interests are jeopardised.[2]

The existing obligations of WTO Members under the WIPO treaties are an important element of the TRIPS minimum standards. Article 2(2) provides that nothing in Parts I to IV of TRIPS is to derogate from existing obligations under the Paris Convention, the Berne Convention, the Rome Convention and the Washington Treaty. Likewise, Article 20 of the Berne Convention, which is incorporated into the TRIPS Agreement,[3] makes provision for future special agreements which are contemplated to involve higher levels of protection: 'The Governments of the countries of the Union reserve the right to enter into special agreements among themselves, in so far as such agreements grant to authors more extensive rights than those granted by the Convention, or contain other provisions not contrary to this Convention'. Article 19 of the Paris Convention, which itself is incorporated into TRIPS,[4] in a similar vein, makes provision for:

---

[2] Reto M. Hilty, 'Ways Out of the Trap of Article 1(1) TRIPS' in Hanns Ullrich and others (eds.), *TRIPS plus 20: From Trade Rules to Market Principles* (Springer Berlin Heidelberg 2016) 187.
[3] TRIPS Agreement art. 9(1).
[4] Ibid. art. 2(1).

'special agreements for the protection of industrial property, in so far as these agreements do not contravene the provisions of this Convention'. Thus, the TRIPS Agreement, together with the WIPO treaties it incorporates, exhibits a relatively coherent intention to mandate a minimum floor of obligations concerning the protection and enforcement of intellectual property rights, below which Member laws may not fall but which Member laws may exceed.[5] Aspects of these minimum standards will have particular relevance in the context of SEIP.

3.1.1.1 Patentability of Computer Programs

Interoperability standards may manifest in the form of computer programs. Neither the TRIPS Agreement nor the Paris Convention mandates that any particular technology (e.g. computer software) be patentable per se; rather, as noted above, Article 27(1) of TRIPS requires that patents shall be available and patents enjoyable without discrimination inter alia as to the field of protection. Thus, purported inventions in a particular field may not be excluded per se, but may be excluded from patentability on grounds that they do not satisfy the applicable standards.

For example, although it would not be permissible to exclude computer software from patentability merely because it is a computer program, it would be permissible to exclude it on the grounds that the relevant invention does not satisfy the threshold requirements of Article 27(1), for example because it is not an 'invention'. This approach is reflected in present UK law.[6] Alternatively, the requirement that patents be available in all fields of technology could be construed to impose a limitation that an invention must be technical in nature.[7] This would seem to be the effect of the exclusion of computer programs from patentability under Article 52 of the European Patent Convention[8] 'as such': in practice such inventions are patentable if they achieve a solution to a technical problem through technical means.

---

[5] Annette Kur, 'From Minimum Standards to Maximum Rules' in Hanns Ullrich and others (eds.), *TRIPS plus 20: From Trade Rules to Market Principles* (Springer 2016) 134.
[6] Patents Act 1977 s. 1(2)(c).
[7] Andreas Neef and Susanne Reyes-Knoche, 'Article 27. Patentable Subject Matter', in Peter-Tobias Stolle, Jan Busche and Katrin Arend (eds.), *WTO-Trade-Related Aspects of Intellectual Property Rights* (Brill Nijhoff 2009) 469, 480.
[8] Convention on the Grant of European Patents (adopted 5 October 1973, entry into force 7 October 1977) (1065 UNTS 199).

3.1.1.2 Special Provision for the Copyrightability of Computer Programs and Compilations of Data

In addition to computer programs, interoperability standards may manifest occasionally in compilations of data. The TRIPS Agreement makes special provision for the copyrightability of both computer programs and compilations of data. In particular, Article 10(1) provides that computer programs, whether in source or object code, shall be protected as literary works. This requirement has since been reinforced in Article 4 of the WIPO Copyright Treaty.[9]

Likewise, Article 10(2) provides that compilations of data or other material, whether in machine readable or other form, which by reason of the selection or arrangement of their contents constitute intellectual creations, shall be protected as such. Nevertheless, it is clarified by the second sentence of Article 10(2) that such protection, which shall not extend to the data or material itself, shall be without prejudice to any copyright subsisting in the data or material itself. Article 10(2) builds on and clarifies the protection accorded pursuant to Article 2(5) of the Berne Convention to collections of literary and artistic works such as anthologies and encyclopaedias, and has subsequently been restated by Article 5 of the WIPO Copyright Treaty.[10]

3.1.2 Certain Provisions of the TRIPS Agreement Exhibiting the Character of Maximum Standards

In recent years, some scholars have criticized the focus of the TRIPS Agreement (and also developments with respect to TRIPS-plus provisions in preferential trade agreements) on the articulation of minimum standards, and have recommended a move towards also articulating maximum standards at the international level, pointing to recent WIPO initiatives regarding access by the visually impaired to copyrighted works as potentially providing a template.[11] Another suggested approach is to embed the provisions of the TRIPS Agreement and TRIPS-plus free trade agreements (FTAs) more deeply within the general body of public international law, taking cognizance of principles of customary international law and general principles of law, as well as provisions of

---

[9] WIPO Copyright Treaty (adopted 20 December 1996, entered into force 6 March 2002) (2186 UNTS 5) art. 4.
[10] Ibid. art. 5.
[11] Kur (n. 5).

international human rights and environmental law pertaining to intellectual property.[12]

A modest number of narrowly crafted provisions of the TRIPS Agreement could be characterized as imposing some degree of maximum standards of protection. Yet, such provisions are at best piecemeal; intellectual property law provides no coherent set of rules for addressing concerns associated with the overprotection of SEIP.

3.1.2.1 Patent Disclosure Requirements

Pursuant to Article 29, WTO Members are obligated to require disclosure of inventions in a manner sufficiently clear and complete for the invention to be carried out by a person skilled in the art. The disclosure requirement imposes an important quid pro quo on inventors in return for the grant of the patent monopoly.[13]

Article 29(1) has something of the character of a maximum standard, as it comprises a formal requirement of the patent application.[14] Article 29(1) has some potential to address concerns associated with access to SEPs, notably in the context of disclosure requirements for computer programs. As discussed further in Chapter 4, better disclosure of software patents would facilitate inventing around SEPs, and in addition would enable access to patented interface specifications necessary for interoperability.

Thus, while Article 27(1) of TRIPS will preclude WTO Members from excluding particular subject matter (e.g. software) from patentability per se, Article 29(1) could nevertheless be applied to ensure that Members impose proper disclosure standards with respect to inventions embodied in computer software.

3.1.2.2 Fairness and Equity in Enforcement Procedures

One example of a potential minimum standard can be found in paragraphs (1) and (2) of Article 41 of TRIPS. Article 41(1) provides for a key overarching obligation in respect of enforcement: WTO Members must

---

[12] See Henning Grosse Ruse-Khan, *The Protection of Intellectual Property in International Law* (Oxford University Press 2016).
[13] Susanne Reyes-Knoche, 'Article 29. Conditions On Patent Applicants', in Peter-Tobias Stoll, Jan Busche and Katrin Arend, *WTO-Trade-Related Aspects of Intellectual Property Rights* (Brill Nijhoff 2009) 521, 524; Antony Taubman, Hannu Wager and Jayashree Watal (eds.), *A Handbook on the WTO TRIPS Agreement* (Cambridge University Press 2012) 101.
[14] Busche and Stoll (n. 13) 524.

ensure that enforcement procedures (as specified in Part III of TRIPS) are available under their law so as to permit effective action against any act of infringement of intellectual property rights covered by the TRIPS Agreement, including expeditious remedies to prevent infringements and remedies which constitute a deterrent to further infringements.

The final sentence of Article 41(1) could be characterized as something of a maximum standard regarding the enforcement of SEIP: Members are affirmatively obligated to apply enforcement procedures in such a fashion as to avoid the creation of barriers to legitimate trade, and to provide safeguards against their abuse. Article 41(2) articulates a further, overarching requirement: enforcement procedures must be fair and equitable, not unnecessarily complicated or costly, or entail unreasonable time limits or unwarranted delays. As Cottier observes, 'The principle of equity essentially stands for the proposition of achieving a fair and just result under the facts of a particular case'.[15] The same author elaborates:

> Recourse to equitable principles amounts to a particular legal methodology suitable for complex configurations entailing conflicting interests and the need to balance them appropriately ... [I]t has great potential to be applied in the field of intellectual property protection, not only in assessing compensation for compulsory licensing, but also in defining and refining the scope of rights and exemptions.[16]

In light of Articles 1(1), 7 and 8 of the TRIPS Agreement, it would seem inappropriate for WTO Members to introduce new, TRIPS-plus measures that failed to adhere to the carefully negotiated balance of rights and obligations reflected in these provisions.

3.1.2.3 Effective Protection against Acts of Unfair Competition

Article 10bis as incorporated into TRIPS obliges WTO Members to assure to nationals of other WTO Members effective protection against unfair competition, namely any act of competition contrary to honest practices in industrial or commercial matters. Such unfair acts are explicitly taken to include: (i) acts of such a nature as to create confusion as to the firms, goods or industrial or commercial activities of a competitor; (ii) false allegations in the course of trade; or (iii) indications or

---

[15] Thomas Cottier, 'Embedding Intellectual Property in International Law' in Pedro Roffe and Xavier Seuba (eds.), *Current Alliances in International Intellectual Property Law Rulemaking: The Emergence and Impact of Mega-Regionals*, vol. 4 (ICTSD/SEPI 2017) 25.
[16] Ibid.

allegations in the course of trade liable to mislead the public as to the goods in question.

Read to its maximum degree of expansiveness, Article 10bis might be interpreted to require WTO Members to enact suitable measures to ensure that SEIP holders do not engage, for example, in anticompetitive abuses in connection with the assertion of their rights.[17] That, however, is a long bow to draw, given that the examples enumerated are directed more towards dishonest or misleading conduct rather than anticompetitive practices as such, and in particular is to be contrasted with the provisions of the Telecommunications Reference Paper, which by their terms clearly are directed to addressing anticompetitive practices.

Moreover, even were it appropriate to read Article 10bis in such expansive fashion, the provision is wholly lacking in such detail as would guide Members as to the nature of the provisions that should be introduced to address the applicable anticompetitive practices.[18] Indeed, Article 10bis may not require Members to introduce any legislation at all.[19]

Nevertheless, Article 10bis does provide a useful foundation in international law to guide Paris Convention contracting parties and WTO Members in framing their laws on unfair competition. Although, as outlined above, it is rather questionable as to whether the provisions of Article 10bis could be construed to extend to cover abuses associated with access to SEIP (being primarily directed to matters of disinformation, consumer protection and the misappropriation of trade secrets), there is nothing in Article 10bis that would prevent Paris Convention contracting parties and WTO Members from giving their laws on unfair competition a broader scope,

---

[17] See, e.g., Christian Riffel, 'Unfair Competition, International Protection', *Max Planck Encyclopaedia of Public International Law* (Oxford University Press) para. 12.

[18] Ibid. para. 1. '*As a result of the uncertainty in the application of Art. 10bis Paris Convention, it has become virtually meaningless for the solution of international disputes, in particular because some countries reduce the regulatory content of this article to a mere restatement of a national treatment obligation ...*'.

[19] Marcus Höpperger and Martin Senftleben, 'Protection against Unfair Competition at the International Level – The Paris Convention, the 1996 Model Provisions and the Current Work of the World Intellectual Property Organisation' in Reto M. Hilty and Frauke Henning-Bodewig (eds.), *Law against Unfair Competition: Towards a New Paradigm in Europe?* (Springer 2007) 63. '*Art. 10bis establishes a flexible, open minimum standard of protection against unfair competition. The obligation to assure effective protection, laid down in paragraph 1, does not require the enactment of specific legislation*'.

including to deal with concerns associated with access to interoperability standard and to SEIP. This is likely to be particularly the case for SEIP-related conduct that clearly involves dishonest practices, such as failure to make proper disclosure of SEPs to a standard-setting organization.

3.1.2.4 The Idea/Expression Dichotomy and Originality in Copyright Protection

The idea/expression dichotomy in copyright law can be said to impose constraints of a generalized nature that can have some bearing on concerns associated with access to interoperability standards and SEIP. Article 9(2) of TRIPS restates the idea/expression dichotomy that is familiar from the laws of numerous Member States: copyright protection shall extend to expressions and not to ideas, procedures, methods of operation or mathematical concepts as such. Article 9(2) has the character of a maximum standard: it would likely be inconsistent with the requirements of the TRIPS Agreement for a Member to extend copyright protection to ideas, methods of operation, mathematical concepts etc. Taubman et al. consider that likewise the requirement of originality present in various Members' law is implicitly included in TRIPS, providing another maximum standard of a kind.[20]

3.1.2.5 Concluding Observations Regarding Maximum Standards in the TRIPS Agreement

The provisions of the TRIPS Agreement exhibit far more concern with laying down minimum standards of protection than with articulating maximum standards with a view to addressing the potential for overprotection of intellectual property, notably for present purposes of SEIP. Whilst an isolated few TRIPS provisions (as discussed in Sections 3.1.2.1–3.1.2.4 above) might be said to have the character of maximum standards, the TRIPS Agreement as a whole does not present a coherent set of standards to address concerns associated with access to SEIP. Nevertheless, stronger adherence by the TRIPS Membership even to these limited maximum standards (e.g. proper disclosure of software patents in line with Article 29) would be beneficial (but not sufficient) in the context of securing access to interoperability standards and SEIP.

---

[20] Taubman, Wager and Watal (n. 13) 41–2.

3.1.3 Significance of the TRIPS Flexibilities

Nevertheless, the minimum protections of the TRIPS Agreement are articulated within an overarching framework that provides for balance with legitimate policy objectives beyond the domain of intellectual property protection, and moreover for considerable flexibility of Members to tailor their regimes for the protection of intellectual property to their own unique circumstances. Such flexibility includes statements of object and purpose (Articles 7 and 8 of TRIPS), provisions dealing with anticompetitive licensing practices (Article 40), relevant exceptions (notably Articles 30 and 13 of TRIPS and Article 9(2) of the Berne Convention, providing for 'three-step tests'), as well as provisions concerning the compulsory licensing of patents.

3.1.3.1 The Fundamental Flexibilities Expressed in the TRIPS Preamble and in Articles 7 and 8

The Preamble to the TRIPS Agreement recognizes the underlying public policy objectives of national systems for the protection of intellectual property, including developmental and technological objectives. Article 1(1) of TRIPS provides that 'Members shall be free to determine the appropriate method of implementing the provisions of this Agreement within their own legal system and practice'. This provision is important in according flexibility to Members from common law and civil law systems to give effect to the TRIPS obligations within the modalities of their own particular legal system.

Articles 7 and 8 of TRIPS, entitled 'Objectives' and 'Principles', respectively, shed crucial light on the objects and purposes of the TRIPS Agreement, as well as lending context to the more specific provisions of the Agreement.

In Article 7, the fundamental importance of technological innovation as the justification for the protection of intellectual property is emphasized.[21] In this sense, Article 7 serves to align the objectives of the TRIPS Agreement with the public policy objectives underlying the protection of intellectual property more broadly. The reference to 'social and economic welfare' is also of considerable importance, affirming that intellectual property protection is intended to promote welfare both in a narrow economic sense (notably dynamic and static efficiency, in

---

[21] Thomas Cottier and Pierre Veron (eds.), *Concise International and European IP Law: TRIPS, Paris Convention, European Enforcement and Transfer of Technology* (3rd ed., Kluwer Law International 2015) 28.

3.1 THE PROVISIONS OF THE TRIPS AGREEMENT

particular through the channel of technological advancement) and also in a broader social sense that includes, for example, notions of distributive justice and the protection of human rights and the natural environment.

Moreover, the reference to 'the mutual advantage of producers and users of technological knowledge' highlights the intentions of the framers of TRIPS to balance the rights of producers and users with the view to maximizing the speed of technological advancement. This articulation is especially helpful in light of the trade-off inherent in the protection of intellectual property between promoting both initial and follow-on innovation, something which is of particular importance in the context of interoperability standards.

Article 8 cites important public policy objectives such as the protection of public health and nutrition, and flags the need for TRIPS-consistent measures to prevent abuses of intellectual property rights or practices that restraint trade or adversely affect technology transfer. Article 8(2) manifests the intentions of the framers of TRIPS that the Agreement should include sufficient flexibility to address abuses of intellectual property rights; the link to the more general doctrine of *abus de droit* underpinning many provisions of the WTO Agreement is apparent.[22] This provision should interoperate seamlessly with more specific provisions of TRIPS dealing with abuse of rights, notably Articles 31 and 40.[23]

WTO panels and the Appellate Body have, in a relatively orthodox fashion, taken Articles 7 and 8 into account as statements of both context, and of object and purpose, relevant to interpretation of the standards of protection outlined in the provisions of TRIPS.[24] In *Australia – Certain Measures Concerning Trademarks, Geographical Indications and Other Plain Packaging Requirements Applicable to Tobacco Products and Packaging*, the Panel reaffirmed the interpretive weight of these provisions: 'Articles 7 and 8, together with the preamble of the TRIPS Agreement, set out general goals and principles underlying the TRIPS Agreement, which are to be borne in mind when specific provisions of the Agreement are being interpreted in their context and in light of the

---

[22] Ibid. 35.
[23] Ibid.
[24] *WTO, United States – Section 211 Omnibus Appropriations Act of 1998 – Report of the Appellate Body (6 August 2001) WT/DS176/R* [8.49], [8.57]; *WTO, European Communities – Protection of Trademarks and Geographical Indications for Agricultural Products and Foodstuffs – Report of the Panel (15 March 2005) WT/DS290/R* [7.209]–[7.210]; *WTO, Canada – Patent Protection of Pharmaceutical Products – Report of the Panel (17 March 2000) WT/DS114/R* [7.26].

object and purpose of the Agreement'.[25] The proper interpretive weight of Articles 7 and 8 was reaffirmed in the Doha Declaration on TRIPS and Public Health,[26] which WTO Panels and the Appellate Body have consistently applied as a subsequent agreement between WTO Members regarding the interpretation of the TRIPS Agreement[27] pursuant to Article 31(3)(a) of the Vienna Convention on the Law of Treaties.[28] Whilst not directly relevant to the measures contemplated in the present treatise, the Doha Declaration does nevertheless emphasize the interpretive relevance of Articles 7 and 8 – albeit in a manner that would obviously result from the application of customary rules of treaty interpretation in any case. Specifically, paragraph 5(a) of the Doha Declaration provides that in applying the customary rules of interpretation of public international law, each provision of the TRIPS Agreement shall be read in the light of the object and purpose of the Agreement as expressed, in particular, in its objectives and principles.

3.1.3.2 Article 40 – Interfacing Intellectual Property and Competition within the TRIPS Agreement

The TRIPS Agreement also outlines, in Article 40, provisions dealing squarely with anticompetitive licensing practices in the context of the protection of intellectual property, which may be conceptualized as building upon and elaborating further the basic principle articulated in paragraph 2 of Article 8,[29] namely that appropriate measures consistent with TRIPS may be needed to prevent the abuse of intellectual property rights. Clearly, Article 40 will be of primary relevance in the context of

---

[25] WTO, *Australia – Certain Measures Concerning Trademarks, Geographical Indications and Other Plain Packaging Requirements Applicable to Tobacco Products and Packaging – Report of the Panel* (28 June 2018) WT/DS435/R, WT/DS441/R, WT/DS458/R, WT/DS467/R [7.2402].

[26] WTO, Doha WTO Ministerial, Declaration on the TRIPS Agreement and Public Health (20 November 2001), WTO Doc WT/MIN(01)/DEC/1.

[27] WTO, *Australia – Certain Measures Concerning Trademarks, Geographical Indications and Other Plain Packaging Requirements Applicable to Tobacco Products and Packaging – Report of the Panel* (28 June 2018) WT/DS435/R, WT/DS441/R, WT/DS458/R, WT/DS467/R [7.2409]; WTO, *United States: Measures Affecting the Production and Sale of Clove Cigarettes – Report of the Appellate Body* (4 April 2012) WT/DS406/AB/R [256]–[268].

[28] Vienna Convention on the Law of Treaties, adopted 23 May 1969, entered into force 27 January 1980 (1155 UNTS 331) art. 31(3)(a).

[29] Mor Bakhoum and Beatriz Conde Gallego, 'TRIPS and Competition Rules: From Transfer of Technology to Innovation Policy' in Hanns Ullrich and others (eds.), *TRIPS plus 20: From Trade Rules to Market Principles* (Springer 2016) 548.

the subject matter of this treatise. A core aspect of this work will be the extent to which licensing practices of SEIP holders can, or should, be characterized as anticompetitive practices in accordance with a Member's law.

Paragraph 2 of Article 40 does not articulate exhaustively the form of such anticompetitive practices, but does specifically mention three classes of such practices, all of which have, from time to time, been observed in connection with SEIP. A further practice not mentioned in paragraph 2 is the refusal to license SEIP, particularly in circumstances where the right holder has previously given undertaking to an SSO to license, for example on FRAND terms. Concomitantly with such refusal to license, SEIP holders may approach the domestic courts, seeking to restrain a user or potential user from practising the SEIP in question.

These practices have been found to be anticompetitive under the laws of a number of WTO Members, including in the EU under Article 102 Treaty on the Functioning of the European Union (TFEU). By its terms, paragraph 2 of Article 40 does not contain an exhaustive list of the relevant anticompetitive practices.[30] Whilst Article 40 does not operate as an exception to other minimum standards imposed by TRIPS (e.g. the requirements of Article 28 and Article 44(2)), it will clearly lend significant interpretive context to those provisions, as well as to the interpretation of Articles 30 and 31.

3.1.3.3 The Flexibilities Conferred by the Three-Step Tests

Although TRIPS does not include general exceptions in the form presented by Article XX of the General Agreement on Tariffs and Trade (GATT) 1994 or Article XIV of the General Agreement on Trade in Services (GATS), it nevertheless includes general exception provisions with respect to specified classes of intellectual property, in the form of the so-called 'three-step tests'. Article 30 provides merely one of numerous three-step tests in international intellectual property law; others can be found in Articles 9, 13 and 26.2 of the TRIPS Agreement, Articles 10(1) and 10(2) of the WIPO Copyright Treaty, Article 16(2) of the WIPO Performances and Phonograms Treaty, Article 9(2) of the Berne Convention, and elsewhere.[31]

---

[30] Ibid. 552; Cottier and Veron (n. 21) 117.
[31] Christoph Geiger, Daniel J Gervais and Martin Senftleben, 'The Three Step Test Revisited: How to Use the Test's Flexibility in National Copyright Law' (2014) 29 American University International Law Review 581, 586.

By its terms, Article 30 is framed in somewhat more liberal terms than its copyright counterpart in Article 13: patent exceptions must be 'limited', whereas copyright exceptions must be confined to cases that are both 'certain' and 'special'. The second step in Article 30 prohibits only 'unreasonable' conflict with normal exploitation of a patent (thus enabling a proportionality assessment), whereas under Article 13, no conflict with the normal exploitation of a copyright is permitted. The third step of the Article 30 test refers explicitly to the 'legitimate interests of third parties', which Article 13 does not, giving more explicit voice to the need to consider broader public interests associated with patent exceptions.

Article 30 has been applied by a single WTO panel in *Canada – Patent Protection of Pharmaceutical Products* (*Canada – Pharmaceuticals*), which involved consideration of the 'three-step test' in the context of two exemptions in Canadian statute to the exclusive rights granted by patents in Canada. The first exemption (regulatory review exception), provided for in section 55(2)(1) of Canada's Patent Act, permitted generic drug manufacturers to infringe pharmaceutical patents in the course of preparing regulatory submissions for approval of the generic drug, before the expiration of the patent term.[32] The second exemption (stockpiling exception), provided for in section 55(2)(2) of the Patent Act, allowed generic manufacturers relying on the regulatory review exception to develop stockpiles of generic drugs before the expiration of the patent term for sale after expiration.[33] The regulatory review exception satisfied all three steps of the test;[34] the stockpiling exception failed the first step, obviating the need to consider its conformity with the remaining two steps.[35]

The copyright three-step tests are provided in Article 9(2) of the Berne Convention and Article 13 of TRIPS.[36] Given the almost identical drafting of these two provisions, their ordinary meaning will be the same, only their contexts and objects and purposes may differ. Moreover, such differing context, objects and purposes will only be relevant to extent

---

[32] WTO, *Canada – Patent Protection of Pharmaceutical Products – Report of the Panel* (17 March 2000) WT/DS114/R (n. 24) [7.2].
[33] Ibid. 7.7.
[34] Ibid. 7.84.
[35] Ibid. 7.38.
[36] Three-step tests have subsequently also been included in the WIPO Copyright Treaty (WCT) and the WIPO Performances and Phonograms Treaty (WPPT).

that conformity with the provisions of the Berne Convention is considered independently of its incorporation into TRIPS.

Article 13 has been the subject of a single WTO panel report. In *United States – Section 110(5) of the Copyright Act*, the panel examined two statutory exceptions to the US Copyright Act. The first, known as the 'homestyle exception', exempted certain small eating and drinking establishments from being required to obtain permission to play music through ordinary 'homestyle' sound equipment.[37] The second, known as the 'business exception', exempted a wider array of food, drink and retail establishments.[38] The 'homestyle exception' was found to satisfy the three-step test provided in TRIPS Article 13, but the 'business exception' failed to satisfy any of the three steps.

Compounding the drafting differences between Article 30 and Article 13, the patent panel in *Canada – Pharmaceuticals* (probably better-credentialed, as it included renowned trade scholar Robert Hudec and former Deputy Director-General of WIPO Mihaly Ficsor) adopted a broader reading of the term 'normal exploitation' in the second step of Article 30, allowing for examination of the underlying policy purposes behind patent protection; by contrast, the copyright panel adhered to a narrower focus on the economic impact of the US copyright exemptions and the numerical size of the exempted classes of business proprietors. Thus, as it stands, the TRIPS Agreement as interpreted by the relevant cases would seem to provide for a considerably broader scope for patent exceptions than for copyright exceptions.

Academic commentary has generally been rather critical of the approach of the panel in US – Section 110, whose 'economic' and 'positivist' approach to the construction of the test has been contrasted unfavourably with the more 'policy-oriented' approach of the patent and trademark panels.[39] Geiger et al., for example, have commented: 'While we do not wish to reexamine the panel's report in detail here, it is essential to indicate how the policy space of national legislators could be unduly curtailed if some of the approach taken by the panel in that dispute was applied too mechanically in future cases'.[40] Some

---

[37] *WTO, United States – Section 110(5) of US Copyright Act – Report of the Panel* (15 June 2000) WT/DS160/R [2.5]–[2.8].
[38] Ibid. [2.9]–[2.10].
[39] Geiger, Gervais and Senftleben (n. 31) 585; Jane C. Ginsburg, 'Towards Supranational Copyright Law? The WTO Panel Decision and the "Three-Step Test" for Copyright Exceptions' (2001) 3 Revue Internationale du Droit d'Auteur 7, 23.
[40] Geiger, Gervais and Senftleben (n. 31) 592.

commentary has gone further, suggesting that an entirely new interpretive approach is needed for the three-step test, and especially for Article 13. One argument made repeatedly is that the three steps of the various tests should be interpreted holistically, rather than broken down into constituent elements and parsed minutely.[41] Other suggestions include reversing the order of consideration of the steps to begin with the third step;[42] and viewing the three-step test as an open list of factors to be considered by tribunals on a case-by-case basis, in a manner similar to the US copyright fair use test.[43]

A Declaration on a Balanced Interpretation of the Three-Step Test in Copyright Law, based on the findings of a multi-institutional research project, crystallized many of these suggestions in a single document which called inter alia for a holistic interpretation of the test,[44] and a normative interpretation of the term 'normal' in the second step.[45] Gervais et al., surveying the various commentary, suggest the following interpretive approach:

> Operationally, if a challenged E&L easily passes two of the steps but is slightly below the threshold for the third, then the E&L could be said to pass the test, bearing in mind that, analytically, there is some degree of overlap between the steps. What may be a small potential miss on one of the steps may thus be compensated by demonstrating that an impugned E&L is clearly valid under the other two.[46]

Such reinterpretive efforts have their critics, who assert that they pay insufficient regard to the words of the three-step tests, and to the negotiating history of the Berne Convention.[47] With persistent clouds hanging over the WTO Appellate Body, these interpretive debates are unlikely to be resolved in the immediate future.

---

[41] Christoph Geiger and others, 'Declaration A Balanced Interpretation of the "Three-Step Test" in Copyright Law' (2010) 1 Journal of Intellectual Property, Information Technology and Electronic Commerce Law 119; Geiger, Gervais and Senftleben (n. 31) 585.

[42] Daniel J. Gervais, 'Towards a New Core International Copyright Norm: The Reverse Three-Step Test' (2005) 9 Marquette Intellectual Property Law Review 1, 28–30.

[43] Kamiel J. Koelman, 'Fixing the Three-Step Test' (2006) 28 European Intellectual Property Review 407, 410.

[44] Geiger and others (n. 41) 120.

[45] Ibid. 121; see also Geiger, Gervais and Senftleben (n. 31) 608.

[46] Geiger, Gervais and Senftleben (n. 31) 611.

[47] Andre Lucas, 'For a Reasonable Interpretation of the Three-Step Test' (2010) 32 European Intellectual Property Review 277; Patrick R. Goold, 'The Interpretive Argument for a Balanced Three-Step Test?' (2017) 33 American University International Law Review 187, 209–11.

3.1.3.4 Flexibilities Regarding Compulsory Licensing

Article 31 of the TRIPS Agreement permits compulsory licensing of patents, including in the case of anticompetitive practices. While Article 31 does not per se confer a right to issue compulsory licences, such a right is provided by the Article 5(2) of the Paris Convention, which is explicitly referenced by the TRIPS Agreement. The provisions of Article 31 retain considerable flexibility and discretion for Members to issue compulsory licences, particularly in circumstances where anticompetitive practices have been established. Given that the competition laws of numerous jurisdictions provide for an excessive pricing discipline, there is the potential for WTO Members to pursue excessive pricing investigations under domestic competition law, as a vehicle for imposing compulsory licences consistently with the requirements of Article 31.

3.1.3.5 Concluding Observations Regarding the TRIPS Flexibilities

As such, international intellectual property law does not require states to take concrete steps to ensure access to interoperability standards and SEIP, but it nevertheless does permit states a considerable measure of discretion in crafting measures tailored to address such concerns.

3.2 The WTO Agreement on Technical Barriers to Trade

Beyond international intellectual property law, there are in essence no international disciplines providing for access to interoperability standards and SEIP. The WTO TBT Agreement includes a Code of Good Practice in relation to standards preparation; however this instrument imposes best endeavours obligations only on regulating Members in respect of the activities of private standard-setting organizations – noting in this regard the fundamental importance of private bodies to the creation of interoperability standards.

By and large, the WTO Agreements (as with most international treaties) do not reach private conduct. The TBT Agreement,[48] which would seem to be the agreement most proximately directed towards matters pertaining to standards, imposes its most detailed obligations only in respect of 'technical regulations', which are laws and regulations of a Member in the domain of product regulation (i.e. 'laying down product

---

[48] Agreement on Technical Barriers to Trade, April 15 1994, Marrakesh Agreement Establishing the World Trade Organization, Annex 1A 1994 (1868 UNTS 120).

characteristics') having mandatory application. This would not include the majority of interoperability standards, which are instruments drafted by private bodies and not having any legal force.

Certain interoperability standards would squarely be captured by the primary obligations of the TBT Agreement – namely those which are given the force of law by a Member – but these are not by any means the majority. An argument could also be made that privately drafted standards which do not have the force of law but which are de facto essential for participation in a market are in fact 'mandatory' and should be treated as such. This argument would not succeed before a WTO panel or the Appellate Body.[49] Apart from anything else, such an approach would give rise to unmanageable problems of attribution: even presuming the standard has become mandatory in a factual sense, this does not answer the question of which WTO Member should be responsible as a matter of international law for the resultant conduct either of the standard-setting body or its Members.

Nevertheless, the TBT Agreement does include some provisions which apply with respect to private standard-setting bodies, namely the Code of Good Practice for Standard-Setting Organizations, provided at Annex 3 to the TBT Agreement. The Code of Good Practice mandates familiar substantive obligations: non-discrimination; non-creation of obstacles to international trade; reliance on international standards; and non-specification of product standards in terms of performance rather than design or descriptive characteristics, together with significant procedural obligations pertaining to transparency, notice-and-comment and the resolution of complaints.

The Code of Good Practice is useful in two key aspects. First, it outlines a set of 'best practices' which private standard-setting organizations (including those involved in the creation of interoperability standards) are encouraged to follow. Second, it imposes some (admittedly quite limited) obligations upon Members to ensure the compliance of non-governmental standard-setting bodies within their

---

[49] WTO, *United States – Measures Concerning the Importation, Marketing and Sale of Tuna and Tuna Products – Report of the Panel (15 September 2011)* WT/DS381/R [7.142]. The Panel noted that the importance of the fact that US measures imposing conditions on access to a 'dolphin-safe' label applied to canned tuna sold in the United States were legally enforceable and binding under US law. The Panel's findings were upheld by the Appellate Body. See *WTO, United States – Measures Concerning the Importation, Marketing and Sale of Tuna and Tuna Products – Report of the Appellate Body (16 May 2012)* WT/DS381/AB/R [199].

3.2 WTO AGREEMENT ON TECHNICAL BARRIERS TO TRADE

respective territories with such 'best practice' obligations. The TBT Agreement, including the Code of Good Practice, is, however, conspicuously silent regarding the relationship between standards and intellectual property rights.

The Code of Good Practice is important in terms of imposing binding obligations upon WTO Members in terms of the activities of private standard-setting bodies within their respective territories. The default rule in public international law is that States are responsible for the actions of private bodies only where such bodies exercise elements of the governmental authority through a legal delegation, or the body acts under the 'effective control' of the State, which would include not only generalized control but in addition a specific control over the impugned action.[50] Beyond this, public international law also imposes certain limited obligations of due diligence upon States to ensure that their territory is not used in a manner contrary to the rights of other States.[51]

Article 4 of the TBT Agreement, consistently with this relatively limited approach in general public international law, imposes a relatively high-level obligation upon Members: Members must take such reasonable measures as may be available to them to ensure that non-governmental standardizing bodies within their territories accept and comply with the Code of Good Practice. In addition, Members shall not take measures which have the effect of, directly or indirectly, requiring or encouraging such standardizing bodies to act in a manner inconsistent with the Code of Good Practice.

These 'best endeavours' type obligations, which are broadly consonant with States' general due diligence obligations under public international law, do not give rise to significant obligations on States to take measures that meaningfully affect the behaviour of SSOs. Perhaps of more significance, they are directed principally towards the activities of SSOs, rather than the private actions of members of such SSOs with respect for the assertion of their SEIP.

Perhaps in the recognition of such limitations, the WTO TBT Committee has progressed work relating to the trade dimensions of private standard setting. Notably, in its Decision on Principles for the Development of International Standards, Guides and Recommendations

---

[50] Articles on the Responsibility of States for Internationally Wrongful Acts 2001 (Yearbook of the International Law Commission, A/CN4/SERA/2001/Add1 (Part 1)) Arts 5, 8.
[51] *Case Concerning Pulp Mills on the River Uruguay* 2010 ICJ Rep 18 45–6.

with relation to Articles 2, 3 and 5 of the Agreement,[52] the Committee outlined six core principles that should guide the development of international standards: transparency, openness, impartiality and consensus, effectiveness and relevance, coherence and development dimension. The provisions of this Decision dealing with openness do recommend that standard-setting bodies maintain open membership practices, but otherwise do not mention a need for all relevant parties to have access to standards. The Decision does not mention intellectual property.

3.3 The WTO Telecommunications Agreement

The WTO Telecommunications Agreement, including the GATS Annex on Telecommunications and the Telecommunications Reference Paper, provide for a comprehensive regime at the international level for access to and use of telecommunications networks and services, including supporting disciplines on anticompetitive practices. However, these instruments include no meaningful constraints in the context of access to interoperability standards or SEIP. The highly detailed and prescriptive requirements of the WTO Telecommunications Agreement may perhaps be considered as a template for what a comprehensive regime dealing with access to interoperability standards might look like in practice. However, these provisions are squarely directed towards the telecommunications industry only and deal only incidentally (and very briefly) with access to interoperability standards.

The framers of the GATS recognized that the sectoral commitments made by Members could be undermined by the anticompetitive actions of entrenched telecommunications monopolies. Telecommunications service supply was in the 1990s, and remains to this day, a natural monopoly service characterized by high fixed and sunk costs, economies of scale, network effects and economies of density. For this reason, the service has in many countries been supplied by vertically integrated monopolies with close links to government. Such monopolies frequently carried universal service obligations in respect of basic telecommunications services.

During the 1990s, telecommunications services in many advanced economies were privatized and liberalized, which in many cases involved

---

[52] WTO Decision of the Committee on Technical Barriers to Trade on Principles for the Development of International Standards, Guides and Recommendations with Relation to Articles 2, 5 and Annex 3 of the Agreement 2000 (G/TBT/9).

3.3 THE WTO TELECOMMUNICATIONS AGREEMENT 73

the imposition of open access regulations upon incumbents, together with strong protections against unilateral conduct. It was seen as necessary to impose a requirement upon WTO Members to provide for such an open access regime to secure the integrity of specific commitments under the GATS.[53]

The core provisions outlining an access regime are paragraph 5 of the Annex and section 2 of the Reference Paper. In particular, paragraph 5 of the Annex imposes an obligation upon Members to ensure that any service supplier of any other Member is accorded access to and use of public telecommunications transport networks and services, on reasonable and non-discriminatory terms and conditions. This is a far-reaching commitment; the property rights of the network owner are significantly circumscribed. Section 2.2 builds on the requirements of paragraph 5 of the Annex, by providing for somewhat more fine-grained obligations in relation to network interconnection. Interconnection must be available at every technically feasible point; there must be no discrimination against competitors, compared with the treatment given to affiliates; it must be supplied on rates that are cost-oriented.

The Annex also includes some recognition of the importance of international standards in the field of telecommunications (paragraph 7 (a)); however, this provision merely provides acknowledgement of such standards rather than requiring any concrete action: 'Members recognize the importance of international standards for global compatibility and inter-operability of telecommunications networks and services and undertake to promote such standards through the work of relevant international bodies, including the International Telecommunications Union and the International Organization for Standardization'. Finally, it is worth noting that the Reference Paper also includes requirements for an antitrust/competition law regime to discipline the conduct of major suppliers. Section 1.1 of the Reference Paper provides: 'Appropriate measures shall be maintained for the purpose of preventing suppliers who, alone or together, are a major supplier from engaging in or continuing anti-competitive practices'. Section 1.2 elaborates on this obligation by providing a non-exclusive illustrative list of examples of 'anti-competitive practices'. In *Mexico – Telecommunications*, the Panel considered that the term 'anti-competitive practices' 'includes practices in

---

[53] Henry Gao, 'Annex on Telecommunications', in Rüdiger Wolfrum, Peter-Tobias Stoll and Clemens Feinäugle (eds.) *WTO-Trade in Services* (Brill Nijhoff 2008) 683, 687–8.

addition to those listed in Section 1.2, in particular horizontal practices related to price-fixing and market-sharing agreements'.[54]

Thus, the access regime mandated by the Annex and the Reference Paper includes a parallel path under antitrust/competition law. Indeed, such laws, if comprehensive in scope and properly enforced, may be sufficient to ensure compliance with paragraph 5(a) of the Annex and section 2.2 of the Reference Paper as well. In this regard the Reference Paper follows the example of numerous domestic regimes applicable to telecommunications. In sum, the WTO Telecommunications Agreement provides an example of how international economic law might deal with access to interoperability standards, rather than providing actual disciplines that might be of relevance.

3.4 The WTO Information Technology Agreement

The Ministerial Declaration on Trade in Technology Products (Information Technology Agreement) was adopted by twenty-nine WTO Members and States or separate customs territories in the process of acceding to the WTO, in Singapore on 13 December 1996.[55]

The scope of the Information Technology Agreement is confined to products, and its substantive commitments are limited to tariff reductions commitments. In particular, parties to the Information Technology Agreement agree to bind and eliminate customs duties and other duties and charges of any kind, within the meaning of Article II:1(b) of the GATT 1994, with respect to all products either falling within the Harmonized System classifications listed in Attachment A, or specified in Attachment B, irrespective of how classified under the Harmonized System (paragraph 2).

Consumer electronics are excluded from the scope of the Information Technology Agreement.[56] Instead, only industrial equipment and components are included.[57] Products covered by the Information Technology Agreement include: computers; semiconductors;

---

[54] *WTO, Mexico – Measures Affecting Telecommunications Services – Report of the Panel* (2 April 2004) WT/DS204/R [7.238].

[55] Ministerial Declaration on Trade in Technology Products (Information Technology Agreement) 1996 (WTO Doc WT/MIN (96)/16).

[56] Barbara A. Fliess and Pierre Sauve, 'Of Chips, Floppy Disks and Great Timing: Assessing the Information Technology Agreement', *Paper prepared for the Institute Francais des Relations Internationales (IFRI) and the Tokyo Club Foundation for Global Studies* (1997) 48.

[57] Ibid.

semiconductor manufacturing equipment; telecommunications apparatus such as telephones and switching equipment; other instruments such as cash registers and electronic calculators; data storage media and software; and parts and accessories for goods in the other categories.

Parties agreed to incorporate these zero tariff commitments into their GATT 1994 tariff schedules, making them available to all WTO Members on a most-favoured-nation basis.[58] Recognizing the 'free rider' problem inherent in this approach, parties to the Information Technology Agreement agreed to meet their commitments only if participants representing approximately 90 per cent of world trade in information technology products had notified their acceptance to the agreement.[59]

One shortcoming of the Information Technology Agreement concerns non-tariff barriers, which include barriers with respect to standards. It was suggested at an early stage of negotiations that the Information Technology Agreement should extend to non-tariff barriers. However, negotiating parties (especially the United States) considered that this would increase the complexity of the negotiations unmanageably; consequently, non-tariff barriers are not addressed by the Information Technology Agreement.

Nevertheless, participants agree to meet periodically under the auspices of the Council on Trade in Goods to, inter alia, consult on non-tariff barriers to trade in information technology products.[60] Participants and academic commentators have made proposals to extend the ambit of the Information Technology Agreement to include non-tariff barriers, including to deal with product standards, noting the risk of protectionist policies by WTO Members in connection with standard-setting; however no concrete steps have been taken in this regard.[61]

3.5 International Competition Law

Beyond these instruments, there is, in essence, no international competition law. Significant international agreement is currently lacking in

---

[58] Information Technology Agreement Annex 1, paragraph 1.
[59] Ibid. Annex, paragraph 4.
[60] Ibid. Annex, paragraph 3.
[61] Alberto Portugal-Perez, José-Daniel Reyes and John S. Wilson, 'Beyond the Information Technology Agreement: Harmonisation of Standards and Trade in Electronics' (2010) 33 The World Economy 1870, 1872; Catherine Mann and Xuepeng Liu, 'The Information Technology Agreement: Sui Generis or Model Stepping Stone' in Richard Baldwin and Patrick Low (eds.), *Multilateralizing Regionalism: Challenges for the Global Trading System* (Cambridge University Press 2009) 212–13.

relation to international competition law, all attempts to negotiate such an agreement having failed.[62]

Disagreement between the United States and the European Union about the substantive contents of an international agreement, including any proposed unilateral conduct provisions, has been identified as a key reason for such ongoing failure.[63] Unsuccessful attempts to negotiate such an agreement included the failed Havana Charter negotiations of the late 1940s, and the failure of talks over an international competition agreement at the WTO Cancún Ministerial Conference of September 2003.[64] The Havana Charter, which sought to create an International Trade Organization (ITO), included provisions regarding international competition law and an international enforcement mechanism.[65] These provisions were controversial and indeed were part of the reason by the Havana Charter was never submitted to the United States Congress for ratification and subsequently lapsed as an international initiative.

At the WTO's Singapore Ministerial Conference of 1996, international competition policy was placed on the list of future WTO negotiations, at the instigation of the European Union; at the same time a WTO Working Group on the Interaction between Trade and Competition Policy was established.[66] The EU submitted more detailed negotiating proposals in 2001.[67] In consequence, the WTO's Doha Ministerial Declaration of 20 November 2001 provided:

> Recognizing the case for a multilateral framework to enhance the contribution of competition policy to international trade and development, and the need for enhanced technical assistance and capacity-building in this area as referred to in paragraph 24, we agree that negotiations will take place after the Fifth Session of the Ministerial Conference on the basis of

---

[62] Anu Bradford, 'International Antitrust Cooperation and the Preference for Nonbinding Regimes' in Andrew T. Guzman (ed.), *Cooperation, Comity and Competition Policy* (Oxford University Press 2011) 322.
[63] Ibid. 327.
[64] Josef Drexl, 'International Competition Policy after Cancun: Placing a Singapore Issue on the WTO Development Agenda' (2004) 27 World Competition 419, 419.
[65] Spencer Weber Waller, 'National Laws and International Markets: Strategies of Cooperation and Harmonization in the Enforcement of Competition Law' (1996) 18 Cardozo Law Review 1111, 1113; E. M. Fox, 'Competition Law and the Millennium Round' (1999) 2 Journal of International Economic Law 665, 666.
[66] Drexl (n. 64) 420.
[67] Ibid.

a decision to be taken, by explicit consensus, at that session on modalities of negotiations.[68]

By the time of the Cancún Ministerial Conference, any support for such agreement had evaporated, due in part to opposition on the part of developing countries; in these circumstances, then-EU Trade Commissioner Lamy decided to jettison the EU's proposal for competition policy negotiations.[69] It is now generally accepted that an international competition agreement is not feasible, at least at this point in time.[70]

Instead, International Competition Law as such consists of domestic competition laws, which are often applied on a cross-border basis. International coordination between domestic jurisdictions in competition law enforcement is also an important mechanism of international competition law. The International Competition Network (ICN) facilitates such coordination but does not administer any international treaties in this area. The Organisation for Economic Co-operation and Development (OECD) is also active in the field of international competition, publishing research reports on a number of important issues in this field.

3.6 Concluding Observations

There does not currently exist any binding multilateral international agreement which is apt to address concerns relating to interoperability standards and standards-essential intellectual property. Nevertheless, there would appear to be considerable flexibility within international economic law, including international intellectual property law, for jurisdictions to take measures considered appropriate to address concerns associated with access to interoperability standards and SEIP.

---

[68] WTO, Doha WTO Ministerial, Declaration on the TRIPS Agreement and Public Health (20 November 2001), WTO Doc WT/MIN(01)/DEC/1 23.
[69] Drexl (n. 64) 419.
[70] See, e.g., Bradford (n. 62) 321; Drexl (n. 64) 427.

PART II

The Impact of Intellectual Property
and Competition Laws

4

Interoperability Standards and Intellectual Property

4.1 The Concept of Standards-Essential Intellectual Property

Intellectual property can be considered 'essential' to the practice of a standard when it is not technically possible to implement the standard without infringing the intellectual property right in question. Although the question of SEPs is extensively examined in the literature (as will be discussed in Section 4.3.1 below), it is equally possible that other types of intellectual property protection could be essential to the practice of standards, most prominently copyrights.

Indeed, a number of salient cases have examined the concept of standards-essential copyrights, albeit without deploying this term. In the United States, the *Apple* v. *Microsoft*, *Donnelley* v. *Bell South*, *Sega* v. *Accolade* and *Computer Associates* v. *Altai* cases, among others, all concerned copyrights which were asserted in a manner which would have had the effect of precluding another party (generally a competitor to the copyright holder) from practicing an interoperability standard. In the EU, the paradigmatic standards-essential copyright case is the *IMS Health* case, which concerned access to the structure of a database which had become de facto essential to participation in the market.

Trade secrets have also been asserted in cases that involve access to interoperability standards, Microsoft's assertion of trade secrets in the EU *Microsoft* case being the most prominent. Standards-essential layout circuits have not presented as a concern; however, this class of right is also examined, given its proximity to high technology markets, including standardized markets.

4.2 The Law and Economics of Intellectual Property Protection

The primary underlying objective of intellectual property protection is to encourage private innovative activity by according to the originators of creative works a time-limited monopoly over the lawful exploitation of their invention or work.¹ Intellectual property laws, by and large, exist because inventions and works can be expensive to produce but cheap to imitate (especially in light of the digitization of content). This can potentially give rise to the situation where the originator of some creative invention or work is unable to recover the fixed costs expended, because competitors can quickly follow, copying the work and selling it at a lower price.

Such a situation can be expected to have detrimental impact on a creator's incentives: creators will be disinclined to create new inventions or works because they will perceive it to be a loss-making endeavour. Another way of putting it is that knowledge has certain public good characteristics: it is non-rivalrous in nature, and in addition it can (absent legal protection) be non-excludable in nature, or at any rate exclusion may be very difficult.²

Because of its public good characteristics, knowledge creation may be said to give rise to a positive externality: new ideas and works confer considerable benefits on society in general, but the innovator or creator may capture only a modest portion of that social benefit. This creates negative incentives, leading to the suboptimal production of creative ideas and works, to the detriment of society. The rate of innovation may potentially be harmed; this despite compelling economic evidence that innovation is the source of most economic growth.³

Intellectual property law seeks to redress this problem by conferring on the creator a time-limited monopoly to either exploit the invention or work herself, or license another person to exploit it on her behalf. In this manner, intellectual property laws seek to enable the private capture of (some) public benefits. Granted, the problems arising from the public good characteristics of intellectual creations could be addressed through other mechanisms, such as public subsidies for creative activity (which, in fact, also exist).

Nevertheless, encouraging innovation through the provision of subsidies for research and development is likely to provide an imperfect solution (or at least, an incomplete solution), given that it is based on

---

[1] Peter S. Menell and Suzanne Scotchmer, 'Intellectual Property Law' in A. Mitchell Polinsky and Stephen Shavell (eds.), *Handbook of Law and Economics*, vol. 2 (North-Holland 2007) 1475.
[2] Ibid. 1477.
[3] Jeffrey D. Sachs and John W. McArthur, 'Technological Advancement and Long-Term Economic Growth in Asia' in Chong-En Bai and Chi-Wa Yuen (eds.), *Technology and the New Economy* (MIT Press 2002) 157.

a centralized approach to knowledge creation, whereas addressing the issue through intellectual property protection takes a decentralized approach. Moreover, as Menell and Scotchmer observe: 'every invention funded with intellectual property creates a Pareto improvement. No one is taxed more than his willingness to pay for any unit he buys; else he would not buy it'.[4] By the same token, the protection of intellectual property, because it can create monopolies,[5] may result in deadweight losses to consumers, and may also retard follow-on innovations.[6] In addition, the mere fact that intellectual property protection can stimulate innovation does not in itself justify the creation of monopolies, since there are other mechanisms that could also promote such innovation and, indeed, depending on factors like industry type, there may already be incentives for innovation in the relevant industry.[7] For example, firms within a particular industry may have strong incentives to innovate in order to gain lead time and first-mover advantages over their competitors; failure to do so may imperil their position in the marketplace. The task of intellectual property laws is to intervene in the marketplace in order to supply incentives for innovation that would otherwise be deficient, and no more. Protection that goes beyond these needs will likely occasion both static and dynamic efficiency losses (e.g. in follow-on innovation precluded), and will likely be unjustifiable on the basis of economic science.

Beyond the economic arguments for and against intellectual property protection per se, there is a further discourse concerning the tailoring of intellectual property rights to achieve optimal outcomes. The key 'policy levers' in this regard include: the threshold for protection; the breadth of protection; the length of protection;[8] administrative requirements; and remedies for infringement.

---

[4] Menell and Scotchmer (n. 1) 1477.
[5] It is important to recall that whether any particular intellectual property right confers a monopoly upon the right holder is a question of fact that needs to assessed on a case-by-case basis, and will depend fundamentally on the availability of substitutes for the invention, process, work etc., including both substitutes that are also protected by intellectual property rights, and substitutes that are in the public domain. That is, consistently with general principles of competition law analysis, the relevant market needs to be defined in terms of substitution possibilities in order to assess the dynamics of competition (e.g. the presence of monopoly) within that market.
[6] Menell and Scotchmer (n. 1) 1477.
[7] Ibid.
[8] Ibid. 1483.

4.3 Patents

4.3.1 Standards-Essential Patents

In terms of SEIP, SEPs have attracted the greatest attention. Not all patents claimed to be essential to a standard are essential as such from a strictly technical perspective. A simple definition of essentiality is: 'A patent is essential to a standard, if making a product or using a method, complying with the standard, requires use of the patent'.[9] Bekkers, Bongard and Nuvolari describe the concept in the following terms:

> These patents are so basic to the interfaces defined by the standard that it is impossible to design any device that complies with these interfaces without infringing the patent. If there are alternative ways to design something that complies with the standard (even when they are more expensive to implement), the particular patent in question will no longer be essential.[10]

The rules or bylaws of SSOs will frequently define 'essentiality', some in technical terms but others in commercial terms, or on the basis of a blend of technical and commercial essentiality.[11]

In any event, essentiality is a factual matter to be determined, rather than something that can simply be claimed by the relevant right holder. Regarding the need for a factual determination of standard-essentiality, it should be noted, by way of observation, the estimate provided by Goodman and Myers that up to 80 per cent of the patents that firms claim to be essential for a mobile telephony standard were in fact not essential.[12] Indeed, it is quite common for technology firms to make

---

[9] Sadao Nagaoka, Naotoshi Tsukada and Tomoyuki Shimbo, 'The Structure and the Emergence of Essential Patents for Standards: Lessons from Three IT Standards' in Uwe Cantner, Jean-Luc Gaffard and Lionel Nesta (eds.), *Schumpeterian Perspectives on Innovation, Competition and Growth* (Springer 2009).

[10] Rene Bongard, Rudi Bekkers and Alessandro Nuvolari, 'An Empirical Study on the Determinants of Essential Patent Claims in Compatibility Standards' (2011) 40 Research Policy 1001, 1002.

[11] Jorge L. Contreras, 'Essentiality and Standards-Essential Patents' in Jorge L. Contreras (ed.), *The Cambridge Handbook of Technical Standardization Law: Competition, Antitrust, and Patents* (Cambridge University Press 2017) 218; Rudi Bekkers and Andrew S. Updegrove, 'IPR Policies and Practices of a Representative Group of Standards Setting Organizations Worldwide' (Committee on Intellectual Property Management in Standard-Setting Processes, National Research Council 2013) 56–7 nap .edu accessed 25 May 2020.

[12] David J. Goodman and R. A. Myers, '3G Cellular Standards and Patents', *2005 International Conference on Wireless Networks, Communications and Mobile Computing* (2005) 5.

overzealous declarations that a patent is essential to the practice of a standard, since this is likely to result in very significant improvement in the commercial value of the patent.[13]

Nevertheless, whether or not a patent is, in fact, standard-essential is best determined by a court or similarly constituted administrative body, generally in the context of a claim by the right holder against an alleged infringer. In this process, only some of the patent claims may be found essential. Thus, it is preferable to regard essentiality as operating at the level of the patent claim, rather than the entire patent.[14] Patent pools also have expertise in determining essentiality, albeit without being in a position to assess either validity or infringement of the applicable patent claims.

Some interoperability standards may involve very large numbers of SEPs. For example, there are thousands of declared SEPs for each of the last three generations of mobile telephony air interface standards agreed under the auspices of ETSI.[15] Goodman and Myers have identified 6,872 patents claimed to be essential for the third generation W-CDMA technology. The authors grouped these 6,872 SEPs into 732 'patent families', where members of a family are patents obtained in different countries for a single invention.[16] Similarly, there may be hundreds or even thousands of essential patents for Wi-Fi technologies.[17]

Two further comments should be made about these estimates: they may not include all claims; and they should not be taken at face value: ultimately it is up to a court to determine if a particular patent is 'essential' to a particular standard, and there may be certain incentives for companies to claim a patent to be 'essential' where such a claim is highly questionable.

In a careful study of patenting practices for three important standards (Moving Picture Experts Group (MPEG), digital versatile disc (DVD) and W-CDMA), Nagaoka et al. observed that the number of patents which truly are technically essential to the practice of these standards has increased significantly over time, and many patents have been applied for after the standard was set. The authors ascribed these observed characteristics to three factors: (i) the growing complexity of the standards,

---

[13] Contreras, 'Essentiality and Standards-Essential Patents' (n. 11) 223–4.
[14] Ibid. 216.
[15] Erik Stasik, 'Royalty Rates and Licensing Strategies for Essential Patents on LTE (4G) Telecommunication Standards' (2010) 3 les Nouvelles 114, 117.
[16] Goodman and Myers (n. 12) 3.
[17] Carl Shapiro and Mark A. Lemley, 'Patent Holdup and Royalty Stacking' (2007) 85 Texas Law Review 1992, 2027.

covering numerous fields of technology; (ii) the large numbers of firms conducting research and development activities in the relevant fields; and (iii) patent laws (notably US patent laws) which permitted firms to apply for patents after the standard was set using early priority dates.[18]

4.3.1.1 Intellectual Property Policies of SSOs

Standard-setting organizations will frequently have intellectual property policies, which impose binding obligations upon members in terms of SEPs. Such policies will become binding upon members through a variety of legal mechanisms: through the SSO's bylaws, rules of procedure, membership agreement, or another mechanism.[19] SSO IP policies may be limited to patents, or may also cover other forms of IP, notably copyrights.[20]

Notwithstanding significant differences between intellectual property policies across SSOs, the following common elements will generally be observed: (i) disclosure obligations: members may be under a duty to disclose potential SEPs; and (ii) undertakings to licence: the policy will generally obligate members to license their SEPs, either royalty-free, or on reasonable and non-discriminatory (RAND) or FRAND terms, or in accordance with some other formulation.

4.3.1.2 Disclosure Obligations

There is considerable heterogeneity among SSOs in terms of disclosure obligations. The most basic of these involves a call for any SEPs to be disclosed during the course of an SSO working group meeting.[21] More significant obligations may require SSO members to disclose any patent that is or may become essential to the standard.[22] Disclosure of pending patents may result in inventions being disclosed that would otherwise not be under patent law; moreover requiring disclosure of potentially essential patents encourages over-disclosure, since the patent holder may not be able to know at the time the standard is developed whether the patent in question will ultimately become essential or not.[23] There is generally

---

[18] Nagaoka, Tsukada and Shimbo (n. 9).
[19] Bekkers and Updegrove (n. 11) 34–41; Justus Baron and others, 'Making the Rules: The Governance of Standard Development Organizations and Their Policies on Intellectual Property Rights' (2019) JRC 115004 131–132 https://ec.europa.eu/jrc accessed 16 May 2020.
[20] Bekkers and Updegrove (n. 11) 49–56.
[21] Ibid. 70–1.
[22] Ibid. 80–1.
[23] Ibid. 81.

no obligation on a member to conduct a search of its patent portfolio;[24] however the SSO policy may impose an obligation of 'best efforts', 'good faith' or 'reasonable efforts' concerning disclosures.[25]

4.3.1.3 Undertakings to License

Obligations to license are likewise heterogeneous in nature. Where imposed, such an obligation may: (i) require licensing on royalty-free terms; (ii) require licensing on RAND or FRAND terms; or (iii) require the non-assertion of SEPs.[26] Baron and Spulber sampled the IP policies of thirty-six SSOs. In their sample, nine SSOs require licensing on FRAND terms; twenty-two SSOs offer members a choice of options, with FRAND licensing being the least restrictive; and six SSOs require either royalty-free licensing or non-assertion.[27] For example: ETSI and 3GPP require FRAND; IEEE, IETF, ISO/IEC, and ITU require either FRAND, royalty-free licensing or another option (generally non-assertion); and W3C requires royalty-free licensing.[28]

Such declarations may be mandated in standard-form, or alternatively may permit members to draft their own licensing declarations; in the latter instance, heterogeneity will also exist as between members to the same SSO. Undertakings generally do not deal explicitly with the right of the SEP holder to seek injunction.[29] Increasingly, undertakings may specify price caps for future licensing royalties. Other notable features of intellectual property policies are: whether or not the policy addresses assignments or other transfers of rights.

The diversity among SSO patent policies is perhaps merely a reflection of the variegated and fragmented nature of the interoperability standard-setting landscape more generally. SSOs compete both to attract members and in terms of their output in the form of standards.[30] As Baron et al. put it:

> SDOs compete not only in the technology market to attract valuable technologies, but they also compete to attract members, and their

---

[24] Ibid. 85.
[25] Justis Baron and Daniel Spulber, 'Technology Standards and Standard Setting Organizations: Introduction to the Searle Center Database' (2018) 27 Journal of Economics & Management Strategy 462, 483.
[26] Ibid. 478.
[27] Ibid.
[28] Ibid. 479.
[29] Bekkers and Updegrove (n. 11) 126–7.
[30] Baron and others (n. 19) 64–6; Knut Blind, 'An Economic Analysis of Standards Competition: The Example of ISO ODF and OOXML Standards' (2011) 35 Telecommunications Policy 373.

standards compete in the product market for implementers. It is unclear whether SDOs are more concerned with attracting the owners of potential SEPs or standard implementers, and it is likely that the balance between implementers and SEP owners varies between industries and technological fields.[31]

Differences among IP policies, which are nominated as a matter of high importance to industry participants,[32] are likely to reflect the nature of such competition: SSOs will choose the policy that will attract the desired membership and result in development of standards that will be competitive in the marketplace. Baron et al. have documented important differences between the views of 'patent-centric' and 'product-centric' firms towards SSP IP policies, with 'product-centric' firms generally preferring more stringent IP policies, and 'patent-centric' firms preferring less stringent policies.[33]

As such, SSOs whose membership is dominated by companies whose core business is IP licensing will likely have more SEP-friendly policies (i.e. weaker duties to disclose and obligation to license); conversely, stronger disclosure and licensing policies are likely to reflect a membership with a higher proportion of members whose core business is the implementation of SEPs in downstream technologies.[34]

An important question will be whether FRAND and similar undertakings will be enforceable in contract law.[35] At least some courts have held that the FRAND undertaking amounts to a binding contract.[36] However, this approach is likely to give rise to serious difficulties, making reliance

---

[31] Baron and others (n. 19) 65.
[32] Ibid. 65–6.
[33] Ibid. 133.
[34] See Benjamin Chiao, Josh Lerner and Jean Tirole, 'The Rules of Standard-setting Organizations: An Empirical Analysis' (2007) 38 The RAND Journal of Economics 905, 927; Josh Lerner and Jean Tirole, 'A Model of Forum Shopping' (2006) 96 American Economic Review 1091.
[35] *Apple, Inc* v. *Motorola Mobility, Inc* [2012] 886 F Supp 2d 1061 (United States District Court for the District of Western Washington) 1083–4; *Unwired Planet International* v. *Huawei Technologies Co Ltd and Huawei Technologies (UK) Co Ltd* [2017] 2017 EWHC 711 (High Court) [142]; *Microsoft Corporation* v. *Motorola, Inc* [2012] 696 F3d 872 (United States Court of Appeals for the Ninth Circuit) 884; Wenwei Guan, 'Diversified FRAND Enforcement and TRIPS Integrity' (2018) 17 World Trade Review 91, 98–9; Jorge L. Contreras, 'A Market Reliance Theory for FRAND Commitments and Other Patent Pledges' (2015) 2 Utah Law Review 479, 501–17.
[36] *Research in Motion Limited, et al.* v. *Motorola, Inc* [2008] 644 FSupp 2d 788 (United States District Court for the Northern District of Texas) 797; *Microsoft Corp* v. *Motorola, Inc* [2012] 854 FSupp2d 993 (United States District Court for the District of Western Washington) 999; *Microsoft Corporation* v. *Motorola, Inc.* (n. 35) 884–5.

on contract a shaky proposition as a generalized approach. To begin with, as explained by Contreras, undertakings to license (where they exist) can take a wide variety of formulations,[37] some of which will more likely suggest a binding contract than others. Furthermore, the FRAND undertaking may extend only to other members of the SSO, limiting its usefulness to non-members who subsequently seek to rely on it.[38] Third, if the undertaking is procedural rather than content-based, it may be better characterized as an undertaking to make a contract, rather than a contractual undertaking per se.[39] Fourth, whether the undertaking is contractual will fall to be considered under the law of the jurisdiction within which the SSO is domiciled, which may not be the jurisdiction where it is sought to be enforced.

For the court to enforce the undertaking as binding in contract, it would need to: (i) take 'judicial notice' of the contract law of the other jurisdiction;[40] (ii) accept that the declaration can be construed within its own jurisdiction, having regard to the contract law of the other jurisdiction; and (iii) accept that the contract under a foreign law gives rise to binding obligations under the law of the court's jurisdiction. Fifth, the patent may be assigned after the undertaking is given, giving rise to the question of whether it binds an assignee. Many of these difficulties have been overcome in at least some instances,[41] but not in others,[42] and it is highly doubtful that the binding force of the FRAND undertaking can be assumed as a matter of course.

In conclusion, any contract existing between an SEP holder and a prospective implementer cannot be assumed to be complete, and indeed it is more likely that there will exist an incomplete (if any) contract between the two parties. This has important implications for the economic theory of 'hold-up', discussed in the next section.

---

[37] Contreras, 'A Market Reliance Theory for FRAND Commitments and Other Patent Pledges' (n. 35) 503.

[38] At least under United States law, the third-party beneficiary doctrine may render such undertakings enforceable by SSO non-members. See ibid. 508–14.

[39] *Unwired Planet International v. Huawei Technologies Co. Ltd and Huawei Technologies (UK) Co Ltd* (n. 35) paras 140–2; Contreras, 'A Market Reliance Theory for FRAND Commitments and Other Patent Pledges' (n. 35) 507.

[40] *Apple, Inc. v. Motorola Mobility, Inc.* (n. 35) 1081–2.

[41] Ibid. 1066–71.

[42] *Unwired Planet International v. Huawei Technologies Co. Ltd and Huawei Technologies (UK) Co Ltd* (n. 35) paras 140–2; Thomas F. Cotter, 'Comparative Law and Economics of Standard-Essential Patents and FRAND Royalties' (2013) 22 Texas Intellectual Property Law Journal 311, 318–19.

4.3.2 Standards-Essential Patents, Hold-Up and Royalty Stacking

As outlined above, in high technology industries, a single consumer product may incorporate hundreds or even thousands of patented components.[43] This can lead to the related concerns of 'patent hold-up' and 'royalty stacking'.[44] The term 'patent hold-up', coined by Lemley and Shapiro, refers to the phenomenon where the commercial value of a final consumer product is much larger than the value of any particular patented feature. Hence, the holder of any particular patent can use the threat of injunction against the final consumer product as a mean of obtaining royalties that may greatly exceed the value of the patented feature.[45]

The term 'hold-up', borrowed from the economics of incomplete contracting, refers to a situation where one party to a transaction has made relationship-specific investments which are difficult to employ elsewhere, and where the contract between the two parties is incomplete. This situation enables the other party to the transaction to 'hold-up' the first party and demand a higher share of the profits from the venture. The risk of this occurring may deter relationship-specific investments from being made in the first place.[46] Generally accepted means of overcoming hold-up include complete contracting and merger between the two parties.

There can be little question that in many cases the contract between the right holder and user of SEPs will be incomplete, if it exists at all. Nevertheless, patent hold-up in the context of SEPs can be seen as somewhat distinct from a classic hold-up, in that the issue is not so much relationship-specific investments as standard-specific investments:

> In the standard-setting context, firms may make sunk investments in developing and implementing a standard that are specific to particular intellectual property. To the extent that these investments are not redeployable using other IP, those developing and using the standard may be held up by the IP holders ... Moreover, this hold up may cause firms to sink less investment in developing and implementing standards.[47]

---

[43] Shapiro and Lemley (n. 17) 1992.
[44] See generally Shapiro and Lemley (n. 17).
[45] See, generally, ibid.
[46] Thomas F. Cotter, 'Patent Holdup, Patent Remedies and Antitrust Responses' (2009) 34 Journal of Corporation Law 1151, 1163–4.
[47] United States Department of Justice and the Federal Trade Commission, 'Antitrust Enforcement and Intellectual Property Rights: Promoting Innovation and Competition' (United States Department of Justice and the Federal Trade Commission 2007) 35 www.ftc.gov accessed 24 May 2019.

The interrelated concern of 'royalty stacking' refers to the risk that the manufacturer or would-be manufacturer of a final consumer product will be unable to produce the final product, or product only in suboptimal quantities, because of the quantum of licensing fees that must be paid to each individual SEP holder.[48] In this situation, SEPs to the same standard are complements, potentially giving rise to concerns of Cournot complements.[49]

This invites assessment of the empirical basis for such concerns: for example, what percentage of the final price of a product such as a smartphone incorporating a standardized air interface is likely to be consumed by royalties? Information available is not comprehensive: there is no requirement for patent holders to publish agreed royalties.[50] Lemley and Shapiro suggest the percentage could be as high as 30 per cent for 3G mobile telephony standards.[51] Others have estimated 10–13 per cent of the total price of a handset for companies with no patents to trade.[52] In relation to the 4G LTE mobile wireless standard drafted under ETSI auspices, Stasik estimates:

> For a company with no essential patents and no bargaining power, however, it is probably not unreasonable to expect little difference between the announced and actual royalty rates. For such licensees, based on the announced figures alone (and as a matter of simple arithmetic) the aggregate cumulative royalty rate for LTE – that is to say the total amount of all royalties paid to all essential patent holders – will be as much as much as 14.80 percent of the sales price of a handset.[53]

Taking into account undeclared patents and the need for multimode capability, Stasik concludes:

> Taking all of this into consideration, it is hard to imagine a comprehensive calculation of LTE royalty rates which would produce an upper-limit for the aggregate cumulative royalty of less than 25–30 percent. Again to clarify, this is an upper limit. Those companies who have negotiation power will pay less – the best ones will pay much less.[54]

---

[48] Shapiro and Lemley (n. 17) 2010–16.
[49] Neil Gandal and Pierre Régibeau, 'Standard-Setting Organisations' in Panagiotis Delimatsis (ed.), *The Law, Economics and Politics of International Standardisation* (Cambridge University Press 2015) 411–12.
[50] Ibid. 414.
[51] Shapiro and Lemley (n. 17) 2026.
[52] Stasik (n. 15) 115.
[53] Ibid. 117.
[54] Ibid.

Nor are these concerns merely theoretical in nature. The demise of the ultra-wide band (UWB) wireless technology in the early 1990s has been directly linked to problems associated with the assertion of patent rights in connection with interoperability standards.[55]

The total royalty payment is likely to be significantly lower where the user also holds relevant SEPs, and is willing to enter into a cross-licensing arrangement. In the context of a cross-licensing discussion, SEPs are likely to be considerably more valuable than non-SEPs.

The formation of collective rights organizations such as patent pools may also go some way to alleviating these issues. A patent pool may be described as follows:

> Patent pools are privately ordered structures in which multiple patent holders agree to charge a single, collective royalty. Patent pools, which have been utilized in connection with some widely adopted standardized technologies ... allow vendors to manufacture and sell standards-compliant products with a high degree of certainty regarding the aggregate royalty burden of SEPs included within the pool.[56]

Patent pools generally involve a common agent who grants licences to patents inside the 'pool'. Revenues from such licensing are distributed to participants according to an agreed formula.[57] A patent pool enables prospective users to obtain licences to all essential patents associated with a technology in a single transaction.[58]

Voluntary patent pools currently exist in many industries, both standardized and non-standardized, including in relation to mobile wireless telephony, wireless LAN, MPEG, compact disc (CD) and DVD technologies. Patent pools can be costly to administer because great care needs to be taken to ensure that non-essential patents are not included in the pool. Perhaps for this reason, far fewer standard-essential patents are included in pools than are subject to FRAND commitments.[59]

Where a standard incorporates technology held by many different firms, it may be difficult to persuade all rights holders to join the pool. As such, it seems unlikely that voluntary patent pools could ever provide more than a partial solution to problems associated with royalty stacking;

---

[55] William Webb, 'The Role of Networking Standards in Building the Internet of Things' (2012) 1 Communications & Strategies 57, 61.
[56] Jorge L. Contreras, 'Fixing FRAND: A Pseudo-Pool Approach to Standards-Based Patent Licensing' (2013) 79 Antitrust Law Journal 47, 54.
[57] Ibid. 75.
[58] Ibid. 75–6.
[59] Ibid. 76–7.

if firms were forced to join a pool this would essentially amount to compulsory licensing.

Another possible solution to the concerns of patent hold-up and royalty stacking involves ex ante voluntary price commitments by SSO members.[60] Lerner and Tirole, for example, suggest that inefficiencies associated with interoperability standard-setting can be addressed if 'IP holders noncooperatively announce price caps on their offerings, were their intellectual property to be included in the standard. The SSO would then select the standard considering the price caps to which IP owners are committed'.[61] Lerner and Tirole concede, however, that this solution is unable to arise independently of regulation because intellectual property right holders can 'forum shop' away from SSOs that impose a stricter regime on rights holders.[62] There is some evidence of price caps featuring in revisions to SSO rules, although it is not widespread.

Another suggestion comes from Lemley and Shapiro (2013), who suggest that owners of standard-essential patents be required to enter into binding 'final offer' arbitration with any potential licensee to determine a royalty:[63] 'Under our proposal, a patentee who makes a FRAND commitment promises to forego court enforcement of its standard-essential patents in favor of arbitration over the royalty rate with any implementer of the standard willing to engage in such arbitration'.[64] Lemley and Shapiro appear to rely on a combination of improvements to SSO policy and voluntary undertakings by rights holders to achieve this result. For example, SSOs are encouraged to state in their IP policies that a right holder's FRAND commitment represents a renunciation of the right to seek an injunction against a willing licensee.[65] Further, SSOs are encourage to require that any arbitration decision is made public.[66] Moreover: 'SSO best practices should include an instruction to the arbitrator to consider all patents declared essential to the standard in

---

[60] Robert A. Skitol, 'Concerted Buying Power: Its Potential for Addressing the Patent Holdup Problem in Standard Setting Symposium: Buyer Power and Antitrust' (2005) 72(2) Antitrust Law Journal 727; Paul H. Saint-Antoine and Garrett D. Trego, 'Solutions to Patent Hold-up beyond FRAND: An SOS to SSOs' (2014) 59 The Antitrust Bulletin 183.
[61] Josh Lerner and Jean Tirole, 'Standard-Essential Patents' (2015) 123 Journal of Political Economy 547, 550.
[62] Ibid.
[63] Mark A. Lemley and Carl Shapiro, 'A Simple Approach to Setting Reasonable Royalties for Standard-Essential Patents' (2013) 28 Berkeley Technology Law Journal 1135, 1138.
[64] Ibid.
[65] Ibid. 1142–3.
[66] Ibid. 1145.

question, not just the portfolio of standard-essential patents submitted to arbitration'.[67] Surveys of SSO rules to date have revealed few bylaws dealing explicitly with rights to seek injunction. The prospects for such revisions in the future are uncertain at best. As Layne-Farrar observes: 'In addition to those fields traditionally characterized by de facto standards, we might also expect to see some migration from cooperative standard setting to de facto standard setting if the rules and regulations attending SSO participation become too onerous for technology contributing firms'.[68] The same author also states:

> If overzealous regulation of cooperative standard setting leads to reduced SSO participation and increased marketplace battles over de facto standards – a result I hope will not come to pass – then de facto standard setting will become even more important to the economy than it already is and fewer 'essential' patents will be bound by FRAND obligations.[69]

The objections expressed by Layne-Farrar are well-founded. As explained in Chapter 2, there is no particular forum required for standard-setting; rather, standard-setting is, on the whole, a rather footloose enterprise which can easily migrate from one forum to another depending upon a variety of considerations, including the applicable legal environment. For this reason, attempts to resolve concerns about access to SEIP by way of amendments to SSO bylaws are unlikely to succeed.

The limited, legal monopoly associated with an SEP and the potential monopolies which often arise in connection with interoperability standards (deriving from network effects) can become a potent combination. The concept of 'double essentiality' could arise, where a particular patent is essential to a standard, and the practice of a particular standard is essential (through network externalities) to participation in the marketplace.

Thus, a single patent could be used, in effect, to preclude the access of a potential competitor into the marketplace. This dynamic has perhaps best been explained by the European Commission in its decision, under Article 102 of the TFEU, in relation to Motorola's SEP licensing practices. In its definition of the relevant market, the Commission explained that Motorola's 'Cudak' patent, which related to mobile telephony (in

---

[67] Ibid. 1150.
[68] Anne Layne-Farrar, 'Moving Past the SEP Rand Obsession: Some Thoughts on the Economic Implications of Unilateral Commitments and the Complexities of Patent Licensing' (2013) 21 George Mason Law Review 1093, 1097.
[69] Ibid.

particular, web browsing functionality) and was declared essential to ETSI's 2.5G General Packet Radio Service (GPRS) standard, could not be substituted for another technology, because: (i) it was not possible for a mobile handset manufacturer to comply with the GPRS standard without infringing the 'Cudak' patent;[70] and (ii) there were no effective substitutes for compliance with the GPRS standard within the European Economic Area; almost all mobile handsets sold within the EEA were GPRS compliant,[71] and 'next-generation' standards such as 3G and 4G still required backwards-compatibility with the GPRS standard.[72] As such the Cudak patent was (claimed to be) essential to the GPRS standard, and compliance with the GPRS standard was (established to be) essential to participation in the EEA mobile telephony market.

Where such 'double essentiality' exists, every single SEP to the relevant standard can be conceptualized as a monopoly, and each SEP holder can effectively become a gatekeeper for access into the relevant market. Any firm wishing to sell a product or service that incorporates or uses the standard (e.g. a smartphone that can make and receive calls) needs to obtain a licence to each and every SEP, to avoid patent infringement lawsuits. Thus, standards can give rise to many monopolies simultaneously – a phenomenon known as Cournot complements.[73]

Since the primary remedy for patent infringement is injunctive relief, the holder of even a single SEP can effectively exclude another firm from the marketplace. Clearly, the concern exists that this dramatic market power could give rise to abuse of a dominant market position by unscrupulous right holders. Particular concerns surrounding FRAND-encumbered SEPs have arisen in a number of situations: (i) in some instances, right holders have participated in a standard-setting process but have left the process without giving a FRAND declaration, possibly deliberately to avoid doing so;[74] (ii) in other instances, right holders have given FRAND undertakings but subsequently demanded very large

---

[70] *Motorola – Enforcement of GPRS Standard Essential Patents (Case AT39985)* (European Commission) [207]. It is worth noting, however, that the Commission based this limb of its assessment on claimed, rather than demonstrated, essentiality, a possible oversight on the Commission's part.
[71] Ibid. 199.
[72] Ibid. 194–8.
[73] Carl Shapiro, 'Navigating the Patent Thicket: Cross Licenses, Patent Pools, and Standard Setting' in Adam B. Laffe, Josh Lerner and Scott Stern (eds.), *Innovation Policy and the Economy*, vol. 1 (MIT Press 2001) 123.
[74] See, e.g., *Rambus Incorporated v. Federal Trade Commission* (2008) 522 522 F3d 456 (United States Court of Appeal for the District of Columbia Circuit); *Summary of*

royalties, arguing that such royalties are indeed fair and reasonable in the applicable circumstances;[75] and (iii) in some instances, right holders have rejected offers to license that users consider to be FRAND, and have sought injunctive relief against infringers, seeking in effect to exclude the infringer from producing the final product.[76]

A somewhat related concern that has been raised is the rise of 'patent assertion entities' or 'patent trolls' which do not produce any products themselves but simply obtain patents (either by undertaking their own research or buying patents from other firms) in order to license them, often backed by aggressive litigation strategies in the event of infringement. In his judgment in *eBay* v. *MercExchange*, Justice Kennedy of the United States Supreme Court opined:

> In cases now arising trial courts should bear in mind that in many instances the nature of the patent being enforced and the economic function of the patent holder present considerations quite unlike earlier cases. An industry has developed in which firms use patents not as a basis for producing and selling goods but, instead, primarily for obtaining licensing fees.
>
> ...
>
> For these firms, an injunction, and the potentially serious sanctions arising from its violation, can be employed as a bargaining tool to charge exorbitant fees to companies that seek to buy licenses to practice the patent.[77]

By contrast, in some industries there is a high degree of vertical integration. In the smartphone industry, for example, a firm such as Samsung is involved in chip design and manufacturing, handset production and other links in the value chain, as well as holding a larger (and highly valuable) portfolio of SEPs. Numerous other holders of significant numbers of smartphone SEPs also have downstream operations. It should be considered whether this vertical integration could give rise to risks of foreclosure under a 'leveraging' theory of conduct. In this context, licence agreements often cover multiple patents and may also involve

---

Commission Decision of 9 December 2009 under Article 102 of the Treaty (Case COMP/ 38636 – RAMBUS) [2009] OJ C 30 (European Commission).

[75] See, e.g., *Microsoft Corporation v. Motorola, Inc, et al* [2013] 2013 WL 2111217 (United States District Court for the District of Western Washington).

[76] See, e.g., *Huawei Technologies Co Ltd v. ZTE Corp, ZTE Deutschland GmbH (Case C/170–13)* [2015] ECLI:EUC:2015:477 (European Court of Justice).

[77] *eBay Inc. v. MercExchange, LLC* [2006] 547 US 388 (United States Supreme Court) 1142.

cross-licences. It may be tacitly accepted that those firms holding large portfolios of patents will be permitted to infringe, whereas firms with few or no patents may be more likely to be sued – a variant of the concept of 'mutually assured destruction'.

4.3.3 Defences to SEP Infringement

Given the concerns that can arise in relation to the protection of SEPs, relevant defences to infringement will be of considerable importance in this context. Here we discuss the two exceptions of the greatest importance in the context of SEPs, namely those of prior use and research defences, with particular regard to the laws of leading jurisdictions such as the USA, EU and China. Compulsory licensing is discussed separately in Section 4.7.1 below. Patent laws do not generally recognize a reverse-engineering exception, since this would be incompatible with the requirement to publish an invention.

4.3.3.1 Prior Use

A number of jurisdictions' patent laws enable a prior user to continue using an invention after the grant of a patent.[78] In the United States, for example, 35 U.S.C. §273 now extends a prior use defence to all patent types.[79] Likewise Chinese patent law provides for a prior use defence;[80] the defence may be found in the laws of a number of European jurisdictions,[81] and furthermore will feature in the Unified Patent Court Agreement (should it enter into force).[82] Generally, the purpose of this exception is to preserve the capability for a prior user who has chosen not to patent an invention to continue to exploit the invention after the grant of the patent. In this way the incentives for innovative activity are optimized.[83] In the context of SEPs, a prior use defence will be

---

[78] 'Exceptions and Limitations to Patent Rights: Prior Use' (World Intellectual Property Organization 2013) SCP/20/6 www.wipo.int accessed 19 September 2017.
[79] Patent Act 1952 (35 USC §§1–376) §273.
[80] Patent Law of the People's Republic of China (as amended up to the Decision of December 27, 2008, regarding the Revision of the Patent Law of the People's Republic of China), 中华人民共和国专利法 1985 Art. 69(2).
[81] Patentgesetz (Patent Act) 1980 (Article 1 of the Act of 8 October 2017 (Federal Law Gazette I p 3546)) s. 12; Patents Act 1977 s. 64; Code de la Propriété Intellectuelle (Intellectual Property Code) 1992 (Act No 92–597 of July 1, 1992 on the Code of Intellectual Property, as published in the Official Journal of July 3, 1992) Art. L613-7.
[82] Agreement on a Unified Patent Court Not yet in force (2013/C 175/01) Art. 28.
[83] 'Exceptions and Limitations to Patent Rights: Prior Use' (n. 78) 2–4.

important in ensuring that the assertion of essential patents (which in some cases could prevent a user from accessing a standard) does not preclude the practice by originators of their prior inventions.

4.3.3.2 Scientific Research and Experiment

Many jurisdictions provide for an experimental use exception to patent protection. A 2013 study undertaken by WIPO indicated that at least seventy-three jurisdictions legislate for such an exception, and another two provide for it through common law.[84] Generally, jurisdictions' laws describe the exception using terms such as 'scientific research', 'research' and 'experiment' but do not define these terms further.[85] In some cases, legislation confines the exception to activities which are 'exclusively' experimental or 'only' for research purposes, for example 'exclusively for trial or experimental purposes', 'solely serving for research on the patented subject matter', 'done only for research and experimental purposes relating only to a patented invention', 'making or using for purely experimental purposes or for scientific research', 'acts done only for the purpose of scientific research'.[86] In some instances, the relevant legislation explicitly cites the objective of furthering technological development.[87]

Potentially, the experimental use exception is important in the context of SEPs, because it would enable implementers of a standard to test and experiment on claimed SEPs with a view to potentially 'inventing around' those SEPs. Nevertheless, such activities are unlikely to fall within an experimental use exception in all cases, since the ultimate purpose of the experimentation may well be commercial, that is, to find another way to develop products compliant with the standard without infringing the SEP in question.

Recent decisions by the US Federal Circuit have dramatically narrowed the scope of the United States experimental use exception. Most notoriously, the Federal Circuit ruled in *Madey* v. *Duke University* that a university's research using a patented laser did not fall within the experimental use exception.[88] Any research or experimental exception

---

[84] 'Standing Committee on the Law of Patents: Exceptions and Limitations to Patent Rights: Experimental Use and/or Scientific Research' (World Intellectual Property Organization 2013) SCP/20/4 4 www.wipo.int accessed 19 January 2018.
[85] Ibid.
[86] Ibid. 4–5.
[87] Ibid. 5.
[88] *John MJ Madey* v. *Duke University* [2002] 307 F3d 1351 (United States Court of Appeals for the Federal Circuit) 1362.

that has survived this decision in the United States is likely to be narrow indeed.[89]

In Europe, the defence is available in most jurisdictions,[90] including in Germany,[91] France[92] and the UK.[93] A broad exception was included in the Community Patent Convention, and although that convention never entered into force, it was reflected in amendments to the legislation of a number of European jurisdictions.[94] Article 27 of the Convention articulated exceptions both for private, non-commercial use and for experimental use, thus implying that the scope of the experimental use exception would extend beyond non-commercial experimentation to encompass experiments undertaken for commercial purposes.[95] Likewise, in China, Article 69(4) of the Patent Law provides for an experimental use exception.[96] The term 'experimental use' has generally been interpreted sufficiently broadly to include research or experimentation whose ultimate goal may be commercial.[97]

An experimental use defence is likely to be important for addressing the 'essential' aspect of SEPs. A claimed SEP is only truly essential in circumstances where the party seeking to practice the standard cannot do so without infringing the SEP, that is, the user is unable to 'invent around' the SEP. Preserving the right to experiment is likely to encourage 'inventing around' SEPs. Thus, the monopoly associated with the SEP can be kept within manageable bounds. Clearly, however, such experimentation is commercial in nature; thus, confining the availability to the defence to non-commercial experimentation only (especially in the dramatic fashion seen in US law) will severely limit the practical usefulness of the exception.

---

[89] Henrik Holzapfel and Joshua D. Sarnoff, 'A Cross-Atlantic Dialog on Experimental Use and Research Tools' (2008) 48 IDEA Intellectual Property Law Review 123, 140–1.
[90] 'Standing Committee on the Law of Patents: Exceptions and Limitations to Patent Rights: Experimental Use and/or Scientific Research' (n. 84) 2.
[91] Germany Patent Act s. 11(2).
[92] France Intellectual Property Code Art. L613-5.
[93] UK Patents Act s. 60(5)(b).
[94] Holzapfel and Sarnoff (n. 89) 150.
[95] Agreement relating to community patents 1989 (OJ L 401) Art. 27; Holzapfel and Sarnoff (n. 89) 150, 155.
[96] China Patent Law Art. 69(4).
[97] Yuhe Wu and Yanfeng Xiong, 'Comparison of the Bolar Exception in China and the United States' (2008) 3 China Patents & Trademarks 13, 18–19.

4.3.3.3 Patent Fair Use

In addition to presently existing exceptions to the exclusive rights granted by a patent, one proposed bears mention: that of importing the 'fair use' defence from United States copyright law across into patent law.[98] O'Rourke, initiating this debate, proposed a five-factor test for determining whether a use is fair, based closely on the existing copyright law fair use test under American law.[99] Unlike for copyright fair use, O'Rourke suggests that courts adjudicating patent fair use should consider whether it is appropriate for the right holder to be compensated for the fair use.[100] Revisiting the same issues a decade later, Strandburg argued that the case for patent fair use had become stronger, and suggested refining O'Rourke's proposal by mandating courts' consideration of the following factors (i) the existence of a justifiable failure to license; (ii) whether the infringer substantially improved the patentee's invention; (iii) the availability of alternative innovation paradigms; and (iv) the degree of knowledge on the part of the infringer concerning infringement.[101]

Such a broad-ranging defence is also likely to create difficulties. First, application of such a defence would require courts to gather significant amounts of information. Second, with the inclusion of provision for compensation of the right holder, Strandburg is, in essence, proposing an all-purpose compulsory licensing scheme, albeit under a different and more familiar label. As with any compulsory licensing regime, a key question will be the overall impact of compulsory licensing on static and dynamic efficiency, a question which is examined in detail in Chapter 6.

4.3.4 Remedies for Patent Infringement

The principle remedies for patent infringement are injunction and an award of damages. It is common for an injunction (interlocutory or permanent) to be sought to prevent future harm to the right holder, and damages to be sought in respect of harm that took place prior to the issuance of injunction.

---

[98] Maureen O'Rourke, 'Toward a Doctrine of Fair Use in Patent Law' (2000) 100 Columbia Law Review 1177.
[99] Ibid. 1205–8.
[100] Ibid. 1209–10.
[101] Katherine J. Strandburg, 'Patent Fair Use 2.0' (2011) 1 University of California Irvine Law Review 265, 300–1.

4.3.4.1 Patent Injunctions

Some international harmonization of the availability of the injunctive remedy is mandated by international intellectual property law, notably the provisions of the TRIPS Agreement, which requires WTO Members to make available fair and equitable enforcement procedures to permit effective action against infringements of intellectual property rights covered by TRIPS, including injunctions (Articles 41 and 44). These provisions build on and reinforce Article 28 of TRIPS, which requires a patent to confer a number of exclusive rights on its owner, including the right to exclude unlicensed third parties from practising the patented invention.

Nevertheless, the TRIPS provisions leave considerable latitude to domestic jurisdictions regarding the grant by courts and/or administrative authorities of injunctions, including the applicable administrative procedures. Therefore, it is necessary to examine the laws of particular WTO Members to gain greater appreciation of the domestic courts' powers to grant injunction.

4.3.4.2 United States

In the United States, the Supreme Court held in *eBay* v. *MercExchange*[102] that the generally applicable test under American law for the award of an injunction also applies in cases of patent infringement, namely: (i) that plaintiff has suffered an irreparable injury; (ii) that remedies available at law, such as monetary damages, are inadequate to compensate for that injury; (iii) that, considering the balance of hardships between the plaintiff and the defendant, a remedy in equity is warranted; and (iv) that the public interest would not be disserved by an injunction.[103]

eBay represented a major step forward in terms of tailoring the injunctive remedy to the particular circumstances of the case at hand, and it seems especially well-suited to addressing longstanding concerns associated with access to SEPs. Automaticity in the award of injunctions, notably for FRAND-encumbered SEPs, has significant potential to engender abuses of patent rights, and in particular patent hold-up. The Supreme Court's judgment also provided an excellent example of the potential for the limiting doctrines in intellectual property law – in this case, the equitable nature of the injunctive remedy – to address concerns

---

[102] *eBay Inc., v. MercExchange, L.L.C.* (n. 77).
[103] Ibid. 1839.

associated with access to SEIP – obviating the need to resort to competition law remedies.

Following the *eBay* decision, US courts have declined to award injunction for infringements of a patent that is subject to a FRAND declaration.[104] In *Apple* v. *Motorola*, the United States Court of Appeals for the Federal Circuit clarified that the availability of injunctive relief in respect of FRAND-encumbered SEPs should be determined by applying the four-factor test outlined by the Supreme Court in *eBay*.[105] Applying the four-factor test, the Circuit denied Motorola's request for injunction because: (i) Motorola's FRAND undertaking provided to ETSI strongly suggested that money damages were adequate to compensate Motorola for any harm suffered arising from the infringement; and (ii) many other implementors were already practising the standard in question, suggesting there was little likelihood of prejudice to Motorola arising from a single additional user.[106] In *Microsoft Corporation* v. *Motorola Inc.*, the Ninth Circuit opined that in the circumstances, 'injunctive relief against infringement is arguably a remedy inconsistent with the licensing commitment'.[107]

These precedents highlights that several of the factors reiterated by the Supreme Court may well militate against injunction in the context of FRAND-encumbered SEPs – notably the second factor. It seems unlikely that damages would be inadequate to compensate an infringer who has given a FRAND undertaking. The first and fourth factor may well lead to similar conclusions in law. In circumstances where the SEP holder has participated extensively in development of the standard and notified SEPs to the SSO, it seems very unlikely that the subsequent practice of the standard will occasion irreparable harm to the right holder. Indeed, widespread infringement is to be expected as a consequence of the success of the standard in gaining widespread acceptance. Likewise, the public interest may be better served by reliance on reasonable royalty damages rather than injunctions in the context of SEPs – a question that is considered further in Chapter 6.

It is important to emphasize that the application of the four-factor test will not always preclude injunctive relief for FRAND-encumbered SEPs;

---

[104] Jorge L. Contreras, 'Injunctive Relief in US Patent Cases' in Rafal Sikorski (ed.), *Patent Law Injunctions* (Wolters Kluwer 2018) 8–9.
[105] *Apple Inc* v. *Motorola, Inc* [2014] 757 F3d 1286 (United States Court of Appeals for the Federal Circuit) 1331.
[106] Ibid. 1332.
[107] *Microsoft Corporation* v. *Motorola, Inc.* (n. 35) 885.

there have been instances where injunctive relief was granted in respect of FRAND-encumbered SEPs, such as in *CSIRO* v. *Buffalo Technology Inc.*,[108] where the United States District Court for the District of Eastern Texas, applying the four-factor test outlined in *eBay*, reached the conclusion that a permanent injunction was appropriate because: (i) CSIRO's research activities[109] would suffer irreparable harm if no injunction were granted; and (ii) damages would be unable to properly compensate CSIRO for the harms suffered; (iii) the balance of hardships favoured injunction because whilst the harm to Buffalo was merely financial, the harm to CSIRO's publicly beneficial research programmes would be far greater; and (iv) in view of CSIRO's research programmes, the public interest favoured grant of an injunction.[110]

This example reinforces the flexible, case by case nature of the analysis encouraged by the Supreme Court in *eBay*, neither mandating nor precluding the award of injunction in any particular case but rather leaving to the courts to decide on the basis of all relevant facts and circumstances whether an injunction is appropriate.

Furthermore, the *eBay* approach has not been applied in the context of exclusion orders under § 1337 of the Smoot-Hawley Tariff Act 1930, under which imports can be prohibited from entering the United States where they infringe a copyright, patent or trademark.[111] The USITC established under the Smoot-Hawley Act[112] cannot award damages; its only available remedies are exclusion orders and cease and desist orders.[113] As such, the *eBay* four-factor test does not apply in the context of USITC investigations.[114] Hence, the commendable application by the Supreme Court in *eBay* of the limiting doctrines in patent law cannot be said to apply uniformly under American law; of most concern, the

---

[108] *Commonwealth Scientific and Industrial Research Organization* v. *Buffalo Technology Inc* [2007] 492 FSupp2d 600 (United States District Court for the Eastern District of Texas).
[109] CSIRO is Australia's national science and development agency.
[110] *Commonwealth Scientific and Industrial Research Organization* v. *Buffalo Technology Inc* (n. 108) 603–607.
[111] Tariff Act 1930 (19 USC §§1301–1683g) §1337(a)(1)(B)–(C), §1337(d)(1); Helen H Ji, 'District Courts versus the USITC: Considering Exclusionary Relief for F/Rand-Encumbered Standard-Essential Patents Note' (2014) 21 Michigan Telecommunications and Technology Law Review 169, 181; *Spansion, Inc* v. *International Trade Commission* [2010] 629 F3d 1331 (United States Court of Appeals for the Federal Circuit) 1358.
[112] Tariff Act §1330.
[113] Ibid. §1337(d)(1).
[114] *Spansion, Inc.* v. *International Trade Commission* (n. 111) 1359.

burden of § 1337 exclusion orders will fall upon foreign users of American intellectual property.

4.3.4.3 European Law

In Europe, a considerable degree of fragmentation is observed, with patent litigation for the most part left to the national courts.[115] There are, however, moves afoot to harmonize patent litigation across the EU. These will include the advent of a European Patent with Unitary Effect, and a Unified Patent Court with competence to rule across all participating jurisdictions.[116]

The basic requirements for Member State laws regarding the availability of injunctions are set out in the EU Enforcement Directive.[117] Article 9(1) requires Member States to ensure that their judicial authorities have powers to issue interlocutory injunctions; Article 11, similarly, provides for awards of permanent injunctions. The Enforcement Directive also includes overarching guidance about the nature in which these powers are to be exercised. Preambular recital (17) stipulates that remedies should be determined in each case in such a manner as to take due account of the specific characteristics of that case, including the specific features of each intellectual property right.[118] Echoing the requirements of the TRIPS Agreement, procedures must be fair and equitable;[119] effective, proportionate and dissuasive, and must be applied in such a manner as to avoid the creation of barriers to legitimate trade and to provide safeguards against their abuse.[120]

The Enforcement Directive, particularly when considered in light of the guidance provided by TRIPS, would seem to provide for a rather flexible and case-sensitive approach to the award of injunctions, thus inviting a case by case approach taking account of all relevant factors, consistently with principles of equity and consonant with the topical methodology. For example, the principle of proportionality can be interpreted to require consideration of matters such as: whether the purposes of patent protection could be achieved through remedies less onerous

---

[115] Katrin Cremers and others, 'Patent Litigation in Europe' (2017) 44 European Journal of Law and Economics 1, 2.
[116] Ibid.
[117] Directive 2004/48/EC of the European Parliament and of the Council of 29 April 2004 on the enforcement of intellectual property rights 2004 (L 157).
[118] Ibid. Recital 17.
[119] Ibid. Art. 3(1).
[120] Ibid. Art. 3(2).

than injunction; whether injunction can achieve a satisfactory balance of competing rights and obligations.[121] Nevertheless, the Directive perhaps does not go far enough in articulating the factors which should be considered by Member State courts on a case by case basis in their decisions on the award of injunction.[122]

Germany is a particularly important European jurisdiction as regards patent enforcement. By some accounts more than half of all patent disputes in Europe are decided before the Regional Court of Dusseldorf in the first instance, and before the Higher Regional Court of Dusseldorf in the second instance.[123] In Germany, permanent injunction will generally be issued upon a finding of infringement, that is, there is essentially an entitlement to injunction.[124] At least in theory, the doctrine of abuse of rights could operate to temper such automaticity, but in practice the defence will rarely succeed.[125] The German Government has sought public comment on amendments to the Patent Law that would temper the automatic entitlement to patent via a test of proportionality.

In the specific context of SEPs, balancing and proportionality have entered German law via the application of competition law, first by way of the decision of the Bundesgerichtshof in Orange-Book-Standard case, and subsequently (and more effectively) following the European Court of Justice (ECJ)'s *Huawei v. ZTE* decision of 2015.[126] This matter is addressed more extensively in the following chapter.

4.3.4.4 Chinese Law

Chinese patent law provides for awards of preliminary and final injunctions for patent infringement.[127] For both interim and permanent injunction proceedings, Chinese law provides for the courts to apply a balanced and proportionate approach to the question of whether

---

[121] Rafal Sikorski, 'Patent Law Injunctions in the European Union Law' in Rafal Sikorski (ed.), *Patent law Injunctions* (Wolters Kluwer 2018) 3.
[122] Ibid. 4.
[123] Arno Risse, 'Injunctions in Germany' in Rafal Sikorski (ed.), *Patent Law Injunctions* (Wolters Kluwer 2018) 22.
[124] Germany Patent Act s. 139(1); Risse (n. 123) 22; Pierre Larouche and Nicolo Zingales, 'Injunctive Relief in FRAND Disputes in the EU? Intellectual Property and Competition Law at the Remedies Stage' (Tilburg Law School 2017) No. 1 of 2017 11–12 https://papers.ssrn.com accessed 9 February 2018.
[125] Risse (n. 123) 27.
[126] Ibid. 29.
[127] China Patent Law Arts 60, 61.

injunction should be awarded. Regarding interim injunctions, in a 2016 ruling by the Guangzhou Intellectual Property Civil Court, the Court outlined six factors that should determine whether interim injunction should be issued: (i) whether the patents in suit are valid and stable; (ii) the likelihood of ongoing infringement; (iii) the possibility of irreparable injury to the Claimant's legitimate interests, absent infringement; (iv) a comparison of the damage to the defendant from ordering injunction with the damage to the plaintiff of not ordering injunction; (v) the public interest; and (vi) provision by the claimant of appropriate security in the form of a bond.[128]

Permanent injunction is the usual remedy for established patent infringements.[129] However a number of defences are available, including: (i) the public interest; (ii) good faith; and (iii) compulsory licensing, including for breaches of the Anti-Monopoly Law (AML). Compulsory licensing for breach of the AML has been the defence most prominently applied in relation to requests for injunction relating to FRAND-encumbered SEPs, including the National Development and Reform Commission (NDRC)'s Qualcomm investigation and the case of *Huawei v. InterDigital*.[130] These cases are discussed in detail in the following chapter.

The Beijing Intellectual Property Court awarded China's first injunction in respect of FRAND-encumbered SEPs, in *Xian Xidian Jietong Wireless Communication Co., Ltd (IWNComm) v. SONY mobile communication products (China) Co. Ltd*. The court considered that the user (Sony) was primarily responsible for the failure of negotiations to produce a FRAND licence, and accordingly awarded permanent injunction.[131] In a more recent dispute between Huawei and Samsung, the Shenzhen Intermediate People's Court carefully analysed the course of negotiations between the parties before reaching the conclusion that award of permanent injunction was appropriate.[132]

An interesting question is whether the defences of public interest and good faith would provide an alternative path under Chinese law to an appropriately tailored injunctive remedy. In 2008, a vice-president of

---

[128] Liguo Zhang, 'Injunctive Relief in China's Patent Law' in Rafal Sikorski (ed.), *Patent Law Injunctions* (Wolters Kluwer 2018) 79.
[129] Ibid. 80.
[130] Ibid. 84–7.
[131] Ashish Bharadwaj and Dipinn Verma, 'China's First Injunction in Standard Essential Patent Litigation' (2017) 12 Journal of Intellectual Property Law & Practice 717.
[132] Zhang (n. 128) 87–8.

China's highest judicial organ, the Supreme People's Court (SPC), indicated in a speech that:

> If an injunction is likely to cause significant imbalance between the parties' interests, or is not in line with the public interest, or practically difficult to enforce, the court may evaluate the interests according to the specific circumstances of the case, and may not award an injunction on condition that sufficient and feasible damage or monetary compensation is awarded.[133]

These views have subsequently been echoed in a judicial interpretation issued by the SPC.[134] Recent amendments to China's patent law have clarified that the doctrine of abuse of rights also forms part of Chinese law, pointing to a further avenue of flexibility that may assume more importance in the future.[135]

4.3.4.5 Calculation of Compensation for Infringement of Standards-Essential Patents

Domestic laws generally provide for such damages in the form either lost profits, account of profits, or payment of reasonable royalties.[136]

Lost Profits Lost profits generally represent the difference between the revenues which the patent holder would have made but for the infringer, and the revenue the patent holder actually made.[137] In the United States, an award of lost profits is generally more difficult to obtain than reasonable royalties; between 2006 and 2015, only 21 per cent of patent damages were based solely on lost profits.[138] Lost profits awards are less commonly awarded in the EU than in the United States.[139] In China, Article 65 of the Patent Law provides for compensation to be determined according to the patentee's actual losses caused by the infringement,[140] although lost profits are rarely awarded in practice.[141]

---

[133] Ibid. 81.
[134] Ibid. 82.
[135] Ibid.
[136] Patent Act §284; Patents Act (Cth) (No 83 of 1990) s. 122(1); UK Patents Act s. 61(1)(c)–(d); China Patent Law s 65; Tokkyohō (Patent Act) 1959 (Act No 121 of April 13, 1959 as amended up to Act No 55 of July 10, 2015) Art. 102(1); Germany Patent Act s. 139(2).
[137] Christopher B. Seaman and others, 'Lost Profits and Disgorgement' in C. Bradford Biddle and others (eds.), *Patent Remedies and Complex Products: Towards a Global Consensus* (Cambridge University Press 2019) 50.
[138] Ibid. 55.
[139] Ibid. 57.
[140] China Patent Law Art. 65.
[141] Seaman and others (n. 137) 58.

The lost profits paradigm implies competition between the right holder and the user, with the infringing sales of the latter detracting from the legitimate sales of the former. The paradigm applies rather awkwardly in the case of SEPs, where the right holder and the standards implementor may not compete. Additionally, SEPs are often present in complex multicomponent products. In this circumstance, any lost profits award should properly allocate to the right holder only those profits associated with the infringing feature, as distinct from all profits associated with sales of the infringing product.

In *Mentor Graphics Corp. v. EVE-USA Inc.*, the United States Court of Appeals for the Federal Circuit declined to undertake any apportionment analysis, awarding all of the lost profits associated with the defendant's semiconductor emulator system to the plaintiff.[142] The Court reasoned that since only Mentor Graphics could have lawfully sold an emulator system that included the patents at issue, and since client Intel was not prepared to purchase a system that did not include the patented feature, Mentor was entitled to recover all profits arising from EVE-USA's wrongful sales.[143]

The Court proceeded on the assumption that the 'patent considered by the jury at trial (United States Patent No. 6,240,376 or '376)' was the only patented feature in EVE-USA's emulator systems.[144] Even where this assumption can be justified, apportionment would be necessary to avoid compensating the patent holder for sales resulting from unpatented but innovative features incorporated into the user's product.[145] In cases where the user's product incorporates multiple patented features, awarding unapportioned lost profits to a plaintiff in relation to an SEP that is merely a component of a complex multi-component product will lead to precisely the same harms identified with respect to awards of injunctions: it will place SEP holders in

---

[142] *Mentor Graphics Corp v. EVE-USA Inc* [2017] 851 F3d 1275 (United States Court of Appeals for the Federal Circuit) 1280.
[143] Ibid. 1289.
[144] Ibid. 1290: 'Consider the laptop example. *If the only patented component is the extended life battery* and a customer will only buy a laptop with this battery (meaning a laptop with a lower quality battery is not an acceptable noninfringing alternative to the customer), then when an infringer who appropriates the patented extended life battery sells a laptop, the infringer has deprived the patentee of the lost profits on the laptop sale which only it could have made' (emphasis added).
[145] Recalling there are other ways for innovators to obtain protection for their inventions, such as trade secrets and lead time.

a bargaining position that far exceeds the value of the SEP and give rise to risks of patent hold-up and royalty stacking.[146]

Account of Profits   In some jurisdictions, disgorgement of the infringer's profits will also be available as a remedy for infringement of SEPs. In the United States, the remedy is not available in respect of utility patents, but is available for design patents.[147] The EU Enforcement Directive makes available the account of profits for unfair profits made by the infringer.[148] Article 65 of China's Patent Act likewise permits compensation based on the benefits acquired by the infringer through the infringement, where it is hard to establish lost profits.

As with lost profits, the remedy of an account of profits is likely to present significant difficulty in the context of SEPs. The benefits of standardization are likely to be optimized in circumstances where profits are earned by both right holders and users; the latter to encourage follow-on innovation. As such, disgorgement of profits should be applied sparingly in the context of SEPs. As with lost profits, any profits disgorged would need to be properly apportioned to the profits resulting from the patented feature in issue, as distinct from all profits arising from sales of the infringing product.

Reasonable Royalties   One of the most common ways to calculate appropriate damages for patent infringement is to estimate the reasonable royalty that would have been negotiated between the patent holder and infringer in an arms-length commercial transaction. The reasonable royalty is likely to be the most appropriate remedy to redress infringement of SEPs, since the essentiality of the patent and its incorporation into a standard implies widespread use. Ordinary principles for the calculation of the reasonable royalty under applicable domestic law will likely be the starting point; however, adjustments will be desirable to tailor the remedy to the specific context of SEPs.

In the United States, the classic formulation was laid down by the United States District Court for the Southern District of New York in *Georgia Pacific Corp. v. United States Plywood Corp.*,[149] which articulated

---

[146] Bernard Chao, 'Lost Profits in a Multicomponent World' (2018) 59 Boston College Law Review 1321, 1342–8.
[147] Seaman and others (n. 137) 75.
[148] EU IPR Enforcement Directive art. 13(1)(a).
[149] *Georgia Pacific Corp v. United States Plywood Corp* [1971] 318 FSupp 1116 (United States District Court for the Southern District of New York).

the fifteen so-called 'Georgia-Pacific' factors. The 'Georgia-Pacific' factors are sufficiently broad to cover most, if not all considerations that would be relevant in the context of calculating reasonable royalties for infringed SEPs (e.g. the commercial relationship between the parties, any existing licences, the nature of the product, and the contribution of the invention to the profits enjoyed by the end product, and expert testimony), although it will be a matter for the courts to tailor them to the particular circumstances of the case. Likewise, EU Member States are required to provide in their laws for calculation of damages on the basis of 'the amount of royalties or fees which would have been due if the infringer had requested authorisation to use the intellectual property right in question'.[150] Chinese patent law likewise provides for reasonable royalties.[151]

Domestic jurisprudence regarding the calculation of reasonable royalties in the context of SEP infringement is developing well, especially in the leading jurisdictions. In a number of cases, domestic courts have calculated reasonable royalties for SEPs, including SEPs subject to FRAND commitments. For example, in *Microsoft* v. *Motorola*,[152] the United States District Court of Western Washington estimated both a pinpoint FRAND royalty, and a permissible FRAND royalty, for sixteen Motorola patents claimed essential to the ITU H.264 standard, and twenty-four patents claimed essential to the IEEE 802.11 standard, in the immediate context of a breach of contract claim by Microsoft and the broader context of a variety of patent infringement claims brought by both parties in various jurisdictions. The District Court, anchoring its estimates of the permissible FRAND rates in the general US law framework for the calculation of reasonable royalties, namely the fifteen 'Georgia-Pacific' factors,[153] developed a comprehensive approach to calculating the FRAND royalty, paying particular attention to: the contribution of the SEPs in question to the ITU and IEEE standards; the valuation of the SEPs established by patent pools; and expert valuation.

A growing number of other United States court decisions have shed light on the proper methodology for calculating a FRAND royalty, including: *In re Innovatio IP Ventures*;[154] *Ericsson*

---

[150] EU IPR Enforcement Directive Art. 13(b).
[151] China Patent Law Art. 65.
[152] *Microsoft Corporation* v. *Motorola, Inc., et al* (n. 75).
[153] Ibid. 87–93.
[154] *In re Innovatio, LLC Patent Litigation* 2013 WL 5593609 (United States District Court for the Northern District of Illinois, Eastern Division).

v. *D-Link*;[155] *CSIRO* v. *Cisco*;[156] and *Golden Bridge Technology* v. *Apple*.[157] There have also been rulings in the EU (*Huawei* v. *Unwired Planet*),[158] China (*Huawei* v. *InterDigital*),[159] Japan (*Samsung* v. *Apple*)[160] and elsewhere. Domestic cases calculating the applicable FRAND royalty[161] are discussed further in Chapter 6.

Generally, domestic courts around the world are making considerable progress in developing reasonable approaches for royalty calculations in the context of SEPs; such efforts are likely to continue. Ordinary principles of domestic law relating the calculation of patent damages will generally be the starting point, adjusted as appropriate to take account of the particular context of interoperability standard-setting, including undertakings to license provided.

4.3.5 SEPs in the Particular Context of Software Patenting

Patents, together with copyrights and trade secrets, are the main vehicles for the protection of computer software intellectual property. It might be hypothesized that one way to address concerns associated with access to SEPs might simply be to exclude all or most computer programs from patent protection. This would seem to draw support from the first sentence of Article 27(1) of TRIPS, which requires that patent protection be available for any inventions which meet the standard threshold requirements (novelty, utility and non-obviousness).

Laws of nature and mathematical formulae are part of the store of knowledge available to humanity at large and are thus generally excluded from patentability. The distinction between, on the one hand, laws of

---

[155] *Ericsson, Inc* v. *D-Link Systems Inc* [2014] 773 F3d 1201 (United States Court of Appeals for the Federal Circuit).

[156] *Commonwealth Scientific and Industrial Research Organisation* v. *CISCO Systems Inc* [2015] 809 F3d 1295 1295 (United States Court of Appeals for the Federal Circuit).

[157] *Golden Bridge Technology* v. *Apple Inc* [2014] 2014 WL2194501 (United States District Court, Northern District of California).

[158] *Unwired Planet International* v. *Huawei Technologies Co. Ltd and Huawei Technologies (UK) Co Ltd* (n. 35).

[159] *Interdigital Communications, Inc* v. *Huawei Investment & Holding Co, Ltd*, Zongji Renmin Fayuan 2013 (Shenzhen Intermediate People's Court).

[160] *Samsung Electronics Co, Ltd* v. *Apple Japan Godo Kaisha* (Grand Panel of the Japanese Intellectual Property High Court).

[161] See generally Anne Layne-Farrar and Koren W. Wong-Ervin, 'Methodologies for Calculating FRAND Damages: An Economic and Comparative Analysis of the Case Law from China, the European Union, India, and the United States' (2017) 8 Jindal Global Law Review 127.

nature, natural phenomena and abstract ideas, which are patent-ineligible, and, on the other hand, claims which integrate such basic building blocks in a manner that provides a technical solution to a technical problem, which are patent-eligible, is methodologically clear. However, under this approach, most if not all interoperability standards embedded in computer programmes will be patent-eligible.

4.3.5.1 United States Law

Section 101 of the United States Patents Act confers patentability in broad terms to 'any new and useful process, machine, manufacture, or composition of matter, or any new and useful improvement thereof'. United States patent law has long held that laws of nature, natural phenomena and abstract ideas are not patentable.[162] As the Supreme Court explained in its landmark decision in *Alice Corp. Pty. Ltd* v. *CLS Bank International*,[163] since laws of nature, natural phenomena and abstract ideas are the basic tools of scientific and technological work, monopolization of those tools through the grant of a patent might tend to impede innovation more than it would tend to promote it, thereby thwarting the primary object of the patent laws.[164]

In other words, these matters are part of a commons available to all inventors, present and future, and are not subject to appropriation via the allocation of private rights. Nevertheless, the Court in *Alice* also acknowledged that at some level, all inventions make recourse to laws of nature, natural phenomena, or abstract ideas; accordingly, the Court sought to distinguish: 'between patents that claim the building blocks of human ingenuity and those that integrate the building blocks into something more ... thereby transforming them into a patent-eligible invention ...'.[165] In *Alice*, the Court applied a two-step test to determine that the claimed invention, a computerized scheme for managing certain types of financial risks,[166] was a patent-ineligible abstract idea. First, the Court held that the claims at issue were directed toward such a patent-ineligible concept.[167] In particular, the claims described the practice of financial hedging, a commonplace economic concept in the financial

---

[162] *Alice Corporation Pty Ltd* v. *CLS Bank International et al* [2014] 134 SCt 2347 (United States Supreme Court) 2354.
[163] Ibid.
[164] Ibid. 2354.
[165] Ibid.
[166] Ibid. 2352.
[167] Ibid. 2355–7.

services industry. Second, the Court considered whether the claims contained an 'inventive concept' sufficient to transform the claimed abstract idea into a patent-eligible application. In particular, the Court observed that 'the mere recitation of a generic computer cannot transform a patent-ineligible abstract idea into a patent-eligible invention'. Moreover, 'Stating an abstract idea while adding the words "apply it with a computer"' is not sufficient to give rise to a patentable invention.[168] The Court considered that the claims did no more than simply instruct a practitioner to implement the abstract idea of intermediated settlement on a generic computer.[169] Thus, all claims were held patent-ineligible.[170]

In the wake of the *Alice* decision, United States courts apply a 'technological arts' test to questions pertaining to the patentability of computer programs. In practice this involves consideration of whether the claims involve a technological solution to a technological problem.[171] The leading case is *Amdocs (Israel) Ltd. v. Openet Telecom, Inc.*,[172] in which the Federal Circuit, after condensing the Supreme Court's two-step *Alice* test into a single-step test, held that four patents that together described an Internet Protocol network protocol billing system were patentable inventions.[173]

Following the reasoning of the Federal Circuit in *Amdocs*, it would seem apparent that many, if not most, technologies embodied in a computer program that contribute to an interoperability standard would be considered to provide a technological solution to a technological problem, and therefore give rise to patentable inventions under American law.

4.3.5.2 European Law

Although on its face European law takes a more restrictive approach to patents, excluding them from patent eligibility 'as such', in practice European law takes an approach that is very similar to American law, where the key issue is the inventiveness of the software functionality, and in particular whether it presents a technical solution to a technical

---

[168] Ibid. 2358.
[169] Ibid. 2359.
[170] Ibid. 2360.
[171] *Amdocs (Israel) Limited v. Openet Telecom Inc* [2016] 841 F3d 1288 (United States Court of Appeals for the Federal Circuit); Joseph Allen Craig, 'Deconstructing Wonderland: Making Sense of Software Patents in a Post-Alice World' (2017) 32 Berkeley Technology Law Journal 359, 375.
[172] *Amdocs (Israel) Limited v. Openet Telecom Inc.* (n. 171).
[173] Ibid. 1291–306.

problem. Again, the logical conclusion is that interoperability standards embodied in computer programs will generally be eligible for patent protection.

European Patent Convention Article 52, provides that to be patentable, the claim(s) must inter alia be for an invention in a field of technology; programmes for computers are not patentable 'as such'.[174] Further clarification may be obtained from the Implementing Regulations to the Convention on the Grant of European Patents, which point to the need for an invention to be in a technical field, be concerned with a technical problem and possess technical features.

The case law of the Board of Appeal and the Enlarged Board of Appeal of the European Patent Office has, over the years, sought to clarify the meaning of article 52 by reference to the fundamental requirement that an invention be technical or possess a technical character, offering a smörgåsbord of legal tests such as requiring a 'technical process' or 'technical contribution';[175] a 'technical effect' or 'further technical effect';[176] the employment of 'technical means';[177] and the possession of a 'technical character'.[178]

The present approach of the Boards of Appeal has been characterized by Ballardini as an 'any hardware' approach,[179] under which: 'What matters having regard to the concept of "invention" within the meaning

[174] Art. 52(1)–(2) Convention on the Grant of European Patents (adopted 5 October 1973, entry into force 7 October 1977) (1065 UNTS 199).

[175] *Method and apparatus for improved digital image processing/Vicom (T208/84)* [1985] OJ 198714 (Boards of Appeal of the European Patent Office) [12]. The Board stated: 'The Board is of the opinion that a claim directed to a technical process which process is carried out under the control of a program (be this implemented in hardware or in software), cannot be regarded as relating to a computer program *as such* within the meaning of Article 52(3) EPC, as it is the application of the program for determining the sequence of steps in the process for which in effect protection is sought' (emphasis in original).

[176] *Data Transfer with Expanded Clipboard Formats/Microsoft (T424/03)* (Boards of Appeal of the European Patent Office) [5.3]; *Asynchronous Resynchronization of a Commit Procedure, International Business Machines (T1173/97)* [1998] OJ 1999609 (Boards of Appeal of the European Patent Office) [5.1-6.6].

[177] *Auction Method/Hitachi (T258/03)* [2004] OJ 2004575 (Boards of Appeal of the European Patent Office) [4.7].

[178] *Controlling Pension Benefits System/PBS Partnership (T931/95)* [2000] ECLI:EP:BA:2000:T09319520000908 (Boards of Appeal of the European Patent Office).

[179] Rosa Maria Ballardini, 'Software Patents in Europe: The Technical Requirement Dilemma' (2008) 3 Journal of Intellectual Property Law & Practice 563, 566–7. This nomenclature is accepted and adopted by Li, see Yahong Li, 'The Current Dilemma and Future of Software Patenting' (2019) 50 International Review of Intellectual Property and Competition Law 823.

of Article 52(1) European Patent Convention (EPC) is the presence of *technical features* of an entity *or the nature of an activity*, or may be conferred to a nontechnical activity by the use of *technical means*'.[180] As such, the present state of EU law would seem to be more closely aligned with the generally applicable tests of: (i) being in a technical field; (ii) solving a technical problem; and (iii) possessing technical features, as derived from the Implementing Regulations, than from the more particularized exclusion of computer programs 'as such' articulated in the EPC itself.

Reflecting this approach, the Board in *Microsoft* (T424/03) did not exclude on the basis of article 52(2) a claim that, in essence, involved simply a computer program which gave instructions to hardware. Although the Board of Appeal sought to explain its decision in a manner that retained consistency with previous decisions, notably *International Business Machines* (T1173/97),[181] it set such a low bar for the requisite 'technical character' as to call into question to requirement that the computer program achieve a 'further technical effect' going beyond the basic interaction between hardware and software.

The 'any hardware' approach would seem to be more satisfactory from a methodological perspective, but it does mean that many, if not most, computer programs will be considered to be patentable inventions on the basis of features possessed by all computer programs – namely that the inventiveness of the computer program manifests in its physical interfaces with computer hardware. This calls into question whether computer programs are really excluded from patentability 'as such' under EU law,[182] or whether, instead, they are merely subjective to the more generally applicable requirement that the invention provide a solution to a technical problem through technical means. Moreover, it is not apparent that the exclusion of computer programs 'as such' adds anything to the exclusion 'as such' of mathematical formulae.

Where the interoperability standard takes the form of a computer program, it would seem (almost by definition) to present the requisite technical character or technical nature, given that its raison d'être is to accomplish the interoperable functionality as between distinct products, programs or services which function together as part of a larger system. This is an inherently technical function, which solves a technical problem

---

[180] *Auction Method/Hitachi (T258/03)* (n. 177) para. 4.5. Emphasis added.
[181] *Data Transfer with Expanded Clipboard Formats/Microsoft (T424/03)* (n. 176) para. 5.3.
[182] See Ballardini (n. 179) 567.

(namely the problem of interoperability), which manifests in an impact on objects external to the program itself.

On balance therefore, and having regard to the current state of EU law, it seems highly unlikely that any interoperability standard that manifests as computer program would be considered not to constitute an 'invention' and hence not be susceptible to patentability. Indeed, it would seem likely that a computer program that is also interoperability standard would also satisfy the more stringent 'further technical effect' required imposed by T1173/97, inasmuch as the standard lays down means of interoperability between products etc., and thus stipulates technical effects that go beyond the basic interactions between software and hardware.

4.3.5.3 Chinese Law

Chinese law appears to closely follow the European example. China's Patent Law contains no per se exclusion for computer programs, but does exclude scientific discoveries and 'rules and methods for intellectual activities'.[183] Nevertheless, the Guidelines for Patent Examination issued by China's State Intellectual Property Office provide: (i) that computer programs per se are unpatentable because they constitute rules and methods for mental activities; but (ii) notwithstanding (i), a claim that also contains technical features shall not be excluded from patentability.[184] The Guidelines further provide that 'inventions relating to computer programs' are patentable; these are: 'solutions for solving the problems of the invention which are wholly or partly based on the process of computer programs and control or process external or internal objects of a computer by the computer executing the programs according to the above-mentioned process'.[185] A software invention can provide the requisite 'technical solution' where: (i) the computer program is executed to control or process external or internal objects, solving one or more technical problems; or (ii) the computer program is executed to process external technical data, which would lead to a 'technical effect regarding data process according to the laws of nature'.[186] Under either of these two pathways, an interoperability standard that is embodied in a computer program is highly unlikely to be excluded from patentability on grounds that it lacks the requisite technical features. The first would seem to be the

---

[183] China Patent Law art. 25(1), (2).
[184] Li (n. 179).
[185] Ibid.
[186] Ibid.

most readily applicable: an interoperability standard controls an external process or objects, thereby solving a technical problem, namely the problem of interoperability as between distinct modules in a network.

4.3.5.4 Software Patenting: Concluding Remarks

It might be hypothesized that one way to address concerns associated with access to SEPs might simply be to exclude all or most computer programs from patent protection. Nevertheless, even if computer programs are excluded from patentability 'as such' and only if and to the extent they present an 'invention', most if not all interoperability standards, which by their nature supply technical solutions to technical problems, will likely satisfy the test of inventiveness (howsoever credibly formulated) and therefore be eligible for patent protection.

4.3.5.5 Disclosure Requirements in Connection with Computer Programs

The TRIPS Agreement mandates disclosure of patented inventions in a manner sufficiently clear and complete for the invention to be carried out by a person skilled in the art,[187] and this requirement is reflected in United States,[188] European Union[189] and Chinese law.[190] Disclosure is the quid pro quo for the time-limited monopoly imposed by a patent;[191] proper disclosure encourages inventions outside the patent scope immediately, enables practice of the invention after the patent expires and discourages infringement by delineating the scope of the invention.[192]

Nevertheless, disclosure requirements for software inventions have become rather lax, especially in the United States, where Federal Circuit case law[193] has held neither source code nor flow charts need to be disclosed, a general description of the function performed by the

---

[187] Agreement on Trade-Related Aspects of Intellectual Property Rights, Annex 1C to the Marrakesh Agreement Establishing the World Trade Organization (adopted 15 April 1994, entered into force 1 January 1995) (1869 UNTS 299) art. 29(1).
[188] Patent Act §112.
[189] Convention on the Grant of European Patents (adopted 5 October 1973, entry into force 7 October 1977) art. 83.
[190] China Patent Law art. 26(3).
[191] Michael J. Walsh, 'Disclosure Requirements of 35 USC 112 and Software-Related Patent Applications: Debugging the System' (1985) 18 Connecticut Law Review 855, 858–9.
[192] Ibid. 857–8.
[193] *Fonar Corp* v. *General Electric Co* [1997] 107 F3d 1543 (United States Court of Appeals for the Federal Circuit) 1549.

program will be sufficient.¹⁹⁴ In the EU, neither source code nor design documents must be disclosed, although disclosure should include a description in natural language.¹⁹⁵

In these circumstances, follow-on inventors would need to reverse-engineer the software in order to make use of the patent disclosure (e.g. by decompilation of the object code); however in many cases this option will be impractical and in the United States, where the research exception is narrowly construed, such reverse engineering will likely give rise to infringement through the use of temporary copies.¹⁹⁶ In short, software developers are able to enjoy patent and trade secret protection in respect of the same invention.

Ballardini recommends that, at the least, software developers disclose flowcharts, pseudocodes and a natural language description of the invention. Depending on the type of software, disclosure of source code may also be required.¹⁹⁷ Burk and Lemley also recommend higher disclosure requirements for software.¹⁹⁸

In the context of SEPs the main concern is that the ability to 'invent around' the SEP will be constrained by the failure of patentees to fully disclose the invention, and by the restrictions on decompilation. This makes it much more difficult for implementers of the standard to find alternatives to the SEP that can still implement the standard. In summary, concerns surrounding access to SEIP may, at least in some measure, arise because of the approach taken by courts and national patent offices towards the particular issues associated with software patenting, and compounded by court decisions which have narrowed the scope of available patent exceptions.

4.4 Copyrights

4.4.1 Standards-Essential Copyright

The terminology of a 'standards-essential copyright', unlike that of a 'standards-essential patent' is rarely encountered either in case law or

---

[194] Dan L. Burk and Mark A. Lemley, 'Designing Optimal Software Patents' in Robert W Hahn (ed.), *Intellectual Property Rights in Frontier Industries: Software and Biotechnology* (AEI Press 2005) 82–4.
[195] Rosa Maria Ballardini, 'The Software Patent Thicket: A Matter of Disclosure' (2009) 6 SCRIPTed 207, 218.
[196] Ibid. 291–20.
[197] Ibid. 228.
[198] Burk and Lemley (n. 194) 94.

literature. But copyright protection is also important in the domain of interoperability standards.

Formal standards promulgated through SSOs are generally copyrighted;[199] the copyright nature of the standard will generally be publicized on the SSO's website, and a copy of the standard may require the payment of a fee which, however, is usually set at a reasonable level to encourage widespread adoption of the standard. To charge excessive fees for copyrighted standards would presumably preclude the widespread uptake of the standard and would therefore be against the interests of the body promoting the standard. Some SSOs lay down detailed policies regarding copyright in their standards (e.g. the ISO's Policies and Procedures for Copyright, Copyright Exploitation Rights and Sales of ISO Publications).[200]

Very few SSO intellectual property policies extend to copyrights.[201] This may be because it has hitherto been considered that standardized interfaces (e.g. software application programming interfaces) cannot be copyrighted. The 2014 decision of the Federal Circuit in *Oracle v. Google* has overturned this assumption under American law. At least one study has concluded that standards-essential copyrights could be quite widespread in the context of SSO activities.[202] Thus, much greater consideration may in future be warranted of standards-essential copyright in the context of formal SSO standard-setting activities.

More complex issues that have arisen in relation to standards-essential copyright (e.g. *IMS Health*[203] and *Microsoft*[204] cases) pertaining to de facto standards. Standards-essential copyrights can also arise in the context of de facto standards, especially standardized interfaces between computers and users or computer software and interoperable software programmes. Indeed, considerable attention has been given to how copyright law will promote or impede interoperability, especially as between computer programmes, as well as the cognate question of the

---

[199] Baron and Spulber (n. 25) 465.
[200] ISO discloses the details of POCOSA only to its members. Email correspondence with ISO, on file with author.
[201] Charles Duan, 'Internet of Infringing Things: The Effect of Computer Interface Copyrights on Technology Standards' (2019) 45 Rutgers Computer & Technology Law Journal 1, 31–6.
[202] Ibid.
[203] *IMS Health GMBH & Co and NDC Health GMBH & Co (Case C-418-01)* [2004] ECR -05039 (European Court of Justice).
[204] *Microsoft (Case COMP/C-3/37/792 – Microsoft)* (European Commission).

copyrightability of interfaces.[205] Reframing this discussion in terms of standards-essential copyrights permits focus on those circumstances in which access to interfaces is indispensable in order to security interoperability.

Copyright attaches to works, including all works in the literary domain, rather than inventions (which can be patented). The phenomenon of standards-essential copyright is made possible by the breadth of modern copyright laws, which extends well beyond the traditional conception of literary artistic and scientific works, to utilitarian endeavours such as computer programs and databases. WIPO, which has played a central role in this process, initially advocated for a sui generis regime to protect computer programs, but influential member states, notably the USA and EU Member States, preferred copyright protection. Ultimately, the copyright approach found widespread acceptance in many countries and has now been mandated in international treaties, notably the WIPO Copyright Treaty and the TRIPS Agreement.[206]

These international instruments mandate the protection of computer programs as literary works, and also mandate protection of the structures of databases, insofar as they constitute intellectual creations. The preference for a copyright approach rather than a sui generis regime appears to have been driven (at least in part) by the desire on the part of the software industry to avoid the publication or formality requirements that a sui generis regime would likely have entailed.[207]

Copyright protection is subject to relatively easily satisfied requirements of originality. Protection extends to both object (i.e. machine readable) code and source code, and to operating software. It also extends to the structure of computer databases. Copyright protection over computer programs and database structures is not only long-lasting, but

---

[205] Pamela Samuelson, 'The Uneasy Case for Software Copyrights Revisited' (2010) 79 George Washington Law Review 1746; Jonathan Band and Masanobu Katoh, *Interfaces on Trial* (Westview Press, Boulder, Colorado 1995); Jonathan Band and Masanobu Katoh, *Interfaces on Trial 2.0* (MIT Press 2011); Jonathan Band, 'Interfaces on Trial 3.0' (2019) www.policybandwidth.com/interfaces-2-0 accessed 4 March 2020; Peter S. Menell, 'API Copyrightability Bleak House: Unraveling and Repairing the Oracle v. Google Jurisdictional Mess' (2016) 31 Berkeley Technology Law Journal 1515; Peter S. Menell, 'Rise of the API Copyright Dead: An Updated Epitaph for Copyright Protection of Network and Functional Features of Computer Software' (2017) 31 Harvard Journal of Law & Technology 305.

[206] TRIPS Agreement Art. 10(1); WIPO Copyright Treaty (adopted 20 December 1996, entered into force 6 March 2002) (2186 UNTS 5) Art. 4.

[207] Yoshiyuki Miyashita, 'International Protection of Computer Software' (1991) 11 The John Marshall Journal of Information Technology & Privacy Law 41, 49.

requires neither publication nor registration in order to secure the right, making it a powerful vehicle for protecting the interests of software developers. Partly to preserve the boundaries between patent and copyright law, copyright protection does not extend to ideas, procedures, methods of operation or mathematical concepts as such.[208]

Highly significant questions in relation to the protection of standardized interfaces under copyright will include: the boundary between protectable ideas and unprotectable expressions in the context of computer programs and database structures; the degree of protection to be accorded to the non-literal elements (such as the structures) of computer programs; the copyrightability of interface specifications, which are essentially functional in nature; whether infringement will occur in respect of similarities of the allegedly infringing program that arise from functional considerations, such as the need for two programs to interoperate with each other; and the availability of limiting doctrines such as fair use to excuse the reverse engineering of interfaces that is undertaken solely for interoperability purposes.

If these questions are resolved in favour of the copyright holder, then the nature of copyright, its breadth and its long life could easily give rise to considerable monopoly power by copyright holders over interface specifications, with significant impacts on incentives for static and dynamic efficiency.

4.4.1.1 Copyright in the Context of Computer Programs

Access to standards-essential copyrights is addressed indirectly through United States case law, and in EU directives and case law, concerning computer program interfaces. As discussed in Chapter 2, the concept of an interface is inextricably intertwined with the concept of an interoperability standard; interoperability standards generally specify either protocols or interfaces (which provide an agreed framework for exchanging information) in order to promote compatibility or interoperability between distinct elements which form part of a larger system. In the specific context of computing, interfaces may exist: (i) between hardware and hardware; (ii) between hardware and software; (iii) between software and software; and (iv) between computer and user.

Copyright protection over an interface (or elements of the interface) could, in some instances, enable the right holder to act as gatekeeper over the standardized technology, in a fashion that is broadly analogous to the

---

[208] TRIPS Agreement art. 2(1).

role performed by SEPs. Yet, copyright protection has a history and modality that operates, in some respects, quite differently to patent law. Concerns associated with access to standards-essential copyright need to be considered in the unique context lent by copyright protection, notably of computer programs. In terms of copyright protection of computer interfaces, much of the litigation has focussed on software-software interfaces, but some high-profile cases have also addressed copyright in the context of computer-user interfaces.

4.4.1.2 Copyright in the Context of Software-Software Interfaces

It is important to note that courts and legislators have generally addressed these issues through the lens of interoperability between programs, rather than of access to standards-essential copyrights – the latter being a subset of the former. Nevertheless, where copyright protection over computer programs allows for relatively broad scope of interoperability defences, this will necessarily also imply a broad scope of access to standards-essential copyrights.

A transatlantic consensus looked to have emerged regarding the copyright protection of software-software interface specifications, prior to the *Oracle* v. *Google* litigation. This consensus position can be summarized in the following principles: (i) the non-literal elements of a computer program (e.g. its structure) are entitled to a lesser degree of protection as compared with literal elements (e.g. its source and object code); (ii) copyright cannot be used as a vehicle to extend a patent-like protection to the ideas embodied in a computer program; (iii) only the literal copying of such non-literal elements can infringe copyright, if at all; and (iv) literal copying of a computer's code is permitted where undertaken for the sole purpose of ensuring interoperability between computer programs.

Thus, courts and legislators on both sides of the Atlantic crafted an approach to standards-essential copyrights that remained faithful to the notion of copyright protection as broad but 'thin'. Such an approach, by avoiding the creation of monopolies over software-software interfaces, implied considerable latitude for software-software interoperability, and thus indirectly ensured a high degree of access to standards-essential copyrights embedded in computer programs. This approach is to be contrasted with the 'patent thickets' and attendant concerns of 'hold-up' and 'royalty-stacking' that subsequently emerged in connection with SEPs.

However, this transatlantic consensus regarding the 'thin' protection to be accorded to interfaces (and hence to standards-essential copyrights) has been called into question in recent times by the United States Court of Appeals for the Federal Circuit's decision on copyrightability in *Oracle v. Google* (noting that this case is currently being considered by the United States Supreme Court). Should this precedent stand, the prospect of limitations arising with respect to access to standards-essential copyrights will need to be addressed squarely. In the United States, two cases, *Computer Associates* and *Sega*, established the key legal precedents regarding the copyrightability and infringement of software-software interfaces.

Computer Associates International, Inc. v. Altai, Inc. In *Computer Associates*,[209] the United States Court of Appeal for the Second Circuit held that the non-literal elements of a computer program are unprotectable under copyright law inter alia where their design has been dictated by functional considerations, including the need for the program to interoperate with another program. In that case, the non-literal elements of job-scheduling software created by Altai necessarily resembled the non-literal elements of the competing job-scheduling software created by rival Computer Associates, because both programs needed to interoperate with IBM mainframe computer operating system software. That is, Program A supplied by Company Z resembled Program B supplied by Company Y because Programs A and B were both designed to interoperate with Program C designed by Company X.

The Court based its reasons on generally applicable principles of American copyright law, namely the distinction between unprotectable ideas and processes and protectable expression, merger and *scènes à faire*, concluding that copyright protection should not extend to non-literal elements whose form had been dictated by functional considerations – this being seen in effect as protection of the underlying idea of the program, a matter that was more appropriately left to patent law.

By limiting the copyright protection given to the non-literal elements of a computer program, notably those elements pertinent to interoperability, Computer Associates implied a fairly limited scope of protection for standards-essential copyrights. The broad scope and long life of copyright protection was thus counterbalanced by its 'thin'

---

[209] *Computer Associates International, Inc v. Altai, Inc* [1992] 982 F2d 693 (United States Court of Appeals for the Second Circuit).

protection, avoiding many of the issues that have arisen in the context of access to SEPs.

Sega Enterprises Limited* v. *Accolade Inc. *Sega*,[210] decided shortly after *Computer Associates*, became its indispensable complement. In this case, Sega sued Accolade for breach of copyright after Accolade designed games that would run on Sega's highly successful games console. Accolade had initially approached Sega and offered to do this under licence, but Sega demanded that Accolade write games only for Sega, and not for other gaming platforms (e.g. Nintendo).[211]

Accolade declined to do so; instead, it purchased a Sega Genesis console and three Sega game cartridges, then decompiled or disassembled the object code from each in order to understand the interface specifications between console and cartridges. Accolade then developed its own games that were compatible with the Genesis console, using the interface specifications it had obtained through disassembly or decompilation. Accolade successfully defended its actions as fair use.

The United States Court of Appeal for the Ninth Circuit accepted that: 'disassembly of copyrighted object code is, as a matter of law, a fair use of the copyrighted work if such disassembly provides the only means of access to those elements of the code that are not protected by copyright and the copier has a legitimate reason for seeking such access'.[212] Sega, unlike Computer Associates, involved the literal copying of computer code. Applying the doctrine of fair use, the Ninth Circuit crafted an exception that would enable access to the relevant interface specifications solely for interoperability purposes. Indeed, the Ninth Circuit's fair use analysis suggested that functional interface specifications were not copyrightable at all.[213] The Ninth Circuit applied similar reasoning in *Sony Computer Entertainment* v. *Connectix*.[214] Together, Sega and Computer Associates enabled would-be developers of compatible software programs to discern interface specifications through decompilation or disassembly of object code, and then develop their own compatible software programs that did not infringe copyright insofar as there was similarity in

---

[210] *Sega Enterprises Ltd* v. *Accolade, Inc* [1992] 977 F2d 1510 (United States Court of Appeals for the Ninth Circuit).
[211] Ibid. 1514.
[212] Ibid. 1518.
[213] Ibid. 1522.
[214] *Sony Computer Entertainment, Inc* v. *Connectix Corp* (United States Court of Appeals for the Ninth Circuit) 602–3.

the structure of the two programs that was dictated by the need for interoperability between the programs.

Indeed, this line of case law went beyond what was strictly necessary to ensure access to standards-essential copyrights, because it involved all interoperability between computer programs, irrespective of whether one of those programs had become a de facto interoperability standard. The Sega and Sony games platforms were clearly interoperability standards. Independent game developers needed access to the applicable interface specifications in order to practice the de facto standard, that is, in order to write games that would run on the Sega or Sony platforms. By limiting the scope of copyright protection enjoyed by the creator of the de facto standard over the interface specifications, the American courts indirectly ensured access to these standards-essential copyrights.

European Law: The Software Directive and *SAS Institute Inc.* v. *World Programming Limited* Compared to American Law, European law develops to a much greater extent through legislation rather than judge-made law (although when the impact of the case law of the European Court of Justice is considered, this difference is apt to be overstated). At roughly the same time that the *Computer Associates* and *Sega* cases were delineating the scope of access to standards essential copyrights in the United States, the European Parliament and Council issued a Software Directive[215] that laid out the applicable law for Member States in a more coherent and comprehensive fashion, albeit in a way that reflected many of the essential principles reflected in the American cases.

The tenth recital of the Directive places a strong emphasis upon interoperability as the key purpose of a computer program:

> The function of a computer program is to communicate and work together with other components of a computer system and with users and, for this purpose, a logical and, where appropriate, physical interconnection and interaction is required to permit all elements of software and hardware to work with other software and hardware and with users in all the ways in which they are intended to function.

This formulation is notable for its comprehensive approach to the concept of the interface, comprising both hardware and software interconnections, as well as the computer-user interface, and contemplating both logical and physical interconnections and interactions.

---

[215] Directive 2009/24/EC of the European Parliament and of the Council of 23 April 2009 on the legal protection of computer programs 2009 (OJ L 111).

The Directive exhaustively states the copyrightability requirements: originality and the protection of expression as distinct from ideas. In the context of interfaces: 'Ideas and principles which underlie any element of a computer program, including those which underlie its interfaces, are not protected by copyright under this Directive'.[216] This provision will preclude from protection either most, or all, program structures insofar as they lay down interface specifications,[217] and is therefore congruent with the Second Circuit's decision in *Computer Associates* and the Ninth Circuit's decision in *Sega*.[218]

Article 5 of the Directive provides defences for interoperability-related acts falling short of decompilation. Article 6 of the Directive then provides an interoperability-related decompilation defence in respect of reproductions of computer code and translation of its form insofar as indispensable to obtaining the information necessary to achieve the interoperability of an independently created computer program with other programs. To invoke this defence, the copyright user must have a legal right to use the information, and the acts of reproduction or translation must be confined to those parts of the program which are necessary to achieve interoperability.

The scope of the defence provided by Article 6 is remarkably similar to that articulated (one year later) by the Ninth Circuit in *Sega*. The indispensability requirement extends to interoperability 'with other programs'; this open-ended formulation is sufficiently broad to encompass both interoperability with the program that has been reverse-engineered (as was the case in *Sega*) and interoperability with a third program – for example where (as in *Computer Associates*) the decompiler seeks to develop a program that will displace the reverse-engineered program.[219]

The decisions of the UK Courts[220] and the European Court of Justice[221] in *SAS Institute* v. *World Programming Limited* provided a reasonably clear and straightforward application of the principles articulated in the Software Directive. Plaintiff SAS Institute Inc. developed the 'SAS System', an integrated set of programs which enabled users

---

[216] Ibid. art. 1(2).
[217] Band and Katoh, *Interfaces on Trial* (n. 205) 242–3; Pamela Samuelson, 'The Past, Present and Future of Software Copyright Interoperability Rules in the European Union and United States' (2012) 34 European Intellectual Property Review 229, 232.
[218] Band and Katoh, *Interfaces on Trial* (n. 205) 256; Samuelson (n. 217) 232.
[219] Band and Katoh, *Interfaces on Trial* (n. 205) 240–1.
[220] *SAS Institute Inc* v. *World Programming Limited* (2013) 69 EWHC (High Court).
[221] *SAS Institute Inc* v. *World Programming Limited* [2012] ECLI:EC:C:2012:259 (European Court of Justice).

to carry out a wide range of data processing and analysis tasks, notably in relation to statistical analysis. Defendant World Programming Limited (WPL) created software which could execute application programs written in SAS language.[222] WPL's program emulated much of the functionality of SAS's programs, to ensure that its customers' application programs would run in the same way on WPL programs as on SAS programs.[223] WPL did not have access to SAS's source code, did not copy any of SAS's source code, and did not copy the structural design of SAS's source code.[224] SAS sued WPL for breach of copyright, alleging inter alia that WPL copied certain SAS instruction manuals; by copying SAS manuals, WPL also indirectly copied SAS's programs. SAS also alleged that WPL used copies of SAS software it had (lawfully) acquired in contravention of the licence terms.[225]

Justice Arnold, sitting for the High Court (Chancery Division), sought guidance from the European Court of Justice on the interpretation of the Software Directive before finalizing his judgment. The Court of Justice confirmed that neither the functionality of a computer program, nor the programming language and the format of data files used in a computer program constitute a form of expression pursuant to Article 1(2) of the Software Directive.[226] The Court of Justice also confirmed that a licensee is entitled to determine the ideas and principles underlying any element of a computer program (in the course of loading, displaying, running etc. that program), and that copyright owners cannot deny these rights via licensing agreements.[227] Based on this guidance from the Court of Justice, Justice Arnold concluded that: 'copyright in a computer program does not protect either the programming language in which it is written or its interfaces (specifically, its data file formats) or its functionality from being copied'.[228] Justice Arnold therefore concluded that WPL had not infringed SAS Institute's copyrights by producing its own program, because such copyrights did not extend to matters such as mathematical formulae, keywords, default values etc., since these are ideas rather than intellectual expressions and are therefore not copyrightable.[229]

[222] Ibid. 3.
[223] Ibid.
[224] Ibid.
[225] Ibid. 4.
[226] Ibid. 10.
[227] Ibid. 12.
[228] Ibid. 16.
[229] Ibid. 52–3.

This case, in addition to providing a straightforward application of the principles articulated in the Software Directive, may be seen as consistent with the position under American law, notably the decisions in *Computer Associates* and *Sega*. It was confirmed that copyright does not extend to programming languages, interfaces (including file formats) or functionality; as in *Computer Associates*, minimal protection is extended to the non-literal elements of programs and, as in *Sega*, the uncopyrightability of interfaces is confirmed. Helpfully, these exclusions were logically linked to the essential distinction between unprotected ideas and protected expressions of those ideas.

Copyright Protection of Software Interfaces under Chinese Law   Chinese law pertaining to the copyright protection of computer programs reflects well-accepted limiting doctrines in copyright law, such as the idea/expression dichotomy.[230] On this basis, the protection accorded to the non-literal elements of a software-software interface is likely to be a thin protection. As such, there would seem to be adequate flexibility under Chinese copyright law to ensure access to standardized software-software interfaces.

Oracle, America Inc. v. Google Inc.   The transatlantic consensus providing for a relatively broad scope of interoperability-related defences in the context of copyrighted computer programs looks to be under a cloud, however, as a result of the long running and, at the time of print of this work, as yet unresolved battle between Oracle and Google over the copyrightability of Oracle's Java platform.

Java (which was acquired by Oracle in 2010 as part of its acquisition of Sun Microsystems) provides both a programming language and a software platform. The Java platform enables software developers to write programs that function across different kinds of hardware, without making modifications.[231] The Java language includes pre-written programs that carry out various commands; these are collectively known as the Java Application Programming Interface (API). The Java API

---

[230] 中华人民共计算机软件保护条例〉的决定 (Regulations on Computer Software Protection) (as amended up to Decision of the State Council of the People's Republic of China of January 30, 2013) 2002 art. 6; Stephen McIntyre, 'Trying to Agree on Three Articles of Law: The Idea/Expression Dichotomy in Chinese Copyright Law' (2010) 1 Cybaris 62, 72–3.

[231] *Oracle, America Inc v. Google Inc* [2012] 872 FSupp2d 974 (United States District Court for the Northern District of California) 977.

comprised (in 2008) 166 'packages', further divided into over 600 'classes', and over 6,000 'methods'.[232]

Google sought to ensure that code written in Java would run on its Android smartphone operating software platform; in addition to this strict interoperability-related purposes, Google also wanted to replicate the structure and names of the Java platform, to appeal to Java programmers.[233] Google copied the sequence, structure and operation (but not the implementing code) of thirty-seven of the 166 Java API packages. This included copying the exact names (over 11,000 lines of declaring code) and exact functions of all thirty-seven packages. In the case of three of the thirty-seven packages, replicating exact names and functions was strictly necessary for interoperability purposes. For the other thirty-four packages, Google copied the names and functions to appeal to programmers who were already familiar with the Java platform, so as to encourage them to write apps for Android.[234]

In ruling on the copyrightability of the Java API, the United States District Court for the Northern District of California advanced the following propositions of law: (i) under the so-called 'names doctrine', names and short phrases are not copyrightable; (ii) copyright protection never extends inter alia to ideas, processes, systems or methods of operation; and (iii) functional elements essential for interoperability are not copyrightable.[235] The third of these propositions of law appears to have derived primarily from the following sentence in the Ninth Circuit's Sega opinion: 'Accolade copied Sega's software solely in order to discover the functional requirements for compatibility with the Genesis console – aspects of Sega's programs that are not protected by copyright'.[236] Applying these principles, the District Court decided that the structure, sequence and organization (SSO) of the thirty-seven API 'packages' constituted an unprotected method of operation under United States copyright law; that these were functional elements essential for interoperability; and that the exact replication of chapter, class and subclass

---

[232] Ibid.
[233] Band (n. 205) 17.
[234] *Oracle, America Inc. v. Google Inc.* (n. 234) 977.
[235] Ibid. 997.
[236] *Sega Enterprises Ltd. v. Accolade, Inc.* (n. 210) 1522; cited at *Oracle America, Inc v. Google Inc, Order re Copyrightability of Certain Replicated Elements of the Java Application Programming Interface* [2012] 872 FSupp2d 974 (United States District Court for the Northern District of California) 994.

names was permissible under the 'names doctrine'. Summarizing its ruling, the District Court explained that:

> So long as the specific code used to implement a method is different, anyone is free under the Copyright Act to write his or her own code to carry out exactly the same function or specification of any methods used in the Java API. It does not matter that the declaration or method header lines are identical.[237]

Oracle appealed; the Federal Circuit, applying Ninth Circuit law, held that the declaring code was protected expression, notwithstanding a proper assessment of merger doctrine[238] and the names doctrine.[239] Regarding the latter, the Circuit accorded protection to the declaring code, not on the basis of the originality or creativity of individual names embodied in the declaring code, but rather based on the creativity in the selection or arrangement of the names as a whole – in effect, according a database-like protection to such names: 'Because Oracle "exercised creativity in the selection and arrangement" of the method declarations when it created the API packages and wrote the relevant declaring code, they contain protectable expression that is entitled to copyright protection'.[240] Regarding Google's borrowing of the SSO of the Java API, the Court ruled that Java API's SSO was found to be original and creative, because the declaring code could have been written any number of ways.[241] The Court's decision on copyrightability of the SSO thus leaned heavily on its findings as to copyrightability of the declaring code, notwithstanding its ostensible separation of the two issues. Moreover, the Circuit held that considerations of interoperability were only relevant as part of Google's fair use defence, and remanded that question for separate consideration; in 2018, the Circuit held that Google's use of thirty-four of the thirty-seven packages was not fair use.

The Federal Circuit's decision is under review by the Supreme Court. In the meantime, the extent to which the principles embodied in Computer Associates and Sega can survive the Federal Circuit's ruling remains to be seen, given that Oracle appears to have enlarged the protection accorded to the non-literal aspects of computer programs. In its decision, the Court drew parallels between computer programs and

---

[237] *Oracle, America Inc.* v. *Google Inc.* (n. 234) 976.
[238] *Oracle, America Inc* v. *Google Inc* [2014] 750 F3d 1339 (United States Court of Appeals for the Federal Circuit) 1361–2.
[239] Ibid. 1362–3.
[240] Ibid. 1363.
[241] Ibid. 1368.

wholly creative, non-functional literary works, notably referencing Dickens' *A Tale of Two Cities*.[242] Moreover, by perceiving creativity in the selection and arrangement of the chapter, class and subclass names embodied in Java's declaring code, the Court accorded to those names a database-like protection that appears to embrace somewhat the 'gestalt' theory advanced by Apple in *Apple* v. *Microsoft* but rejected by the District Court in that case.

After Oracle, the uncopyrightability of APIs and interface specifications cannot be presumed. If it stands, Oracle seems to preserve the reverse engineering defence permitted in Sega, which was not invoked by Google in its fair use defence. However, Oracle could limit the uses programmers can make of interface specifications decompiled or disassembled consistently with Sega, in a manner that potentially undermines the *Computer Associates* precedent. Notably, it would seem that Oracle will only permit non-literal similarities between interoperating programs insofar as those similarities arise solely due to the need for interoperability in a strict (i.e. physical) sense, rather than in a broader sense that encompasses consideration of the user learning curve. In sum, American law looks to be in a state of flux on this issue, with the general trend being back towards the copyright protection of interface specifications. Should this trend continue, it will inevitably give rise to questions about access to standard-essential copyrights.

4.4.1.3 Copyright in the Context of Computer-User Interfaces

American case law concerning access to copyrighted computer-user interfaces has, like the pre-Oracle approach with respect to software-software interfaces, permitted fairly broad latitude for interoperability-related exceptions. In *Apple* v. *Microsoft and Borland Software*, the courts excused both literal (Borland) and non-literal (Apple) copying of user interfaces, according a very narrow scope of copyright protection. The District Court in *Apple* notably linked this narrow scope of protection to ensuring that no one company was able to assert copyright over an emerging industry standard.

Apple Computer, Inc. v. Microsoft Corporation In this case, originally filed in 1988, Apple sued Microsoft and Hewlett-Packard, arguing that Microsoft's Windows operating system software and HP's New Wave

[242] Ibid. 1363.

application software infringed copyrights protecting the visual displays of the graphical user interface (GUI) of Apple's Macintosh personal computer. Since Microsoft did not copy Apple's code, this amounted to alleged infringement of the non-literal features of Apple's GUI.

Although Apple furnished the District Court with a series of detailed lists of visual similarities between the competing Apple, Microsoft and HP products, it articulated a 'gestalt' theory of infringement, namely that Microsoft's and HP's borrowing of the various features appropriated the 'look and feel' of the Apple Macintosh experience.[243]

For Apple, the GUI was like a desktop, which Apple emphasized by showing the Court a computer screen displaying the image of a desk.[244] Microsoft countered with its own analogy: the GUI was more like the layout of the dashboard, steering wheel, brakes and clutch in a car – arranged as such for essentially functional reasons. The 'dashboard' analogy was found more persuasive and adopted by the Court in its decision; the Court further likened the GUI to the arrangement of dials and knobs on a television, video recorder or stove.[245] Moreover, the District Court linked the 'gestalt' of the Apple GUI to standardization: 'The similarity of such functional elements of a user interface or their arrangement in products of like kind does not suggest unlawful copying, but standardization across competing products for functional considerations'.[246] The Court appreciated that overly broad copyright protection of a standard would preclude the full realization of network effects, and that a balance needed to be struck between rewarding innovation and permitting follow-on endeavours; in any event, Apple had already benefited from lead time, diminishing its need for copyright protection.[247] Apple's 'look and feel' theory was dismissed as an attempt to seek protection for idea as distinct from expression, without the formalities imposed under patent law.[248] The District Court was not inclined to let Apple assert copyright protection over an emerging industry standard that Apple had contributed to, rather than originating.

Reverting to a feature by feature analysis, the District Court found that most of Microsoft's and HP's allegedly similar features were permitted

---

[243] *Apple Computer Inc v. Microsoft Corporation* [1992] 799 FSupp 1006 (United States District Court for the Northern District of California) 1016, 1022.
[244] Ibid. 1021.
[245] Ibid. 1023.
[246] Ibid.
[247] Ibid. 1025.
[248] Ibid. 1026.

under the terms of a 1985 licensing agreement between Apple and Microsoft. The rest were permitted on grounds that: the equivalent Apple features were not original; they represented ideas rather than protectible expression; or they were constrained by functional considerations which gave rise to the defences of merger and *scènes à faire*.[249] The decision was upheld by the United States Court of Appeals for the Ninth Circuit.[250] This case provided an early indication from United States courts that the non-literal elements of computer programs providing for interoperability between computers and users would be accorded minimal protection, especially where the facts tended to indicate that those elements had become industry standards. Thus, the decision is readily reconciled with American case law dealing with software-software interoperability, notably *Computer Associates* and *Sega*.

Lotus Development Corporation v. Borland Software, Inc. In this case, Borland Software's spreadsheet program copied entirely the words and structure of rival Lotus 1-2-3's menu command hierarchy, without copying any of the underlying code. Borland did so because its potential customer base was already familiar with the Lotus menu tree, so this would make it more convenient for users switching from Lotus to Borland.[251]

The United States Court of Appeals for the First Circuit clearly distinguished *Computer Associates* on the facts: *Computer Associates* concerned non-literal copying of code, whereas *Borland* concerned literal copying of the menu command hierarchy.[252] The First Circuit decided that the menu command hierarchy was an unprotectable method of operation, because it 'serves as the method by which the program is operated and controlled'.[253] In particular: 'Without the menu command hierarchy, users would not be able to access and control, or indeed make use of, Lotus 1-2-3's functional capabilities'.[254] Because the menu command hierarchy was a 'method of operation', whether it contained expression or could have been designed differently was immaterial.[255]

---

[249] Ibid. 1027–41.
[250] *Apple Computer, Inc v. Microsoft Corp* [1994] 35 F3d 1435 (United States Court of Appeals for the Ninth Circuit).
[251] *Lotus Development Corporation v. Borland International, Inc* [1995] 49 F3d 807 (United States Court of Appeals for the First Circuit) 810.
[252] Ibid. 814–15.
[253] Ibid. 815.
[254] Ibid. 815.
[255] Ibid. 816.

Thus, American case law concerning access to copyrighted computer-user interfaces has permitted fairly broad latitude for interoperability-related exceptions. This work defines interoperability standards in terms of written specifications; yet there is clearly consonance between written interface specifications and the intangible standard encapsulated in the GUI. The GUI is especially prone to indirect network effects in the form of the user learning curve; as much was acknowledged in Apple.[256]

More recently in Oracle, such user learning effects were seen, not so much as a reason to deny protection, but rather as the fruits of Oracle's creative endeavours which should not simply be appropriated by Google. As such, the Federal Circuit decision in Oracle also places under threat the historically narrow protection accorded to user interfaces.

European and Chinese Law European law regarding the protection of graphical user interfaces takes its starting point from the provisions of the Software Directive discussed immediately above in the context of computer programs. The European Court of Justice in 2011 clarified that while graphical user interfaces are not copyrightable under the provisions of the Software Directive, they can be protected under general European copyright law as reflected in the provisions of Directive 2001/29/EC (Information Society Directive), where they are the author's own intellectual creation and where the requisite originality does not arise solely from components differentiated only by their technical function.[257]

In China, graphical user interfaces are potentially protectable as compilations under China's copyright law.[258] In the *TP-Link* case,[259] protection was denied at second instance by the Guangdong High Court on the basis that the GUI at issue failed to meet the requisite creativity threshold. In addition:

> In the second instance court of the TP-LINK case, the Court held that, although there are a number of identical places or similarities between the GUIs for two WLAN Router products at issue, the GUIs are designed in accordance with the users' requirements; and the GUIs under the present

---

[256] *Apple Computer Inc. v. Microsoft Corporation* (n. 246) 1019.
[257] *Bezpečnostní softwarová asociace – Svaz softwarové ochrany v Ministerstvo kultury (Case C-393/09)* [2010] ECR-13971 (European Court of Justice) I-1402-I-1405.
[258] Ling Jin and Yihong Ying, 'Why Copyright Protection Falls Behind the Requirement for Protecting Graphic User Interfaces: Case Studies on Limitations of Protection for GUIs in China' (2012) 3 IP Theory 6, 7–8.
[259] Shenzhen Jixiang Tengda Tech. Co. Ltd. v. Shenzhen Pulian (TP-LINK) Tech. Co. Ltd., YGFMSZZ No. 92 (Guangdong High Ct. 2005) (广东省高级人民法院(2005)粤高法民三终字第92号民事判决书).

case must have referred to the common elements of existing GUIs, due to similar functions to be rendered and similar user requirements.[260]

This subtle jurisprudence gives careful consideration to the proper scope of protection to be given to the non-literal elements of the GUI; it is clearly consonant with the Second Circuit's decision in *Computer Associates*.

4.4.1.4 Copyright in the Context of Database Structures

International treaties have harmonized in significant degree the principles for the protection of compilations of data. Compilations which by reason of the selection or arrangement of their contents constitute intellectual creations are copyrightable; such protection shall not extend to the data or the material itself and is without prejudice to any copyright protection of that data or material.[261]

United States copyright law reflects these principles. In the Supreme Court's landmark decision in *Feist* v. *Rural Telephone Service*,[262] Justice O'Connor, writing for the Court, explained with impeccable clarity that while the discovery of facts is not creative and that therefore facts cannot be copyrighted, creativity may be found in the selection and arrangement of such facts: 'These choices as to selection and arrangement, so long as they are made independently by the compiler and entail a minimal degree of creativity, are sufficiently original that Congress may protect such compilations through the copyright laws'.[263] Furthermore, only those components of the compilation original to the author were held to be copyrightable.[264] The Court considered that Rural Telephone Service's selection, arrangement and coordination of uncopyrightable facts (i.e. names, towns and telephone numbers) failed to satisfy even the low bar set under American copyright law for originality. The white pages listings were ordered alphabetically – not at all creative.[265]

Telephone directories possess some features of interoperability standards, facilitating the exchange of information between diverse groups of companies and individuals; the design of a directory will be subject to network effects because once classified advertisers and users have

---

[260] Jin and Ying (n. 258) 11.
[261] TRIPS Agreement art. 10(2); WCT art. 5.
[262] *Feist Publications, Inc v. Rural Telephone Service Company, Inc* [1991] 499 US 340 (United States Supreme Court).
[263] Ibid. 1289.
[264] Ibid.
[265] Ibid. 1297.

invested time to understand the functioning of the directory they will be reluctant to use any other directory unless it uses a highly similar structure.[266] For this reason, in the *Donnelley* case (described in the subsection below) an essential facilities doctrine was pled.

BellSouth Advertising & Publishing Corporation v. Donnelley Information Publishing, Inc. BellSouth Advertising & Publishing Corporation (BAPCO) was a wholly owned subsidiary of the Southern Bell local telecommunications monopoly, which published a 'yellow pages' telephone directory for the Greater Miami area. Defendant Donnelley began promoting and selling classified advertisements in the Greater Miami area. He gave a copy of BAPCO's yellow pages to a data entry company, and instructed them to create a database of all the listings in BAPCO's directory, which he used to create 'lead sheets'. Donnelley used these lead sheets to create his own competitive directory for the Greater Miami area. BAPCO sued Donnelley inter alia for copyright infringement and unfair competition; Donnelley counterclaimed, arguing violation of antitrust law, including the essential facilities doctrine.

The District Court for the Southern District of Florida granted BAPCO's copyright claim on summary judgment, finding that BAPCO held a valid copyright in its classified directory and that Donnelley had copied it; three specific acts of copying were identified: (i) entry of subscriber information into a computer database by data entry firm ACS; (ii) printout of sales lead sheets from this database; and (iii) publication of Donnelley's competing directory.

On appeal, the United States Court of Appeals for the Eleventh Circuit reiterated some essential aspects of copyright protection for factual compilations: (i) facts are not copyrightable; and (ii) a compiler's selection, arrangement or coordination, if original, will be the only protectable elements of a factual compilation. The Circuit held that listings, consisting of subscribers' names, towns of residence and telephone numbers were uncopyrightable facts. Further, it was held that the District Court erred in according copyright protection to the collection of facts in the BAPCO directory.[267] The Circuit dismissed BAPCO's arguments concerning the originality of its database, holding that the arrangement of the yellow pages was 'entirely typical', and 'not only unoriginal, it is

---

[266] Marc Rysman, 'Competition between Networks: A Study of the Market for Yellow Pages' (2004) 71 The Review of Economic Studies 483.

[267] *BellSouth Advertising & Pub Corp* v. *Donnelley Information Pub Inc* [1993] 999 F2d 1436 (United States Court of Appeals for the Eleventh Circuit) 1441.

practically inevitable'.[268] The Circuit further held that BAPCO's directory did not survive application of the merger doctrine: 'Because this is the one way to construct a useful business directory, the arrangement has merged with the idea of a business directory, and thus is uncopyrightable'.[269]

Donnelley had argued before the District Court that the yellow pages was an essential facility, a claim which was not dismissed out of hand.[270] Donnelley claimed that BAPCO held a monopoly in the market for the sale of advertising, and had wilfully maintained its monopoly by not providing Donnelley with enough information, such as business classifications and updates, allegedly essential to compete in the directory business, in a timely fashion so as to enable Donnelley to publish a competing directory.[271]

In a sense, the *Donnelley* case shows how the careful application of limiting doctrines in copyright law (such as the merger doctrine) can obviate the need to engage antitrust or competition laws by characterizing either the information in question or indeed the copyright itself as an 'essential facility'.

While in the United States, *Feist* brought the demise of the 'sweat of the brow' doctrine, the EU signalled a different approach in its Database Directive of 1996. The Directive clarifies the copyright protection accorded to database structures; this is complemented by a sui generis right accorded to the contents of database. The term 'database' is defined as a collection of independent works, data or other materials arranged in a systematic or methodical way and individually accessible by electronic or other means.[272]

Article 3 of the Directive largely replicates existing international instruments, imposing a requirement that the database exhibit creativity in the selection or arrangement of its contents, and limiting the protection accorded to the structure as distinct from the contents of the database. The exclusive rights enjoyed by the author of the database include reproduction, adaptation, arrangement and distribution or

---

[268] Ibid. 1442.
[269] Ibid.
[270] *BellSouth Adv & Pub* v. *Donnelley Inf Pub* [1988] 719 FSupp 1551 (United States District Court for the Southern District of Florida) 1566.
[271] Ibid. 1565.
[272] Directive 96/9 of the European Parliament and of the European Council of 11 March 1996 on the legal protection of databases 1996 (OJ L 77) art. 1(2).

communication to the public;²⁷³ limited exceptions are provided for private use, research and teaching and public security.²⁷⁴ Restatement of the distinction between unprotectable ideas and protectable expressions of those ideas is notably absent from the Directive.

The *IMS Health* case, involving the protection of a database structure under German copyright law giving effect to the requirements of the Database Directive, illustrates how database protection can impact on access to interoperability standards and SEIP.

4.4.1.5 The *IMS Health* Case

The *IMS Health* case concerned a 'brick' structure used by IMS Health to market regional sales data to pharmaceutical companies, refined in close collaboration with those customers. Data was segmented by 1,845, later 1,860 and then 2,847 geographical areas known as 'bricks'. The 'bricks' were developed by IMS Health, taking account of municipal boundaries, postcodes, population densities, transport connections and the locations of pharmacies and doctors' surgeries. Pharma Intranet Information AG (PII), established by a former IMS Health employee, sought to supply competing sales data presented in a 2,201 'brick' structure, but its prospective clients were reluctant because they were accustomed to either an 1,860 or 2,247 'brick' structure. PII heeded its customer base and moved to 1,860 and 3,000 'brick' structures very similar to those used by IMS Health.²⁷⁵ PII was subsequently acquired by National Data Corporation Health Information Services (NDC).

IMS Health sought interlocutory injunctions from the German courts, prohibiting NDC from using IMS Health's 1,860 'brick' structure or derivatives thereof; orders were granted by the Landgericht Frankfurt am Main (Frankfurt District Court) and upheld by the Oberlandesgericht Frankfurt am Main (Frankfurt Higher Regional Court). The Oberlandesgericht held that the 'brick' structure was a database protected under German copyright law.²⁷⁶

At this juncture, NDC complained to the European Commission that IMS Health was abusing its dominant position in the German market for pharmaceutical sales data. The Commission agreed that the 'brick'

---

²⁷³ Ibid. art. 5.
²⁷⁴ Ibid. art. 6.
²⁷⁵ *IMS Health GMBH & Co. and NDC Health GMBH & Co (Case C-418–01)* (n. 203) I–5073.
²⁷⁶ Ibid.

structure was, indeed, indispensable to such competition inter alia because it had become an industry standard:

> this structure is a de facto industry standard ... the overwhelming majority of surveyed pharmaceutical companies would not change the current 1 860 structure or could not accept a new structure which would require them to modify their current sales territory. The 1 860 brick structure is a 'common' language for communicating information between all players in the pharmaceutical industry...[277]

The Commission concluded that IMS Health had engaged in abuse of a dominant market position,[278] and required IMS to license the 'brick' structure to its competitors on a non-discriminatory basis and for reasonable fees.[279]

Further appeals to the European courts ensued. After the European Court of Justice had, upon a request for a preliminary ruling from the Oberlandesgericht, restated the legal test for abuse of dominant market position in the context of a refusal to license an intellectual property right,[280] the dispute was settled following a further decision of the Oberlandesgericht. The Oberlandesgericht, reiterating that the 'brick' structure was copyright, nevertheless explained that:

> The defendant or third parties could not simply be prohibited from developing freely and independently a brick structure that is similarly based on a breakdown by district, urban district and post-code district and for that reason comprise more or less the same number of bricks. ... In particular, the defendant or third parties could not be expected to produce a data structure that does not sufficiently satisfy the practical requirements simply in order to keep as much distance as possible from the plaintiff's product. Instead, variations cannot be demanded where the overlaps are based on material technical requirements and, in the light taking into account 'the need of availability' for competitors, the appropriate performance of the technical task depends on these features).[281]

The Oberlandesgericht also clarified that it would not be an infringement of copyright for IMS Health's competitors to develop similar databases of

---

[277] *NDC Health/IMS Health: Interim Measures (Case COMP D3/38044)* [2001] OJ 59 (European Commission) [89].
[278] Ibid. 179.
[279] Ibid. 215.
[280] *IMS Health GMBH & Co. and NDC Health GMBH & Co (Case C-418-01)* (n. 203) I-5081-I-5086.
[281] Excerpted in *NDC Health/IMS Health: Interim Measures (Case COMP D3/38044)* [2003] OJ 268 (European Commission) 71.

their own.[282] Hence, the Oberlandesgericht limited the protection enjoyed by the database structure on account of its extensive basis in commonplace elements. After some prodding by the European Commission and the Court of Justice, the Oberlandesgericht was able to discover some limiting principles in German copyright law that obviated the need for the application of the unilateral competition law doctrines, recalling the outcome of the *Donnelley* case.

Together, *Donnelley* and *IMS Health* illustrate that concerns associated with access to interoperability standards and SEIP could manifest in the copyright protection of databases as well as of software. So far, these issues have arisen particularly in cases where the compilation of data involves extensive collaboration between the compiler and suppliers of information (i.e. telephone subscribers or pharmaceutical companies), transforming the compilation into a means of facilitating the exchange of information between disparate groups, that is, an interoperability standard.

Network effects were not mentioned in the Commission's *IMS Health* interim measures decision, and it is unclear whether users of pharmaceutical sales data gain an incremental benefit as more users of the same data join the 'network'. Moreover, it is unclear whether the dominance of the IMS brick structure arose through path dependency, or whether there was really only one way, or a limited number of ways, to present the data in a manner that was optimized to the requirements of its customers.

4.4.2 Remedies for Infringement of Standards-Essential Copyright

In United States law, with particular reference to the jurisprudence of the United States Court of Appeals for the Federal Circuit, there seems to be an emerging trend to find in favour of the copyrightability of interfaces, and a diminishing tendency to apply the limiting doctrines in the context of standard-essential copyrights, notably the Federal Circuit's 2014 and 2018 decisions in *Oracle* v. *Google*. This trend, if it continues, is likely to shine a brighter spotlight on applicable remedies associated with standards-essential copyrights.

4.4.2.1 Injunctions

As with SEPs, questions regarding the availability of injunctions are likely to loom large. Injunctions for infringement of copyright remain the

---

[282] Alison Jones and Brenda Sufrin, EU Competition Law (5th ed., Oxford University Press 2014) 532.

norm in American law.[283] Although there is clearly the prospect for the *eBay* v. *MercExchange* decision to impact on the availability of injunctions in respect of copyright infringement, the actual impact of *eBay* remains uncertain: a study of copyright infringement cases post-*eBay* found the Supreme Court's dicta had been cited relatively infrequently, and moreover that injunctions had issued in the overwhelming majority of cases where infringement was established.[284]

In the EU, as in the case of patents, there is overarching guidance from the European Commission, notably in the form of the 2004 Enforcement Directive, which articulates a number of important safeguards concerning the availability of injunctions. Notably, remedies (including injunctions) are to be effective, proportionate and dissuasive, and shall be applied so as to avoid the creation of barriers to legitimate trade and to provide safeguards against their abuse.[285] Article 11 mandates the availability of the injunctive remedy, but Article 12 would seem to preserve flexibility for Member State courts not to award injunction for innocent infringement, in circumstances where pecuniary compensation is available and an injunction would cause disproportionate harm.[286] Nevertheless, harmonization of European law in this area remains modest, and decisions on the merits are left to the Member State courts.

In China, injunction will generally be granted on establishment of infringement, absent special circumstances.[287] Permanent injunctions require a finding that infringement is ongoing or there is a likelihood of recurrence.[288] Judicial policy guidance issued by China's Supreme Court in 2009 indicated that, 'Permanent injunction may be denied under specific circumstances if the granting thereof would cause imbalance between the major interests of the parties, or be contrary to public interest, or be practically unenforceable and alternative measures such as

---

[283] J. Liu, 'Copyright Injunctions After eBay: An Empirical Study' (2012) 16 Lewis & Clark Law Review 215, 228.

[284] Ibid.

[285] EU IPR Enforcement Directive art. 3(2).

[286] Reto M. Hilty, 'The Role of Enforcement in Delineating the Scope of Intellectual Property Rights' in Hans-W. Micklitz and Andrea Wechsler (eds.), *The Transformation of Enforcement: European Economic Law in Global Perspective* (Hart Publishing 2016) 240–1.

[287] Guangliang Zhang, 'Rules for Denying Copyright Permanent Injunctions in China: Fog Needs to Be Cleared Part I' [2015] Journal of the Copyright Society of the USA 341, 343.

[288] Ibid. 346.

adequate damages should be adopted',[289] suggesting a relatively broad measure of judicial discretion.

At this stage, the movement towards increased copyrightability of interface specifications appears to be limited to the United States, with the European Union in particular maintaining a more balanced approach. If the decision in *Oracle* v. *Google* stands, this is likely to throw increasing focus on the automatic entitlement to injunction in United States copyright law, which appears to have survived the Supreme Court's decision in *eBay* v. *MercExchange*. Calls for flexibility and balance in copyright remedies – including a greater focus on liability rules – are likely to increase.[290]

4.4.2.2 Methodologies for the Calculation of Damages

A move towards greater copyrightability of interfaces is also likely to throw a spotlight on methodologies for the calculation of copyright damages. Copyright damages can take the following forms: lost profits of the copyright holder; disgorgement of the infringer's profits; reasonable royalty; statutory damages; and additional damages.

Disgorgement of profits need to be approached with caution; apportionment methodologies will be of particular relevance to ensure that the right holder does not appropriate creative elements of the implementation that are better attributable to the user's own efforts. Statutory damages, whilst a useful shorthand for courts, could provide an unduly arbitrary measure given the intricacies of standards-essential copyrights. Additional damages should not necessarily be removed as a possibility: this will depend on all the facts and circumstances of the case, including the extent to which the user has engaged in 'hold-out' behaviour. Reasonable royalty may in many cases be the most appropriate remedy, especially where the course of negotiations between the user and right holder tends to indicate hold-up rather than hold-out as its characteristic feature.

---

[289] Ibid. 347.
[290] Orit Fischman Afori, 'Flexible Remedies as a Means to Counteract Failures in Copyright Law' (2011) 29 Cardozo Arts & Entertainment Law Review 1; Abraham Bell and Gideon Parchomovsky, 'Restructuring Copyright Infringement' (2020) 98 Texas Law Review 689; See, e.g., Jake Phillips, 'EBay's Effect on Copyright Injunctions: When Property Rules Give Way to Liability Rules II. Copyright – Note' – Berkeley Technology Law Journal 405; B. J. Ard, 'More Property Rules than Property? The Right to Exclude in Patent and Copyright' (2019) 68 Emory Law Journal 685.

4.4.2.3 United States Law

Under United States copyright law, an infringer is liable to pay such damages as the copyright holder has suffered arising from the infringement, as well as all the profits which the infringer shall have made from the infringement that are not taken into account in the calculation of actual damages.[291]

Lost Profits Lost profits seek to compensate the copyright owner for actual damage suffered as a result of the infringement.[292] Where lost profits take the form of lost royalties, they can be calculated on the basis of the royalty that would have been agreed at arms-length between right holder and infringer[293] – in which case they will resemble the reasonable royalty familiar from patent law.[294] Such an approach is consistent with the topical methodology, and in the context of standards-essential copyright is likely to provide a sound means for properly allocating the benefits of standardization as between creators and users of standardized solutions.

Account of Profits Where an account of profits is awarded in relation to infringement of standards-essential copyrights (notably in the context of de facto standards), proper apportionment of profits as between the infringer and the right holder will assume considerable importance. United States law permits disgorgement only of those profits attributable to the infringement;[295] however, much will depend on how this broad formulation is applied in practice.

In the *Oracle* v. *Google* litigation, the District Court, on remand from the Federal Circuit, expressed some preliminary views about the apportionment analyses of the two parties, in its Memorandum Opinion of 2 May 2016 on Oracle's motions to exclude several of Google's apportionment estimates.[296] Google offered a range of estimates between $85,000 and $203 million, based on six different scenarios which its

---

[291] Copyright Act 1976 (17 USC §§ 101–801)§504(b).
[292] *Cohen* v. *United States* 100 Fed Cl 461 (United States Court of Federal Claims).
[293] *Chase Jarvis Inc* v. *K2 Inc* [2007] 486 F3d 526 (United States Court of Appeals for the Ninth Circuit) 533.
[294] Kevin Bendix, 'Copyright Damages: Incorporating Reasonable Royalty from Patent Law' (2012) 27 Berkeley Technology Law Journal 527, 530.
[295] *Sheldon* v. *Metro-Goldwyn Pictures Corp* [1940] 309 US 390 (United States Supreme Court) 399–403.
[296] *Oracle America, Inc* v. *Google Inc* [2016] WL 1743154 (United States District Court for the Northern District of California).

expert, Dr Leonard, divided into 'bottom-up' and 'top-down' scenarios. The 'bottom-up' scenarios considered the value of those elements of Android other than the code copied from Java, whereas the 'top-down' scenarios sought to value the portions of the copied code directly.[297] Dr Leonard's four 'bottom-up' scenarios all examined the costs that would have been incurred by Google in using non-infringing alternatives to the copied lines of code.

By contrast, Oracle's expert, Dr Malackowski, suggested apportioning damages of $8.8 billion – all of the Android platform's contribution to search and advertising revenues on Android devices – on the basis that infringing and non-infringing code were so closely commingled as to preclude any attempt to separate the respective contributions of Oracle and Google.[298] The District Court has not, to date, ruled on the merits of these vastly different estimates, but did cast doubt on Oracle's ambit claims for a zero apportionment: 'Nevertheless, to the extent Malackowski engages in the exercise of apportionment, he must offer a methodology tied to the purpose of making a reasonable approximation of the profits attributable to the allegedly infringing elements of Android'.[299] The District Court also disallowed Google's four 'bottom-up' methodologies, on the basis that, while the availability of non-infringing alternatives will be relevant to assessing costs to the plaintiff in terms of lost licensing revenues, such alternatives will not be relevant to the apportionment of lost profits. As the District Court explained:

> The idea behind Section 504(b) is to hand over to the copyright owner the actual profits made by the infringer using his copyrighted work. If a copyright infringer could avoid disgorgement by claiming he could have substituted some noninfringing alternative, the infringer would rarely be discouraged from infringing and the purpose of the disgorgement remedy would be eviscerated. Indeed, the remedy of disgorgement would rarely exceed the simple cost of a license (the clearest alternative to infringement), the recovery of which is already available to a copyright owner through the distinct remedy of actual damages. The law cannot be read to permit an infringer to short circuit the disgorgement analysis in this manner.[300]

---

[297] Ibid. 1–2; see David McGowan, 'The Apportionment Problem in Copyright Law' (University of San Diego School of Law 2017) 17–307 www.ssrn.com accessed 2 May 2020.
[298] *Oracle America, Inc. v. Google Inc.* (n. 296) 1–3.
[299] Ibid. 6.
[300] Ibid. 4.

This logic is impeccable, if the integrity of the distinction between losses to the copyright holder and disgorgement of the infringer's profits is to be preserved. Moreover, the District Court's reasons go to the heart of the disgorgement remedy, which is tinged with moral condemnation of the defendant's conduct, and aims to deter future infringements. Yet, the purpose of developing a platform such as Java is to realize the full extent of network effects associated with the standardized platform, by gaining as many incremental users as possible. If the platform itself, or significant elements of it, is copyrightable then widespread infringement is to be expected as a matter of course – unless every prospective user is to negotiate a licence with Oracle/Java, which in practice is likely to present formidable transaction costs.

As such the disgorgement remedy, in discouraging infringement, may be inadequate – absent careful re-evaluation of the proper apportionment methodology – to set an efficient price for access to the copyrighted platform. Inasmuch as the costs of infringement include lost licensing revenues, limiting damages to such losses only and excluding disgorgement entirely would generate a result analogous to the reasonable royalty. Any apportionment of lost profits on top of such lost licensing revenues should leave intact at least some of the infringer's profits, since profit from the practice of the standardized platform by its users is part of the rationale for developing the standardized platform in the first place.

Other Measures of Damages: Statutory Damages, Additional Damages and Reasonable Royalties The United States Copyright Act also provides for statutory damages[301] and additional damages.[302] For statutory damages, no loss on the part of the right holder or gain on the part of the infringer need be established.[303] Statutory damages have been criticized as being, on occasion, untethered from any reasonable calculation of an assessment of the appropriate damages.[304] Yet, the language of the

---

[301] Copyright Act §504(c).
[302] Ibid. §504(d).
[303] *Sony BMG Music Entertainment* v. *Tenenbaum* [2011] 719 F3d 487 (United States Court of Appeals for the First Circuit); *Adobe System Inc* v. *Feather* [2012] 895 FSupp2d 297 (United States District Court for the District of Connecticut); *Malibu Media LLC* v. *Kurt Schelling* 31 FSuppD 910 (United States District Court for the Eastern District of Michigan).
[304] Pamela Samuelson and Tara Wheatland, 'Statutory Damages in Copyright Law: A Remedy in Need of Reform' (2009) 51 William and Mary Law Review 439; Ben Depoorter, 'Copyright Enforcement in the Digital Age When the Remedy Is the Wrong' (2019) 66 UCLA Law Review 400; James DeBriyn, 'Shedding Light on Copyright

Copyright Act regarding statutory damages would seem to provide greater flexibility than in respect of the lost profits/disgorgement pathway; such damages are to be not less than $750 or more than $30,000 'as the court considers just'.[305] This reference to the justice of the case invokes the equitable roots of intellectual property remedies, and would seem to permit a balanced assessment of all the relevant facts of the matter – notwithstanding the approaches actually adopted by the courts.

Additional damages represent statutory damages in excess of the prescribed thresholds for wilful infringement. Although the Copyright Act does not provide for damages on the basis of reasonable royalty, the remedy has occasionally been applied in circumstances where none of the other classes of damages is available.[306] While reasonable royalties would appear to present certain advantages in the context of damages for infringement of standards-essential copyright, this remedy is legally questionable under American law.[307]

4.4.2.4 European Law

European law presents a relatively flexible and well-considered framework for the calculation for damages concerning standards-essential copyrights. The inclusion of provision for reasonable royalty as a basis for damages calculation is particularly encouraging. Building on the TRIPS requirements, the EU Enforcement Directive requires Member States to ensure that their competent authorities are empowered to order an infringer who knowingly, or with reasonable grounds to know, engaged in infringing activity, to pay the right holder damages appropriate to the actual prejudice suffered by him/her as a result of the infringement.[308] Article 13(2) directs Member States to a choice between, on the one hand, lost profits, unfair profits and moral prejudice[309] and, on the other hand, the hypothetical reasonable royalty which would have been agreed in an arms-length transaction.[310]

Trolls: An Analysis of Mass Copyright Litigation in the Age of Statutory Damages' (2012) 19 UCLA Entertainment Law Review 79.

[305] Copyright Act §504(c)(1).
[306] *Deltak, Inc* v. *Advanced Systems, Inc* [1985] 767 F2d 357 (United States Court of Appeals for the Seventh Circuit) 362.
[307] See David Nimmer, 'Investigating the Hypothetical Reasonable Royalty for Copyright Infringement' (2019) 99 Boston University Law Review 1.
[308] EU IPR Enforcement Directive Art. 13(1).
[309] Ibid. Art. 13(2)(a).
[310] Ibid. Art. 13(2)(b).

4.4.2.5 Chinese Law

Article 49 of China's Copyright Law provides for damages in the first instance to compensate the copyright holder for the actual injury suffered. Only where this is difficult to compensate are lost profits to be awarded. Where neither method is feasible, the court may calculate the damages based on all relevant information (i.e. using the topical methodology), although an upper limit on damages of RMB 500,000 is placed on calculation via this approach. Nevertheless, this ceiling may be exceeded in circumstances where there is evidence that the infringement damage or profit obviously exceeds the statutory compensation ceiling.[311] These three methods of calculation are thus sequential and mutually exclusive.[312] As with the European regime for damages, the Chinese regime would seem to preserve sufficient flexibility to ensure a proper calculation of damages in the context of infringement of standards-essential copyrights. Notably, provision is made for reasonable royalties.

4.4.2.6 Remedies for Infringement of Standard-Essential Copyrights: Concluding Observations

Up to this time, the courts of the United States and the European Union have tended to resolve difficult questions regarding access to standards-essential copyrights, notably where these present in the form of standardized interfaces, through careful attention to questions of copyrightability and infringement, rather than through the lens of the applicable remedies. However, should the trend towards increased copyrightability of interfaces represented by the Federal Circuit's *Oracle v. Google* decision continue, questions pertaining to remedies will assume greater importance; automatic entitlement to injunction in particular is likely to be question, and the intricacies of copyright damage calculation methodologies will also warrant reconsideration in terms of whether the provide appropriate incentives for both creators and users of standardized technologies. Measures of compensation which equate to an estimation of the reasonable royalty are likely to be superior in this regard.

---

[311] *Notice of the Supreme People's Court on Issuing the Opinions on Several Issues concerning Intellectual Property Trials Serving the Overall Objective under the Current Economic Situation* [2009] No 23 (Supreme People's Court) [16].

[312] Yong Wan, 'Copyright Damages in China' [2013] Journal of the Copyright Society of the USA 517, 528.

4.5 Protection for the Layout Topographies of Integrated Circuits

Laws protecting the layout of integrated circuits generally confer a 'thin', copyright-like protection rather than a 'thick', patent-like protection. Such protection is generally limited to the 'layout' or 'topography' of the integrated circuit, and not to ideas, processes, methods of operation etc. Furthermore, protection is generally denied to topographies that are 'commonplace', 'staple' or 'familiar'. Reverse-engineering defences are generally provided. For these reasons, a layout-circuit design is unlikely to be essential to the practice of a standard. It is noteworthy that such laws often already provide for liability rules, in cases where innocent infringement subsequently becomes knowing.

Although a significant number of cases have arisen concerning standards-essential patents in relation to the semiconductor industry (notably, litigation on both sides of the Atlantic concerning Qualcomm and Rambus), those cases have not involved layout-circuit designs. This may be a reflection of the 'thin', copyright-like protection afforded to layout-designs, or simply of the industry's preference to rely on patent law to protect their innovative designs. Alternatively, it may be because it is unlikely that any particular semiconductor configuration would become essential to the practice of an interoperability standard, since standards are generally expressed in terms of performance requirements rather than design or descriptive characteristics.

4.6 Trade Secrets

Trade secrets can be seen as providing a counterpoint to the patent system. Whilst the successful exploitation of a patent can carry considerable rewards, there are also attendant risks. By patenting her invention, the patentee may disclose information sufficient to enable a competitor to 'invent around' the patent, thus effectively losing patent protection. Moreover, the patent may be found invalid by a court even after it is granted. Indeed, in some jurisdictions, the patent application is published a fixed period after its submission, whether the patent is granted or not – meaning that if the inventor chooses to seek a patent the invention will be disclosed, even if the patent application is unsuccessful. In addition, securing and enforcing a patent is costly, and the intrinsic value of the invention may be too low to justify patenting.

4.6 TRADE SECRETS

For these reasons, inventors may prefer secrecy to patenting.[313] Unless some protection is given to unpatented (or unpatentable) secrets, firms will likely expend greater resources preserving the secrecy of their inventions, and such resource expenditures are likely to be wasteful from a social welfare perspective.[314] Moreover, the protection of trade secrets can encourage investment in the production of ideas by securing a return on such investments – that is, a justification similar to that provided for other types of intellectual property protection.[315] Where an innovation is kept secret, rather than disclosed as part of a patent application, it may still attract some degree of protection. However, approaches to the protection of trade secrets vary from jurisdiction to jurisdiction; the trade secret may not be treated as an intellectual property right as such.

Concerns in relation to standards-essential trade secrets arise occasionally. In *United States* v. *Microsoft Corporation*, Microsoft argued that the US Government's proposed remedies, including forward-looking remedies which would require Microsoft to disclose APIs and communication protocols, would infringe its valuable intellectual property; nevertheless Microsoft never provided detailed argument about the extent to which its APIs and protocols were protected by trade secret law, nor did the courts give detailed consideration to this issue.[316] However one of Microsoft's economic experts testified that because Microsoft relied on trade secrets to protect its software intellectual property, disclosure would enable Microsoft's competitors to clone Microsoft's products without infringing copyright.[317]

By contrast in the EU *Microsoft* cases, Microsoft provided greater specificity as to how trade secret law entitled it not to disclose to Sun those protocol specifications that remained undisclosed.[318] The EU's Court of First Instance was relatively dismissive of Microsoft's claims, explaining that trade secrets are, by their nature, a lesser form of right, and therefore overriding them to address competition law violations does not in itself raise significant public policy concerns:

---

[313] See William M. Landes and Richard A. Posner, *The Economic Structure of Intellectual Property Law* (Harvard University Press 2009) 356–9.

[314] Mark F. Schultz and Douglas C Lippoldt, 'Approaches to Protection of Undisclosed Information (Trade Secrets): Background Paper' (OECD Publishing 2014) 62 135.

[315] Ibid.

[316] Harry First, 'Microsoft and the Evolution of the Intellectual Property Concept' [2006] Wisconsin Law Review 1369, 1405.

[317] Ibid. 131.

[318] Ibid. 1405; *Microsoft* v. *Commission of the European Communities (Case T-201/04)* [2007] 2007 ECR II-03601 (European Court of First Instance) [273].

> The case-law on compulsory licensing does not as such apply to trade secrets and the protection that such secrets enjoy under national law is normally more limited than that given to copyright or patents. While there may be a presumption of legitimacy of a refusal to license an intellectual property right 'created by law', the legitimacy under competition law of a refusal to disclose a secret which exists solely as a result of a unilateral business decision depends more on the facts of the case and, in particular, the interests at stake. In the present case, the value of the secret' concerned lies not in the fact that it involves innovation but in the fact that it belongs to a dominant undertaking.[319]

Nevertheless, the Court of First Instance ultimately proceeded on the basis that Microsoft's APIs and protocols were protected by trade secret law, without informing itself as to the precise scope of such protection.[320] Perhaps the United States and European courts should have given greater consideration to Microsoft's trade secret claims. Notwithstanding their variegated nature, which might imply a relative lack of importance, trade secrets are in fact very important to business and the economy generally, and in particular provide an important alternative to other forms of intellectual property (e.g. patents). Further, the disclosure of a trade secret (e.g. to redress anticompetitive behaviour) effectively destroys any such rights that exist, which derive value solely from their secrecy.

Hence, the forced disclosure of a trade secret is qualitatively different to the imposition of a liability rule with respect to patents, copyright or trade secrets. By the same token, trade secret laws generally (albeit with significant variations from jurisdiction to jurisdiction) allow a liberal reverse-engineering defence. Therefore, one option for courts to consider would be to step back and allow competitors to exercise their legal rights to reverse engineer interoperability information, rather than stepping in and thereby destroying the trade secret.

4.7 Compulsory Licensing of Intellectual Property Rights

4.7.1 Compulsory Licence for Established Contravention of Competition Law

Many countries' laws confer powers on courts or regulatory bodies to impose compulsory licences to redress a breach of competition laws, including laws with respect to unilateral conduct (e.g. abuse of

---

[319] *Microsoft* v. *Commission of the European Communities (Case T-201/04)* (n. 330) para. 280.
[320] Ibid. 289.

4.7 LICENSING OF INTELLECTUAL PROPERTY RIGHTS

a dominant market position). Such an approach to compulsory licensing necessarily involves the application of two bodies of law simultaneously: competition law and intellectual property law. This can give rise to complexity, overlap and uncertainty.

The licence may be granted under competition law or under the relevant intellectual property law (e.g. patent law). In either case the relevant decision-maker may be required to take cognizance of the applicable principles of both bodies of law. Where the power to issue a compulsory licence is issued pursuant to competition law, the power may well apply across all forms of intellectual property. By contrast where the power is granted under intellectual property law, it is more likely to be confined to a particular type of intellectual property (e.g. patents or copyrights). The power may exist concurrently in both competition law (applicable to all intellectual property rights) and relevant intellectual property laws. This is the case in numerous jurisdictions, for example, Australia,[321] China,[322] Germany.[323] The decision-maker could be a competition authority, an intellectual property authority, a political decision-maker (e.g. a Minister) or the courts.[324]

4.7.1.1 United States Law

In the United States, the powers of the courts to impose a compulsory licence as a remedy for breach of the antitrust laws arises from case law, as illustrated by the decision of the United States District Court of the District of Columbia in the *Microsoft* case,[325] which was subsequently upheld by the United States Court of Appeals for the District of Columbia Circuit.[326] In that case, the remedies imposed by the District Court included orders to: (i) disclose (for the sole purpose of

---

[321] Competition and Consumer Act (Cth) 2010 1974 s. 80(1); see also subs. 50(3); Australian Patents Act s. 133(2)(b).
[322] Anti-Monopoly Law (Promulgated by Order No. 68 of August 30, 2007) of the People's Republic of China, 中华人民共和国反垄断法 Article 47; China Patent Law ch. VI.
[323] 'Survey on Compulsory Licences Granted by WIPO Member States to Address Anti-Competitive Uses of Intellectual Property Right' (World Intellectual Property Organization 2011) CDIP/4/4 Rev./Study/Inf/5 3 www.wipo.int accessed 4 August 2017.
[324] Ibid. 11–13.
[325] *State of New York, et al.* v. *Microsoft Corporation, Final Judgment* [2002] 224 FSupp2d 76 (United States District Court for the District of Columbia); *State of New York et al* v. *Microsoft Corporation* [2002] 224 FSupp2d 76 (United States Court of Appeals for the District of Columbia).
[326] *Commonwealth of Massachusetts, ex rel* v. *Microsoft Corporation* [2004] 373 F3d 1199 (United States Court of Appeals for the District of Columbia Circuit) 1215–25.

interoperating with a Windows Operating System product) APIs and related Documentation used by Microsoft Middleware to interoperate with a Windows Operating System Product,[327] and (ii) make available for use by third parties, for the sole purpose of interoperating or communicating with a Windows Operating System Product, on reasonable and non-discriminatory terms, any communications protocol implemented in a Windows Operating System Product installed on a client computer, and used to interoperate with a Microsoft server operating system product.[328]

To facilitate these orders, the District Court also required Microsoft to license any intellectual property rights owned or licensable by Microsoft, as required to exercise any of the options or alternatives expressly provided in the final judgment, on reasonable and non-discriminatory terms.[329] From the *Microsoft* judgment it is clear that this power (i) arises from case law;[330] and (ii) extends to all types of intellectual property rights. In the *Microsoft* case, Microsoft's patents, copyrights and trade secrets were potentially impacted by this ruling.

4.7.1.2 European Law

The power of EU courts and the European Commission (EC) to order compulsory licences in respect of infringements of competition law emanates from TFEU Article 105(1), which empowers the Commission to investigate suspected cases of infringement, and propose appropriate measures to bring such infringement to an end.[331]

In the foundational case of *Commercial Solvents*[332] (which did not involve any intellectual property right), the EC intervened in a situation where supply had been discontinued, and simply mandated that supply continue on the previously agreed terms,[333] thus obviating the need to determine an access price on the basis of economic principles.

---

[327] *State of New York, et al.* v. *Microsoft Corporation, Final Judgment* (n. 325) 268–9.
[328] Ibid. 269–70.
[329] Ibid. 271–2.
[330] *State of New York et al* v. *Microsoft Corporation, Memorandum Opinion* [2002] 231 FSupp2d 203 (United States District Court for the District of Columbia) 249–50.
[331] Consolidated Version of the Treaty on the Functioning of the European Union ([2008] OJ C115/13) Art. 105.
[332] *Istituto Chemioterapico Italiano SpA and Commercial Solvents Corporation* v. *Commission of the European Communities (Cases 6 and 7/73)* [1974] ECR 00223 (European Court of Justice).
[333] *Commercial Solvents (72/457/EC)* [1972] 1972 OJ 29951 (European Commission).

4.7 LICENSING OF INTELLECTUAL PROPERTY RIGHTS

By contrast in *Magill*[334] the EC (in a decision subsequently upheld by the ECJ) mandated supply where none had previously existed, but set out only in very general terms the required conditions of such a licence.[335]

The Commission outlined a more robust process in *IMS Health*,[336] where it had found a copyrighted database to constitute a de facto standard indispensable to competition in a market. The Commission, in addition to requiring IMS Health to grant a licence without delay to all undertakings present in the market, on non-discriminatory terms and for a reasonable fee, outlined a process whereby IMS would in the first instance negotiate such a licence with the relevant undertakings and, should those negotiations fail, the Commission would appoint an independent, expert arbitrator to determine the relevant licensing terms.[337]

Likewise in *Microsoft*, the Commission ordered the supply of certain interoperability information to relevant undertakings. Microsoft was required to keep the interoperability information updated in a timely manner. Microsoft was further required to establish an evaluation mechanism that would give interested undertakings a workable possibility of informing themselves about the scope and terms of use of the interoperability information.[338] Similarly in *Huawei v. ZTE*, the ECJ outlined the negotiating process that should be followed with regards to the negotiation of a FRAND licence. Where such negotiations failed, the ECJ indicated that the parties may, by common agreement, request that the amount of the royalty be determined by an independent third party, by decision without delay.[339]

Hence, the Commission and the European Courts have, from time to time, applied (or threatened to apply) the remedy of compulsory licensing but have avoided engaging in detailed consideration of the terms of such licence. Instead they have: (i) required that supply continue on previously agreed terms (*Commercial Solvents*); (ii) required that a licence be granted on fair, reasonable and/or non-discriminatory terms (*Magill, IMS Health, Microsoft, Huawei*); (iii) proposed or required independent third-party arbitration in the event of the failure of

---

[334] *Radio Telefis Eirann v. Commission of the European Communities* [1991] European Court of First Instance T-69/89, II–00485 ECR.
[335] *Magill TV Guide/ITP, BBC and RTE* (89/205/EEC) [1988] OJ 78 43 (European Commission).
[336] *NDC Health/IMS Health: Interim Measures (Case COMP D3/38.044)* (n. 277).
[337] *NDC Health/IMS Health: Interim Measures (Case COMP D3/38.044)* (n. 277).
[338] *Microsoft (Case COMP/C-3/37/792 – Microsoft)* (n. 204) 299–300.
[339] *Huawei Technologies Co. Ltd v. ZTE Corp., ZTE Deutschland GmbH (Case C/170–13)* (n. 76) para 68.

negotiations (*IMS Health*, *Huawei*); and/or (iv) proposed other relevant measures (e.g. establishment of an evaluation mechanism in *Microsoft*).

4.7.1.3 Other Countries' Laws

Many other countries maintain compulsory licensing regimes directed specifically to addressing anticompetitive practices by a right holder. A survey undertaken by WIPO during 2014 indicated that forty-seven WIPO Member States provide for compulsory licensing of patents on grounds of 'anti-competitive practices and/or unfair competition'.[340] For example, Article 48(2) of China's 1984 Patent Law provides for the State Council to grant a compulsory licence to exploit a patent where it has been legally determined that the enforcement of the patent right by the patentee is an act of monopoly, to avoid or to eliminate the adverse effects caused to competition.[341]

In other cases, compulsory licensing regimes may be directed towards more general purposes, but in terms sufficiently broad to potentially encompass the case of SEIP. This will include circumstances where a compulsory licence is available: to prevent abuses of rights (see, e.g. German[342] and Hong Kong law[343]); to promote the public interest at large, and in furtherance of multiple policy objectives (e.g. Portuguese[344] and Chinese[345] laws).

4.8 Concluding Remarks about Standards-Essential Intellectual Property

Laws protecting intellectual property seek to overcome the public goods nature of ideas and information by providing a time-limited monopoly to creators of innovators and works to exploit the fruits of their endeavours. Intellectual property protection remains critical to providing the requisite incentives for the creation of new and revised interoperability standards. At the same time, it is important to pay attention to the impacts of intellectual property protection on incentives for follow-on innovation,

---

[340] 'Exceptions and Limitations to Patent Rights: Compulsory Licences and/or Government Use (Part I)' (World Intellectual Property Organization 2014) SCP/21/4 Rev. 5 www.wipo.int accessed 5 August 2017.
[341] China Patent Law.
[342] Germany Patent Act ss. 24, 81–85a.
[343] Patents Ordinance (HK), Chapter 514 1997 ss. 64–7.
[344] 'Exceptions and Limitations to Patent Rights: Compulsory Licences and/or Government Use (Part I)' (n. 352) para. 11.
[345] Ibid.

4.8 CONCLUDING REMARKS ABOUT SEIP

notably the implementation of existing standards, such as developing new consumer products (e.g. mobile phones, laptops) based on standardized technologies.

Intellectual property rights can become 'standards-essential' in the sense that it is not possible to implement an interoperability standard without first obtaining a licence to practise certain intellectual property embodied in the standard. Patents, copyrights and trade secrets, in particular, have from time to time been found by the courts to be standards-essential. Where intellectual property becomes standards-essential, the holder of the SEIP can effectively deny prospective users access to utilizing the standard. Since standards create positive externalities in the form of network effects, denial of access to standards through the assertion of intellectual property rights could limit the realization of network effects, to the detriment of society generally.

Patent protection, which is best-suited to protecting inventions, including those inventions embodied in computer programs and databases, has received the most attention, with a well-developed literature discussing concerns associated with SEPs, such as 'patent hold-up' and 'royalty stacking'. These concerns are increasingly being addressed, at least in the United States and, on early indications elsewhere (e.g. Japan) inter alia by the courts tailoring the availability of the injunctive remedy to take account of the standard-setting context, including in particular undertakings to license, such as so-called 'FRAND declarations', given by the right holder.

In other jurisdictions such as the EU and China, the same concerns are being addressed through the application of unilateral disciplines in competition law, including in some cases the imposition of compulsory licences. Other facets of patent protection, such as the nature and scope of obligations to disclose the invention and defences to infringement (e.g. an experimental use exception) will also impact on addressing concerns such as hold-up and royalty stacking. Collective rights organizations such as voluntary patent pools may also be apt to address at least some of these concerns.

Standards-essential copyrights provide a more 'thin' protection than patent laws, and as such patents, rather than copyrights, are increasingly the preferred means of protection in high technology industries such as computer software and databases. Nevertheless, standards-essential copyrights can also arise, notably in cases of computer programs and databases, for example where standardized protocols or interfaces are copyrightable.

Although phenomena such as 'hold-up' and 'royalty stacking' are not observed in connection with standards-essential copyright, nevertheless some cases before the courts have involved claims of copyright protection which, had they succeeded, could have had detrimental impacts on the implementation of standardized technologies. Many of these claims, however, have been rejected on the basis of the limiting doctrines in copyright law, which include the distinction between protectable expressions and unprotectable ideas, the need for originality, merger doctrine, *scènes à faire* and fair use. Because of the widespread application of the limiting doctrines, there has been relatively less need to address concerns regarding standards-essential copyright through remedies, including the availability of the injunctive remedy.

Nevertheless, more recent US cases addressing the copyrightability of interfaces, such as *Oracle* v. *Google*, would seem to reflect a greater inclination on the part of the Federal Circuit in particular to recognize the copyrightability of interfaces. If this trend continues, it will invite greater scrutiny inter alia upon the remedies generally awarded for infringement of standards-essential copyrights. Automaticity of injunctions is likely to be particularly questioned. There will also likely be greater scrutiny of methodologies for the calculation of damages. Reasonable royalty, the methodology most likely to ensure a quantum of damages that provides for appropriate incentives for initial and follow-on innovation, is available under EU and Chinese law, but is only available under United States law in very limited circumstances; in any case its place in American law is tenuous. The proper principles for calculation of lost profits and disgorgement of profits will likely require further consideration and clarification in the context of standards-essential copyrights.

Other types of intellectual property, for example trade secrets, do, on occasions, become standards-essential (as was seen in the EU *Microsoft* case), but this phenomenon will generally be rare, since standardization generally requires the applicable protocols and interfaces to be placed in the public domain.

To the extent that concerns about access to interoperability standards, and in particular to access to SEIP, remain unaddressed through (e.g.) application of the limiting doctrines in intellectual property law, there will likely be increasing occasion for competition laws, notably unilateral disciplines in competition law such as the essential facilities doctrine, to be applied, as discussed in the chapter to follow.

5

Interoperability Standards and Competition Law

5.1 Introductory Comments

As Chapter 4 explains, the assertion of intellectual property rights (notably patents, copyright and trade secrets) in the context of interoperability standards could result in restricting the access of market participants to those standards. The question logically arises as to whether competition laws, which seek to promote competition through disciplining the attainment and exercise of market power, should be called upon to ensure access to interoperability standards and SEIP. An essential facilities doctrine would seem to be an obvious candidate for the task. This Chapter weighs the case for applying competition law rules to ensure access to interoperability standards and SEIP through the lens of a possible international instrument.

5.2 The Essential Facilities Doctrine

This section examines whether the essential facilities doctrine should form the basis for such an international instrument. This Chapter highlights two fundamental concerns with such an approach. First, such an approach will be infeasible because there are entrenched differences among leading jurisdictions (notably the United States, the European Union and China) regarding, not merely the precise circumstances in which a doctrine should apply, or how or whether it should apply in the context of interoperability standards or SEIP, but indeed whether such a doctrine should exist at all. Second, this chapter flags concerns about the optimality of mandating an essential facilities doctrine at the international level. At this point in time it cannot be said that a law and economics approach would justify the imposition of the doctrine in the context of access to interoperability standards and SEIP. Proceeding topically, this section traces the history and intellectual foundations of the doctrine, from its origins in the writings of the English jurist Lord

Hale, to its modern articulation by the European Court of Justice in *Bronner*. Next, the interface between the doctrine and intellectual property rights is examined – particularly under EU law, since the American doctrine has for all intents and purposes been abolished and the Chinese doctrine is in its infancy. Third, the extent to which a doctrine could be justified on the basis of law and economics is assessed.

5.2.1 Historical Development and Intellectual Foundations of the Essential Facilities Doctrine

5.2.1.1 Lord Hale's Manuscript Originates the Doctrine

The origins of the essential facilities doctrine may perhaps be traced to the writings of Lord Matthew Hale, a seventeenth century English legal scholar.[1] In his essay entitled *De Portibus Maris* (which concerned access to the sea), Hale considered the distinction between wharfs or cranes established under exclusive licence from the Crown, as compared with wharfs or cranes held privately and subject to market competition:

> A man for his own private advantage may in a port town set up a wharf or crane, and may take what rates he and his customers may agree for cranage, wharfage, &c; for he doth no more than is lawful for any man to do, vis. make the most of his own, &c-If the kind or subject have a public wharf, unto which all persons that come to that port must come and unlade or lade their goods, as for the purpose, because they are the wharfs only licensed by the queen, according to the st. 1 Eliz. c. 11., or because there is no other wharf in that port, as may fall out where the port is newly erected; in that case there cannot be taken arbitrary and excessive duties for cranage, wharfage, &c, neither can they be enhanced to immoderate rates; but the duties must be reasonable and moderate, though settled by the king's licence or charter; for now the wharf and crane and other conveniences are affected with the public interest, and they cease to be *juris privati* only. As if a man set out a street in a new building on his own land, it is now no longer bare private interest but it is affected with the public interest.[2]

From this excerpt it is apparent that Hale's (later classic) phrase 'affected with the public interest' was notably applied by its author to instances of both: (i) public monopoly, for example a monopoly conferred by statute;

---

[1] See generally Richard Epstein, *Principles for a Free Society* (Perseus Publishing 1998) ch 9.
[2] Chief Justice Lord Matthew Hale, 'A Treatise in Three Parts. Pars Prima. De Jure Maris et Brachiorum Ejusdem. Pars Secunda. De Portibus Maris. Pars Tertia. Concerning the Customs of Goods Imported and Exported' in *Collection of Tracts Relative to the Law of England* (E Lynch 1787) 77–8.

and (ii) private monopoly, for example monopoly gained through first mover advantage; in both cases the monopoly was 'affected with the public interest' and consequently rates charged needed to be 'reasonable and moderate'.

5.2.1.2 Impact of Hale's Manuscript on English Law

Hale's manuscript lay unpublished for over a century, until it was published in 1787 along with a collection of other works of various authors.[3] Once published, however, its influence began to be felt almost immediately; in 1800, an English court ruled in *Bolt* v. *Stennett*[4] that the owner of a licensed crane was required to make a crane situated at a public quay available for use, on reasonable terms and conditions.[5]

In the 1810 English case of *Allnutt* v. *Inglis*,[6] which concerned access to a wine storage facility, the defendant was the treasurer of the London Dock Company, which had an exclusive statutory right to store wines imported into England; the nub of the dispute was whether or not the London Dock Company could charge any storage charge it wished, or whether there was any constraint upon its pricing. Chief Justice Lord Edward Ellenborough's opinion, drawing on Hale's treatise, stated:

> The question on this record is whether the London Dock Company have a right to insist upon receiving wines into their warehouse house for hire and reward arbitrary to their will and pleasure, or whether they were bound to receive them for a reasonable reward only. There is no doubt that the general principle is favored in both law and justice, that every man may fix what price he pleases upon his own property or the use of it; but if, for a particular purpose, the public have a right to resort to his premises and make use of them, and he have a monopoly in them for that purpose, if he will take the benefit of the monopoly, he must as an equivalent perform the duty attached to it on reasonable terms.[7]

5.2.1.3 The Doctrine Crosses the Atlantic

Munn* v. *Illinois The first application of Lord Hale's principle in American law was in *Munn* v. *Illinois*,[8] a case involving access to grain

---

[3] Hale (n. 2); see Breck P. McAllister, 'Lord Hale and Business Affected with a Public Interest' (1930) 43 Harvard Law Review 759, 759.
[4] *Bolt* v. *Stennett* [1800] 101 Engl Rep 1572 8 Term Rep 606 (Court of King's Bench).
[5] Ibid. 1573; see McAllister (n. 3) n. 35.
[6] *Allnutt* v. *Inglis* [1810] 104 Engl Rep 206 1810 12 East 527 (Court of King's Bench); see also Epstein (n. 1).
[7] *Allnutt* v. *Inglis* (n. 6) 210–11; see also Epstein (n. 1).
[8] *Munn* v. *Illinois* [1876] 94 US 113 (United States Supreme Court).

elevators. The Supreme Court was asked to consider whether the State of Illinois could lawfully, under the US Constitution, pass a statute fixing a maximum charge for the use of grain elevators. In particular, the Court was called upon to consider whether Illinois's law violated the Fourteenth Amendment to the Constitution, which provides that no State shall 'deprive any person of life, liberty or property, without due process of law, nor deny to any person within its jurisdiction the equal protection of the laws'.

In holding that the impugned Illinois statute did not, in fact, violate the Fourteenth Amendment, Chief Justice Waite observed that when the United States separated from Great Britain, the various States retained the powers of the British Parliament. The laws inherited by the States included the principle outlined by Hale in his treatise and applied in Allnut. Chief Justice Waite thus held: 'Enough has already been said to show that, when private property is devoted to a public use, it is subject to public regulation. It remains only to ascertain whether the warehouses of these plaintiffs in error, and the business which is carried on there, come within the operation of this principle'.[9] Mr Justice Field, writing in the same case, found his Chief Justice's statement of the law overbroad, and that it could conceivably lead to rate regulation of all commodities, 'from a calico gown to a city mansion'.[10] Mr Justice Field suggested that Lord Hale's principle should apply only to property dedicated to the public interest in a strict legal sense.[11]

The 'Granger' Cases Munn was one of eight US cases known as the 'Granger cases' – the only one that did not directly concern rates charged by railroads (although the business of grain elevators was closely linked to the railroad business). The 'grangers' were associations of farmers and other businessfolk who were greatly concerned about the wealth and political influence of the 'robber barons' who had built the railroads. They felt that railroad proprietors were able to exercise greater influence over the livelihoods of the grangers, in some respects, than government itself. They backed their calls for rate control by references to 'popular sovereignty' and cited concerns about growing concentrations of industry and of wealth, along with the political influence of the railroad proprietors. Government intervention through rate regulation was seen

---

[9] Ibid. 94.
[10] Ibid. 153.
[11] Ibid. 141.

as legitimate because government was able to make manifest the will of the people.[12]

The principle outlined by Chief Justice Waite in *Munn v. Illinois* was upheld twenty years later by the Supreme Court in *German Alliance Insurance Co v. Lewis*,[13] concerning Kansas State legislation which controlled fire insurance rates.[14] In that case, Mr Justice McKenna, writing for the majority, opined that regulation was permitted where the matter concerned 'a broad and definite public interest'.[15] Shortly afterwards in *Block v. Hirsch*,[16] Mr Justice Holmes, writing for the majority, justified rent control laws on more pragmatic grounds relating to the particular circumstances at hand: a scarcity of housing; the character of housing as a necessity; the appropriateness of rate control regulation in view of the public interest at stake; and the temporary nature of the measure.[17]

5.2.1.4 *United States v. Terminal Rail Road Association of St Louis*: The First Essential Facilities Case

Block v. Hirsch was issued shortly after the Supreme Court's now-famous 1912 *Terminal Railroad* decision,[18] generally seen as the foundational case for the doctrine.[19]

The Facts of *Terminal Railroad* The Terminal Railroad Association, a Missouri corporation composed of erstwhile competing rail terminal and rail bridge companies, had secured complete control of St Louis's union station, its only rail bridge, and every rail terminal on either side of the river Missouri that could be used to approach the bridge. Terminal Railroad consolidated its position by obtaining stock control of the Merchants' Bridge Company, which owned the only competing St Louis rail bridge, and by taking control of the Wiggins Ferry Company, which provided the only alternative means at that time to

---

[12] Paul Kens, 'Property, Liberty and the Rights of the Community: Lessons from Munn v Illinois' (2011) 30 Buffalo Public International Law Journal 157, 161–6.
[13] *German Alliance Insurance Co v. Lewis* [1914] 233 US 389 (United States Supreme Court).
[14] McAllister (n. 3) 771.
[15] Ibid. 772.
[16] *Block v. Hirsch* [1921] 256 US 135 (United States Supreme Court).
[17] McAllister (n. 3) 773.
[18] *United States v. Terminal Railroad Association of St Louis* [1912] 224 US 383 (United States Supreme Court).
[19] Robert Pitofsky, Donna Patterson and Jonathan Hooks, 'The Essential Facilities Doctrine Under United States Antitrust Law' (2002) 70 Antitrust Law Journal 443, 445.

convey freight across the Missouri.[20] The cost of constructing bridges over the Missouri necessarily limited their number.[21]

Thus, Terminal Railroad had succeeded in monopolizing all rail approaches to the Missouri on either side of the river: any freight undertaking seeking to convey goods across the river needed to deal with the company. The Court observed that the constituent documents of the Terminal Railroad Company effectively excluded membership by prospective rail users, conditioning their membership on the unanimous consent of all the existing members.[22]

Having secured control of all rail approaches to the Missouri, Terminal Railroad then prescribed transportation charges for its members on a cost-recovery basis; there was no indication that non-member rail companies had been excluded from using Terminal Railroad's facilities, nor that non-members had been required to pay higher charges than members.[23] The constituent agreement obliged Terminal Railroad members forever to use the company's facilities, in practice foreclosing the future construction of competing facilities.[24] Summing up the situation, the Court surmised:

> That through their ownership and exclusive control they are in possession of advantages in respect to the enormous traffic which must use the St. Louis gateway, is undeniable. That the proprietary companies have not availed themselves of the full measure of their power to impede free competition of outside companies, may be true. Aside from their power under all of the conditions to exclude independent entrance to the city by any outside company, their control has resulted in certain methods which are not consistent with freedom of competition.[25]

Certain practices of the Terminal Railroad company were condemned by the Court; for example, the company applied a rate schedule which was alleged to discriminate arbitrarily against short-haul traffic.[26] Exceptions allowed to the usual rates appeared to favour traffic originating in the East St Louis area, to the benefit of that region and the corresponding detriment of other regions.[27] Terminal Railroad relied on the evidence of

---

[20] *United States* v. *Terminal Railroad Association of St Louis* (n. 18) 391–4.
[21] Ibid. 395.
[22] Ibid. 399–400.
[23] Ibid. 400.
[24] Ibid.
[25] Ibid. 401.
[26] Ibid. 407.
[27] Ibid. 408.

Mr Albert L. Perkins, an experienced engineer, to justify the efficiency benefits arising from its combination. Mr Perkins testified that the public benefit was served where all the railroad terminals serving a large city were unified insofar as possible – but that the company operating the unified terminals should be 'the agent of every company', and furthermore that its services 'Should not be for profit or gain'.[28]

Terminal Railroad: **the Court's Decision** The Court, swayed perhaps by the evidence of Mr Perkins, sought to preserve the advantages obtained by the consortium, but to modify the agreement between Terminal Railroad and its member companies so as to 'constitute the former the bona fide agent and servant of every railroad line which shall use its facilities'.[29] The case was remanded to the District Court with instructions to secure from the defendant companies plans for the reorganization of their contracts with the Terminal Railroad company, including: (i) to admit any existing or future railroad company to membership; (ii) to allow to non-member companies use of the facilities 'upon . . . just and reasonable terms and regulations'; and (iii) to abolish certain of Terminal Railroad's arbitrary charging practices.[30]

Subsequent Characterization of the *Terminal Railroad* Decision *Terminal Railroad* has on occasion been characterized as a case involving foreclosure,[31] although this is not apparent from the Supreme Court's judgment. Moreover, it now seems reasonably clear (e.g. based on the testimony of Mr Perkins) that terminal rail services in St Louis were, in fact, a natural monopoly.[32] While Terminal Railroad was able to exercise control over all rail freight entering or exiting St Louis, in practical terms its monopoly was only effective in respect of goods

---

[28] Ibid. 405–6.
[29] Ibid. 410–11.
[30] Ibid. 411–12.
[31] Daniel E. Troy, 'Unclogging the Bottleneck: A New Essential Facility Doctrine' (1983) 83 Columbia Law Review 441, 452; David J. Gerber, 'Rethinking the Monopolist's Duty to Deal: A Legal and Economic Critique of the Doctrine of "Essential Facilities"' (1988) 74 Virginia Law Review 1069, 1079; Gregory J. Werden, 'The Law and Economics of the Essential Facility Doctrine' (1987) 32 St Louis University Law Journal 433, 444.
[32] See David Reiffen and Andrew N. Kleit, 'Terminal Railroad Revisited: Foreclosure of an Essential Facility or Simple Horizontal Monopoly?' (1990) 33 The Journal of Law and Economics 419, 420. A natural monopoly is sub-additive in the sense that no combination of two or more suppliers can provide the relevant good or service at lower cost than can a single supplier.

moving westward, particularly coal from Illinois; shippers of goods moving eastwards were able to use many other bridges across the Missouri located in other towns. Presumably this explains why Terminal Railroad was only able to impose additional charges (in the form of a 'Bridge Arbitrary' of two cents per hundredweight of goods) on goods moving westwards.[33] There are some indications that the company was able to use its position to earn economic rents.[34]

Although it has frequently been cited as the origin of the doctrine, it is possible to analyse *Terminal Railroad* as a case of joint collusion rather than of single-firm conduct;[35] it has also been interpreted as tantamount to public utilities regulation.[36] Railroads at the time were regulated by the Interstate Commerce Commission, and the Supreme Court may have been influenced by those regulatory arrangements in crafting its remedy in the *Terminal Railroad* case.[37] On balance, *Terminal Railroad* is best viewed as involving elements of both collective conduct and the beginnings of an essential facilities doctrine. Had the Supreme Court viewed the combination as either a cartel or an illegal merger, it might have ordered divestiture of the relevant combination; yet the Court clearly did not want to do this, in view of the overriding efficiency benefits resulting from combining all of St Louis's rail terminals within a single enterprise. Instead, the Court preferred to allow the combination to operate as a single entity, and instructed the lower courts to devise suitable open-access obligations.

5.2.1.5 *Associated Press v. United States*

A similar fact pattern can be observed in the next landmark Supreme Court decision, *Associated Press v. United States*,[38] which involved the Associated Press, an association comprised of the publishers of more than 1200 newspapers.[39] The Associated Press gathered news from

---

[33] Ibid. 429–31.
[34] Ibid. 434.
[35] Abbott B. Lipsky and J. Gregory Sidak, 'Essential Facilities' (1998) 51 Stanford Law Review 1187, 1195; Reiffen and Kleit (n. 32) 425; James R. Ratner, 'Should There Be an Essential Facility Doctrine' (1988) 21 U.C. Davis Law Review 327, 336.
[36] Edward H. Levi, 'The Antitrust Laws and Monopoly' (1947) 14 The University of Chicago Law Review 153, 157.
[37] Ratner (n. 35) 337.
[38] *Associated Press et al v. United States* [1945] 65 Ct 1416 (United States Supreme Court).
[39] Ibid. 1417.

5.2 THE ESSENTIAL FACILITIES DOCTRINE

various sources, which it then distributed to its members under a non-profit arrangement.[40]

The United States Government brought antitrust claims against the Associated Press, focussing primarily on its by-laws, which: (i) prohibited member organizations from passing news to non-members; and (ii) enabled members to block their competitors from joining the association.[41] Justice Black, writing for the Court, opined:

> Inability to buy news from the largest news agency, or any one of its multitude of members, can have most serious effects on the publication of competitive newspapers, both those presently published and those which but for these restrictions, might be published in the future. ... The net effect is seriously to limit the opportunity of any new paper to enter these cities. Trade restraints of this character, aimed at the destruction of competition, tend to block the initiative which brings newcomers into a field.[42]

Furthermore, the Court stated that:

> While it is true in a very general sense that one can dispose of his property as he pleases, he cannot "go beyond the exercise of this right, and by contracts or combinations, express or implied, unduly hinder or obstruct the free and natural flow of commerce in the channels of interstate trade" ... The Sherman Act was specifically intended to prohibit independent businesses from becoming 'associates' in a common plan which is bound to reduce their competitor's opportunity to buy or sell the things in which the groups compete.[43]

The Court dismissed argument that access to AP membership was not 'indispensable' because AP and its member publishers had not 'deprived the reading public of AP news', since members of the public in whichever city they found themselves could purchase a newspaper supplied by the AP news network.[44] The Court considered that if it accepted such arguments, it would thereby render the Sherman Act a dead letter.[45] The Court upheld the decree of the District Court that prohibited AP from observing the impugned by-laws, or from agreeing to any new or revised by-law having the same effect.[46]

---

[40] Ibid. 1416.
[41] Ibid. 1417.
[42] Ibid. 1421.
[43] Ibid. 1422.
[44] Ibid. 1424.
[45] Ibid.
[46] Ibid. 1425–6.

5.2.1.6 *Otter Tail Power Company* v. *United States*: The First Single-Firm Conduct Case

The Supreme Court later extended the principles articulated in *Terminal Railroad* and *Associated Press* to single-firm conduct. *Otter Tail Power Company* v. *United States* concerned the activities of a company retailing electric power to 465 towns in Minnesota, North Dakota and South Dakota.[47] Otter Tail operated a vertically integrated business that extended from generation to transmission, distribution and retail. Four towns within Otter Tail's service area wished to replace Otter Tail as their retailer and distributor and instead operate a 'municipal system' under which the townships would rely on Otter Tail for generation and transmission but supply their own distribution and retail services.

Otter Tail sought to prevent the establishment of these municipal systems, predominantly by: (i) refusing to supply wholesale electric power to these municipalities; and (ii) refusing to 'wheel' electric power supplied by other wholesale suppliers over its transmission network. Two of the municipalities (Elbow Lake and Hankinson) were able to obtain wholesale electricity from other sources but required Otter Tail to wheel it; Otter Tail refused. Otter Tail also commenced litigation against the four towns with a view to preventing them from establishing municipal systems.

The Supreme Court held that Otter Tail had attempted to monopolize a market, in violation of section 2 of the Sherman Act.[48] The Court considered that Otter Tail had 'used its monopoly power in the towns in its service area to foreclose competition or gain a competitive advantage, or to destroy a competitor'.[49] The Court further cited the District Court's findings that Otter Tail had 'a strategic dominance in the transmission of power in most of its service area and that it used this dominance to foreclose potential entrants into the retail area from obtaining electric power from outside sources of supply'.[50] Finally, the Court relied on the District Court's finding that requiring Otter Tail to wholesale and wheel electric power was technically feasible and would not cause damage to Otter Tail's network.[51]

---

[47] *Otter Tail Power Company* v. *United States* [1973] 410 US 366 (United States Supreme Court).
[48] Ibid. 1022.
[49] Ibid. 1029.
[50] Ibid.
[51] Ibid. 1031.

5.2 THE ESSENTIAL FACILITIES DOCTRINE

On these grounds the Supreme Court upheld the District Court's decree that enjoined Otter Tail from refusing to wholesale electric power, and also from refusing to wheel electric power generated from other sources.[52] It was noted by the Court that Otter Tail was subject to utilities regulation by the Federal Power Commission, but that the regulatory scheme was primarily voluntary in nature and did not empower the Commission to order Otter Tail to wheel electric power.[53] It should be noted that the Supreme Court: (i) did not mention an essential facilities doctrine by name; and (ii) couched its decision in such terms that it could equally have been characterized as based on a theory of 'monopoly leveraging'.

5.2.1.7 The Doctrine Attains Maturity in American Law

The doctrine was first named by scholar A. D. Neale in the second edition of his work, The Antitrust Laws of the United States of America:[54]

> The Sherman Act requires that where facilities cannot practicably be duplicated by would-be competitors, those in possession of them must allow them to be shared on fair terms. It is an illegal restraint of trade to foreclose the scarce facility.[55]

The doctrine was approaching maturity when it was enunciated as follows by the United States Court of Appeals for the Ninth Circuit in *Alaska Airlines Inc. v. United Airlines Inc.*: '[T]he essential facilities doctrine imposes liability when one firm, which controls an essential facility, denies a second firm reasonable access to a product or service that the second firm must obtain in order to compete with the first'.[56]

MCI Communications **Case** The doctrine received perhaps its most coherent treatment with the United States Court of Appeals for the Seventh Circuit's decision in *MCI Communications Corporation and MCI Telecommunications Corporation v. American Telephone &*

---

[52] Ibid. 1028, 1032.
[53] Ibid. 1028.
[54] Spencer Weber Waller, 'Areeda, Epithets and Essential Facilities' [2008] Wisconsin Law Review 359, 361.
[55] A. D. Neale, *The Antitrust Laws of the United States of America: A Study of Competition Enforced by Law* (Cambridge University Press, 2nd ed., 1970) 67.
[56] *Alaska Airlines, Inc. v. United Airlines, Inc.* [1991] 948 F.2d 536, 542 (United States Court of Appeals for the Ninth Circuit).

Telegraph Company.⁵⁷ MCI Communications wished to enter the long-distance telecommunications business, which at that time was dominated by the incumbent, the American Telephone & Telegraph Company (AT&T). MCI's business consisted of microwave transmission towers capable of routing telecommunication traffic between certain major cities.

MCI did not have facilities that would enable it to carry calls all the way to a customer's end-premises; rather it relied on AT&T to complete the origination and termination of long-distance calls between ordinary customers. MCI also did not have facilities to transmit long-distance calls between all cities, and sought access to AT&T's services in respect of those long-distance routes which it did not currently serve. MCI obtained approval from the Federal Communications Commission to supply long-distance telephone services, but its efforts were severely hampered by incumbent AT&T's refusal to interconnect its facilities with MCI's facilities.

The industry was regulated under the Federal Communications Commission (FCC) Act 1934, and a number of regulatory determinations were made by the FCC in the matter, binding on both MCI and AT&T; nevertheless, the Seventh Circuit held that the provisions of the Sherman Act applied concurrently in relation to AT&T's conduct.⁵⁸

The Seventh Circuit described the essential facilities doctrine in the following terms:

> A monopolist's refusal to deal under these circumstances is governed by the so-called essential facilities doctrine. Such a refusal may be unlawful because a monopolist's control of an essential facility (sometimes called a 'bottleneck') can extend monopoly power from one stage of production to another, and from one market into another. Thus, the antitrust laws have imposed on firms controlling an essential facility the obligation to make the facility available on non-discriminatory terms.⁵⁹

The Circuit then proceeded to outline the test for application of the doctrine:

> The case law sets forth four elements necessary to establish liability under the essential facilities doctrine: (1) control of the essential facility by

---

⁵⁷ *MCI Communications Corporation and MCI Telecommunications Corporation v. American Telephone and Telegraph Company* [1983] 708 F2d 1081 (United States Court of Appeals for the Seventh Circuit).
⁵⁸ Ibid. 1102–3.
⁵⁹ Ibid. 1132.

a monopolist; (2) a competitor's inability practically or reasonably to duplicate the essential facility; (3) the denial of the use the facility to a competitor; and (4) the feasibility of providing the facility to a competitor.[60]

Applying the test it had articulated to the facts of the case, the Circuit held that: (1) AT&T held complete control of the local facilities required by MCI; (2) the facilities in question were 'essential facilities' because it would have been uneconomic for MCI to duplicate AT&T's facilities, which were considered to be a natural monopoly; (3) AT&T had denied interconnection; and (4) it was feasible for AT&T to provide interconnection. Furthermore, the Circuit held that there was no reasonable business or technical justification for AT&T to deny interconnection.[61] The Court remanded the case to the District Court for reconsideration on the question of damages; the case was eventually settled.[62]

5.2.1.8   Origins of the Doctrine in Anglo-American Law: Concluding Observations

Reviewing the origins of the Anglo-American essential facilities doctrine, the history and genealogy of the doctrine reveals it to be more legal than economic in nature, and to be grounded primarily in considerations of justice and fairness, rather than the efficient allocation of resources. Indeed, some of the antecedents of the doctrine, such as the 'Granger cases' of the nineteenth century, bear the hallmarks of populism and concerns about the unwarranted privileges enjoyed by the wealthier and better-connected classes.

5.2.1.9   Criticisms of the Doctrine

The doctrine flourished in American law during the era of the 'inhospitability tradition' towards market power, guided by the Harvard School of Antitrust Law.[63] With the rise of the law and economics approach in American scholarship, the essential facilities doctrine, with its patchy theoretical underpinnings, was clearly vulnerable, especially when the inhospitality tradition came under increasing attack from scholars of the Chicago School, wielding the bright sword of law and economics to call

---

[60] Ibid. 1132–3.
[61] Ibid. 1133.
[62] Waller (n. 54) n. 21.
[63] O. E. Williamson, 'Symposium on Antitrust Law and Economics: Introduction' (1979) 127 University of Pennsylvania Law Review 918, 920.

into question many of the comfortable assumptions of antitrust law at the time – including in relation to the so-called 'unilateral disciplines'.

The essential facilities doctrine has been roundly criticized in law and economics literature[64] – yet this literature has been far from uniform in its criticisms. Keszbom and Goldman, for example, have argued that some of the cases that had been decided on the basis of the doctrine could have been decided on other well-accepted bases such as monopoly leveraging, abuse of monopoly power or refusal to deal.[65] Hylton has argued that forced sharing would give rise to risks of collusion,[66] and would undermine firms' incentives to make investments with large sunk costs.[67] Werden criticized the doctrine for overlooking the benefits of vertical integration.[68] A number of papers have invoked the single monopoly profit theorem.[69] A further criticism has been that courts are ill-equipped to supervise the sharing of an essential facility.[70]

Summarizing the Criticisms: the Areeda Article of 1989 In a seminal article published in 1989 that encapsulated many of the concerns held by the Chicago School, scholar Phillip Areeda criticized the doctrine harshly, observing:

> Indeed, the cases support the doctrine only by implication and in highly qualified ways. You will not find any case that provides a consistent rationale for the doctrine or that explores the social costs and benefits or the administrative costs of requiring the creator of an asset to share it with a rival. It is less a doctrine than an epithet, indicating some exception to the right to keep one's creations to oneself, but not telling us what those exceptions are.[71]

Areeda proposed six principles for limiting the application of the doctrine:

---

[64] Waller (n. 54) n. 31.
[65] Allen Keszbom and Alan V. Goldman, 'No Shortcut to Antitrust Analysis: The Twisted Journey of the "Essential Facilities" Doctrine' (1996) 1996 Columbia Business Law Review 1, 5.
[66] Keith N. Hylton, 'Economic Rents and Essential Facilities' [1991] Brigham Young University Law Review 1243, 1252–3.
[67] Ibid. 1261–2.
[68] Werden (n. 31) 462–4.
[69] Ibid. 469–70; Gerber (n. 31) 1084–6.
[70] Werden (n. 31) 472; Troy (n. 31) 462.
[71] Phillip Areeda, 'Essential Facilities: An Epithet in Need of Limiting Principles' (1989) 58 *Antitrust Law Journal* 841.

5.2 THE ESSENTIAL FACILITIES DOCTRINE

1. There is no general duty to share and compulsory access should be an exceptional remedy
2. The facility of a single firm should only be considered essential where it is critical to the plaintiff's vitality and the plaintiff's presence is essential for competition in the marketplace
3. No person should be forced to deal unless to do so is likely to substantially improve competition in the marketplace
4. Notwithstanding the above principles, a defendant's conduct should be excused when it carries a legitimate business purpose
5. When considering the defendant's purposes, a mere intention to exclude is insufficient; there must be an intention to exclude by improper means
6. No court should impose a duty to deal which it cannot properly supervise on an ongoing basis.[72]

Areeda might equally have described the doctrine as one in need of supporting principles. In any case, careful scrutiny of Professor Areeda's six limiting principles suggests that the doctrine could have survived even under this formula, albeit in heavily circumscribed form. If the Areeda formulation were law, then plaintiffs might, at least in some cases, be able to establish a case for forcible access, for example where both natural monopoly and exclusionary conduct could be established. Indeed, the Areeda formulation does not look so far distant from contemporary European law, particularly as applied in the context of refusals to license intellectual property rights.

5.2.1.10 Demise of the Doctrine in American Law: the *Trinko* Case

Nevertheless, Areeda's six limiting principles never became law; instead, the United States Supreme Court in *Verizon Communications, Inc. v. Law Offices of Curtis V. Trinko LLP*,[73] referring with approval to Areeda's article and discussing the doctrine in disparaging terms, held that any such doctrine (if it existed) could only be invoked where access to the facility in question is unavailable, and that this will not be the case 'where a state or federal agency has effective power to compel sharing and to regulate its scope and terms'.[74] Thus a statutory path to access (such as

---

[72] Ibid. 852–3.
[73] *Verizon Communications, Inc v. Law Offices of Curtis V Trinko, LLP* [2004] 540 US 398 (United States Supreme Court).
[74] Ibid. 411.

was available in respect of Verizon's conduct under the US Telecommunications Act of 1996) will preclude operation of a more general doctrine.

The tenor of the Supreme Court's commentary, praising the virtues of monopoly and describing the doctrine in harsh terms, made abundantly clear the Court's view that the doctrine no longer formed part of American law.[75] It is thus probably correct to view the Court's *Trinko* decision as the 'end of the line' for the doctrine that began its life with the *Terminal Railroad* decision.

5.2.1.11 Arguments for Revival of the Doctrine in American Law

While the doctrine no longer forms part of American law, a number of scholars have argued for its revival.[76] One approach that bears mention is that of Brett Frischmann and Spencer Weber Waller, who consider that it is appropriate to apply the doctrine to 'infrastructure';[77] the authors provide the following examples: '(1) transportation systems, such as highway and road systems, railways, airline systems, and ports, etc.; (2) communication systems, such as telephone networks and postal services; (3) governance systems, such as court systems; and (4) basic public services and facilities, such as schools, sewers, and water systems'.[78] Lao observes, in similar terms: 'A common feature in the key essential facilities cases is that they all involved networks and/or natural monopolies that provide necessities or form part of society's infrastructure'.[79] Frischmann and Waller outline the following three-part test for determining whether an asset is infrastructure:

1. The resource may be consumed non-rivalrously;
2. Social demand for the resource is driven primarily by downstream productive activity that requires the resource as an input; and
3. The resource is used as an input into a wide range of goods and services, including private goods, public goods, and/or non-market goods.[80]

---

[75] See Waller (n. 54) 364–5.
[76] Brett Frischmann and Spencer Weber Waller, 'Revitalizing Essential Facilities' (2008) 74 Antitrust Law Journal 1; Marina Lao, 'Networks, Access and "Essential Facilities": From Terminal Railroad to Microsoft' (2009) 62 Southern Methodist University Law Review 557.
[77] Waller (n. 76) 4.
[78] Ibid. 11.
[79] Lao (n. 76) 567.
[80] Waller (n. 76) 12.

Frischmann and Waller distinguish between commercial, public and social infrastructure. All involve non-rivalrous or partially non-rivalrous input, but the difference lies in the outputs produced.[81] Commercial infrastructure is used in the production of private goods; public infrastructure in the production of public goods; and social infrastructure in the production of non-market goods.

Under this approach the question would be whether interoperability standards, which in essence are information, can be characterized as 'infrastructure'; Frischmann and Waller answer in the affirmative, noting however that this will depend on downstream use of the standard.[82] The authors consider that the case for applying the doctrine to commercial infrastructure is considerably weaker; as such many interoperability standards, which would most likely fall within Frischmann and Waller's conceptualization of commercial infrastructure, need not necessarily be subjected to the doctrine.[83]

Might the doctrine be revived in the future in American law? The possibility cannot be dismissed. But merely reviving hoary legal principles without a solid theoretical foundation can hardly be recommended. A revived doctrine in American law would need to pay heed to the criticisms of scholars like Areeda, and should be established upon proper foundations, such that it cannot be dismissed as a mere epithet.

5.2.1.12 Intellectual Foundations and Historical Development of a European Doctrine

Whilst the doctrine is for all intents and purposes deceased in the United States, it remains good law in the European Union, under the guise of the law of abuse of a dominant market position, one of the founding precepts of the common market now enshrined in Article 102 of the Treaty on the Functioning of the European Union,[84] which by its terms encompasses refusals to supply goods or services.

5.2.1.13 Is it Proper to Speak of a European Essential Facilities Doctrine?

EU cases have occasionally made reference to an 'essential facilities doctrine', generally in connection with recognized public utilities such

---

[81] Ibid. 15.
[82] Ibid. 38.
[83] Ibid. 19–20.
[84] Damien Gerardin, 'Limiting the Scope of Article 82 EC: What Can the EU Learn from the U.S. Supreme Court's Judgment in Trinko in the Wake of Microsoft, IMS and Deutsche Telekom?' (2004) 41 Common Market Law Review 1519, 1525–6.

as ports,[85] but the term has not been used by the Court of Justice. While the matter is debated among the authorities,[86] it would seem that the differences between the general 'refusal to supply' obligations in Article 102 of the TFEU and the United States essential facilities doctrine are so marginal as to warrant reference to an EU doctrine, albeit as a convenient label rather than as a formal legal test.

5.2.1.14 Origins of the European Doctrine

American Influences There can be little doubt that the founders of European integration were influenced by United States doctrine as it existed in the late 1940s and 1950s; the United States was instrumental in both the reconstruction of post-war Germany (including the establishment of the post-war legal order), and in the creation of the forerunner organizations to the EU, namely the European Coal and Steel Community (ECSC) and the European Economic Community (EEC). The United States Military Governor of Germany, John McCloy, was himself an antitrust lawyer, and the competition law provisions of the 1951 Treaty of Paris (establishing the ECSC) were drafted by Professor Robert Bowie, an American antitrust specialist recruited by McCloy for the task.[87] The provisions drafted by Bowie were then reworked in a more European language by French jurist Maurice Lagrange.[88] Thus,

---

[85] Alison Jones and Brenda Sufrin, *EU Competition Law* (5th ed., Oxford University Press 2014) 514–16.

[86] John Temple Lang, 'Defining Legitimate Competition: Companies' Duties to Supply Competitors and Access to Essential Facilities' (1994) 18 Fordham International Law Journal 437, 483; Barry Doherty, 'Just What Are Essential Facilities?' (2001) 38 Common Market Law Review 397, 435; Cyril Ritter, 'Refusal to Deal and "Essential Facilities": Does Intellectual Property Require Special Deference Compared to Tangible Property?' (2005) 28 World Competition 281, 282–5; Thomas Eilmansberger, 'The Essential Facilities Doctrine Under Art. 82: What Is the State of Affairs after IMS Health and Microsoft?' (2005) 16 King's Law Journal 329, 329; James Turney, 'Defining the Limits of the EU Essential Facilities Doctrine on Intellectual Property Rights: The Primacy of Securing Optimal Innovation' (2005) 3 Northwestern Journal of Technology and Intellectual Property 179, 186–8; Mercer H. Harz, 'Dominance and Duty in the European Union: A Look through Microsoft Windows at the Essential Facilities Doctrine Comment' (1997) 11 Emory International Law Review 189; Jacques Pelkmans, 'Making EU Network Markets Competitive' (2001) 17 Oxford Review of Economic Policy 432, 448–9; Sebastien J. Evrard, 'Essential Facilities in the European Union: Bronner and Beyond' (2004) 10 Columbia Journal of European Law 491, 505.

[87] Nicola Giocoli, 'Competition versus Property Rights: American Antitrust Law, the Freiburg School, and the Early Years of European Competition Policy' (2009) 5 Journal of Competition Law & Economics 747, 765–6.

[88] David J. Gerber, *Law and Competition in Twentieth Century Europe: Protecting Prometheus* (Oxford University Press 1998) 338–9.

US law and practice influenced the creation of pan-European competition rules.[89]

Ordoliberalism and the European Doctrine Yet undue weight should not be placed on these American influences, especially with regards to the unilateral disciplines, which have always been more reflective of European thought, including the influence of German ordoliberals.

Walter Eucken, an economics professor and perhaps the intellectual leader among the founding ordoliberals, perceived the economy is comprising two distinct orders: the transaction economy (*Verkehrswirtschaft*) and the centrally administered economy (*Zentralverwaltungswirtschaft*). The two orders were not merely commingled; the intrusion of one into the domain of the other would actually impair its functioning. For example, excessive governmental intervention in the economy would cause harm to the transaction economy.[90] Competition was essential to the functioning of the transaction economy, and the preferred form of competition was 'complete competition', namely competition in which no firm has market power[91] (akin to the notion of perfect competition in neoclassical economics).

Ordoliberalism is thus a doctrine grounded, in equal measure, in law, economics and political science. It does not, as with the Chicago School doctrine, set political concerns aside and focus exclusively on matters pertaining to the efficient allocation of resources. This, more than anything, may explain why the two schools of thought are to some degree irreconcilable. To a degree, the need for forceful action to curb monopolistic practices recommended by the ordoliberal thinkers reflects a hostility to market power itself – a view which aligns ordoliberalism in some ways with the American Harvard School.[92] Indeed, some early ordoliberal thinkers, such as Franz Böhm, considered that any agglomeration of monopoly power, howsoever obtained, should be addressed aggressively through legal measures, including the measure of divestiture.[93]

---

[89] Giocoli (n. 87) 766; Gerber (n. 88) 338–9.
[90] Gerber (n. 88) 244.
[91] Ibid. 244–5.
[92] But one difference between the two schools is that, whilst the Harvard School saw structure, conduct and performance as linked sequentially, ordoliberals perceive these elements as mutually interdependent, without causality proceeding in any particular direction. Peter Behrens, 'The Ordoliberal Concept of "Abuse" of a Dominant Position and Its Impact on Article 102 TFEU' in Fabiana di Porto and Rupprecht Podszun (eds.) (Edward Elgar 2018) 10–11.
[93] Giocoli (n. 87) 773–4.

Other ordoliberals (e.g. Leonhard Miksch) took a more 'regulatory' view of monopoly: firms with market power should be forced to behave as if they were subject to competition. Miksch developed his thinking based on a distinction already evident in German competition law, between 'performance competition', involving the supply of higher quality goods or services at lower prices, and 'impediment competition', involving predatory conduct aimed at inhibiting rivals.[94] Thus, monopolistic enterprises would be forced to behave as if they were in a competitive market, by strict constraints on 'impediment competition', that is, anticompetitive behaviour.

German ordoliberals exercised a profound influence, not merely on the establishment of German competition rules post–World War II, but also in the formation of European competition policy, rules and institutions.[95]

Ordoliberalism and the Unilateral Disciplines Unilateral disciplines were included in the 1951 Treaty of Paris,[96] which created the European Coal and Steel Community, and the 1957 Treaty of Rome,[97] which created the European Economic Community. The inclusion of strong competition law protections in the Treaty of Paris, and, subsequently, in the Treaty of Rome, was seen as essential to the core purposes of these treaties, namely the creation, development and preservation of the common market.[98]

Ordoliberal influence of the unilateral disciplines did not cease with the drafting of the Treaties of Paris and Rome, but rather informed conception of the disciplines as they were developed by the European Commission's DG Competition and the European Court of Justice.[99]

---

[94] Ibid. 774.

[95] Ibid. 776–80; Ian Rose and Cynthia Nqwe, 'The Ordoliberal Tradition in the European Union, Its Influence on Article 82 EC and the IBA's Comments on the Article 82 EC Discussion Paper Papers from the Chicago Conference' (2007) 3 Competition Law International 8, 8.

[96] Treaty between the Federal Republic of Germany, the Kingdom of Belgium, the French Republic, the Italian Republic, the Grand Duchy of Luxembourg and the Kingdom of the Netherlands instituting the European Coal and Steel Community 1951 (261 UNTS 140).

[97] Treaty Establishing the European Economic Community 1957 (4300 UNTS 11).

[98] Indeed, this remains a core purpose of the TFEU to this day; see Article 3(3). Behrens observes: 'This link of competition to integration is the specific European perspective that determined and still determines the interpretation of TFEU Article 102'. Behrens (n. 92) 10.

[99] Ibid. 7; Laurent Warlouzet, 'The EEC/EU as an Evolving Compromise between French Dirigism and German Ordoliberalism (1957–1995)' (2019) 57 JCMS: Journal of Common Market Studies 77, 82.

5.2 THE ESSENTIAL FACILITIES DOCTRINE

This influence was channelled through figures such as Ernst-Joachim Mestmäcker, described as 'a leading representative of the second generation of ordoliberals', who served as special advisor to DG Competition.[100]

Ordoliberal thought developed the view that a dominant firm should not be permitted to use its market power to foreclose the freedom of other economic operators to participate in the market, nor the freedom of consumers to choose the products of their choice.[101]

How Ordoliberal is TFEU Article 102? Recent scholarship has sought to re-examine the true extent of ordoliberal influence in European competition law. It has been pointed out, for example, that Article 102 TFEU does not reflect the ordoliberal ideal, since it attempts to regulate the behaviour of dominant firms, which pure ordoliberals would consider unachievable.[102] It has also been suggested that Article 102 reflects a compromise between the various European partners, and shows other influences, such as the regulatory approach to dominant firms present in many European competition laws.[103]

Beyond US influence, and the considerable influence of the ordoliberal movement, other sources of the European competition tradition must be acknowledged, in particular the 'administrative control' model found in many European countries during the 1920s. Such laws tended to permit intervention against monopolistic practices where they threatened the key interests of the economy or society at large. Provisions were often vague, and accorded to administrative officials a wide margin of discretion.[104]

Nevertheless, the influence of ordoliberalism cannot be dismissed; for example, as Larouche and Schinkel observe:

> Accordingly, even if Article 102 TFEU does not embody the model of direct intervention against market power advocated by ordo-liberals, the distinctive features identified above can nonetheless be traced back to ordo-liberal thought. Such is certainly the case for the focus on the

---

[100] Behrens (n. 92) 7–8.
[101] Ibid. 13.
[102] Pinar Akman, *The Concept of Abuse in European Competition Law: Law and Economic Approaches* (Hart Publishing 2012).
[103] Pierre Larouche and others, 'Continental Drift in the Treatment of Dominant Firms: Article 102 TFEU in Contrast to Section 2 Sherman Act' in *The Oxford Handbook of International Antitrust Economics*, vol. 2 (Oxford University Press 2014).
[104] Gerber (n. 88) 174.

protection of the competitive process, the insistence on competition on the merits and the special responsibility of the dominant firm.[105]

Ahlborn and Evans, for example, have characterized the European Commission's decision in the *Microsoft* case as ordoliberal in nature, pointing in particular to the clear distinction drawn between 'performance competition' and 'impediment competition', as well as the use of structural presumptions and an overall form-based approach.[106]

5.2.2 Development of the Essential Facilities Doctrine in European Cases

Having examined the intellectual foundations of the European essential facilities doctrine, it is instructive to examine how the doctrine has been developed through the cases, especially those adjudicated by the European Court of Justice. The *Bronner* decision represents a modern and authoritative articulation of the doctrine in instances where no intellectual property rights can be asserted. However, the origins of the European doctrine can be traced back to the *Commercial Solvents* decision of the early 1970s.

5.2.2.1 *Commercial Solvents* case

The first case to apply an essential facilities doctrine (in substance but not in name) in European law was *Commercial Solvents*.[107] In that case Commercial Solvents Corporation, a United States company, acquired a controlling stake in Istituto Chemioterapico Italiano SpA (Istituto), an Italian enterprise which resold within the European Economic Community ethambutanol, an intermediate chemical product used in the manufacture of pharmaceuticals, supplied by Commercial Solvents.

One of Istituto's customers was Laboratorio Chemico Farmaceutico Giorgia Zoja SpA (Zoja), another Italian enterprise. Zoja cancelled its contract with Istituto (because it had cheaper sources of supply available), but then subsequently sought further supplies, which Istituto was unable to provide because Commercial Solvents refused. Zoja, finding

---

[105] Larouche and others (n. 103).
[106] Christian Ahlborn and David S. Evans, 'The Microsoft Judgement and Its Implications for Competition Policy Towards Dominant Firms in Europe' (2008) 75 Antitrust Law Journal 887, 911–12.
[107] *Istituto Chemioterapico Italiano SpA and Commercial Solvents Corporation v. Commission of the European Communities (Cases 6 and 7/73)* [1974] ECR 00223 (European Court of Justice).

5.2 THE ESSENTIAL FACILITIES DOCTRINE

(after conducting a search on the world market) that there were no alternative sources of supply available, complained to the European Commission, which found Commercial Solvents and Instituto to have contravened Article 86 of the Treaty of Rome and required them to supply the relevant chemical products 'at a price not exceeding the maximum price charged for those two products', under penalty of significant fines, along with an additional fine concerning the initial refusal to supply.[108]

Istituto and CSC sought annulment of the Commission's decision before the European Court of Justice. The Court of Justice rejected the applications and upheld the Commission's decision. Having upheld the Commission's finding that Istituto and CSC held a dominant market position, the Court considered the core question of whether the refusal to supply could be characterized as an abuse; it stated (in a classic early articulation of the law):

> it follows that an undertaking which has a dominant position in the market in raw materials and which, with the object of reserving such raw material for manufacturing its own derivatives, refuses to supply a customer, which is itself a manufacturer of these derivatives, and therefore risks eliminating all competition on the part of this customer, is abusing its dominant position within the meaning of Article 86.[109]

The Court of Justice upheld the supply obligations which had been imposed by the Commission, although it reduced the fines imposed.[110]

Two aspects of this decision are to be noted. First, the requisite 'abuse' was satisfied on the basis of the removal of a single competitor from the market – note the breadth of the phrase 'eliminating all competition *on the part of the customer*' (emphasis added). Second, the Commission (and on review, the Court) neatly sidestepped the problem of supervising the supply of the solvents on an ongoing basis (a concern highlighted by Areeda and others in their criticisms of the American doctrine) by simply mandating supply at prices already charged in the marketplace.

5.2.2.2 *Sea Containers* v. *Stena Sealink*

The term 'essential facilities' does not appear much in EU jurisprudence (the term has never been applied by the Court of Justice), and

---

[108] Ibid. 227.
[109] Ibid. 251.
[110] Ibid. 255–7.

has primarily been applied in the context of access to infrastructure such as seaports.

In *Sea Containers* v. *Stena Sealink*,[111] Sea Containers had sought access to the port of Holyhead for the purpose of operating a fast ferry service between Wales and Ireland. Sealink owned and operated the Port of Holyhead. Negotiations between Sea Containers and Sealink proceeded very slowly; in the meantime, Sealink had begun operating its own fast ferry service on the Wales-Ireland route. Sea Containers complained to the Commission; in its 1993 decision, the Commission did apply the term:

> An undertaking which occupies a dominant position in the provision of an essential facility and itself uses that facility (i.e. a facility or infrastructure, without access to which competitors cannot provide services to their customers), and which refuses other companies access to that facility without objective justification or grants access to competitors only on terms less favourable than those which it gives its own services, infringes Article 86 if the other conditions of that Article are met ... The owner of an essential facility which uses its power in one market in order to protect or strengthen its position in another related market, in particular, by refusing to grant access to a competitor, or by granting access on less favourable terms than those of its own services, and thus imposing a competitive disadvantage on its competitor, infringes Article 86.[112]

This remains one of the few explicit references to the doctrine in European law. While it might be argued therefore that a European doctrine as such applies only to physical infrastructure such as ports, rail networks, electricity grids etc., this would seem an unduly semantic approach, given that the relevant principles applied in *Stena Sealink* do not seem materially different from those applied cases not involving physical infrastructure.

5.2.2.3 *Oscar Bronner GmbH & Co KG* v. *Mediaprint Zeitung*

In *Oscar Bronner*,[113] the Austrian Oberlandesgericht Wien (Vienna Higher Regional Court) made a reference to the European Court of Justice under Article 177 of the Treaty of Rome, seeking guidance as to whether conduct by Mediaprint (a large Austrian media enterprise)

---

[111] *Sea Containers v. Stena Sealink (Case IV34/689)* [1993] 1993 OJ L158 (European Commission).
[112] Ibid. 66.
[113] *Oscar Bronner GmbH & Co KG v. Mediaprint Zeitung (C-7/97)* [1998] ECR -07791 (European Court of Justice).

5.2 THE ESSENTIAL FACILITIES DOCTRINE

would give rise to an abuse of a dominant market position under Article 86 of the Treaty. Mediaprint's Neue Kronen Zeitung and Kurier newspapers together held a dominant market share in Austria's daily newspaper market. Mediaprint had established a national home delivery network to support its dominant position in the daily newspaper market.

Oscar Bronner was the publisher of the daily newspaper *Der Standard*, which held a relatively small market share. Oscar Bronner sought access to Mediaprint's home delivery network, but this was refused; it was noted that another Austrian daily newspaper (Wirtshaftsblatt) unaffiliated with Mediaprint had been given access to Mediaprint's delivery network, as part of a deal with Mediaprint that included all printing and distribution services. Wirtshaftsblatt was a daily financial newspaper; as such it was less likely than Der Standard to compete with Mediaprint's offerings but rather would likely have been seen by Mediaprint as complimentary to its existing offerings and therefore it would have been attractive for Wirtshaftsblatt to be made available to Mediaprint customers via Mediaprint's home delivery network.

The Court considered Mediaprint's refusal would not amount to an abuse of a dominant market position. In particular, it considered (in light of principles established in *Commercial Solvents*) that the refusal would be unlikely to eliminate all competition on the part of Oscar Bronner, since other distribution channels were available to Oscar Bronner, such as sale in shops or kiosks.[114] Moreover the Court did not perceive there to be any technical, legal or economic obstacles to Oscar Bronner establishing its own home distribution network;[115] and that it was untenable for Oscar Bronner to maintain the contrary merely on the grounds that its circulation was too small to support the establishment of such a distribution network.[116]

While the Court of Justice did cite to Commercial Solvents, its reference to the lack of economic impediments to Oscar Bronner developing its own network, and its dismissal of Oscar Bronner's reference to economies of scale, seemed to indicate a certain distancing by the Court from the Commercial Solvents decision, and a movement towards a more 'economic' approach.

Oscar Bronner is generally regarded as reflecting settled EU law in cases where no intellectual property rights are involved. It can be

---

[114] Ibid. I-7831.
[115] Ibid.
[116] Ibid. I-7832.

regarded as the intellectual and historical progenitor of the doctrine originated by Lord Hale. Much like the doctrine as practiced in pre-*Trinko* American law, the *Oscar Bronner* decision displays an understanding of applicable economic concepts (notably, those of natural monopoly and economies of scale), but without engaging in a systematic exegesis of the doctrine from firm economic foundations.

It is to be contrasted with the narrower articulation of the doctrine where intellectual property rights are affected, notably the principles expounded in the *Magill* and *IMS Health* cases. To complicate matters further, a number of the cases that do involve intellectual property rights also concern interoperability standards (both de facto, as in *IMS Health* and *Microsoft*, and formal standards, as in *Huawei* v. *ZTE*).

5.2.3 The Doctrine in the Context of Intellectual Property and Interoperability Standards

This section examines European and Chinese law on the interface between the doctrine and intellectual property rights.

5.2.3.1 The EU Essential Facilities Doctrine and Intellectual Property Rights

Under EU law, a refusal to supply an input protected by intellectual property rights could amount to an abuse of a dominant market position as could, in certain circumstances, a refusal to license an intellectual property right. At the outset, it is important to clarify that the legal test for the doctrine in the context of intellectual property is narrower than the legal test for the modern doctrine where no intellectual property right can be claimed, as represented by the *Bronner* test.

The orthodox position of EU law is reflected in two decisions of the Court of Justice, in *Magill* and *IMS Health*. The decisions of the European Commission and the European Court of First Instance in Microsoft departed from the settled *Magill/IMS Health* test, and implied a broader doctrine in the context of access to interoperability standards, including those protected by intellectual property rights.

One way to synthesize these somewhat conflicting decisions might be that the *Magill/IMS Health* test reflects relatively settled law (at least for refusals to license), but that where the undertaking complained against holds an exceptionally high degree of market power (such as Microsoft's 96 per cent market share for PC operating systems) and has manifestly relied on 'impediment competition' rather than 'performance

5.2 THE ESSENTIAL FACILITIES DOCTRINE

competition' to protect its market position, the ordoliberal principles underlying Article 102 will likely to lead the courts to a find an abuse, even where the *Magill/IMS Health* test cannot be satisfied.

Nevertheless, this view is somewhat speculative, and in the absence of further and definitive guidance from the European Court of Justice, a more straightforward reading of the state of the law is that it is unsettled, with multiple legal tests apparent, and that there is a need for reconciliation among the leading cases.

Magill **Case** The *Magill* case[117] arose from the refusal of three state broadcasters (Radio Telefís Eirann (RTE)), Independent Television Publications Ltd (ITP) and the British Broadcasting Corporation (BBC) to supply to Magill TV Guide Ltd (Magill) weekly television programme listings. RTE, ITP and BBC copyrighted their TV programme listings, and provided daily programme listings to certain newspapers free of charge and subject to licensing restrictions; they each published their own separate TV guides. Magill, an independent publisher, wished to publish a comprehensive weekly TV guide, a product that did not currently exist in the market and for which there was customer demand. RTE, ITP and the BBC prevented Magill from doing so by obtaining injunctions from the UK courts against Magill for infringement of copyright.[118]

The European Court of Justice affirmed the findings of the Commission and the Court of First Instance that RTE, ITP and BBC had engaged in abuse of a dominant market position. Having established the existence of a dominant market position, the Court observed that the refusal to supply fell within the exclusive rights conferred by the relevant copyrights, but that such refusal could nevertheless amount to an abuse in 'exceptional circumstances'. Without seeking to define exhaustively what those exceptional circumstances might be, the Court found such refusal to be abusive on two grounds: (i) RTE, ITP and the BBC had sought to prevent the emergence of a new consumer product, a weekly comprehensive television programme guide, which was currently not available on the market and for which there was demonstrated customer demand; and (ii) RTE, ITP and the BBC had attempted to reserve for themselves the market for weekly TV guides (whether comprehensive or

---

[117] *Radio Telefís Eirann (RTE) and Independent Television Publications (ITP) v. Commission of the European Communities (C-241/91 and C-242/91 P)* [1995] ECR -00743 (European Court of Justice).
[118] Ibid. I-812.

not) by excluding Magill from the market. The conduct was unjustified either by the needs of the broadcasting sector, or the particular activity of publishing television magazines.[119]

IMS Health GMBH & Co. and NDC Health GMBH & Co *IMS Health GMBH & Co. and NDC Health GMBH & Co*[120] is a notable refusal to license case; the facts have been described in Chapter 4. In that case, the Landgericht Frankfurt am Main (Frankfurt Regional Court) decided to seek a preliminary ruling from the European Court of Justice concerning whether IMS Health's enforcement of its intellectual property rights amounted to the abuse of a dominant market position.

The relevant statement of the applicable law was provided by the ECJ:

> It is clear from that case-law that, in order for the refusal by an undertaking which owns a copyright to give access to a product or service indispensable for carrying on a particular business to be treated as abusive, it is sufficient that three cumulative conditions be satisfied, namely, that that refusal is preventing the emergence of a new product for which there is a potential consumer demand, that it is unjustified and such as to exclude any competition on a secondary market.[121]

Regarding the first factor, the so-called 'new product' test, the ECJ stated:

> Therefore, the refusal by an undertaking in a dominant position to allow access to a product protected by an intellectual property right, where that product is indispensable for operating on a secondary market, may be regarded as abusive only where the undertaking which requested the licence does not intend to limit itself essentially to duplicating the goods or services already offered on the secondary market by the owner of the intellectual property right, but intends to produce new goods or services not offered by the owner of the right and for which there is a potential consumer demand.[122]

Regarding the second factor, the existence of objective justification, the ECJ did not offer an opinion, as it was unable to do so on the facts provided by the Landgericht.[123]

---

[119] *Radio Telefis Eirann v. Commission of the European Communities* [1991] European Court of First Instance T-69/89, II–00485 ECR II–521; *Radio Telefis Eirann (RTE) and Independent Television Publications (ITP) v. Commission of the European Communities* (C-241/91 and C-242/91 P) (n. 117) I–824.

[120] *IMS Health GMBH & Co and NDC Health GMBH & Co (Case C-418-01)* [2004] ECR-05039 (European Court of Justice).

[121] Ibid. I–5082.

[122] Ibid. I–5085.

[123] Ibid.

5.2 THE ESSENTIAL FACILITIES DOCTRINE

Concerning the third of these three cumulative elements, namely the question of the exclusion of all competition on a secondary market, the ECJ considered that the crucial question was whether the 'brick structure' constitutes an indispensable factor in the supply of German regional sales data for pharmaceutical products. The ECJ, however, reserved it to the national court to determine whether, in fact, IMS's refusal was likely to exclude all competition in this market.[124]

Although the Court was limited by the terms of the preliminary reference from the Landgericht and did not comprehensively apply the legal test it had articulated to the facts of the case, its decision provides confirmation of the doctrine are expounded in *Magill*, with some additional detail provided, including a careful restatement of the requirements of the so-called 'new product' test.

Microsoft Corporation v. Commission of the European Communities In the *Microsoft* case,[125] Microsoft was found to have twice abused a dominant market position, by: (i) refusing to supply full interoperability information to Sun Microsystems for purposes of ensuring interoperability between personal computers running Microsoft's Windows client PC operating system and servers running Sun's Solaris server operating system ('client-server interoperability') and between servers running Microsoft's Windows server operating system and Sun's Solaris ('server-server interoperability'); and (ii) making the availability of the Windows client PC operating system conditional on the simultaneous acquisition of the Windows Media Player software.

The Commission's case regarding 'interoperability information' was essentially that Microsoft withheld from its competitors in the server operating systems market interface information indispensable for competing server operating systems to interoperate and operate seamlessly with personal computers running Windows. The focus of Sun's request was a 'reference implementation' that would enable Sun servers interoperating with Windows PCs to execute group and user administration and file and print services.

The case revealed the ability of Microsoft, as the dominant supplier of PC operating system software, to disclose varying levels of interoperability information to its customers, application software developers and

---

[124] Ibid. I–5084.
[125] *Microsoft (Case COMP/C-3/37/792 – Microsoft)* (European Commission); *Microsoft v. Commission of the European Communities (Case T-201/04)* [2007] 2007 ECR II-03601 (European Court of First Instance).

server operating system software competitors. The APIs shared with applications developers were insufficient for purposes of enabling full server-server and client-server interoperability. Thus, Microsoft had developed a de facto interoperability standard, the Windows suite, while keeping certain of its interfaces secret. Microsoft's dominance arose from indirect network effects.[126] The popularity of an operating system depends on the availability of application programs to run 'on top of' the operating system. More popular operating systems have more applications written for them.[127]

Once a particular operating system has become the established 'platform' in the market, the Commission found that it would be very difficult for rival platform operators to enter the market because they would need to either: (i) attract a large number of applications developers to write to their proposed alternative platform; or (ii) replicate the interfaces of the existing platform, for example by reverse-engineering the object code presented by the dominant platform.[128] In the *Microsoft* case, neither of these options was considered commercially feasible. Both had been tried by IBM during its unsuccessful attempt to promote its OS/2 operating system as a competitor to Microsoft windows.[129] The latter was attempted by Sun Microsystems but abandoned when the cost and time-consuming nature of such a reverse engineering exercise became apparent.[130]

Legal Tests Both the Commission and, on review, the European Court of First Instance, acknowledged that the Court of Justice's decision in *Magill* reflected settled law concerning refusals to supply in the context of intellectual property rights.[131] Nevertheless, in applying this allegedly settled test to the facts, both the Commission and the Court of First Instance departed from the *Magill* test in two key respects: first, they relaxed the requirement for the refusal to exclude all competition, instead requiring only the exclusion of all effective competition; and second, they relaxed the third factor (the so-called 'new product' test), requiring only that the refusal have a limiting effect on technical development. The

---

[126] *Microsoft (Case COMP/C-3/37/792 – Microsoft)* (n. 125) para. 450.
[127] Ibid. 449.
[128] Ibid. 449–59.
[129] Ibid. 457.
[130] Ibid. 455.
[131] Ibid. 551; *Microsoft v. Commission of the European Communities (Case T-201/04)* (n. 125) II–3726.

Commission and the Court of First Instance also carefully examined, and rejected, Microsoft's proffered justifications for its refusal to supply the interoperability information. This aspect of EU law was given much less detailed treatment in *Magill* and *IMS Health*. As such, this element of the doctrine is particularly open to conjecture under current EU law.

Exclusion of Effective Competition in a Neighbouring Market The Commission held that Microsoft's refusal to supply the interoperability information risked eliminating competition from the workgroup server operating system market owing to the indispensability of that information to competition in the market. The Commission noted in particular the rapid decline in market share of Microsoft's key competitors, and concluded that this trend (which was likely to continue) was driven fundamentally by Microsoft's unwillingness to make available to requisite interoperability information to these competitors.[132] There was extensive debate before the Court of First Instance as to whether all competition must be eliminated, or whether abuse may occur where the refusal results in the elimination of all effective competition.[133] The Court of First Instance considered that the latter test is sufficient to ground an abuse:

> Nor is it necessary to demonstrate that all competition on the market would be eliminated. What matters, for the purpose of establishing an infringement of Article 82 EC, is that the refusal at issue is liable to, or is likely to, eliminate all effective competition on the market. It must be made clear that the fact that the competitors of the dominant undertaking retain a marginal presence in certain niches on the market cannot suffice to substantiate the existence of such competition.[134]

On this basis, the Court of First Instance agreed with the Commission that the requisite risk of elimination had been established, notwithstanding the potential for competitors such as Novell and Linux to maintain marginal positions in the workgroup server operating systems market.[135]

Emergence of a New Product for Which There Is Potential Consumer Demand Regarding the likely impact of Microsoft's refusal on technical development, the Commission observed that Microsoft's customers were increasingly locked into homogenous, Windows-only solutions, which

---
[132] *Microsoft (Case COMP/C-3/37/792 – Microsoft)* (n. 125) paras 585–692.
[133] *Microsoft v. Commission of the European Communities (Case T-201/04)* (n. 125) II–3793.
[134] Ibid. II–3794.
[135] Ibid. II–3803.

effectively denied them access to innovative features that could potentially be supplied by Microsoft's competitors.[136] The Commission further opined that:

> If Microsoft's competitors had access to the interoperability information that Microsoft refuses to supply, they could use the disclosures to make the advanced features of their own products available in the framework of the web of interoperability relationships that underpin the Windows domain architecture.[137]

The Commission seemed to accept that Microsoft's competitors were not necessarily seeking to supply 'new products' as such (in the same way that Magill proposed to supply a weekly comprehensive television guide, which was not currently being supplied); rather, they were seeking to supply much the same product, albeit with 'advanced features' not present in the case of Microsoft's products. The Court of First Instance upheld the approach of the Commission, observing:

> The circumstance relating to the appearance of a new product, as envisaged in *Magill* and *IMS Health*, cited in paragraph 107 above, cannot be the only parameter which determines whether a refusal to license an intellectual property right is capable of causing prejudice to consumers within the meaning of Article 82(b) EC. As that provision states, such prejudice may arise where there is a limitation not only of production or markets, but also of technical development.[138]

The Court of First Instance noted in particular that, if they had access to the interoperability information, Microsoft's competitors would be in a position to differentiate their products in aspects other than interface specifications.[139]

Objective Justifications Proffered by Microsoft for its Refusal to Supply Microsoft sought to justify its refusal to supply the interoperability information to Sun inter alia on the basis that the relevant interface specifications were innovative and protected by intellectual property rights, and that requiring Microsoft to share this information to its competitors would diminish its incentives to innovate.[140] The

---

[136] *Microsoft (Case COMP/C-3/37/792 – Microsoft)* (n. 125) para. 694.
[137] Ibid. 700.
[138] *Microsoft v. Commission of the European Communities (Case T-201/04)* (n. 125) II-3818.
[139] Ibid. II-3821.
[140] *Microsoft (Case COMP/C-3/37/792 – Microsoft)* (n. 125) para. 709.

5.2 THE ESSENTIAL FACILITIES DOCTRINE

Commission rejected these arguments through the application of a 'balancing test':

> a detailed examination of the scope of the disclosure at stake leads to the conclusion that, on balance, the possible negative impact of an order to supply on Microsoft's incentives to innovate is outweighed by its positive impact on the level of innovation of the whole industry (including Microsoft).[141]

The Commission found that 'it is dubious whether an order to supply would have any negative impact on Microsoft's incentives to innovate'.[142] The Commission also observed that Microsoft had already disclosed significant interoperability information to its competitors, without any apparent negative impact on its incentives to innovate,[143] and that Microsoft's incentives to innovate would be stronger if its competitors survived in the market.[144] Before the European Court of First Instance, Microsoft argued that the Commission had erred by applying a 'balancing test'.[145] Unhelpfully, the Court of First Instance responded by denying that the Commission had applied a balancing test,[146] before simply affirming the reasoning of the Commission, and dismissing Microsoft's arguments on this point without further elaboration.[147]

Microsoft – Concluding Observations   Microsoft thus appears to depart from *Magill* and *IMS Health* in three crucial respects: first, not all competition needs to be eliminated from the downstream market, provided that any remaining competitors are confined to niche positions; second, there is no need to establish the suppression of a new product as such, merely that a mandatory supply obligation would stimulate dynamic efficiency, for example by encouraging product differentiation; and third, that a defendant's proffered efficiency rationale can be dismissed by reference to a 'balancing test' that weighs the potential benefits of forced sharing to competitors, in the form of increased innovation and competition, with the detriment to the monopolists' (or near-monopolists) own incentives for innovation.

---

[141] Ibid. 783.
[142] Ibid. 729.
[143] Ibid. 728.
[144] Ibid. 725.
[145] *Microsoft v. Commission of the European Communities (Case T-201/04)* (n. 125) II–3825.
[146] Ibid. II–3836.
[147] Ibid. II-3836-II-3837.

The third is perhaps of most concern, since it appears to be based on an improper comparison between the incentives of the monopoly on the one hand and the incentives of the entire market on the other. Were such a balancing test to be applied, it should weigh the negative impacts to dynamic efficiency for the market as a whole with the positive impacts on dynamic efficiency for the market as a whole. Of course, even such a construct would be open to the criticism of the Neo-Chicago theorists that courts, lacking perfect information and prone to errors, are poorly placed to undertake such a balancing exercise. Time will tell whether *Microsoft* represents a new direction in European law, or whether it will be confined to its unique facts, notably the super-dominance of Microsoft in the vital market for personal computer operating software.

5.2.3.2 The Doctrine under Chinese Law

Article 6 of China's Anti-Monopoly Law provides that any business with a dominant position may not abuse that dominant position to eliminate or restrict competition. Article 55 of the AML provides clarifies the interrelation between the AML and intellectual property rights:

> This Law does not govern the conduct of business operators to exercise their intellectual property rights under laws and relevant administrative regulations on intellectual property rights; however, business operators' conduct to eliminate or restrict market competition by abusing their intellectual property rights shall be governed by this Law.

A number of observations can be made about these provisions of the AML. First, no reference is made to an essential facilities doctrine. Earlier drafts of the AML did include such a specific reference, which was deleted in subsequent drafts.[148] Nevertheless the drafting of Article 17 is very similar to Article 102 of the EU's TFEU, and quite clearly embraces an abuse of a dominant market position discipline. Furthermore Article 17(3), by its clear terms, addresses refusals to supply, and moreover incorporates a defence of 'justifiable cause'.

Article 17(1) provides for the somewhat controversial discipline of excessive pricing. Article 55 seeks to mediate the relationship between competition law provisions and intellectual property. In the specific context of unilateral disciplines such as refusal to supply, Article 55 can be expected to give rise to interpretations quite similar to the EU concept

---

[148] Yong Huang, Elizabeth Xiao-Ru Wang and Roger Xin Zhang, 'Essential Facilities Doctrine and Its Application in Intellectual Property Space under China's Anti-Monopoly Law' (2015) 22 George Mason Law Review 1103, 1124.

of abuse in 'exceptional circumstances'. Furthermore, while explicit reference to the essential facilities doctrine was omitted from the provisions of the AML itself, the doctrine has been referenced in drafts of the Anti-Monopoly Law Antitrust-IP Guidelines issued by the State Administration for Industry and Commerce (SAIC).[149]

More recently, China's Ministry of Commerce (MOFCOM) published a document entitled, 'Anti-Monopoly Guidelines on the Abuse of Intellectual Property Rights (Draft for Comments)'. This document includes a chapter on abuse of dominance involving intellectual property rights, which spells out in some detail how Chinese authorities propose to address Article 17 in the context of intellectual property rights. These Guidelines include explicit reference to an essential facilities doctrine with respect to intellectual property rights.[150]

The *Qualcomm* case provides additional guidance as to how Chinese authorities would likely approach such questions. China's NDRC investigated Qualcomm's licensing practices and concluded on 10 February 2015 that Qualcomm had contravened the AML. The NDRC considered that each of Qualcomm's SEPs effectively gave rise to a dominant market position.[151] Qualcomm was found to have abused its dominant market position by charging unfairly high patent royalties, tying licences of SEPs to non-SEPs, and imposing unfair licensing terms.[152] Qualcomm agreed to pay a fine of $975 million (which amounted to 8 per cent of its China revenue for the year 2013)[153] and to adjust its royalty rates charged to licensees in China. The *Qualcomm* case did not invoke the essential facilities doctrine by name; nevertheless, it has given rise to controversy in particular because of its apparent reliance on notions of unfair or excessive pricing.

5.2.4 Application of the Doctrine to Interoperability Standards and Standards-Essential Intellectual Property

In the United States the doctrine is no longer recognized as law, and moreover has never been applied by name by the Supreme Court (nor

---

[149] Ibid. 1104.
[150] Koren W. Wong-Ervin, 'An Update on the Most Recent Version of China's Anti-Monopoly Guidelines on the Abuse of Intellectual Property Rights' [2017] Competition Policy International 1.
[151] Jianmin Dai, Zhisong Deng and Song K. Jung, 'Antitrust Enforcement against Standard Essential Patents in China' (2017) 62 The Antitrust Bulletin 453, 456.
[152] Ibid.
[153] Ibid.

mentioned in any statute), including in leading cases such as *Terminal Railroad*, *Associated Press* and *Otter Tail*. Similarly, in the EU, the doctrine is not named in the TFEU or another relevant Community law, nor has it been applied by name in the jurisprudence of the European Court of Justice. Likewise, in China, the doctrine is not named in the AML, and has not (yet) been applied by name by the Supreme People's Court; it presents in a number of official policy guidelines and a small number of cases. Accordingly, delineating the doctrine with precision and distilling common principles across jurisdictions is a fraught exercise.

Nevertheless, there would appear to be strong similarities between the doctrine applied by the US lower courts in its 'mature' phase (e.g. *MCI Communications*) and the existing state of EU law concerning refusals to supply, as encapsulated in *Bronner*, *Microsoft* and *IMS Health/Magill*; the Chinese doctrine, however, appears to be of a more vigorous nature, more like a doctrine of excessive pricing, and may benefit from further explanation of its underlying principles.

Taking the dicta of the leading pre-*Trinko* US case, *MCI Communications*, as our starting point, the doctrine involves application of the following four-part test: (i) control of the essential facility by a monopolist; (ii) a competitor's inability practically or reasonably to duplicate the essential facility; (iii) the denial of the use the facility to a competitor; and (iv) the feasibility of providing the facility to a competitor.

In the EU, an essential facilities doctrine can be conceived under the rubric of a number of legal tests, including the *Bronner* test (applicable to sharing across the economy generally), the *IMS Health/Magill* test (for refusals to license intellectual property rights),[154] the *Microsoft* test (a more expansive version of the *IMS Health/Magill* test) and perhaps a further test, as articulated in *Huawei* v. *ZTE*, for refusals to licence FRAND-encumbered SEPs.

Taking cognizance also of the present position in Chinese law, it is apparent that there are entrenched differences among the leading jurisdictions as to the advisability of having an essential facilities doctrine at all, much less applying it in the context of intellectual property rights. Under a strict approach much influenced by law and economics, and in particular by the single monopoly profit theorem propounded by the

---

[154] The *Commercial Solvents*, *Microsoft* and *Huawei v. ZTE* cases could perhaps supply a third, fourth and even a fifth formulation for an EU doctrine.

Chicago School, American law has abolished the doctrine and is unlikely to revive it. European law, guided by a blend of German ordoliberalism and the French regulatory tradition, is disposed to apply the doctrine, including to protect individual competitors (see *Commercial Solvents* and indeed *Bronner*) and even where intellectual property rights may be asserted.

These differences in the law would seem to reflect deeper disagreement about the principles underlying the unilateral disciplines – in particular whether economic efficiency should be the sole consideration or whether broader concerns (e.g. political considerations such as the preservation of democratic institutions, distributive justice, or perhaps industry policy) should also be addressed through competition laws. Disagreement at the level of principle makes these differences especially intractable.

5.2.5 The Law and Economics of the Essential Facilities Doctrine

In addition to the problem of entrenched inter-jurisdictional differences noted above, it is also worth considering whether a sound basis in public policy for mandating an essential facilities doctrine at the international level can be established. A law and economic approach to competition law proceeds on the basis that economic theory provides a basis for competition law, and further that extensions of competition law can only be justified by reference to economic theory. Thus, the sole purpose of (and justification for) competition law should be to promote economic efficiency.[155]

5.2.5.1 Standards-Essential Intellectual Property as an Essential Facility

An initial issue is whether an intellectual property right (e.g. a patent), the practice of which is necessary in order to obtain access to an essential facility, can in itself be considered an essential facility, or whether access to SEIP should properly be characterized merely as an aspect of the larger question of access to the facility itself, that is, the physical or information infrastructure to which access is sought.

It should be questioned whether it is really helpful to characterize an intellectual property right – even one that is standards-essential – as an 'essential facility'. An intellectual property right is, in essence, a bundle of legal rights and entitlements awarded to the innovator by the competent

---

[155] Richard A. Posner, *Antitrust Law* (2nd ed., University of Chicago Press 2001), 2.

authorities. To consider a *chose en action* such as a patent or copyright as an 'essential facility' akin to a rail network or electricity grid is to draw a long bow indeed. This goes beyond 'information infrastructure' to a notion of 'legal infrastructure'.

Such an approach moreover invites questions regarding the role of the competent authorities in the creation of such essential facilities, and leads directly to the situation where the holder of the *chose en action* could abuse its dominant market position merely by asking the courts to enforce the rights granted by the competent authorities, for example by the patent office. The more methodologically sound approach would seem to be that it is the interoperability standard (and perhaps in some instances its technological subcomponents), rather than the SEIP, which should be characterized as the essential facility. But even on this approach, the desirability of forcible licensing as a matter of law and economics should be considered squarely.

5.2.5.2 Monopoly and Consumer Welfare

The principles of competition law are based on a static neoclassical approach to evaluating the economic costs associated with monopoly. Under the classic analysis, a monopoly is thought to raise its price and reduce its output until its marginal cost is equal to marginal revenue. Since the monopoly's demand curve is also the market's demand curve, this results in a lower level of output and a higher price that would hold in the competitive equilibrium. In addition to a transfer of surplus from consumers to producers, this also results in a deadweight loss. This deadweight loss arises because consumers substitute to other goods (or simply do not purchase), even those goods may be more costly to produce, because the monopoly good has now become more expensive.[156] Thus, from a static efficiency perspective, the presence of monopoly generally results in a welfare loss.

5.2.5.3 Law and Economics Objections to Limitations on an Enterprise's Right to Refuse Supply

As outlined above, the essential facilities doctrine has been severely criticized in law and economics literature. Whilst these criticisms are somewhat heterogeneous in nature, a number of key objections to the doctrine have emerged (which will necessarily extend to the cognate doctrine of monopoly leveraging): (i) dominant firms have adequate

---

[156] See Jean Tirole, *The Theory of Industrial Organization* (MIT Press, 1988), 66–8.

incentives to supply in the absence of any mandated duty to supply; (ii) a mandatory duty to supply could have negative impacts on dynamic efficiency; (iii) account needs to be taken of the potential for harm to consumers; and (iv) courts are poorly placed to supervise mandatory access on an ongoing basis, both in terms of price- and non-price terms of supply.

In the specific context of a mandatory duty to license an intellectual property right, a fifth concern may be added: since the very reason for granting the right is to promote innovation, mandating a duty to license is likely to raise pervasive concerns of detrimental impacts on dynamic efficiency. The so-called 'Neo Chicago' school has raised the further criticism that courts have imperfect information and are prone to error; as such they should not be tasked with important resource allocation decisions.

5.2.5.4 Incentives to Supply: Chicago and Post-Chicago Schools

The Chicago School criticized the so-called inhospitability tradition developed by the Harvard School towards unilateral refusals to supply. The Chicago School lawyers and economists applied static neoclassical price theory to demonstrate that even a monopolist would have no incentive to leverage his monopoly into a vertically adjacent market, and that such refusals would generally be justified on efficiency grounds.

The 'fixed-sum' or 'chain link' theory of monopoly posited that a firm holding a monopoly at one vertical layer (where there is effective competition at other layers) would be able to extract the full monopoly profit already. Therefore, the firm would not benefit from leveraging its monopoly power into a vertically adjacent layer. Indeed, any attempt to raise the price at the adjacent layer would reduce the returns to the monopoly, since the final price would thereby increase above the efficient monopoly level.[157]

Chicago theorists further considered that vertical refusals to supply could likely be justified on economic efficiency grounds, for example monopolizing a downstream market would permit rationing in order to achieve efficient price discrimination.[158] The essential principles of the single monopoly profit theorem remain generally accepted.

---

[157] The efficient monopoly price is at the intersection of the Marginal Revenue and Marginal Cost curves. Any increase above the efficient monopoly price will decrease demand and also decrease the revenue earned by the monopolist.

[158] Ward S. Bowman, 'Tying Arrangements and the Leverage Problem' (1957) 67 Yale Law Journal 19.

Post-Chicago scholars accepted many of the basic premises of the Chicago School, including that: economic reasoning should be the sole basis for imposing antitrust liability; and that single firm conduct should only be condemned where it resulted in efficiency losses. However, the post-Chicago theorists found a number of problems with the single monopoly profit theorem. In particular, they found instances where monopoly leveraging would be both attractive to the monopolist, and detrimental to overall welfare.

Whinston found two such instances in which tying would be profitable: first, where there exists a second, inferior substitute for the tying product; and second, where the tied product has alternative uses, such that not all consumers would wish to purchase a bundle of the tied and the tying product (e.g. a replacement parts market). Whinston noted, however, that the welfare implications of these extensions were uncertain, and as such, crafting an appropriate legal rule would be difficult.[159] Similarly, Carlton and Waldman showed that a monopolist would have an incentive to leverage in order to protect the tying market from competition. Again, these authors noted that the welfare effects of their work were unclear.[160]

Thus, although the post-Chicago scholarship has cast doubt on the ubiquitous application of the single monopoly profit theorem, it has not conclusively shown that intervention to address conduct such as tying or refusal to supply would enhance welfare. Some authors have expressed support for an essential facilities doctrine that incorporates a rule of reason type analysis.[161] However it is not clear precisely what kind of analysis the courts should pursue under such a rule. The types of information relied on by the post-Chicago models would not be easy for courts to obtain.

5.2.5.5 Potential to Inhibit Economically Efficient Investment in New Facilities

Since monopoly is generally understood to give rise to a static efficiency loss, any mandatory duty to supply could engender ex post, static efficiency gains by obtaining the supply of goods or services at lower cost to

---

[159] Michael D. Whinston, 'Tying, Foreclosure, and Exclusion' (1990) 80 The American Economic Review 837.

[160] Dennis W. Carlton and Michael Waldman, 'The Strategic Use of Tying to Preserve and Create Market Power in Evolving Industries' (2002) 33 The RAND Journal of Economics 194.

[161] Troy (n. 31).

5.2 THE ESSENTIAL FACILITIES DOCTRINE

consumers. Nevertheless, it is important also to take account of potential ex ante dynamic efficiency losses. A mandatory duty is likely to reduce the expected returns from an investment. As such, there is a very real risk of negative incentives to new investments, since it will be understood that any new investments will need to be shared with competitors.[162]

For any unilateral refusal to supply law to be welfare-enhancing, supply should only be mandated where it is likely to encourage more investment than it discourages. Some economists have proposed a case by case balancing exercise: for example, Kaplow suggested that courts should balance the reward to a patentee against the monopoly loss accruing from exploitation of the patent.[163] Such a 'balancing exercise' will, however, be very difficult for courts to undertake.[164] For this reason a per se legality approach may be preferable, even where intellectual property rights are not concerned, with any mandatory duty to supply limited to regulated utilities through the operation of statute.[165]

5.2.5.6 Need to Establish Harm to Consumers

One important criticism of any rules mandating supply or licensing is that there needs to be a clear identification of likely harm to consumers.[166] If competitors are harmed but consumers do not suffer, it is unclear how the conduct will diminish economic efficiency. Most of the cases in which the essential facilities doctrine has been invoked involved inputs into the production of final consumer goods or services – for example interoperability information, an input into server software, itself an input into the production of end-products and services to consumers. Or rail terminal services, an input into freight services, itself an input into the shipment of end-consumer products. To establish a case for mandatory access, one of the prerequisites is likely to be a showing that end-consumers will suffer detriments in the form of higher prices,

---

[162] William J. Baumol, *Free Market Innovation Machine* (Princeton University Press 2002) 121; Gerardin (n. 84) 1549; Einer Elhauge, 'Defining Better Monopolization Standards' (2003) 56 Stanford Law Review 253, 300–5.
[163] Louis Kaplow, 'The Patent-Antitrust Intersection: A Reappraisal' (1984) 97 Harvard Law Review 1813, 1816.
[164] George A. Hay, 'A Monopolist's "Duty to Deal": The Briar Patch Revisited' (2002) 3 Sedona Conference Journal 1, 5; Elhauge (n. 162) 301.
[165] Hay (n. 164) 7; Richard A. Posner, *Antitrust Law* (2nd ed., University of Chicago Press 2001) 243–4; Herbert Hovenkamp, *The Antitrust Enterprise* (Harvard University Press 2005) 270.
[166] Francois Leveque, 'Innovation, Leveraging and Essential Facilities: Interoperability Licensing in the EU Microsoft Case' (2005) 28 World Competition 71, 76.

diminished quality, less choice or value, diminished levels of aftersales service, etc. If this cannot be shown, mandatory supply obligations may simply protect intermediaries whose presence in the market is not essential for consumer welfare.

5.2.5.7 Ability of Courts to Supervise Mandatory Supply

Concerns have been raised about the ability of the courts to supervise the terms of mandatory supply.[167] Whilst some of the United States essential facilities cases did involve regulated industries where supply could be supervised by a regulatory agency, others went beyond these confines.[168] Where there has been a disruption of previous terms of supply, one possibility would be to mandate supply at the previous terms – as was done by the European Court of Justice in *Commercial Solvents*. Nevertheless, this is likely to give rise to unmanageable difficulties where such terms of supply are complex and need to be updated frequently. In any case, it cannot be assumed, absent careful analysis, that the existing terms of supply represent an economically efficient outcome. Another option, explored in the EU *Microsoft* case, would be to establish an independent, expert monitoring authority to supervise mandatory access – but this would seem to push a competition law remedy towards public utilities regulation.

5.2.5.8 The Special Situation of Intellectual Property Rights: Dynamic Efficiency Considerations

The protection of intellectual property is primarily justified on the basis that the creator of the work or invention should be given a limited monopoly in order to commercially exploit the work or invention. As such, any competition law offence dealing with refusal to license an intellectual property right needs to take particular account of dynamic efficiency considerations.[169] Thinking about this question systematically, it seems that the considerations are essentially the same for intellectual property as for other refusals to supply:[170] the concern surrounding disincentives to investment will equally arise regardless of whether or

---

[167] Werden (n. 31) 472; Posner (n. 165) 257; Hovenkamp (n. 165) 270; Lipsky and Sidak (n. 35) 1223.
[168] Werden (n. 31) 460.
[169] Gerardin (n. 84) 1541.
[170] Richard J. Gilbert and Carl Shapiro, 'An Economic Analysis of Unilateral Refusals to Licence Intellectual Property' (1996) 93 Proceedings of the National Academy of Sciences of the United States of America 12749, 12750; Ritter (n. 86).

not there would be a compulsory licence issued. Not all innovations are protected by intellectual property rights.

A compulsory licence may have positive effects on static efficiency (by making available goods and services to consumers at lower prices), but negative effects on dynamic efficiency.[171] These negative effects on dynamic efficiency, as with other forms of property, arise in the form of reduced incentives for investments in innovative products or services. Importantly, both market incumbents and other future, prospective entrants could be affected by reduced incentives for efficient investment arising from the imposition of open access obligations. Forced sharing could have other impacts: it could reduce efficiency even in the short run, by encouraging inefficient licensing.[172] It could also have positive impacts on dynamic efficiency if it stimulates the production of innovative new goods and services that rely on the intellectual property in question.

Ideally, a court or regulator would have the capability to measure the size of each of these possible effects, and then decide whether forcible sharing would, in sum, encourage or discourage dynamic efficiency. However, keeping in mind the imperfect information held by courts, and the attendant risk of regulatory error, such an approach is unlikely to be practicable.[173] As Leveque puts it:

> competition authorities are not well equipped to regulate innovation. They lack the scientific and technical expertise.[174]

The various approaches adopted by European courts and by the European Commission have been criticized on the basis of law and economics. Leveque, for example, criticized the new product test in *Magill* and *IMS Health*, pointing out that it is unlikely to provide a useful proxy for estimating harm to consumers.[175] A further problem is how precisely to define a new product.[176]

The approach of the Commission in *Microsoft* has been subjected to particular criticism.[177] Leveque, for example, criticized the Commission

---

[171] Christian Ahlborn, David S. Evans and A. Jorge Padilla, 'The Logic & Limits of the Exceptional Circumstances Test in Magill and IMS Health' (2004) 28 Fordham International Law Journal 1109, 1130-6; Hay (n. 164) 3-6.
[172] Gilbert and Shapiro (n. 170) 12753.
[173] Gerardin (n. 84) 1542.
[174] Leveque (n. 166) 80.
[175] Ibid. 76.
[176] Gerardin (n. 84) 1531.
[177] Leveque (n. 166) 78-80.

for assuming that Microsoft would have greater incentives to innovate in a competitive market, even though economic theory has not established conclusively whether monopolies or competitive firms have greater incentives to innovate. Leveque also pointed out that the Commission failed to acknowledge that Microsoft's incentives to innovate with respect to interoperability information would diminish if it could no longer make exclusive use of the information.[178]

On one view, the narrower *IMS Health/Magill* test provides an appropriate set of 'screens',[179] which courts can use to identify the conduct which will most likely cause harm to competition without impacting negatively on incentives for innovation. For example, Ahlborn, Evans and Padilla support the 'exceptional circumstances' test as applied by the European Court of Justice in *Magill* and *IMS Health* (however they express concerns about the test applied by the Commission in *Microsoft*). These authors consider that the 'exceptional circumstances' test, which is limited to situations of very high market power, foreclosure and the prevention of new consumer products, can be successful in identifying those situations where the combined dynamic and static efficiency gains from forced sharing outweigh the attendant dynamic efficiency losses.[180]

However, it is unclear that even such a narrowly crafted essential facilities doctrine would unambiguously promote economic efficiency. Forced sharing could have significantly negative impacts on incentives for innovation (of both the monopoly and other firms in the industry).

The concept of the 'new product' is moreover inherently indeterminate, and it cannot be assumed in advance that every product deemed 'new' (e.g. a weekly television guide) will lead to large increases in dynamic efficiency. The price of access will also be important: if it is set too low it will not only discourage future innovative activities but also encourage inefficient production.[181] Furthermore, the courts will likely be drawn into an ongoing supervisory role that is beyond their capacities, in terms of both time and expertise.

Finally, the question of whether a monopolistic or a competitive market structure will optimize the speed of innovation will depend on

---

[178] Ibid. 79.
[179] David S. Evans and A. George Padilla, 'Designing Antitrust Rules for Assessing Unilateral Practices: A Neo-Chicago Approach' (2005) 72 University of Chicago Law Review 73, 86.
[180] Ahlborn, Evans and Padilla (n. 171) 242–4.
[181] Gilbert and Shapiro (n. 170).

a multiplicity of factors such as symmetry between the competing firms and when they enter the industry. The size and nature of network externalities, along with the consumer preferences which guide and structure those externalities, will also be of crucial importance.[182]

Another problem with the *Magill/IMS Health* test is that one of the factors for consideration is the adequacy of the economic efficiency rationale proposed by the monopolist. Assessment by the courts of the efficiency rationale of the monopolist injects inherent indeterminacy into the test. In the *Microsoft* case, for example, the Commission applied a 'balancing test' in response to Microsoft's claim that its incentives to innovate had been harmed. Generally, courts are not well-placed to carry out such an assessment. On balance, therefore, it cannot be assumed that even a narrowly crafted essential facilities doctrine, such as that implied by the *Magill* and *IMS Health* cases, will promote economic efficiency. Therefore, such a rule should not, as a matter of law and economics, be proposed as a mandatory rule at the international level.

Nevertheless, the range of potential situations encompassed by the *IMS/Magill* test is small; in the European case law, only in *Magill* were the requirements of the test clearly established. The test was most likely not satisfied in *IMS Health*, since the competing 'brick' structures could hardly have been characterized as new products. Nor was it satisfied in *Microsoft*: complete foreclosure was not demonstrated, and it is highly questionable whether Sun or other competitors of Microsoft were seeking to supply new products in the *Magill* sense. Few of the American 'essential facilities' cases would have satisfied this standard – certainly not *Terminal Railroad*, where no foreclosure is apparent from the record, and there was no indication that the production of new products had been inhibited. As such, the very narrowness of the 'modified per se legality' test suggests that, even if it may on balance reduce economic efficiency, such a diminution is likely to be small.

5.3 Request for Injunction in Relation to Standards-Essential Patents as a Competition Law Breach

Where the holder of an intellectual property right that is essential to the practice of a standard and is subject to a commitment to license seeks an injunction in relation to that right, some jurisdictions consider there may

---

[182] Willow Sheremata, 'Barriers to Innovation: A Monopoly, Network Externalities, and the Speed of Innovation' (1997) 42 The Antitrust Bulletin 937.

potentially be a breach of the competition laws. This issue has to date arisen mostly in connection with standards-essential patents subject to obligations to license on FRAND terms to a standard-setting body. Yet there is a close connection to the EU case law in connection with standards-essential copyrights, for example *IMS Health* and *Magill*, given that the anticompetitive conduct in question in those cases consisted of seeking (and obtaining) injunctions from the UK and German courts, respectively, concerning the use of standard-essential copyrights.

5.3.1 United States Law

In the United States it seems fairly clear that section 2 of the Sherman Act[183] will not apply with respect to attempts to obtain injunctions with respect to FRAND SEPs; whether section 5 of the Federal Trade Commission Act[184] will apply, however, remains an open question. Section 5 prohibits unfair methods of competition and unfair acts and practices. It may only be enforced by the Federal Trade Commission.

An important limitation is provided by the *Noerr-Pennington* doctrine, which provides immunity from US antitrust law for petitioning the Government, including for bringing good-faith legal proceedings before a court or government agency.[185] The application of the *Noerr-Pennington* doctrine to the FTC Act is unclear. There is limited jurisprudence from United States courts as to whether such actions will succeed; one district court has ruled that the owner of a SEP does not violate section 2 of the Sherman Act by seeking an exclusion order before the USITC.

In *Apple, Inc. v. Motorola Mobility, Inc* (heard before the United States District Court for the Western District of Wisconsin), Apple made counterclaims against Motorola arising from an ITC investigation that had been initiated by Motorola. Apple argued inter alia that Motorola's request for injunctive relief infringed section 2 of the Sherman Act. The court dismissed Apple's claims pursuant to the *Noerr-Pennington* doctrine.[186]

The FTC has entered into consent agreements with two SEP holders pursuant to section 5 of the FTC Act, on the grounds they sought to

---

[183] Sherman Antitrust Act 1890 (15 USC §§1–38) §2.
[184] Federal Trade Commission Act 1914 (15 USC §§ 41–58).
[185] *Apple, Inc v. Motorola Mobility, Inc* [2012] 886 F Supp 2d 1061 (United States District Court for the District of Western Washington) 1075.
[186] Ibid. 1077.

5.3 REQUEST FOR INJUNCTION IN RELATION TO SEPS

enforce their SEPs by way of injunctive relief. In its public statements, the FTC explicitly disputed that the *Noerr-Pennington* doctrine applied in these situations. In particular, the FTC argued that these companies waived any *Noerr-Pennington* rights by providing FRAND undertakings.[187] Since these matters were not heard by the courts, this fact remains in question; nevertheless, the FTC's views would seem directly contradictory with the District Court's ruling in *Apple v. Motorola*.

5.3.2 European Law

In the European context, by contrast, it is now clear from the *Motorola*, *Samsung* and *Huawei* decisions that Article 102 is potentially applicable in the context of requests by FRAND SEP holders for injunctions. The logical connection between the analytical matrix of the Court in *Huawei* and the Commission in *Motorola* and *Samsung*, as compared with the approaches in the traditional refusal to supply or refusal to license cases (e.g. *IMS Health* and *Magill*) remains unclear.

In *Motorola*, the Commission did not explicitly apply the 'refusal to supply' obligations included in Article 102, following the *Bronner-IMS Health-Microsoft* line of cases, although it did refer to those cases in footnotes.[188] Instead, drawing on more general Article 102 jurisprudence, the Commission crafted bespoke grounds of Article 102 liability, based on: (i) Apple's manifest willingness to enter into a licence agreement; (ii) harm to consumers arising from a temporary ban on Apple products as a result of the injunction; (iii) Apple's acceptance of anticompetitive licensing terms; and (iv) possible negative impacts on standard-setting.[189] Nevertheless in its assessment of Motorola's dominance, the Commission noted the indispensability of the GPRS standard to participation in markets for the supply of mobile handsets.[190]

In *Huawei*, the Court of Justice drew a somewhat more explicit link to the traditional refusal to supply cases when it observed:

---

[187] *Statement of the Federal Trade Commission, In the Matter of Google Inc* [2013] Federal Trade Commission C-4336; *Statement of the Federal Trade Commission, In the Matter of Robert Bosch GMBH* [2013] Federal Trade Commission C-4377.
[188] *Motorola – Enforcement of GPRS Standard Essential Patents (Case AT39985)* (European Commission) 255, 256.
[189] Ibid. 280.
[190] Ibid. 227–30.

It is characterised, first, as the referring court has observed, by the fact that the patent at issue is essential to a standard established by a standardisation body, rendering its use indispensable to all competitors which envisage manufacturing products that comply with the standard to which it is linked.[191]

There was no discussion of whether Huawei's refusal was likely to eliminate all competition in the relevant market (which on the facts seemed unlikely), nor whether Huawei's refusal was preventing the emergence of a new consumer product for which there was consumer demand.

Thus, *Huawei*, *Motorola* and *Samsung* are better viewed as a new strand of cases, rather than a continuation of the principles laid down in *Commercial Solvents*, *Bronner*, *IMS Health* and *Magill*. In these cases, the 'essential facility' is perhaps the SEP or, more likely, the technology upon which the SEP reads and which is essential to the practice of a standard which, itself, is essential to participation within the relevant market.

5.3.2.1 Huawei Technologies v. ZTE

The leading case is *Huawei v. ZTE*, upon which the Court of Justice issued judgment on 16 July 2015.[192] Huawei held a European patent in connection with the synchronization of cellular telephony signals. Huawei provided notification to ETSI that its patent was essential to the LTE 4G mobile telephony standard. Accordingly, Huawei undertook to ETSI to license its patent on FRAND terms.

Huawei and ZTE Corporation (both Chinese multinational enterprises engaged in the telecommunications business) sought to negotiate a licence but did not reach agreement; ZTE meanwhile put products on the market which used the LTE standard (and therefore practised Huawei's patent), without paying any royalty to Huawei. Huawei brought proceedings before the Landgericht Dusseldorf, seeking injunction, damages and the recall of products from the market. The Landgericht referred the matter to the ECJ for a preliminary ruling as to whether Huawei's petitions might amount to the abuse of a dominant market position. The Landgericht stated in its application for preliminary

---

[191] *Huawei Technologies Co Ltd v. ZTE Corp, ZTE Deutschland GmbH (Case C/170–13)* [2015] ECLI:EUC:2015:477 (European Court of Justice) [49].
[192] Ibid.

5.3 REQUEST FOR INJUNCTION IN RELATION TO SEPS

reference that Huawei's patent was essential to the practice of the 4G LTE standard; that Huawei held a dominant market position was uncontested; the Court's decision therefore focused on the question of abuse.

After recalling the doctrine of 'exceptional circumstances' and citing *Magill, IMS Health* and *Volvo*, the Court distinguished those cases on the basis of: (i) the status of the patent as essential to practice of a standard established by a standardization body; (ii) the giving of the irrevocable FRAND undertaking; and (iii) the ability of the patent holder, by seeking injunction, to reserve to itself the manufacture of products compliant with the 4G LTE standard.[193] In particular, the Court explained that the giving of the FRAND undertaking gave rise to legitimate expectations that a FRAND licence would be granted.[194]

The Court also noted the requirements of the EU Enforcement Directive, notably the need for effective measures to redress patent breaches and the rights of patent holders to have recourse to such proceedings. Seeking to balance intellectual property and competition law considerations in the context of the legitimate expectation of a licence occasioned by the FRAND undertaking, as well as the broader standardization context, the Court laid down the following statement of the applicable law:

> Accordingly, the proprietor of an SEP which considers that that SEP is the subject of an infringement cannot, without infringing Article 102 TFEU, bring an action for a prohibitory injunction or for the recall of products against the alleged infringer without notice or prior consultation with the alleged infringer, even if the SEP has already been used by the alleged infringer.[195]

In laying down this statement, the Court was confronted with the reality that the presence of an abuse would depend heavily on the precise course of negotiations between the right holder and the user of the SEP. In the eight paragraphs following the above statement, the Court laid down a set of instructions to guide the two parties in their licensing negotiations: first, the SEP holder must alert the alleged infringer as to the SEP and the alleged infringement; then, having expressed its willingness to conclude a FRAND licence, the SEP holder must present such a licence to the alleged infringer; the alleged infringer must respond diligently to the offer; if it rejects the offer, it should promptly make a counter-offer;

---

[193] Ibid. 49–52.
[194] Ibid. 53.
[195] Ibid. 60.

the alleged infringer must provide appropriate security for any unlicensed use of the SEP; and the alleged infringer should not be precluded from challenging validity.[196]

The prescriptiveness and conditionality of the Court's judgment shows the difficulty of applying the competition laws in the context of FRAND licensing negotiations. If any of these instructions is not met, either by the right holder or the user, is there an abuse for purposes of Article 102? Might both the right holder and user be found in contravention of the competition laws if their behaviour during the negotiations does not meet the requisite standards?

Nevertheless, the *Huawei* judgment has given considerable certainty to the telecommunications industry regarding FRAND licensing practices. The Court's statement of the law in Huawei is nevertheless somewhat brief and was necessarily confined by the boundaries of the request for preliminary reference. A much more detailed examination of the applicable principles was provided by the Commission in its *Motorola* decision.

5.3.2.2 *Motorola – Enforcement of GPRS Standard Essential Patents*

Prior to *Huawei*, the European Commission concluded an infringement of Article 102 in *Motorola – Enforcement of GPRS Standard Essential Patents*.[197] The case concerned Motorola's GPRS 'Cudak' patent, which Motorola declared essential to ETSI's GPRS standard, known in the industry as 2.5G. The Cudak patent concerned the transmission of data packets in a wireless communication system. Motorola gave a FRAND declaration in accordance with ETSI's intellectual property policy. During April 2011, Motorola sought injunctions from the Mannheim District Court in Germany against Apple Sales International, with a view to ordering Apple inter alia to cease and desist from selling in Germany any Apple products that implemented the asserted patents, including the Cudak patent.[198]

During the German injunction proceedings, Apple made six licensing offers to Motorola. Following Apple's third licensing offer, the Mannheim District Court granted an injunction against Apple with respect to the Cudak patent. Apple appealed to the Karlsruhe Appellate Court. This appeal was rejected. Following further Apple clarifications to

---

[196] Ibid. 61–9.
[197] *Motorola – Enforcement of GPRS Standard Essential Patents (Case AT.39985)* (n. 188).
[198] Ibid. 115–16.

5.3 REQUEST FOR INJUNCTION IN RELATION TO SEPS   207

its sixth licensing offer, Apple and Motorola signed a Settlement Agreement during 2012.

The Settlement Agreement included terms and conditions highly favourable to Motorola: it covered all German patents and German parts of European patents held by Motorola and claimed by Motorola to be essential for a number of applicable standards; the royalties both for future and past use of the patents were to be set by Motorola 'according to its equitable discretion and according to the FRAND standard in the industry. Whether the royalties are FRAND shall be subject to examination and be changed with retroactive effect by a court'; and Apple agreed to unconditionally withdraw all pending nullity complaints, oppositions or utility model cancellation requests against the licensed patents. If Apple filed a new nullity complaint, opposition or utility model cancellation request against any of the licensed patents, Motorola retained the right to terminate the Settlement Agreement.[199]

In considering whether Motorola had infringed Article 102, the Commission found that the technology upon which the Cudak SEP read constituted its own product market, since it had no effective substitutes. Notably, there were no substitutes for GPRS within the EEA; and furthermore, the Cudak SEP was essential to the GPRS standard. The Commission based this latter finding on Motorola's declaration of essentiality, rather than assessing whether the Cudak patent was in fact essential to the GPRS standard.[200]

The Commission (unsurprisingly) found that Motorola was dominant in the relevant market,[201] with a 100 per cent market share. Moreover, the Commission found that: 'Due to the wide adoption of GPRS in the EEA and the need of operators and device manufacturers to base their services and products on the same air interface technology, so that devices can communicate with the network, industry players are locked-in to the GPRS technology'.[202] As to whether Motorola had abused its dominant market position, the Commission stated:

> a patent holder, including a holder of SEPs, is generally entitled to seek and enforce injunctions as part of the exercise of its IP rights. The seeking and enforcement of injunctions cannot therefore, in itself, constitute an abuse of a dominant position. The exercise of an exclusive right by its owner may, however, in exceptional circumstances and absent any

[199] Ibid. 163.
[200] Ibid. 207.
[201] Ibid. 269.
[202] Ibid. 231.

objective justification involve abusive conduct. The list of exceptional circumstances is not exhaustive.[203]

The exceptional circumstances present in the *Motorola* case were the GPRS standard-setting context and Motorola's FRAND commitment. Concerning the GPRS standard-setting context, the Commission outlined the importance of the GPRS standard and Motorola's active participation in the GPRS standard-setting process, before concluding: 'Once GPRS, based on the agreement of patent holders to grant access to their SEPs on FRAND terms and conditions, was widely implemented and the industry became locked in, a SEP holder may be able to behave in anti-competitive ways, for example by 'holding-up' implementers of the standard after its adoption'.[204] Concerning Motorola's FRAND commitment, the Commission concluded: 'Therefore, in the case at hand, Motorola has committed to make available and monetise the Cudak GPRS SEP on FRAND terms and conditions, rather than to make use of the Cudak GPRS SEP in a manner which excludes others from using it'.[205] The Commission explained that the fact that an act by an autonomous judicial body (i.e. the granting of an injunction) was a precondition for the likely anticompetitive effects did not affect the abusive nature of the conduct, because Motorola's act of seeking an injunction was an autonomous act which Motorola was not required to take.[206] The Commission found that Motorola's behaviour was capable of having the following anticompetitive effects: a temporary ban on the online sale of Apple's GPRS-compatible products in Germany; the inclusion in the Settlement Agreement of licensing terms disadvantageous to Apple, and a negative impact on standard-setting.[207]

The Commission reached similar findings in its investigation of Samsung's conduct. In response to the Commission's Statement of Objections, Samsung made binding commitments which the Commission accepted.[208]

Together, these cases provide a relatively coherent jurisprudence concerning the application of Article 102 in the context of requests for injunction concerning FRAND-encumbered SEPs. Nevertheless,

---

[203] Ibid. 278.
[204] Ibid. 289.
[205] Ibid. 299.
[206] Ibid. 309–10.
[207] Ibid. 310–11.
[208] *Samsung – Enforcement of UMTS Standard-Essential Patents (Case AT39939)* [2014] OJ C35008 (European Commission) [121].

5.3 REQUEST FOR INJUNCTION IN RELATION TO SEPS

a number of questions remain. First, the requisite 'essentiality' of the SEP was definitively established in *Huawei*, by the referring Landgericht, but was only inferred in *Motorola* on the basis of Motorola's declaration to ETSI. Second, complications will arise in circumstances where the FRAND undertaking has not been given, is ambiguous in its terms, or where the standard is de facto rather than formal.

5.3.3 Chinese Law

Anti-monopoly guidelines in China by NDRC also foreshadow the possibility that seeking injunctions in relation to FRAND-encumbered SEPs could violate the AML: 'Standard essential patentees with market dominance use injunctive relief applications to force licensees to accept unfairly high license fees or other unreasonable licensing conditions, which may exclude or restrict competition'.[209] NDRC provided the following factors to guide whether seeking the injunctive remedy might engage the AML: (i) the performance and actual willingness expressed by the parties in the negotiation; (ii) the commitments undertaken by SEPs regarding injunction; (iii) the licensing conditions proposed by the parties in the negotiation; (iv) the influence of the injunction imposed on the licensing negotiation; and (v) the competition in the relevant market and downstream market, and the interests of consumers.[210] This provides at least the indication that the seeking of such injunctions could engage the AML, and the relevant factors to be applied in the context of such an assessment, but little more. Further elaboration is expected through cases. The guidelines remain in draft.

5.3.4 Merits of Applying the Unilateral Disciplines to Address Injunctions for FRAND-Encumbered SEPs

Scholars are divided on the merits of competition law's intrusion into the FRAND arena to date. Some venerable antitrust scholars remain sceptical.[211] Ginsburg et al., for example, suggest that problems

---

[209] 'Anti-Monopoly Guidelines on the Abuse of Intellectual Property Rights (Draft for Comment), 公开征求《关于滥用知识产权的反垄断指南（征求意见稿的意见)' (23 March 2017) http://fldj.mofcom.gov.cn/ accessed 18 May 2020 art. 26.
[210] Ibid. art. 26.
[211] Mark A. Lemley, 'Ten Things to Do About Patent Holdup of Standards (and One Not To)' (2007) 48 Boston College Law Review 149, 167–8.

associated with SEPs have been overblown[212] and that antitrust intervention is likely to impact negatively on incentives for innovation.[213] Others are more positively disposed to intervention along the lines of the EU approach.[214]

A number of observations can be made regarding a competition law approach to this question. First, such an approach should be applied only to SEIP that is established to be essential to the implementation of an interoperability standard. In *Motorola*, such 'essentiality' was presumed on the basis of declarations given by the relevant right holder, whereas in *Huawei*, the question of 'essentiality' had been determined definitively by the referring Landgericht.

As discussed in Chapter 4, empirical examination of SEPs has demonstrated that many patents declared as standards-essential to SSOs are not, in fact, standards-essential in a strictly technical sense.[215] It would seem problematic to impose supply obligations under Article 102 in respect of SEPs for which technical alternatives exist. Moreover, establishing as a matter of technical fact whether a particular patent is, or is not, standards-essential is a complicated matter, best performed by a court or similarly constituted administrative body with a high degree of competence in the construction of patent claims. Competition agencies may not be well-placed to undertake such an assessment.

Furthermore, application of competition rules in this context will need to be reconciled with general principles of law in the applicable jurisdiction concerning the right of access to courts and tribunals. In the United States, a person is generally immune from antitrust immunity merely for approaching the courts and seeking a legal remedy, by operation of the *Noerr-Pennington* doctrine. Likewise, in EU law the right of access to the courts is enshrined as a fundamental right under Article 47 of the Charter of Fundamental Rights.[216]

---

[212] Douglas H. Ginsburg and others, 'The Troubling Use of Antitrust to Regulate FRAND Licensing' (2015) 10 CPI Antitrust Chronicle 2, 4–6.
[213] Ibid. 6–7.
[214] Roberto Grasso, 'The ECJ Ruling in Huawei and the Right to Seek Injunctions Based on FRAND-Encumbered SEPs under EU Competition Law: One Step Forward' (2016) 39 World Competition 213.
[215] See Sadao Nagaoka, Naotoshi Tsukada and Tomoyuki Shimbo, 'The Structure and the Emergence of Essential Patents for Standards: Lessons from Three IT Standards' in Uwe Cantner, Jean-Luc Gaffard and Lionel Nesta (eds.), *Schumpeterian Perspectives on Innovation, Competition and Growth* (Springer 2009).
[216] Charter of Fundamental Rights of the European Union ([2016] OJ C 202) Art. 47.

Yet while the US courts have treated the *Noerr-Pennington* principle as a more or less complete defence in this context, the Commission in *Motorola* and *Samsung*, and the ECJ in *Huawei*, read Article 47 more narrowly, holding that the right of access to the courts is not unlimited.[217] Nevertheless, questions are likely to persist about whether it can be an infringement of competition law merely to ask a court for a remedy which the court is empowered (and may indeed be inclined) to grant.

Further analysis is also recommended as to how the EU's approach in *Huawei* can be reconciled with the more general principles concerning Article 102, refusals to supply and the essential facilities doctrine. In the Huawei decision there was no mention of the *IMS Health/Magill* test. Generally, the mere act of seeking injunctions in relation to FRAND-encumbered SEPs will not satisfy the *IMS Health/Magill* test for liability.

First, the SEP may not be 'indispensable' if it is only claimed to be essential to the standard, but essentiality is not established as a legal fact following a careful construction of the relevant claims. It may also not be 'indispensable' if there are other competing alternatives to the particular standard in question. Second, the refusal may not reserve all competition to the refusing right holder: the right holder may in fact be prepared to licence to other prospective licensees (e.g. those holding significant portfolios of SEIP or those prepared to pay higher licensing fees). Indeed, it may not even reserve all 'effective' competition to the right holder (adopting the lower threshold applied by the Commission in the *Microsoft* case), if there are other licensees undertaking viable competing businesses, which is usually the case. Third, it is unclear whether the 'new product' test will be satisfied if the user is proposing to supply a product which is minimally differentiated from many other products currently available in the marketplace.

Perhaps, given that EU bodies have relatively greater competence in the arena of competition laws than in the arena of intellectual property law, and that some differences in the practices of EU Member States with respect to the protection of SEPs by way of the injunctive remedy are observed, the approach using competition law to address the overprotection of intellectual property law may represent the most practicable way forward. Although applying competition rules may in some ways be a 'blunt instrument' to address concerns associated with access to interoperability standards and to SEIP, it is a tool that is nevertheless

---

[217] Grasso (n. 214) 236.

available and if no other remedy is at hand it seems inevitable that competition rules can, and indeed should, be applied to deliver some kind of workable solution.[218]

5.4 Excessive or Unfair Pricing

While many jurisdictions maintain competition laws dealing with unfair pricing, it is well-accepted that any action should be weighed carefully, particularly in innovation-intensive industries. As Hayek explains in his classic paper, prices play a fundamental role in directing an economy's resources towards their most valuable (and therefore socially productive) uses.[219]

In the case of new, innovative products, the correct analysis may be to compare welfare in the case of monopoly pricing with welfare in the alternative scenario, in which the new product is not created at all. Furthermore, regulating monopoly prices can have significant negative impacts on dynamic efficiency. Investing in innovative ventures is akin to a lottery where most investments become worthless and a few yield supranormal profits. But by capping the profits of successful ventures, the expected return of all entrepreneurs is reduced and therefore in the future such innovative activity may not occur.[220]

United States antitrust law does not include any excessive or unfair pricing offence. European[221] and Chinese[222] law do, however, consider that unfair or excessive pricing can amount to an abuse of a dominant market position. In the EU, Article 102(a) would appear to be applicable in the context of intellectual property licensing negotiations, but cases on the books are lacking. By contrast, Article 17(1) of China's AML has been applied in the context of SEP licensing negotiations.

---

[218] See Herbert Hovenkamp, 'Standards Ownership and Competition Policy' (2007) 48 Boston College Law Review 87, 109.

[219] Friedrich Hayek, 'The Use of Knowledge in Society' (1945) 35 American Economic Review 519.

[220] David S. Evans, Vanessa Yanhua Zhang and Xinzhu Zhang, 'Assessing Unfair Pricing under China's Anti-Monopoly Law for Innovation-Intensive Industries' (University of Chicago 2014) 20–22 https://chicagounbound.uchicago.edu accessed 21 May 2019.

[221] Consolidated Version of the Treaty on the Functioning of the European Union ([2008] OJ C115/13) Art. 102(a).

[222] Anti-Monopoly Law (Promulgated by Order No. 68 of August 30, 2007) of the People's Republic of China, 中华人民共和国反垄断法 Art. 17(1).

5.4.1 European Law

In the EU, TFEU Article 102(a) on its face clearly extends to excessive pricing abuses, referring to 'directly or indirectly imposing unfair purchase or selling prices or other unfair trading conditions'. The case law of the European Court of Justice indicates that such an abuse could arise where an undertaking with a dominant market position in the relevant market imposes a price which is excessive in relation to the economic value of the service provided.[223] This has been reflected in the case law of the Member States, for example by the UK Court of Appeal in *Attheraces Ltd* v. *BHB Ltd*, in which Mummery LJ stated: 'a fair price is one which represents or reflects the economic value of the product supplied. A price which significantly exceeds that will be prima facie excessive and unfair'.[224] Several decisions by the Court of Justice concerning the practices of monopoly copyright collecting societies have indicated that, while an excessive pricing discipline could, in principle, be applied in the context of intellectual property licensing, in practice this is likely to be a difficult matter.[225]

These decisions cannot, however, be regarded as addressing directly the imposition by an SEIP holder of excessive royalties, since the dominant market position arose from the monopolies held by the collecting societies rather than from the relevant copyrights per se.

An excessive pricing argument under Article 102(a) of the TFEU in the context of FRAND-encumbered SEPs was considered and rejected in 2017 by the UK High Court in *Unwired Planet* v. *Huawei*.[226] Birss J clarified in that case that the difference between a FRAND and a non-FRAND royalty was distinct from the difference between a fair and an unfair of excessive price for purposes of Article 102(a).[227] He rejected

---

[223] *Kanal 5 and TV 4 (Case C-52/07)* [2008] EU:C:2008:703 (Court of Justice of the European Communities (Fourth Chamber)) I-9321; *General Motors NV v. Commission of the European Communities (Case 26/75)* [1975] ECR 1975 – 01367 (European Court of Justice) 1379; *United Brands Company and United Brands Continentaal BV v. Commission of the European Communities (Case 27/76)* [1978] ECR 00207 (European Court of Justice) 301.

[224] *Attheraces Ltd & Anor v. The British Horseracing Board Ltd & Anor* 2007 EWCA Civ 38 (Court of Appeal) [204].

[225] *Autortiesību un komunicēšanās konsultāciju aģentūra/Latvijas Autoru apvienība (Case C-177/16)* [2017] ECLI:EU:C:2017:698 (European Court of Justice); *Kanal 5 and TV 4 (Case C-52/07)* (n. 223).

[226] *Unwired Planet International v. Huawei Technologies Co Ltd and Huawei Technologies (UK) Co Ltd* [2017] 2017 EWHC 711 (High Court) 756–64.

[227] Ibid. 757.

Huawei's arguments that Unwired Planet's offers were per se unfair because they were well above a FRAND rate, and indicated that detailed economic evidence would be required for the proper assessment of such a claim.[228]

This decision tends to indicate that the availability of an excessive pricing remedy in the EU in the context of SEIP royalty negotiations cannot be excluded out of hand. Yet it seems unlikely that plaintiffs in the EU would go to the expense and time needed to muster the economic evidence necessary to support such a claim, rather than simply relying on *Huawei* v. *ZTE* to challenge the patent holder's application for injunction under Article 102.

5.4.2 Chinese Law

Article 17(1) of China's AML provides for an abuse of a dominant market position where an undertaking sells commodities at unfairly high prices. Article 17(1) has been applied to intellectual property licensing practices, including in the context of SEPs. Qualcomm was investigated by China's NDRC[229] in 2015, in relation to its licensing practices of SEPs in China. Qualcomm was found inter alia to have violated Article 17(1) of China's AML for charging excessive royalties for its 3G licences. The NDRC considered that each SEP consisted of a single product market for market definition purposes.[230]

NDRC's finding of unreasonably high royalties was not made on the basis of consideration of the prices charged either in absolute or relative terms. Rather, NDRC inferred that royalties were too high based on two findings: (i) Qualcomm offered a price list for licensing patents but did not specify which patents it was offering, thus giving rise to the risk that licensees were paying for invalidated patents; and (ii) Qualcomm demanded a royalty-free cross-licence in return.[231] In addition, Qualcomm was found to have bundled SEPs with non-SEPs, and to

---

[228] Ibid. 760.
[229] Prior to 2018, NDRC was one of three Chinese agencies with responsibilities for competition law enforcement. From March 2018, enforcement responsibilities have been consolidated in a single agency, the State Administration for Market Regulation (SAMR).
[230] Liyang Hou, 'Qualcomm: How China Has Invalidated Traditional Business Models on Standard Essential Patents' (2016) 7 Journal of European Competition Law & Practice 686, 687.
[231] Ibid.

5.5 FRAUD IN THE CREATION OF STANDARDS 215

have sold chipsets on condition that purchasers would not challenge the validity of any of Qualcomm's patents.[232]

Qualcomm opted to settle the matter rather than challenge the NDRC's findings through the Chinese courts. The NDRC accepted undertakings from Qualcomm in relating to its licensing practices, including an undertaking to reduce the basis of royalties to 65 per cent of the net selling price of branded devices sold for use within China. Qualcomm further agreed: not to charge for expired patents; not to demand cross-licences without fair compensation; and not to bundle SEPs and non-SEPs without justification. Qualcomm also agreed to pay a fine of 6.088 RMB (approximately USD975 m at prevailing exchange rates).[233]

5.4.3 Excessive Pricing: Concluding Observations

Therefore, while it would be appropriate for domestic jurisdictions to maintain laws with respect to excessive pricing (and many do), these laws should apply very rarely (if ever) to prices asked by intellectual property right holders. Indeed, it would be consistent with economic theory not to apply such laws to intellectual property right holders at all. Excessive pricing intervention could therefore not be regarded as a routine tool of intervention to address overpricing by SEP holders. It is probably too controversial to recommend as a basis for international action.

5.5 Misconduct or Fraud in the Creation of Standards

Competition laws could also be engaged in circumstances where participants in a standard-setting process engage in some species of fraud or misconduct. Examples include where participants fail to properly disclose SEPs to a standard-setting body during the development phase, or leave the SSO before the standard is complete without providing appropriate undertakings to license, and subsequently refuse to license or demand supra-FRAND royalties.

The practice of both the United States Federal Trade Commission and the European Commission supports the application of antitrust or competition laws in these situations, and there is further support notably in

---

[232] Ibid.
[233] Yan Bing Li, 'Antitrust Correction for Qualcomm's SEPs Package Licensing and Its Flexibility in China' (2016) 47 International Review of Intellectual Property and Competition Law 336, 344–5.

the Third Circuit's opinion in *Broadcom v. Qualcomm*.[234] Nevertheless, judicially established contraventions are few. Cases against perpetrators of 'patent ambush' have generally asserted a two-stage course of wrongful conduct: first, before the standard was established, the right holder behaved deceptively, to induce an SSO to include a patented technology into a standard; and second, after the standard was established, the patent holder sought to recoup unjustifiably high royalties.

However, if the courts assess the ex ante and ex post aspects of the SEP holder's allegedly fraudulent conduct separately, neither may sound as a breach of competition law. Deceptive conduct in itself may not rise to the level of anticompetitive behaviour, unless stringent factual requirements can be proven (e.g. that but for the deceptive course of conduct, another technology would have been selected by the SSO); and seeking an excessively high royalty in licensing negotiations will rarely of itself contravene competition or antitrust laws.

As such, although a role for competition laws in disciplining instances of fraud or misconduct cannot be excluded, it seems that the limiting doctrines in intellectual property law or elsewhere (e.g. contract, equitable waiver or estoppel) will be more likely to resolve these sorts of disputes.

5.5.1 United States Law

In the absence of Supreme Court guidance, and with conflicting approaches from District of Columbia Circuit in *Rambus* and the Third Circuit in *Broadcom v. Qualcomm*, United States law looks somewhat unsettled at this point in time.

5.5.1.1 Rambus v. *Federal Trade Commission*

In *Rambus v. Federal Trade Commission*,[235] the United States Court of Appeals, District of Columbia Circuit set aside an administrative decision of the Federal Trade Commission, imposed in relation to Rambus' alleged misconduct in the context of standard-setting. The FTC had brought suit against Rambus under § 5(a) of the Federal Trade Commission Act,[236] alleging monopolization in contravention of § 2 of

---

[234] *Broadcom Corp v. Qualcomm Inc* [2007] 501 F3d 297 (United States Court of Appeals for the Third Circuit).
[235] *Rambus Incorporated v. Federal Trade Commission* (2008) 522 522 F3d 456 (United States Court of Appeal for the District of Columbia Circuit).
[236] US Federal Trade Commission Act.

5.5 FRAUD IN THE CREATION OF STANDARDS

the Sherman Act.[237] The FTC alleged that Rambus had breached the intellectual property policies of the Joint Electron Device Engineering Council (JEDEC), by failing to disclose patent interests which it was required to disclose. By so doing, Rambus monopolized four markets: one for each of the patents asserted.[238]

Rambus held patents over innovative computer memory technologies that provided a faster architecture for dynamic random-access memory chips (DRAMs). Rambus participated in standard-setting activities sponsored by JEDEC which ultimately produced two synchronous DRAM standards: synchronous DRAM (SDRAM) and double data rate synchronous DRAM (DDR-SDRAM). However, Rambus withdrew from JEDEC before the DDR-SDRAM standard was completed, noting that its proposed licensing terms might not be consistent with JEDEC's policies.[239] The completed DDR-SDRAM standard became very successful, and ultimately around 90 per cent of all DRAMs worldwide were DDR-SDRAM compliant.[240] Rambus asserted four patents it held in relation to DDR-SDRAM.[241]

The FTC issued a lengthy and detailed decision holding that Rambus' conduct amounted to exclusionary conduct that significantly contributed to its acquisition of monopoly power in licensing markets for the four SEPs.[242] The FTC concluded that but for Rambus' misconduct, one of two outcomes would have resulted: (i) JEDEC would have selected different technologies for inclusion in the DDR-SDRAM standard; or (ii) JEDEC would have obtained from Rambus FRAND declarations, resulting in lower licence fees to users of these technologies.[243]

On appeal, the United States Court of Appeals for the District of Columbia Circuit set aside the Commission's orders, on the basis that (i) the first possible outcome was not proven;[244] and (ii) the second possible outcome was not anticompetitive.[245]

Regarding the first possible outcome, the DC Circuit assumed without deciding that if it could be proven that but for Rambus'

---

[237] Sherman Antitrust Act.
[238] *Rambus Incorporated v. Federal Trade Commission* (n. 235) 461.
[239] Ibid. 460.
[240] Ibid. 459.
[241] Ibid. 461.
[242] *In the Matter of Rambus, Inc (2006-2 Trade Cases P75364)* [2006] WL 2330117 (Federal Trade Commission) [57].
[243] Ibid. 40.
[244] *Rambus Incorporated v. Federal Trade Commission* (n. 235) 463-4.
[245] Ibid. 467.

misrepresentations, the patented technologies would not have been included in the standard, this would amount to anticompetitive conduct. However, on the facts, it could not be proven that, absent such misrepresentations, Rambus' technologies would have been excluded. Thus, the Commission's first claim failed.[246] Regarding the second possible outcome, the Court reiterated that deceptive conduct enabling an enterprise to charge higher prices was not exclusionary per se.[247] The District of Columbia Circuit made clear that antitrust claims in the context of 'patent ambush' needed to go beyond allegations of excessive pricing: But an otherwise lawful monopolist's use of deception simply to obtain higher prices normally has no particular tendency to exclude rivals and thus to diminish competition.[248] Thus, the Circuit, by separately analysing the ex ante and ex post phases of Rambus' conduct, concluded that neither had breached the antitrust laws. The Circuit also made clear that it would not entertain excessive pricing claims brought under the guise of alleged deceptive conduct.

5.5.1.2 Broadcom Corp. v. Qualcomm Inc.

In a decision rendered slightly earlier, the United States Court of Appeals for the Third Circuit took a different approach, laying down the following legal test:

> We hold that (1) in a consensus-oriented private standard-setting environment, (2) a patent holder's intentionally false promise to license essential proprietary technology on FRAND terms, (3) coupled with an SDO's reliance on that promise when including the technology in a standard, and (4) the patent holder's subsequent breach of that promise, is actionable anticompetitive conduct.[249]

The United States Court of Appeals for the Third Circuit affirmed in part, and reversed in part, the decision of the District Court for the District of New Jersey to dismiss Broadcom's antitrust claims for failure to state a claim, and remanded for further consideration.[250] No further decision on remand was issued.

The Third Circuit's decision is difficult to reconcile with the approach of the DC Circuit in Rambus. Notably, the Third Circuit sought to

---

[246] Ibid. 463.
[247] Ibid. 464.
[248] Ibid.
[249] *Broadcom Corp. v. Qualcomm Inc.* (n. 234).
[250] Ibid. 323.

combine the ex ante deceptive conduct and ex post exploitative conduct into a single cause of action. Moreover, it did not require, as in Rambus, that a plaintiff prove that, but for the patent holder's misrepresentation to the SSO, the SSO would have selected a different technology for inclusion in the standard.

On the facts, a core aspect of Qualcomm's alleged monopolization was its ex post demand for supra-FRAND royalties.[251] Thus, a key problem with the Third Circuit's approach is whether its legal test can be distinguished from an excessive pricing discipline, or indeed the reintroduction of an essential facilities doctrine; the Third Circuit in its reasons cited the *Aspen Skiing* case as an exception to a monopolist's right to refuse to deal, and even distinguished the *Trinko* case on facts.[252]

In a final chapter to the long-running dispute between the two companies, the United States Court of Appeals for the Federal Circuit held in December 2008 that Qualcomm's failure to comply with SSO[253] disclosure requirements gave rise to an implied waiver of its right to assert its SEPs against Broadcom.[254] Thus, doctrines limiting the assertion of the SEPs – in this instance emanating from equity rather than patent law – resolved the dispute, rather than enforcement of the antitrust laws.

5.5.2 European Law

In the EU there have been no judicial findings of misconduct, although Rambus settled its case with the European Commission, in which the Commission alleged that Rambus had engaged in intentionally deceptive conduct in the standard-setting process. In that matter, it was alleged that Rambus had intentionally failed to disclose the existence of patents and patent applications which it later claimed were relevant to the standard. The Commission stated:

> The Commission took the preliminary view that Rambus' practice of claiming royalties for the use of its patents from industry standard-compliant DRAM manufacturers at a level which, absent its allegedly

---

[251] *Broadcom Corp.v. Qualcomm Inc.* [2006] 2006 WL 2528545 (United States District Court for the District of New Jersey) [2]; *Broadcom Corp. v. Qualcomm Inc.* (n. 234) 304.
[252] *Broadcom Corp. v. Qualcomm Inc.* (n. 234) 316–17.
[253] The SSO in question was the Joint Video Team (JVT), a joint project of the Video Coding Experts Group of the ITU, the MPEG and the IEC, established to develop video compression technologies.
[254] *Qualcomm Incorporated v. Broadcom Corporation* United States Court of Appeals for the Federal Circuit 2007-1545, 2008-1162 1022.

intentional deceptive conduct, it would not have been able to charge raised concerns as to the compatibility with Article 102 of the Treaty on the Functioning of the European Union ('TFEU').[255]

Thus, the Commission was inclined to evaluate the ex ante and ex post phases of Rambus' actions as a single course of conduct inconsistent with TFEU Article 102.

The Commission found that, but for Rambus' alleged deceit, JEDEC Members would likely have designed around Rambus' patents to ensure the standard remained patent-free.[256] The Commission considered that there was a broad range of alternative technologies to those that were eventually included in the JEDEC DRAM standard.[257] The Commission considered that there were considerable barriers to entry into the market and the industry was locked into the JEDEC DRAM standards.[258]

In June 2009, Rambus offered to the Commission a series of licensing commitments in relation to its DRAM products. The Commission assessed that Rambus's proffered commitments were sufficient to meet its concerns, and that there was therefore no longer grounds for action on its part, and that the proceedings should be brought to an end.

The European Commission also investigated Qualcomm's licensing practices in connection with the WCDMA standard developed by ETSI. The Commission investigated whether Qualcomm had failed to offer licences on FRAND terms, in breach of its undertaking to ETSI. The Commission closed its investigation against Qualcomm without issuing a Statement of Objections.[259] This may have reflected reservations by the Commission about the strength of its case. It is noteworthy that neither the *Rambus* nor the *Qualcomm* investigations resulted in a judicial finding that an abuse of a dominant market position had occurred.

5.5.3 Chinese Law

These issues are yet to arise in China, although the NDRC's disposition of the Qualcomm matter suggests that misconduct claims would have a better chance of succeeding under Chinese law.

---

[255] *Summary of Commission Decision of 9 December 2009 under Article 102 of the Treaty (Case COMP/38636 – RAMBUS)* [2009] OJ C 30 (European Commission) [3].
[256] Ibid. 43.
[257] Ibid. 46.
[258] Ibid. 47.
[259] European Commission, 'Antitrust: Commission Closes Formal Proceedings against Qualcomm' (24 November 2009) http://europa.eu accessed 29 November 2017.

5.5.4 Conclusions Regarding Fraud and Misconduct in Standard-Setting

A fundamental question with these cases is whether they are, in substance, excessive pricing cases. The basis of liability seems to be that the right holder, through various species of misconduct, deceptively secures a position where excessive licensing fees can be charged, inconsistently with the FRAND undertaking that was (or, as the case may be, was not) given.

Distinguishing such conduct from excessive pricing requires the misleading or deceptive conduct to be given significance under competition law, and combining the ex ante deception and ex post exploitation phases of the conduct at issue. Judicial support for this approach remains patchy at best. Contract, equity and the limiting doctrines in intellectual property law may provide better-tailored means of redressing concerns associated with such allegations of misconduct.

5.6 Tying

The competition law offence of tying (i.e. mandatory bundling of products or services) is very similar to refusal to supply, and could also manifest in the context of SEIP and interoperability standard-setting.

In the US *Microsoft* case, Microsoft was accused of tying (from both a contractual and a technological perspective) sales of its Internet Explorer web browser to sales of its dominant Windows operating system. Initially, the District Court found a violation of section 2 of the Sherman Act, applying a per se test; this was overturned by the District of Columbia Circuit, which opined that a rule of reason analysis should instead be conducted;[260] the tying claim was not pursued subsequently. The District of Columbia Circuit preferred a rule of reason approach inter alia because:

> the pervasively innovative character of platform software markets, tying in such markets may produce efficiencies that courts have not previously encountered and thus the Supreme Court had not factored into the per se rule as originally conceived. For example, the bundling of a browser with OSs enables an independent software developer to count on the presence of the browser's APIs, if any, on consumers' machines and thus to omit them from its own package.[261]

---

[260] *State of New York, et al. v. Microsoft Corporation, Final Judgment* [2002] 224 FSupp2d 76 (United States District Court for the District of Columbia) 89–95.
[261] Ibid. 93.

As the Circuit emphasized, the efficiency benefits of tying need to be considered carefully before enjoining such conduct in high technology markets.

In the EU *Microsoft* case, Microsoft was found to have abused its dominant market position by tying sales of Microsoft's Windows Media Player to sales of its Microsoft Windows Operating System. This was found to have attracted content providers and software developers to write to Media Player, despite it being rated less favourably than its competitors on objective measures of quality. The Commission found that network effects were strong in the media player market and, as such, content providers and software developers were much more likely to write only for a single media player. As such, Microsoft's tying reinforced the network effects already present on the market.[262] By way of remedy, Microsoft was ordered to make available a version of Microsoft Windows that did not include Windows Media Player.[263]

Likewise, in the China National Development and Reform Commission's Qualcomm investigation, Qualcomm was found liable under Article 17(1) of China's Anti-Monopoly Law, inter alia for tying licencing of SEPs to licencing of non-SEPs. This tying was found to have two anticompetitive effects. First, it forced licensees to pay higher licence fees since they were effectively forced to pay for patents they did not need. Second, it precluded the market opportunities to license of technology firms with competing patents.[264]

The law and economics of tying is broadly similar to that of refusal to supply. For example, the single monopoly theorem is also applicable in the context of tying.[265] There is, if anything, greater scope for economic efficiencies arising from tying arrangements than from refusals to supply (including economies of scale and scope, product quality and lower transaction costs).[266] Ahlborn et al., for example, suggest that tying should be legal except in circumstances where there is strong evidence that the tying conduct harms consumers.[267] Layne-Farrar and Salinger

---

[262] *Microsoft (Case COMP/C-3/37/792 – Microsoft)* (n. 125) paras 835–954.
[263] Ibid. 300.
[264] Hou (n. 230) 687.
[265] Anne Layne-Farrar and Michael A. Salinger, 'Bundling of RAND-Committed Patents' (2016) 45 Research Policy 1155, 1156–7; Bowman (n. 158).
[266] Christian Ahlborn, David S. Evans and A. Jorge Padilla, 'The Antitrust Economics of Tying: A Farewell to Per Se Illegality Antitrust in the US and EU: Converging or Diverging Paths' (2004) 49 Antitrust Bulletin 287, 319–21.
[267] Ibid. 290.

have observed that, on the one hand, tying SEPs to non-SEPs could enable right holders to evade FRAND commitments but that, on the other hand, it can achieve efficiencies through lower contracting and litigation costs; therefore the authors suggest that such tying be permitted, but remain subject to FRAND obligations; moreover it is demonstrated that tying would tend to lower the FRAND licensing fees charged.[268]

The application of general competition law disciplines such as tying will likely continue to generate difficult cases in the specific context of interoperability standards; nevertheless, noting in particular the close connection between tying and refusal to supply obligations, the analysis in preceding sections regarding the essential facilities doctrine will apply also in the context of tying cases; if anything tying disciplines should be applied more sparingly than refusal to supply obligations.

5.7 Horizontal Conduct

Standard-setting could also be a venue for horizontal anticompetitive practices, such as illegal price-fixing or market sharing agreements. Indeed, a number of purported standardization attempts have been shown to be little more than fronts for cartel conduct.[269] For this reason there will always likely be some degree of scrutiny by competition regulators of standard-setting bodies. Discussions in standard-setting forums about pricing could give rise to suspicions of price-fixing. Likewise, collective rights organizations such as patent pools need to adhere to certain standards of conduct to avoid being viewed as collusive agreements. Nevertheless, in recognition of the profound benefits to society arising from standard-setting processes in general, competition regulators are generally inclined to take a permissive approach to the assessment of standard-setting activity.

5.7.1 United States Law

In the United States, although standardization activities could, in principle, offend §1 of the Sherman Act, the Standards Development Organization Act of 2004 confirms that the practices of SSOs are to be

---

[268] Layne-Farrar and Salinger (n. 266) 1156.
[269] Hovenkamp (n. 218) 91–3.

evaluated under the rule of reason: the conduct is to be judged on the basis of its reasonableness, taking into account all relevant factors affecting competition.[270] The Department of Justice on occasion has assessed the intellectual property policies of SSOs under the rule of reason standard,[271] for example in 2015 when Acting Assistant Attorney General Hesse issued a business review letter to IEEE, concluding that amendments to IEEE's patent policy had the potential to benefit competition and consumers by mitigating patent hold-up and royalty stacking, and were unlikely to harm competition. The Department thus indicated that it did not intend to take antitrust enforcement action against IEEE at that point in time, but reserved the right to do so in due course, should implementation of the revised patent policy lead to anticompetitive results.[272]

Assistant Attorney Hesse's letter also expressed some insightful limitations as to the Department's review:

> The Department's task in the business review process is to advise the requesting party of the Department's present antitrust enforcement intentions regarding the proposed conduct. It is not the Department's role to assess whether IEEE's policy choices are right for IEEE as a standards-setting organization ('SSO'). SSOs develop and adjust patent policies to best meet their particular needs. It is unlikely that there is a one-size-fits-all approach for all SSOs, and, indeed, variation among SSOs' patent policies could be beneficial to the overall standards-setting process. Other SSOs, therefore, may decide to implement patent policies that differ from the Update.[273]

Hence, the Department emphasized that while it was able to highlight for an SSO where the 'red lines' of antitrust liability were to be found (and avoided), it remained a matter for the SSO to determine the intellectual property policy settings that would best meet its specific technology needs. Notably, this passage indicated that SSO patent policies could remain consistent with the Sherman Act, notwithstanding the absence of patent policy provisions equivalent to those introduced by the IEEE.

---

[270] Standards Development Organization Act 2004 (15 USC §§ 4301–4306) §4302(2).

[271] Renata B. Hesse and Frances Marshall, 'US Antitrust Aspects of FRAND Disputes' in Jorge L. Contreras (ed.), *The Cambridge Handbook of Technical Standardization Law: Competition, Antitrust and Patents* (Cambridge University Press 2017) 267–9.

[272] Renata B. Hesse, 'Response to Electrical and Electronics Engineers Request for Business Review' (2 February 2015) 16 www.justice.gov accessed 20 June 2020.

[273] Ibid. 1–2.

5.7.2 Chinese Law

Under China's Anti-Monopoly Law, standardization agreements could potentially infringe the prohibition on monopolistic agreements set out in Article 13, which prohibits inter alia agreements among competing undertakings limiting the development of new products or new technology.[274] This would be on the basis that by establishing a standard, the SSO participants (many of whom will compete in one market or another) are effectively reducing or excluding the adoption of competing technologies; in cases where there is no obligation on the part of the SSO's members to adopt the standard this risk is likely to be diminished.

Article 15(i) of the AML provides a safe harbour in respect of agreements made to improve technology, or to research and develop new products, but even in such case it would need to be shown that the agreement allows consumers to share the benefits derived from the agreements and will not entirely eliminate competition in the relevant market.[275] Article 55 of the AML will also be relevant: the law does not apply to conduct by undertakings lawfully implementing their intellectual property rights, but is applicable to conduct by undertakings to eliminate or restrict market competition by abusing intellectual property rights.

Clearly, such a Delphic exclusion in relation to the conduct of intellectual property holders warrants clarification in the particular context of standard-setting activities. Guidelines issued by China's NDRC in 2015 indicate that antitrust review of standardization agreements will involve consideration of whether the agreement excludes any specific operators, excludes particular proposals by a specific operator, prohibits the implementation of other standards, or causes 'necessary and reasonable mechanism to restrict IP right enforcement related to the standard'.[276]

5.7.3 European Law

In the EU, the Competition Commission of the European Commission in its Communication on Horizontal Co-operation Agreements has

---

[274] China Anti-Monopoly Law art. 13(d).
[275] Ibid. art. 15.
[276] Nigel Naihung Lee, 'The Recent Development of China's Anti-Monopoly Law on Standard Setting Organization's Patent Pooling Arrangements and the Issues of Incorporating Patent Misuse Doctrine as the Antitrust Review Standard' (2015) Maryland Series in Contemporary Asian Studies 1, 19–20.

indicated that standard-setting activities could potentially engage the prohibition on anticompetitive agreements outlined in TFEU Article 101. In particular, standard-setting can give rise to restrictive effects on competition by potentially restricting price competition and limiting or controlling production, markets, innovation or technical development; technologies not included in a standard may potentially be excluded from the market; and standard-setting can give rise to opportunities for foreclosure where the process for selecting technologies in the standard is de facto controlled by one or more stakeholders or where the standard-setting process is biased towards one or more participants.[277]

Standardization agreements that will not infringe the prohibition outlined in Article 101(1) will not need to be justified by reference to their economic benefits by reference to Article 101(3). In this regard, the Commission recognizes that:

> Where participation in standard-setting, as well as the procedure for adopting the standard in question, is unrestricted and transparent, standardisation agreements which set no obligation to comply with the standard and provide access to the standard on fair, reasonable and non-discriminatory terms do not restrict competition within the meaning of Article 101(1).[278]

Since standard-setting organizations will need to meet these standards of conduct in order to avoid the application of the prohibition in Article 101(1), this implies a role for competition authorities to regulate the activities of SSOs, for example by scrutinizing with care the by-laws of the SSO, including its intellectual property policy, to ensure that they do not give rise to risks of anticompetitive conduct either by the SSO itself or by its members; indeed, the Competition Commission has undertaken this role, communicating to SSOs the instances where their intellectual property policies fall short of these conduct standards.[279]

Notably, even where the SSO by-laws might raise concerns pursuant to Article 101(1) of the TFEU, they would then fall to be assessed pursuant to Article 101(3), in terms of their contribution to promoting technical or

---

[277] Communication from the Commission: Guidelines on the Applicability of Article 101 of the Treaty on the Functioning of the European Union to Horizontal Co-operation Agreements [2011] OJ C11/1 68.
[278] Ibid. C 11/59.
[279] Nicolo Zingales and Olia Kanevskaia, 'The IEEE-SA Patent Policy Update under the Lens of EU Competition Law' (2016) 12 European Competition Journal 195, 201–5; Maurits Dolmans, 'Standards for Standards European Union Law' (2002) 26 Fordham International Law Journal 163, 181.

economic progress. Even SSO policies that fail to meet the Competition Commission's conduct standards for the avoidance of infringement of Article 101(1) might still satisfy the requirements of Article 101(3) and therefore not contravene the competition laws.

5.7.4 Concerted Practices and Interoperability Standards – Analysis

Even where competition authorities are inclined to rely on concerted practices disciplines to regulate the activities (notably, the intellectual property policies) of SSOs, the authority will need to consider carefully whether the policy privileges the rights of either creators or users of intellectual property; a policy favouring the former presents risks of hold-up, whereas a policy favouring the latter will present risks of hold-out; a policy that balances the rights of each group will be most likely to withstand competition law scrutiny.[280]

In any case, the capability of national competition regulatory authorities to police the activities of SSOs should not be overstated. The ultimate sanction available to the competition authority where it is unsatisfied with the by-laws of the SSO will be a cartel investigation, occasioning prosecutions and the usual remedies (e.g. fines, other orders). This would represent a heavy-handed response which would likely serve to discourage standardization activities and encourage them to migrate to a more favourable jurisdiction. For this reason, the leverage held by competition authorities over the intellectual property policies of SSOs is best applied sparingly and in a nuanced fashion.

Furthermore, the ultimate goal of both standardization activities and the protection of intellectual property is to encourage dynamic efficiency. Competition regulatory agencies may lack the analytical tools to impose on SSOs the set of intellectual property policies which is apt to optimize technological development for the benefit of right holders and users (as acknowledged in the Department of Justice's 2015 business review letter to IEEE). SSOs are primarily fora where engineers come together to set highly detailed and specialized technical specifications; it would be difficult for competition regulators to determine ex ante which set of intellectual property policies is best adapted to achieve the specific technology goals of the SSO.

In the case of SSO bylaws which are manifestly inadequate in terms of addressing the risks associated with hold-up, or which are

---

[280] Zingales and Kanevskaia (n. 279) 203–5.

demonstrably biased in favour of the interests of either creators or users of standardised technologies, there may be a role for competition regulators to intervene – most likely via communications with the SSO and the issuance of letters of assurance in respect of its by-laws – in order to secure the remedy of such defects. However, for competition regulators to adopt a heavy-handed approach and seek to determine the finer details of SSO intellectual property policies is likely to be counterproductive in terms of securing the optimal degree of dynamic efficiency.

5.8 Competition Law Approaches to SEIP: Conclusions

This chapter has examined the various ways in which competition laws are applicable in the context of interoperability standards, including in relation to access to SEIP. Perhaps the most controversial, and widely considered, question is the extent to which an essential facilities doctrine could be instrumental in securing access to interoperability standards, and to SEIP; a number of jurisdictions, led by the EU, have applied the doctrine to this end. The essential facilities doctrine has been applied in a variety of situations, for example refusal to supply interoperability information, refusal to license SEIP or seeking injunctions from a competent court in respect of SEIP.

The precise conditions under which the doctrine will, or should, apply in each of these situations remains somewhat unclear. EU law, for example, appears to apply a different analytical matrix for the last-mentioned situation (see *Huawei, Motorola*) from the other two (see *IMS Health, Magill, Microsoft*), in addition to the existing difference under EU law between refusals to supply generally and refusals to license intellectual property.

The underlying policy basis for these differences could benefit from further exploration, and explanation. Law and economics assessment of the essential facilities doctrine highlights that it should only be applied sparingly, if ever. Moreover, very significant transatlantic differences are apparent: in the USA the doctrine no longer exists, whilst in the EU it applies relatively commonly. Other jurisdictions, including China, are adopting the EU approach.

Because there are entrenched differences between jurisdictions regarding the applicability of the doctrine, and because the foundations in law and economics of the doctrine are tenuous, the doctrine is not recommended as a basis for international agreement to address concerns

5.8 COMPETITION LAW APPROACHES TO SEIP

associated with access to interoperability standards and to SEIP. Inter-jurisdictional differences are likewise present in relation to the related question of whether seeking a court-ordered injunction in relation to SEIP (notably in the context of FRAND-encumbered SEPs) amounts to a breach of the competition laws.

Another unilateral conduct doctrine, that of excessive pricing with respect to intellectual property rights, is also available but is even more controversial and less-well accepted. Another potential basis of liability is tying, whose law and economic assessment bears many similarities to that of refusal to supply. Whilst jurisdictions have considered other bases of liability (e.g. misconduct or fraud in the creation of standards), it is unclear precisely how these actions will, or should, sound in competition law.

Regarding antitrust and competition laws disciplining concerted practices such as cartels or other anticompetitive agreements, these will clearly apply to standard-setting practices which are simply fronts for price-fixing or other cartel conduct. Regarding more legitimate standard-setting activity, these disciplines will apply at least in theory, but in practice are more likely to supply broad guidelines than facilitate intrusive regulation by competition authorities of the precise detail of an SSO's intellectual property policy.

Surveying these diverse (and increasingly divergent) jurisdictional practices, it would seem reasonable to recommend that jurisdictions should continue to apply their generally applicable competition laws in the context of interoperability standards, and SEIP. Yet, it may be stretching the fabric of competition law too far to see competition law as the primary remedy for securing access to interoperability standards and SEIP. Inventing novel bases of liability in competition law (such fraud or misconduct, or breach of FRAND) should be done sparingly and with considerable care. Also to be borne in mind is whether other bodies of law (including contract, equity and the limiting doctrines in intellectual property law) can address these issues in a more straightforward and streamlined fashion.

Finally, our survey reveals that the policy basis for the application of competition laws is equally as important as the requirements of the laws themselves, since this policy foundation will guide courts in 'hard cases'. Any international initiative in this area needs to take cognizance of fundamental policy differences between jurisdictions.

PART III

Towards Liability and Compensation

6

Exclusive Property Rules or Liability Rules for Interoperability Standards and Standards Essential Intellectual Property?

6.1 Exclusive Property Rules, Liability Rules and Inalienability Rules

To find a way forwards in terms of access to interoperability standards and SEIP, it will be useful to consider a framework that is broad enough to encompass both intellectual property and competition law. One particularly helpful approach derives from the distinction drawn in law and economics literature between liability rules and exclusive property rules. This branch of law and economics derives from a groundbreaking paper published by Guido Calabresi and Douglas Melamed in the *Harvard Law Review* in 1972.[1] However the roots of this modality of thought may be traced back further, to the pioneering law and economics scholarship of Ronald Coase, which in many ways laid the foundations for the analysis which was to follow.

6.1.1 The Coase Theorem

Ronald Coase outlined his key insight into law and economics in his groundbreaking paper entitled 'The Problem of Social Cost'.[2] The Coase Theorem provides that in a zero-transaction cost world, the initial allocation of rights and the legal rule applied will not matter because private agents will costlessly bargain to find the most efficient solution, which will occur where the entitlement rests with the agent who values it most highly. The Coase Theorem reminds us that from an economic efficiency perspective, distributive considerations are not relevant. Nevertheless,

---

[1] Guido R. Calabresi and A. Douglas Melamed, 'Property Rules, Liability Rules, and Inalienability: One View of the Cathedral' (1972) 85 Harvard Law Review 1089.
[2] Ronald Coase, 'The Problem of Social Cost' (1960) 3 Journal of Law and Economics 1.

where the assumption of zero transaction costs is relaxed, initial allocations and legal rules do matter. If transaction costs exceed the benefit to the parties of a transaction, the transaction will not take place and therefore the initial allocation will be final. Therefore, policymakers should craft initial allocations and legal rules so as to ensure that transaction costs do not prevent the realization of the most efficient outcome, that is, entitlements being held by those who value them the most.[3]

Since the foundational work of Coase, many scholars have applied his reasoning to different contexts. This includes situations where hold-up may occur. Demsetz, for example, demonstrated that provided the assumption of zero transaction costs holds, hold-up or other strategic behaviour will not prevent the final efficient allocation of rights, although it may well alter the internal distribution of the contractual surplus between the parties.[4]

6.1.2 *The Calabresi and Melamed Framework*

The distinction between liability and exclusive property rules was outlined in Calabresi and Melamed's classic 1972 paper, which described the distinction as follows: 'An entitlement is protected by a property rule to the extent that someone who wishes to remove the entitlement from its holder must buy it from him in a voluntary transaction in which the value of the entitlement is agreed upon by the seller'.[5] Likewise, 'Whenever someone may destroy the initial entitlement if he is willing to pay an objectively determined value for it, an entitlement is protected by a liability rule'.[6] Calabresi and Melamed also discuss a third type of rule, which they term an 'inalienability rule', as follows: 'An entitlement is inalienable to the extent that its transfer is not permitted between a willing buyer and a willing seller'.[7] Inalienability rules are not generally applied in the context of intellectual property and are not of particular assistance to the analysis which follows. Polinsky formulates the same nomenclature in similar terms.[8]

---

[3] See Francesco Parisi, 'Coase Theorem', *The New Palgrave Dictionary of Economics* (2nd ed., Palgrave Macmillan 2008).
[4] Harold Demsetz, 'When Does the Rule of Liability Matter?' (1972) 1 The Journal of Legal Studies 13, 22–5; Parisi (n. 3).
[5] Calabresi and Melamed (n. 1) 1092.
[6] Ibid.
[7] Ibid.
[8] A. Mitchell Polinsky, 'On the Choice between Liability Rules and Property Rules' (1980) XVIII Economic Inquiry 233, 233.

6.1 EXCLUSIVE PROPERTY RULES, LIABILITY RULES 235

According to Calabresi and Melamed, society has two key issues to decide: who will hold an entitlement and which rule the entitlement will be protected by.[9] In the context of the tort law of nuisance, and in particular a transaction involving two economic agents A and B, these considerations can result in four possible scenarios: (i) A has the entitlement, protected by a property rule; (ii) A has the entitlement, protected by a liability rule; (iii) B has the entitlement, protected by a property rule; and (iv) B has the entitlement, protected by a liability rule.

Suppose that A operates a barbecue, driving noxious smoke onto B's property. Suppose the smoke blackens sheets which B is drying on his clothesline (this borrows from Coase's famous example).[10] B brings a claim against A in the courts, alleging nuisance. The court can make four possible orders. First, it can decide that B has an entitlement (the right to clean sheets), protected by a property rule. Thus, the court finds a nuisance against A, and grants B an injunction. A cannot continue to send smoke over to B's property unless he negotiates with B and pays a price that is acceptable to B. With zero transaction costs, this will occur if the value to A of using his barbecue exceeds the cost to B of the blackening of his sheets (we assume that B derives no utility from A's smoke). Alternatively, the court could find nuisance against A, but refuse to grant an injunction, instead ordering A to compensate B for the damage done to his sheets. Thus, B holds the entitlement, protected by a liability rule. Third, the court could find no nuisance. This is effectively giving A an entitlement to emit smoke from his barbecue, protected by a property rule: B can only stop A from emitting smoke by paying him a price which is acceptable to A.

Calabresi and Melamed also identified a (somewhat obscure) fourth situation, where A holds the entitlement, protected by a liability rule. In this case B can require A to stop the smoke but B must compensate A for the costs associated with doing so, at a valuation determined by the court. Again, with zero transaction costs, A and B can bargain around this entitlement to achieve a potentially Pareto optimal solution.

Calabresi and Melamed also stimulated discussion of the circumstances in which a property or a liability rule might be preferred. They began by classifying the sorts of considerations society might take into account into three categories: (1) economic efficiency; (2) distributional goals; and (3) other justice reasons. As regards economic efficiency, the

---

[9] Calabresi and Melamed (n. 1) 1090–2.
[10] See Coase (n. 2).

authors propose the use of 'potential Pareto' or Kaldor-Hicks efficiency: the optimal outcome is reached where no further alteration is possible where the gains to the winners exceed the losses to the losers, such that the winners could (potentially) compensate the losers and still remain better off.[11]

In terms of efficiency considerations, Calabresi and Melamed concluded that economic efficiency would dictate a set of entitlements that favours knowledgeable choices between social benefits and the social costs of avoiding them, and furthermore: 'that this implies, in the absence of certainty as to whether a benefit is worth its costs to society, that the cost should be put on the party or activity best located to make such a cost-benefit analysis'.[12] In circumstances where that party is difficult to identify: 'the costs should be put on the party or activity which can with the lowest transaction costs act in the market to correct an error in entitlements by inducing the party who can avoid social costs most cheaply to do so'.[13] Calabresi and Melamed provide an example of a case where a liability rule would be superior to a property because of strategic behaviour or 'hold-out' on the part of land owners – which is a surprisingly similar scenario to the issues arising concerning SEPs in the context of formal standard-setting activities.[14] The example is given of a tract of land which is proposed to be turned into a public park; for this to occur, each of the landholders will have to sell at a price approximating to the valuation of his or her land. If sufficient landholders hold-out for a higher price, the total price rises to a level at which the transactions do not proceed and therefore the park does not come into existence.

The authors treat this as an example of transaction costs: a transfer does not occur because the cost of establishing the value of the entitlement is too high.[15] But equally, it could be interpreted as an instance of Cournot complements, with each of the landowners holding a monopoly over his parcel of land, and each parcel being essential to the establishment of the park. There is strategic behaviour on the part of the landowners: each tries to obtain for himself a share of the profits to be had from the creation of the park that exceeds the value that is properly attributable to the parcel. This has the ultimate result of

---

[11] Calabresi and Melamed (n. 1) 1096.
[12] Ibid. 1096.
[13] Ibid. 1097.
[14] Ibid. 1106–8.
[15] Ibid. 1106.

precluding the establishment of the park, which would be Pareto efficient. Thus, Calabresi and Melamed's example, which is intended to provide an illustration of possible situations in which a liability rule may be preferable to a property rule, anticipates the problems associated with access to SEIP.

6.1.3 Extensions of the Calabresi and Melamed Framework

Following from the initial analytical work undertaken by Calabresi and Melamed, many scholars considered the implications of this work, notably the circumstances in which either a liability rule or an exclusive property rule might be preferable. Kaplow and Shavell supplied the useful overarching hypothesis that a liability rule is preferable for harmful externalities, but that a property rule is preferable in relation to the taking of things. In relation to the taking of things where bargaining is possible (the most relevant situation), these authors consider that bargaining between property holders and takers is possible under both property and liability rules. However, property rules are preferred for a number of reasons, notably that: (i) owners will be reluctant to bargain because of a multiplicity of would-be takers; (ii) reciprocal takings are a problem; and (iii) excessive taking will lead to wasteful investments in technologies to prevent and facilitate taking.[16]

Polinsky explained that for negative externalities, under conditions of strategic behaviour, complete information on the part of the collective authority and lump sum transfers not being available, there will generally be no advantage of liability rules over property rules, observing: 'the choice between property rules and liability rules is interesting only if the collective authority has preferences regarding the distribution of income between the parties. Otherwise, given perfect information, the rules are equally desirable since either one can achieve the efficient outcome'.[17] Krier and Schwab argued that it is a necessary corollary of the Coase Theorem that where transaction costs are zero or minimal, judges need not concern themselves with economic efficiency considerations and can instead decide on the basis of other justice considerations alone. Where an initial allocation is economically inefficient, economic agents will bargain at zero or minimal cost to reallocate the right to the

---

[16] Louis Kaplow and Stephen Shavell, 'Property Rules Versus Liability Rules: An Economic Analysis' (1996) 109 Harvard Law Review 713, 774.
[17] Polinsky (n. 8) 235.

agent who places the highest value upon it.[18] By contrast, where transaction costs are significant, courts must consider which is the most economically efficient initial allocation – and in doing so must take the nature and quantum of transaction costs into account.[19] Krier and Schwab cited (and proceeded to critique) the conventional wisdom advanced by the post-Calabresi and Melamed scholarship: 'Hence the familiar piece of conventional wisdom that amounts to virtual doctrine: When transaction costs are low, use property rules; when transaction costs are high, use liability rules'.[20] Krier and Schwab take issue with this conventional wisdom, suggesting that it is not only transaction costs that are relevant. Rather we should also consider assessment costs to the courts of gathering the information necessary to assess the quantum of damages for a liability rule, along with the costs imposed by the courts' errors. Krier and Schwab summarize their position as follows:

> In short, when (a) assessment costs promote inaccurate damage awards by the judge, and (b) bargaining between the parties is at the same time impeded by transaction costs, there is no a priori basis for favoring liability rules over property rules. If (a) and (b) are the real-world conditions-and we think they regularly are-then the conventional preference for liability rules makes no sense.[21]

Under this analytical lens, the task for judges is to assess whether transaction costs are likely to be greater or less than a court's own assessment costs.[22]

In sum, the law and economics scholarship has not provided a clear position in favour of either liability rules or exclusive property rules, nor indeed even an agreed approach to discerning when one particular approach or another is to be preferred. Generally, however, there emerges, particularly from the work of Krier and Schwab, and also Polinsky, a degree of scepticism as to the value of property rules over liability rules, and an indifference as between to the two, particularly in circumstances where transaction costs are not so high as to prevent efficient bargaining away from an initial allocation of rights and obligations.

---

[18] James E. Krier and Stewart J Schwab, 'Property Rules and Liability Rules: The Cathederal in Another Light' (1995) 70 New York University Law Review 440, 443.
[19] Ibid. 449.
[20] Ibid. 451.
[21] Ibid. 455.
[22] Ibid. 459.

The next step in our analysis is to consider how the framework of liability rules and exclusive property rules has generally been applied in the context of intellectual property rights, including in the particular context of SEIP.

6.2 Standards-Essential Intellectual Property: Exclusive Property Rules or Liability Rules?

Much of the development of the framework of liability rules and exclusive property rules relates to tort law, notably accidents and nuisance, both of which are examples of harmful externalities. Whilst some scholars (notably Kaplow and Shavell)[23] have extended their analysis to possessory things, they focus on unique and specific assets (like houses). By contrast, the information protected by intellectual property is generally non-rivalrous in nature; as a result, conclusions reached in relation to fixed assets like houses will not necessarily apply in the context of intellectual property. A number of scholars have given consideration to these issues in the context of intellectual property, including SEIP, although in many cases the analysis is not framed in the terms outlined by Calabresi and Melamed.

6.2.1 Existing Scholarship

Merges noted the advantages of exclusive property rules for intellectual property rights, pointing to Arrow's 'paradox of information': without property rights, inventors have a dilemma because if they disclose the invention they have nothing to trade but if they do not, the buyer cannot discern if the idea is valuable.[24] Merges considers that transaction costs are high in the context of intellectual property rights, but disputed that this is a sound reason for preferring liability rules: rather, high transaction costs encourage creators and users of intellectual property to form collective rights organizations,[25] he also observed that: 'More importantly for property rights theory in general, the property rule facilitates this adjustment. By contrast, statutory liability rules work against the flexible, voluntary institutions that are formed to overcome the costs

---

[23] Kaplow and Shavell (n. 16).
[24] Robert P. Merges, 'Of Property Rights, Coase and Intellectual Property' (1994) 94 Columbia Law Review 2655, 2657–8.
[25] Ibid. 2662.

faced by transactors'.[26] Applying the Calabresi and Melamed framework, Merges argued:

> IPR cases fit the criteria set up by Calabresi and Melamed for application of a property rule: (1) there are only two parties to the transaction; (2) the costs of a transaction between the parties are otherwise low; and, most importantly, (3) a court called on to set the terms of the exchange would have a difficult time doing so quickly and cheaply, given the specialized nature of the assets and the varied and complex business environments in which they are deployed.[27]

In a similar vein, Smith considered a spectrum of possible approaches to intellectual property, from a commons approach to exclusivity regimes, without specifically considering liability rules;[28] he expressed a preference for property rules, because their greater modularity results in information cost savings.[29]

In his seminal 1996 paper, Merges contended that private collective rights organizations, where creators and users of intellectual property rights 'contract into' liability rules, exhibit superior efficiency compared with either statutory or court-ordered liability rules. Merges further argued that property rules are superior as they encourage agents to join efficient collective rights organizations (including patent pools).[30] Merges also includes some interesting allusions in his paper to 'foundational' or 'exceptional' patents which earned higher royalties,[31] and 'exceptional inventions' which were excluded from informal patent pool arrangements.[32] Lemley, in a counterpoint article to Merges' piece, argues that contracting around liability rules is also feasible. Undertaking a careful study of settlement practices in patent and copyright law, Lemley concludes that property rules do not appear to offer superior outcomes in terms encouraging greater settlement of cases, and that parties appear to be equally capable of negotiating around liability rules.[33]

---

[26] Ibid.
[27] Ibid. 2664.
[28] Henry E. Smith, 'Intellectual Property as Property: Delineating Entitlements in Information' (2007) 116 Yale Law Journal 1742, 1758.
[29] Ibid. 1817–18.
[30] Robert P. Merges, 'Contracting into Liability Rules: Intellectual Property Rights and Collective Rights Organizations' (1996) 84 California Law Review 1293, 1293.
[31] Ibid. 1343–4.
[32] Ibid. 1351–2.
[33] Mark A. Lemley, 'Contracting Around Liability Rules' (2012) 100 California Law Review 463, 476, 477–83.

Antonelli conceptualizes technological knowledge as an essential facility, owing to economics of density arising from the possibility of allocating the fixed costs of innovation among all possible users.[34] Antonelli considers that, while intellectual property rights provide an important signalling function and facilitate the emergence of specialized markets for disembodied knowledge, the imposition of property rules for intellectual property results in 'knowledge rationing', resulting in: (i) decreased allocative and technical efficiency; (ii) reduced dynamic efficiency owing to the reductions in the dissemination of knowledge; (iii) costs of litigation and other transaction costs; and (iv) duplication and coordination problems. To redress the problems associated with exclusivity, Antonelli proposes a 'compensatory liability' regime.[35] Antonelli sees telecommunications access regulation as an important precedent, separating exclusive ownership from open-access use, and also sees compulsory licensing as a useful reference point.[36] Antonelli considers that compensation should be ex post and court-determined, based on the court's assessment of the proper share which the right holder should receive of the economic value generated by the innovative product of the user.[37]

Noting traditional arguments in favour of property rules, namely that the transaction costs of patent licensing are smaller than the information costs of liability rules (e.g. in the form of compulsory licences),[38] Depoorter questions this conventional wisdom on the basis that: (i) patent valuation is also difficult for patent holders and prospective licensees, not just for third party arbiters such as courts; (ii) the difficulties in establishing patent boundaries increase the cost of patent licensing; and (iii) positive externalities arising from the complementary nature of diverse patented inventions means that some innovative solutions will not be pursued.[39]

In his 2001 paper, Carl Shapiro coined the phrase 'patent thicket' and introduced concerns surrounding 'patent holdup'.[40] Building on

---

[34] Cristiano Antonelli, 'Technological Knowledge as an Essential Facility' (2007) 17 Journal of Evolutionary Economics 451, 464.
[35] Ibid. 456–7.
[36] Ibid. 457–8.
[37] Ibid. 461.
[38] Ben Depoorter, 'Property Rules, Liability Rules and Patent Market Failure' (2008) 01 Erasmus Law Review 59, 66.
[39] Ibid. 67–73.
[40] Carl Shapiro, 'Navigating the Patent Thicket: Cross Licenses, Patent Pools, and Standard Setting' in Adam B. Laffe, Josh Lerner and Scott Stern (eds.), *Innovation Policy and the*

Shapiro's work, Lemley and Shapiro suggested that for firms which do not practise their patent, injunctions should not be available in situations where costs of redesign exceed the value of the patented feature.[41] If the redesign cost is small and the infringer is able to design around the patent, the authors suggest a permanent injunction should be awarded, but a stay granted to give the infringer time to design around the patent.[42] In all cases of infringement, reasonable royalties should be paid to the patent holder.[43] Lemley and Weiser suggested that liability rules are preferable to property rules in industries strongly characterized by component patenting, where an injunction in relation to a single patented component would potentially prohibit significant non-infringing conduct.[44] Lemley and Weiser suggest the courts develop core cases where injunctions are viewed as presumptively appropriate or presumptively inappropriate.[45] The authors further state:

> It is quite clear to us, for example, that courts should cast a sceptical eye at claims for injunctive relief where the patent owner is not a direct competitor of the defendant, where the defendant did not copy the invention from the patent owner, and where the patented invention is only a small part of an overall product. In such cases, an injunction does not seem necessary for market exclusivity or deterrence purposes, and it is likely to cause significant harm to the makers of products.[46]

By way of a general rule, Lemley and Weiser suggest: 'We believe that when injunctive relief results in a shutdown of significant noninfringing uses along with the infringing uses, the use of a property rule is inappropriate'.[47] Lemley and Weiser lay down three lessons that should be borne in mind when setting liability rules: (i) liability rules should be clearly defined; (ii) liability rules should be appropriately limited so that

---

Economy, vol. 1 (MIT Press 2001). See also Mark A. Lemley, 'Ten Things to Do About Patent Holdup of Standards (and One Not To)' (2007) 48 Boston College Law Review 149, 166-7.

[41] Carl Shapiro and Mark A. Lemley, 'Patent Holdup and Royalty Stacking' (2007) 85 Texas Law Review 1992, 2037-8. The authors suggest a further requirement: that the user have invented the feature independently rather than copied it from the right holder.

[42] Ibid. 2038.

[43] Ibid. 2037-8.

[44] Mark A. Lemley and Philip J. Weiser, 'Should Property or Liability Rules Govern Information?' (2006) 85 Texas Law Review 783, 798.

[45] Ibid. 799.

[46] Ibid. 799-800.

[47] Ibid. 803.

they do not undermine investment incentives; (iii) setting and enforcing liability rules can be quite costly.[48]

Very similar conclusions emerge from the work of Cotter (2009), who suggests that, while injunctive relief should be the norm in patent infringement cases,[49] damages alone should be sufficient (without the award of an injunction) when 'patent holdup' is present. Cotter defines patent hold-up as:

> When a component patent owner (2) is able to exploit its bargaining position vis-à-vis downstream users (3) due to the possibility that the patent owner will be able to enjoin the manufacture, use, or sale of an end product that incorporates the patent invention, (4) in such a way as to threaten either (a) static deadweight losses far out of proportion to any likely increases in dynamic efficiency; or (b) dynamic efficiency losses due to downstream users' reduced incentives to invest in standard-specific technology or to engage in follow-up innovation.[50]

Cotter also suggested a liability rule in the context of SEIP, citing the work of Oliver Williamson and observing that a patent holder may 'hold-up' a user in order to extract a greater share of the gains from trade, once the user has made asset-specific investments in the relationship, and that the risks of hold-up occurring may deter the user from making such asset-specific investments.[51] Cotter further argued that hold-up may produce little, if any, benefit in terms of dynamic efficiency because the patent system should seek to align rewards with an inventor's contribution; allowing the patent holder to reap the benefits of the user's creative activity through hold-up is thus unlikely to encourage dynamic efficiency.[52] Cotter also notes the concerns regarding Cournot complements.[53] Cotter confines his suggestions to situations where a number of additional conditions are met: (i) the patent must contribute to some end product, rather than constituting an end product in itself;[54] (ii) the thesis only applies where the patent holder and the user do not compete in a downstream market;[55] and (iii) the thesis only applies where the user sells a multicomponent end

---

[48] Ibid. 813.
[49] Thomas F. Cotter, 'Patent Holdup, Patent Remedies and Antitrust Responses' (2009) 34 Journal of Corporation Law 1151, 1175.
[50] Ibid. 1153–4.
[51] Ibid. 1163.
[52] Ibid. 1168.
[53] Ibid. 1169.
[54] Ibid. 1171.
[55] Ibid.

product.[56] In colloquial terms, then, Cotter confines his thesis to situations where both 'patent trolls' and 'patent thickets'/'royalty stacking' are present.

6.2.2 Analysis: Liability or Exclusive Property Rules for Standards-Essential Intellectual Property?

First, we proceed on the basis that economic efficiency considerations are paramount, and that (per the framework of Calabresi and Melamed), distributive and other justice considerations are not especially important in this context. It is fairly well accepted that intellectual property laws seek to balance static efficiency losses associated with the market power (or even monopoly) of the right holder with (net) dynamic efficiency gains resulting from improved incentives for innovation. This basic framework is adequate to guide us not just for intellectual property rights generally but also for the specific case of SEIP.

To unpack this further, granting an intellectual property right (e.g. a patent), in circumstances where the grant of that right gives rise to market power or monopoly, will result in the usual static efficiency losses associated with monopoly pricing but may not occasion any corresponding static efficiency gains. In terms of dynamic efficiency, the grant of the right (and its enforcement via either an exclusive property or a liability rule) could potentially give rise to both dynamic efficiency gains and losses. Dynamic efficiency gains can be expected to arise due to positive externalities associated with the creation of knowledge: the intellectual property right enables the inventor or creator to capture a larger slice of the total social benefits associated with the invention or work. This in turn is likely to provide incentives to other inventors and creators to invest time and resources in efficient creative activities.

However, in industries characterized by a high degree of cumulative innovation, the protection of intellectual property rights could also result in dynamic efficiency losses resulting from impacts on follow-on innovation. In markets involving SEIP, a trade-off may be observed between, on the one hand, incentives to invest in innovative activities that will lead to the development of new standards or revised versions of existing standards (e.g. new or revised mobile air interface standards) and, on the other hand, incentives to develop new and innovative consumer

---

[56] Ibid.

products and services on the basis of existing standards (e.g. innovative new mobile handset designs).

In markets where follow-on innovation is significant, establishing the efficient price for intellectual property that will result inadequate incentives for both initial and follow-on innovation is likely to be extremely difficult, particularly for a judicial or regulatory body.

In general, therefore, the ideal regime for intellectual property rights is likely to be one where the dynamic efficiency gains associated with the protection of the intellectual property outweigh the combined static and dynamic efficiency losses associated with that protection. This is the basic cost-benefit analysis that should be applied both to intellectual property generally, and to SEIP in particular. Furthermore, it is reasonable to assume (based on the Neo-Chicago framework of scholars such as Evans and Padilla)[57] that courts are not, in general, well-placed to undertake such a balancing of static and dynamic effects. Instead, clear rules are needed that provide bright lines to courts, such that courts are not required to undertake a detailed analysis of the likely static and dynamic efficiency effects on a case by case basis.[58]

Turning to the question of transaction and assessment costs, we consider that three broad categories need to be considered: (i) transaction costs, notably the costs to private parties of negotiating licences under the shadow of either an injunction or a damages award; (ii) the costs associated with strategic behaviour, such as 'hold-up' and 'hold-out' scenarios, similar to that presciently described by Calabresi and Melamed; and (iii) assessment costs incurred by courts in determining the appropriate quantum of damages, including the costs imposed by incorrect valuations imposed in court orders.

Finally, it should be noted that it is not the purpose of this book to consider whether, in general, property rules or liability rules are to be preferred for intellectual property rights (noting, however, that the literature universally favours exclusive property rules as the general case for intellectual property). Rather our analysis is confined to the particular case of SEIP. We begin our analysis with an assessment of applicable static efficiency considerations.

---

[57] David S. Evans and A. George Padilla, 'Designing Antitrust Rules for Assessing Unilateral Practices: A Neo-Chicago Approach' (2005) 72 University of Chicago Law Review 73.
[58] Ibid.; see Christian Ahlborn, David S. Evans and A. Jorge Padilla, 'The Logic & Limits of the Exceptional Circumstances Test in Magill and IMS Health' (2004) 28 Fordham International Law Journal 1109.

6.2.2.1 Static Efficiency Considerations

Cournot Complements The issue raised most prominently in the law and economics literature in support of liability rules for SEIP is based on the theory of Cournot complements, initially put forward by French economist Augustin Cournot in the first half of the nineteenth century. Cournot demonstrated that where two producers of complementary inputs (e.g. copper and tin) merge to create a monopoly producing a final good that is the composite of the two complementary inputs (e.g. brass), prices will be lower.[59] As separate firms, the producers do not take account of each other's prices in setting their own. Where each is a monopoly, each will charge at the monopoly level. As an integrated firm, a single monopoly rent is charged, resulting in a lower overall price. This result was confirmed more recently by Economides and Salop, who demonstrated that in complex markets characterized by combinations of complementary and competing goods, integration that internalizes vertical externalities (between complements) while maintaining competition between competing goods (described as 'composite goods competition') provides superior results to maintaining fully independent production.[60]

It is appropriate to apply the Cournot complements model to SEIP, such as the case where multiple patents (more precisely, multiple patent claims dispersed across multiple patents) are essential to the practice of a standard.[61] Each SEP can be characterized as a monopoly, since a prospective user cannot (legally) practice the standard without the consent of each right holder.[62] Multiple SEPs in respect of a given interoperability standard should be characterized as complements, rather

---

[59] Antoine Augustin Cournot, *Researches into the Mathematical Principles of the Theory of Wealth, 1838* (Nathaniel T. Bacon tr., MacMillan 1929); Nicholas Economides and Steven C. Salop, 'Competition and Integration Among Complements, and Network Market Structure' (1992) 40 The Journal of Industrial Economics 105, 106.

[60] Economides and Salop (n. 59) 114–16.

[61] Mark A. Lemley and Carl Shapiro, 'Patent Holdup and Royalty Stacking' (2007) 85 Texas Law Review 1992–2049 (p. 2013); Cotter (n. 49) 1169–70; Joseph Farrell and others, 'Standard-Setting, Patents and Hold-Up' (2007) 74(3) Antitrust Law Journal 603–70 (642–4); Damien Gerardin, Anne Layne-Farrar and A. Jorge Padilla, 'The Complements Problem Within Standard Setting: Assessing the Evidence on Royalty Stacking' (2008) 14 Boston University Journal of Science, Technology and Law 144–76 (145–9) ('certainly the complements theory behind royalty stacking has stood the test of time. The relevant question is not whether royalty stacking is possible, though, but whether it is common enough and costly enough in actuality to warrant policy changes').

[62] See, e.g., *Motorola – Enforcement of GPRS Standard Essential Patents (Case AT39985)* (European Commission) [207]–[208].

than substitutes, since a licence to practise each SEP is required to practise the standard, and one SEP cannot be substituted for another. As monopolists, each SEP holder may (at least in theory) seek to price at the monopoly level.

This will mean that a prospective user must pay many different monopoly rents to multiple SEP holders. In the extreme case, the net result of such 'royalty stacking' may be that the sum of the licence fees becomes so high that the prospective user chooses not to produce the final product – especially if the prospective developer does not hold SEPs that could be included in a cross-licensing agreement. Indeed, the countervailing bargaining power associated with SEPs held by a prospective user will be of no account to a patent assertion entity which does not practise the standard.

Some observations are in order, however. First, for this view to retain its currency, the patent must truly be essential to practice of the standard; claimed essentiality is insufficient. Generally, only a court (or another body with a high level of expertise in intellectual property matters, e.g. a patent pool) can provide a definitive view on the question of essentiality. Second, the possibility of competition between multiple standards (or between standardized and non-standardized marketplace solutions) should not be excluded, although this is rarely addressed in the literature.[63] Standards which exhibit 'patent thickets' are likely to be disadvantaged, and may lose out to standards in respect of which such issues are effectively addressed (including through collective rights organizations).[64] Of course, competition between standards may be severely limited by the phenomena of (direct or indirect) network externalities, positive feedback loops and tipping, which may incline the market towards the dominance or even monopoly of a single standard – but this would need to be established on a case by case basis, since not all markets characterized by interoperability standards tend towards monopoly.

Depending on the strength of network externalities in any given market, the market may 'tip' towards a single dominant standard (as seen in markets for personal computer operating systems and mobile wireless interfaces), or it may tolerate multiple, competing standardized solutions (currently the case with mobile payment solutions). In case of the latter, the need for effective, court-ordered access to SEIP will be

---

[63] But again see ibid. 194–206 which included careful consideration of this issue.
[64] For example, one of the reasons why the BETA standard lost out to VHS was that VHS had more open licensing terms.

weakened because the prospective user can simply avoid the patent thicket by selecting a competing standardized solution.

Hold-up Where there is an incomplete contract between two firms and one of the firms makes relationship-specific investments, part of the returns from these sunk investments can be appropriated ex post by the other party to the relationship. Noting the risks of hold-up, the first party will not make the investment; thus, investment will be below the socially optimal level.[65] Standards-essential intellectual property may present a case of hold-up in the sense that, after a standard has been drafted, approved and established in the marketplace, SEIP holders can 'hold-up' users of the standard (and perhaps also other holders of SEIP), and appropriate some of the returns of the relationship-specific (i.e. standard-specific) investment.[66] As a result of this 'hold-up', licence fees for SEIP may exceed the contribution of the SEIP in question to the value of the final product.[67]

This phenomenon appears to be most prevalent at the moment for SEPs negotiated in the context of formal SSOs, where there are potentially many, many disparate holders of SEPs in respect of any given standard, which could also give rise to 'royalty stacking'.[68] Where the prospective licence fees payable to many SEPs become prohibitively high, end-users may decline to make socially optimal downstream investments based on the standard.[69] This could result in losses to both static and dynamic efficiency (noting that much if not all innovation is follow-on in nature). Nevertheless, it should be conceded (as critics of the 'hold-up' theory' contend)[70] that at this point in time, empirical evidence to support the existence of hold-up is lacking. Of course, if that argument were taken to its logical conclusion, it needs to pointed out that the

---

[65] O. E. Williamson, 'Transactions-Cost Economics: The Governance of Contractual Relations' (1979) 22 Journal of Law and Economics 233.
[66] Shapiro and Lemley (n. 41); Farrell and others (n. 61).
[67] Farrell and others (n. 61).
[68] Shapiro and Lemley (n. 41); Farrell and others (n. 61); Cotter (n. 49).
[69] Shapiro and Lemley (n. 41) 2012; Farrell and others (n. 61) 647.
[70] See, e.g., Gerardin, Layne-Farrar and Padilla (n. 61); Alexander Galetovic and Stephen Haber, 'Innovation Under Threat? An Assessment of the Evidence for Patent Hold-Up and Royalty Stacking in SEP-Intensive, IT Industries' (2016) 3 Competition Policy International Journal; Alexander Galetovic and Stephen Haber, 'The Fallacies of Patent Holdup Theory' (2017) 13(1)Journal of Competition Law & Economics 1, 6–10; J. Gregory Sidak, 'What Aggregate Royalty Do Manufacturers of Mobile Phones Pay to License Standard-Essential Patents?' (2016) 1 The Criterion Journal on Innovation 701.

empirical evidence in support of intellectual property protection generally is also not strong: if policy action were taken only after the accumulation of robust empirical evidence, it is doubtful that intellectual property would be protected in the first place. It is not recommended that a different evidentiary basis be adopted for addressing abuses associated with SEIP, as distinct from the evidentiary base needed for the protection of intellectual property in the first place. Rather, the better approach is to proceed on the basis of a sound policy case based on economic theory alone.

It cannot be excluded that hold-up could also occur in the context of standards-essential copyrights or trade secrets. The nature of the protection afforded by copyright law (which attaches to the creative expression of ideas rather than to the underlying ideas themselves) traditionally implied that a single right holder (where an SSO, consortium or individual firm) would generally hold the copyright in relation to the entire standard. It is conceivable, however, that SSO member contributions to interoperability standards could include copyrighted materials. Concerns regarding access to such copyrights have not arisen to date. However, this could have been because it was traditionally considered that copyright protection did not extend to standardized interfaces; the *Oracle* v. *Google* decisions have questioned this assumption.

Should concerns of 'copyright hold-up', 'copyright royalty stacking' and 'copyright thickets' arise as a consequence of the *Oracle* v. *Google* precedent (which is presently before the Supreme Court), then our analysis in respect of SEPs will also apply in the context of such standards-essential copyrights. Indeed, given the broad scope of protection, the de minimis nature of the originality requirements generally imposed, the lack of formalities and the relatively long term of protection enjoyed by copyrighted works, a case could be made for a broader application of liability rules to standards-essential copyrights.

Trade secrets are not well suited to the joint development of standards by hundreds of innovators simultaneously, since the invention would usually need to be disclosed to the other joint inventors in the first instance, and later to users, resulting in the loss of both secrecy and legal protection;[71] trade secrets are better suited to single-firm

---

[71] The facts of the US and EU *Microsoft* cases presented the unusual situation where the standards developer was able to promulgate the standard whilst still maintaining significant trade secrets. This probably results from the peculiar nature of computer software; in any case, Microsoft did not develop either Windows or its communication protocols jointly with other firms, so there was no Cournot complements problem. In addition,

innovation. Thus, Cournot complements and hold-up problems are much less likely to occur in respect of standards-essential trade secrets.

It should be noted that critics of the 'hold-up' hypothesis have suggested that there is not a classic hold-up in the sense described by scholars such as Williamson.[72] However there is little argument that a situation of many SEPs simultaneously asserting rights in connection with a given standard gives rise to Cournot complements; and whether or not the situation represents a classic 'hold-up' situation as such does not necessarily detract from the policy case for intervention.

Intellectual Property Rights Protecting Components, and Non-infringing Conduct Many patents cover only a single component of a highly complex multicomponent product (e.g. a mobile handset). The final product may incorporate hundreds or even thousands of patented inventions, both SEPs and non-SEPs. Using the threat of injunctions, SEP holders may be able to threaten to remove the end product from the market unless adequate royalties are paid. If the SEP holder's arguments are accepted by a court, and an injunction is granted, this will likely impose static efficiency losses far in excess of any possible dynamic efficiency gains. Moreover, merely by threatening to exclude the final product from the market, the SEP holder will be able to extract a royalty that exceeds the value of the patented invention to the final product.[73] It should be noted that this phenomenon is equally applicable to non-standardized industries.

There could also be similar situations in relation to other intellectual property rights, notably copyright asserted in relation to computer software. Given the collaborative nature of the software development process, any given programme may incorporate multiple protected expressions.[74] Furthermore, a final consumer product such as a computer or smartphone will necessitate the use of many different software programmes simultaneously – and interoperability of those programmes will be essential if the device is to function properly. For

---

Microsoft, whilst unquestionably a monopolist, was probably not pricing anywhere near the monopoly level, and its pricing practices had probably not had any detrimental impact on market uptake of the Windows operating system.

[72] Galetovic and Haber, 'The Fallacies of Patent Holdup Theory' (n. 70) 23–9.
[73] Shapiro and Lemley (n. 41) 2009–10.
[74] Microsoft Corporation, 'Supreme Court, Google v. Oracle: Brief of Microsoft Corporation as Amicus Curiae in Support of Petitioner' (2019) 9 https://supremecourt.gov accessed 22 June 2020.

example, the assertion of copyright over interfaces in the context of an Internet of Things could give rise to serious risks of market fragmentation, and create 'copyright thickets' analogous to the patent thickets seen most prominently during the smartphone patent wars.[75]

Undertakings to License Standards-Essential Intellectual Property In assessing any request for an injunction, courts are likely to consider carefully the precise terms of any undertaking to license given in connection with SEIP, such as a so-called 'FRAND declaration'. As discussed earlier, such declarations will vary from one SSO to another. Since secondary markets for SEIP are well-developed, in some cases the SEIP may be traded to another entity after the declaration is given, calling into question whether the new owner is bound by the declaration. In many if not most cases the declaration can be viewed as part of an 'incomplete bargain' between the right holder and the potential user, facilitating the prospect of 'hold-up'.

Giving careful and precise meaning to the terms of any undertaking to license provided will likely form a central part of a court's analysis of issues concerning access to SEIP. Whilst in some instances the declaration may be found to constitute a binding contract between the right holder and the potential user, this is unlikely to be the case in all or even most circumstances. In other cases, equitable remedies, in particular either a careful consideration of whether injunctions should be awarded, or other equitable doctrines such as estoppel, will likely be found more useful by the courts, because of the inherently flexible and open-ended nature of a court's considerations with respect to these equitable doctrines.

Concerning injunctions, a court may reach the view that where an undertaking is provided, damage to the right holder arising from use of the SEIP is unlikely to be irreparable, and moreover that damages are likely to be an adequate remedy (since the right holder has already agreed to license). Applying estoppel, a court may reach the view that, having given an undertaking to license, the right holder should be estopped from enforcing her patent rights such as obtaining an injunction.

There may also be scope for SSOs to improve the standard form of undertakings given, in order to provide greater clarity to right holders

---

[75] See Lu Tan and Neng Wang, 'Future Internet: The Internet of Things', *2010 3rd International Conference on Advanced Computer Theory and Engineering (ICACTE)* (2010) 379; Joseph A. Gratz and Mark A. Lemley, 'Platforms and Interoperability in Oracle v Google' (2018) 31 Harvard Journal of Law & Technology 603, 612–13.

and users concerning the precise legal nature of the undertaking. Greater clarity surrounding undertakings can be seen to move towards a more complete contracting regime, thus addressing concerns of 'hold-up'. Nevertheless, mandating such improvements is not recommended, because standard-setting activity is footloose and will likely migrate away from fora which are seen to be overly hostile to the interests of right holders.

Collective Rights Organizations An important consideration for the courts will be whether the relevant intellectual property rights are available through a collective rights organization (CRO) such as a patent pool. CROs are voluntary and thus the right holder is not seen to be coerced into licensing the SEIP, which may be better from the perspective of preserving dynamic efficiency incentives. Furthermore, CROs are 'one-stop shops' where users can secure licences to use many SEIP rights in a single transaction, resulting in significant savings of transaction costs. CROs use panels of experts to value SEIP; such experts may be more skilful than the courts in placing a value on particular intellectual property rights.[76] Better pricing of intellectual property rights is likely to be crucial to balancing the incentives and interests of creators and users of intellectual property rights, promoting higher levels of dynamic efficiency.

Nevertheless, there are also limits to the usefulness of CROs, principally because right holders are not required to join them. Thus, while a patent pool may give a user access to many SEPs, it will almost certainly not provide access to all; there will be hold-outs, and those hold-outs may well be those right holders seeking the highest licensing fees. For this reason, CROs are unlikely to provide a complete solution. Furthermore (from a logical perspective) it is unclear why the right holder can only voluntarily license the intellectual property rights when he has already given an undertaking to the SSO to license the intellectual property rights in question. Finally, if courts are more active in applying liability rules rather than property rules, this may provide right holders with incentives to join CROs. Given the benefits of CROs enumerated, providing such incentives is likely to be efficient and beneficial.

---

[76] Merges (n. 30) 1317. Of course, a court can also rely on expert testimony, which has happened already in cases where access prices for SEIP have been assessed, including in relation to FRAND-encumbered SEPs.

6.2.2.2 Other Considerations

Cross-Licensing and Patent Assertion Entities Another relevant factor will be whether the right holder is practising, or is likely to practise, the standard, or whether the right holder is a 'non-practising entity' or 'patent assertion entity' ((PAE), colloquially, a 'troll'). Right holders who practise a standard will need access to SEIP held by other entities and will therefore have certain incentives to license. Negotiations between two practicing entities will include cross-licences, with a 'net-off' payable to the party considered to have the more valuable portfolio of relevant intellectual property rights.

This dynamic has important implications for market entry. New entrants into downstream markets which use SEIP may find themselves paying very high licence fees for SEIP. However, this problem can be addressed by the entrants engaging in research and development with a view to obtaining their own SEIP. Once the new entrants have their own portfolios of SEIP they will have a stronger hand in cross-licensing negotiations. Thus, with respect to practising entities, higher licence fees are likely to stimulate higher levels of efficient research and development activity into new or upgraded standards.

PAEs, however, are immune to such pressures because they do not practise the standard. They will be able to obtain very high licence fees even from those entities which also hold very significant portfolios of SEIP. For this reason, both Lemley and Shapiro and Cotter consider that liability rules should apply only with respect to PAEs, not to all right holders generally.[77] Even in this case, however, it would appear that for multicomponent products, the ability to shut the end-user product out of the market on the basis of the violation of only one patent would seem vastly disproportionate to any dynamic efficiency gains associated with protection of the patent.

A final point to note is that practising entities may have incentives to 'leverage' the market power into the downstream market in order to reduce competition in downstream markets for which SEIP is important. In the USA, courts are not concerned about such 'leverage' because of the legacy of the Chicago School, which considers leverage to be irrational and, in any case, most likely efficient. However other economic traditions (including the post-Chicago School) acknowledge that leveraging may be rational for the right holder. For jurisdictions which do not wholly accept the Chicago School approach, confining liability rules to PAEs only may

---

[77] Shapiro and Lemley (n. 41) 2036; Cotter (n. 49) 1171–2.

be less attractive. As such, while the nature and extent of downstream competition between a right holder and user should unquestionably be taken into account by the courts, the existence of such competition should not act as an outright bar to the imposition of a liability rule.

Incentives to License Courts may wish to consider the extent to which right holders have incentives to license and therefore liability rules are not needed. Yes, SEIP generally has a higher market value. But for the SEIP to hold this higher value, the standard must be 'standard' – that is, it must have attained widespread marketplace acceptance. Purported standards which do not attain widespread marketplace acceptance will never produce high-value SEIP (one exception being where the standard is made mandatory through law). Purported standards for which the relevant intellectual property right is not available upon suitably open terms may never attain marketplace acceptance.

Furthermore, we would expect that even where a standard has attained widespread marketplace acceptance, that the standard can lose this status if it ceases to be perceived by the marketplace as superior. It is worth noting at this juncture that the theory that an entire market can be 'locked into' an inferior standard through entrenched network externalities remains contentious within the economics fraternity. Therefore, SEIP holders will likely have incentives to license in order to preserve the market position of the standard. Furthermore, where SEIP holders are overly opportunistic and do not respond to these longer-term incentives (e.g. because of strategic behaviour or a Cournot complements problem), we may over time see markets adjust by moving away from the existing standard towards a newer standard where licensing terms are more open.

It is important in this regard to view the market power associated with an interoperability standard as transitory rather than permanent. The market power associated with network externalities arising from an interoperability standard is unlikely to become entrenched in the same way that public utilities with a legacy of government ownership and protection can obtain very long-term market power.

6.2.2.3   Dynamic Efficiency Considerations

Optimal Innovation in New and Revised Standards The terms and conditions of access (including price-related terms and conditions) to SEIP are very important for preserving incentives for innovative activity pertaining to the creation of new or revised standards. Underpricing of

SEIP will likely discourage firms from undertaking the costly research and development essential to the creation of new or revised standards. Where injunctions are available this will likely enable right holders to extract higher licence fees, using the threat of denying the user from valuable downstream markets. Adopting the Schumpterian perspective, we can anticipate that, in the medium to long term, higher licence fees for SEIP will be likely to encourage more research and development into possible future standards. Whilst there is a question as to whether such research and development would be wholly efficient, in general given the high societal value associated with standardized technologies it is reasonable to assume that it would be.

Optimal Innovation Based on Existing Standards Much if not most innovation is follow-on in nature and builds on existing technologies. It is equally important to ensure that adequate incentives are preserved for innovations based on existing standards (e.g. mobile handset designs which utilize existing wireless communications technologies). Overpricing of access to SEIP may encourage research and development in new standards, but at the cost of efficient innovation based on existing standards. Therefore, a balanced approach is called for.

6.2.2.4 Transaction and Assessment Cost Considerations

Bargaining Costs Clearly, negotiation of licences to use SEIP involves costs that may be considerable in scope. Nevertheless, well-resourced suppliers and acquirers of SEIP can be expected to have developed sophisticated intellectual property licensing capabilities. Moreover, as Merges points out, private actors are able to address these bargaining costs through forming CROs such as patent pools.[78] And as observed by Gerardin et al.,[79] such bargaining costs do not appear to be precluding private actors from entering into licensing transactions. On balance, while transaction costs in the context of SEIP licensing may well be high, they are unlikely to be so high as to prevent Coaseian bargaining to reach an optimal solution. Strategic behaviour is more likely to be the culprit.

Strategic Behaviour There appears to be little disagreement that strategic behaviour, of a kind that is very similar to the 'hold-out' scenario

---

[78] Merges (n. 31).
[79] Gerardin, Layne-Farrar and Padilla (n. 61).

discussed by Calabresi and Melamed,[80] is evident in markets for the licensing of SEIP, and is most likely occurring both by holders of SEIP ('hold-up') and acquirers of SEIP ('hold-out'). The transaction cost effects of such strategic behaviour are likely to be magnified by the impact of Cournot complements, component patenting and the indirect network externalities associated with interoperability standards. Therefore, it is reasonable to assume that the transaction costs associated with such strategic behaviour are considerable. However, compelling evidence that this strategic behaviour has reached such a level that efficient bargains for the licensing of SEIP are not being struck, and that nascent technologies are not being developed due to concerns about 'hold-up' and 'royalty stacking', appears to be lacking. Nevertheless, strategic behaviour may well have reached a level where SEP holders are able to extract from users a disproportionate benefit arising from the implementation of interoperability standards.

Assessment Costs There is little contention that courts will encounter considerable assessment costs in relation to determining the appropriate quantum of damages for the infringement of SEIP. Consideration has not been given to the question highlighted by Krier and Schwab, namely whether the transaction costs and the assessment costs associated with infringement of SEIP are correlated, or whether one is larger than the other. However, one significant factor here is that where courts are asked to grant an injunction for infringement of SEIP, they are generally asked at the same time to award damages in respect of the infringement that has already occurred. Thus, assessment costs are generally incurred in any case, even where the outcome is the award of an injunction (i.e. an exclusive property rule).

This leaves the question of errors by the courts. In our view it is reasonable to assume that, whilst court-established licence fees (whether in the form of damages, a reasonable royalty or a compulsory licence) are likely to involve errors, such errors are equally likely to overprice or underprice access to the right (since the court is likely to hear expert testimony from both sides before deciding on damages). If anything, existing scholarship (e.g. Lemley and Shapiro) seems to indicate that courts (at least in the United States) are inclined to award damages for infringements of SEIP that are too high rather than too

---

[80] Calabresi and Melamed (n. 1) 1106–8.

low[81] – a shortcoming that is unlikely to be redressed by the imposition of an exclusive property rule.

6.2.3 The Choice between Exclusive Property Rules and Liability Rules for Standards-Essential Intellectual Property: Concluding Observations

There is a fairly robust literature identifying static efficiency losses associated with exclusive property rules in relation to SEIP. These static efficiency losses arise from Cournot complements, hold-up and component patenting which can give rise, at least in theory, to royalty stacking, although empirical evidence for this phenomenon could be developed further. In terms of dynamic efficiency, there appear to be both gains and losses from an exclusive property rule – gains to creators of new standards or revised standards but losses to firms seeking to innovate based on existing standards. Where the sum of the static and dynamic efficiency losses associated with an exclusive property rule outweighs the associated dynamic efficiency gains, a liability rule is to be preferred.

In the case of SEIP, it would seem reasonable for the courts to prefer liability rules to exclusive property rules for SEIP where two criteria are satisfied: (i) there exists a Cournot complements problem arising from the simultaneous, horizontal assertion of a large number of SEIP rights in respect of a standard; and (ii) the imposition of an exclusive property rule, for example in the form of an injunction, will likely prohibit very significant, legitimate innovative activity, such as court-award injunctions covering end-consumer products which implement an interoperability standard, but which are found to infringe one or a small number of SEPs. Thus while, in general, the preference for exclusive property rules in the context of intellectual property is to be retained, in certain limited circumstances, the costs associated with strategic behaviour (or the potential for strategic behaviour) by certain right holders suggest that a move to liability rules will be optimal in these cases.

Nevertheless, whether a liability or an exclusive property rule should be imposed by a competent court in the context of any particular factual pattern should, consistently with the topical methodology, depend on the consideration of all relevant factors, which will likely include: (i) the technical characteristics of the standard in question; (ii) the existence of SEIP, that is, whether a valid intellectual property right is essential to the

---

[81] Shapiro and Lemley (n. 41) 2029–35.

practice of a standard; (iii) whether the SEIP is infringed by the user in the particular circumstance; (iv) whether there is other SEIP in relation to the same standard and if so, how many individual rights exist and how many right holders the user will need to deal with in order to gain access to the standard; (v) whether the right holder is currently practising the standard; (vi) the terms of the relevant SSO's policies on intellectual property (where they exist); (vii) the terms of any undertaking to license provided in relation to the SEIP; (viii) whether the SEIP is available by way of a CRO; (ix) the course of negotiations between the right holder and the user, and in particular whether evidence exists of either hold-up by the right holder or hold-out by the user; and (x) the applicability of relevant principles of competition, contract, estoppel and other bodies of law. It is not recommended, however, that courts engage in extensive consideration of the static and dynamic efficiency losses or gains associated with an exclusive property or a liability rule. Generally, courts are poorly placed to undertake such detailed economic analysis.[82]

6.3 Exclusive Property Rules, Liability Rules and Refusals to Supply

There has been relatively little law and economics scholarship applying the Calabresi and Melamed framework to competition law, including refusals to supply interoperability information and refusals to license SEIP. For example, Lemley and Weiser consider whether liability or property rules should govern information, but do not squarely consider how this would apply in the context of competition rules[83] (although they do consider the implications of their analytical framework for compulsory licensing).[84]

Nevertheless, these matters have been much discussed in the law and economics literature, albeit outside the Calabresi and Melamed framework, and that analysis can readily be incorporated within the Calabresi and Melamed framework. Where the holder of the interoperability information has no legal duty to share, this represents an exclusive property rule. By contrast, where a duty to deal is imposed under competition law, the exclusive property rule is transformed into a liability rule: the prospective user may take the interoperability information, but must pay to

---

[82] See Evans and Padilla (n. 57).
[83] Lemley and Weiser (n. 44).
[84] Ibid. 824–41.

the owner of the information compensation adjudged to be adequate in the circumstances.

Although the point is contested in the literature, it would seem reasonable to suggest that where competition law imposes an obligation to license an intellectual property right, for example by way of the issuance of a compulsory licence, this again constitutes the imposition of a liability rule. Lemley considers that this situation is not a liability rule, but rather one party to the transaction is prevented from enforcing a property rule.[85] Depoorter, by contrast, treats this situation as a liability rule.[86] Disentitlement of a property rule is not one of the four rules envisaged by Calabresi and Melamed.

A judicially ordered licence could conceivably be treated as either Rule 2 (right holder owns the intellectual property right, protected by a liability rule), or Rule 3 (user has a legal right to use the information, protected by a property rule). Treating judicially ordered compulsory licences as Rule 3 cannot be correct, however, because the right holder still owns the intellectual property and remains entitled to a stream of compensation for breach. Lemley's substantive point is that few courts actually set the price for the licence, which is generally left to market participants to negotiate. But against this, it is contended that such negotiation occurs under the shadow of a court-determined valuation of the price of the licence, and if courts rarely reach this point it is because the mere finding of liability in competition law generally gives the parties adequate incentives to settle. In substance, then, if not in form, court-enforced disentitlement of a property rule, for example through finding of a contravention of applicable competition law, is tantamount to a liability rule held by the right holder: the user is free to use the information but must compensate the right holder in terms which might be negotiated freely in the first instance but ultimately in the event of disagreement will be fixed by a court.

As such, the analysis undertaken in Chapter 5 concerning the advisability of mandating access to interoperability standards and SEIP under competition laws, for example by way of an essential facilities doctrine, can be reconceptualized within the framework of exclusive property and liability rules, without altering the assumptions reached, namely that it would be equally appropriate for domestic laws to provide either a per se legality rule, or a 'modified per se legality rule' along the lines suggested

---

[85] Lemley (n. 33) n. 44.
[86] Depoorter (n. 38) 62.

by Evans and Padilla (2005),[87] where courts apply a series of 'screens' to isolate exclusionary conduct that is unlikely to involve significant dynamic efficiency benefits.

Regarding refusals to supply interoperability information, as was the subject of the EU *Microsoft* litigation, the two criteria outlined above for the imposition of a liability rule are unlikely to apply. In particular, there is unlikely to be a Cournot complements issue where the information in question (e.g. standards-essential communication protocols) is held by a single monopolistic firm. Furthermore, adopting a per se legality rule, that is, an exclusive property rule, is very unlikely to have the consequence of prohibiting significant non-infringing conduct. On the contrary, applying an exclusive property rule in this context does not prohibit the user of the information from doing anything (although it does mean that the user may not receive the information in question).

Of course, if the prospective user is able to obtain the information in some way, for example by way of reverse engineering the relevant object code (as did, in fact, occur in *Sega* v. *Accolade*),[88] then it would fall to the owner of the interoperability information to assert any such valid intellectual property rights as it may possess before a competent court (note this never actually happened in either of the *Microsoft* cases). At that point in time, it is for the court to assess whether an exclusive property rule (in the form of an injunction) or a liability rule (in the form of damages or a reasonable royalty but no injunction) would be more appropriate. The same considerations as outlined in the paragraphs above will apply in this situation: there does not appear to be a strong case for the substitution of an exclusive property rule for a liability rule; as such, an injunction will be the preferred remedy (noting, however, that the injunctive remedy is often equitable in nature and as such consideration of all relevant issues will nevertheless be warranted).

As an alternative to an exclusive property rule in the form of an injunction, it may be appropriate to apply a modified per se legality rule, employing a series of 'screens' as suggested by Evans and Padilla: if these requirements are met the court would then decline to award an injunction and instead award damages or reasonable royalty only. For example, Ahlborn, Evans and Padilla noted with approval the liability rule applied by the European Court of Justice in *IMS Health* and *Magill*:

---

[87] Evans and Padilla (n. 57).
[88] *Sega Enterprises Ltd* v. *Accolade, Inc* [1992] 977 F2d 1510 (United States Court of Appeals for the Ninth Circuit).

(i) access to the information is indispensable to compete in a secondary market; (ii) failure to license the intellectual property would eliminate competition in that secondary market; (iii) the intellectual property is needed to create a new product for which there is likely consumer demand; and (iv) there is no objective justification for the refusal to license.[89]

Concerning refusal to license SEIP, the same analysis will apply: absent Cournot complements and component intellectual property rights, the preferred approach will be either an exclusive property rule (i.e. an injunction), or a liability rule (i.e. no injunction), following an assessment that applies a series of 'screens' to identify problematic exclusionary conduct by the right holder.

6.4 Implications for Injunctions and Compensation

6.4.1 Implications for Injunctions

Our analysis above highlights one strong case for the imposition of a liability rule (e.g. court-awarded damages only for infringement of SEIP but no injunction), where two factors are satisfied: (i) the dispersion among many holders of SEIP gives rise to a Cournot complements problem; and (ii) an injunction would have the effect of prohibiting significant non-infringing conduct.[90] It highlights a further situation where the imposition of a liability rule would be acceptable (but not necessarily recommended), namely where: (i) access to the information is indispensable to compete in a secondary market; (ii) failure to license the intellectual property would eliminate competition in that secondary market; (iii) the intellectual property is needed to create a new product for which there is likely consumer demand; and (iv) there is no objective justification for the refusal to license.[91]

It is further recommended, consistently with the topical methodology, that courts have regard to all relevant factors in making such a determination. Such factors would include: (i) the nature of the intellectual property; (ii) the standard(s) in question; (iii) any undertakings to license given in connection with the SEIP; (iv) the course of negotiations between the right holder and the user, including whether the right holder has engaged in 'hold-up' and whether the user has

---

[89] Ahlborn, Evans and Padilla (n. 58) 1144–5; see also Evans and Padilla (n. 57) 87–8.
[90] See Lemley and Weiser (n. 44).
[91] See Ahlborn, Evans and Padilla (n. 58).

engaged in 'hold-out'; (v) the nature and extent of competition between the right holder and the user in downstream markets; (vi) the dispersion of SEIP in relation to the standard(s) in question; (vii) whether the final end-consumer product or service supplied by the user incorporates many other non-infringing innovations, or whether in contrast the user is merely copying the innovations of the right holder; and (viii) applicable competition rules.

It is not recommended, however, that courts attempt to balance the static and dynamic efficiency effects associated with the choice of either a liability rule or an exclusive property rule, as courts are unlikely to have either the information or indeed the competence to engage in an exercise of this nature; as such, a balancing exercise of this nature is likely to lead the courts into error. For the common law jurisdictions, this will be readily accommodated within the courts' existing equitable discretion as to whether or not to award injunction, as seen in *eBay* and its progeny and, to a lesser degree, in the UK courts in *Unwired*.

For civil law jurisdictions, in particular where there is basically an automatic entitlement to permanent injunction upon a finding that the SEIP is infringed, this may be more difficult without legislative change. The enactment of laws articulating the relevant factors to be taken into account in connection with injunctions for SEIP may be the most appropriate way forward for these jurisdictions. Pending the entry into force of such laws, competition law (in particular the unilateral disciplines, e.g. abuse of a dominant market position) may provide a practical workaround to temper the automatic entitlement to injunction. Other principles of general law may also be relevant, such as good faith (especially where there is a FRAND undertaking), abuse of rights and estoppel, may also be useful in this regard.

Notably, our proposed formulation does not give undue prominence to undertakings to license (e.g. FRAND declarations) given by the right holder, although this will unquestionably be a matter for the courts to consider in their analysis. Issues of concern have also arisen outside the confines of formal SSO standards, and our rule needs to be broad enough to deal with such situations. One can easily imagine situations where a liability rule would likely be inappropriate, for example where a patented invention was included in an interoperability standard without a right holder's knowledge or even against that right holder's wishes. In such cases the courts would presumably order an injunction as a matter of course. In general terms, however, it is proposed that the availability (or unavailability) of undertakings to license merely be one of

6.4 IMPLICATIONS FOR INJUNCTIONS AND COMPENSATION

the various factors which the courts take into account, having regard to all relevant factors in each case.

Our proposed approach applies equally as between formal standards negotiated and drafted under the auspices of a formal SSO, and de facto standards (e.g. those drafted by consortia or single firms). Nevertheless, Cournot complements will be less likely in the case of de facto standards, where the relevant SEIP tends to be held among a much smaller number of participating right holders. Cournot complements are most commonly seen where many parties come together to draft an interoperability standard under the auspices of a formal SSO.

Our proposed approach will apply equally as between different types of intellectual property rights, notably patents and copyrights. Within the domain of copyright, the application of other limiting doctrines in copyright law, such as the distinction between unprotectable ideas and protectable expressions, merger, *scènes à faire* and fair use, may obviate the need to apply liability rule in the place of the usual exclusive property rules (i.e. injunctions). Given that the *Oracle* v. *Google* decisions have called into question the scope and applicability of these limiting doctrines, questions concerning access to standards-essential copyrights could loom much larger in the future. At this point in time, it is clear that in circumstances where Cournot complements apply in the context of standards-essential copyrights, our proposed approach will clearly also apply. 'Copyright thickets' by some accounts are on the increase as a result of trends such as object-oriented software programming.[92]

Cournot complements will be rarely seen in the case of trade secrets, which generally manifest in de facto standards (e.g. the fact pattern in the EU *Microsoft* case); disclosure of a trade secret to a standard-setting body will extinguish the trade secret.

6.4.2 Implications for Compensation

6.4.2.1 Implications for Calculation of Damages

Whilst, in general, principles for the calculation of damages under domestic law are likely to be adequate in respect of SEIP, reasonable royalties (discussed at Section 6.4.2.2 below) are, in most cases, likely to provide a superior approach. Concepts such as lost profits, account of profits, wilfulness, statutory damages, and additional or punitive damages, whilst they will doubtless remain available and may be awarded

---

[92] Clark D. Asay, 'Software's Copyright Anticommons' (2016) 66 Emory Law Journal 265.

from time to time, are generally less well-suited to striking an appropriate balance between the competing interests of the right holder and the user of SEIP.

An award of lost profits seems an awkward fit for SEIP, given that the purpose of standardization is to encourage follow-on innovation based on a common standard. Standards (whether formal or de facto) are generally widely used and indeed, intended to be so. Indeed, network externalities imply that the more people using the standard, the greater benefit accruing to each user. Therefore, it does not make sense to penalize a user for taking sales away from a competing right holder, since the underlying logic of standardization dictates that both should be permitted to apply the standard. More particularly, an unapportioned award of lost profits in respect of a complex multicomponent product would, in a similar fashion to an injunction, overcompensate the right holder and facilitate patent hold-up and royalty stacking.

As with lost profits, account of profits should be applied in the context of SEIP with care. The logic of standardization suggests that profits associated with implementation of the standard should be shared between right holders and users, and not accrue exclusively or predominantly to right holders. Proper apportionment of damages between right holder and user will assume particular importance. Enabling the infringer to recoup all profits associated with its use of a de facto standard is likely to discourage use of the standard and therefore prevent the realization of the full network externalities associated with the standard. In general, awards of lost profits or an account of profits will be best suited to cases of manifest hold-out by the user; courts should carefully consider whether reasonable royalties are available in law and better suited to compensate the right holder appropriately for harm suffered arising from an infringement.

Whilst there may be some justification for additional, punitive or statutory damages SEIP where clear evidence of 'hold-out' exists, this can quite easily be accommodated through adjustments to the reasonable royalty calculation. A reasonable royalty calculation which takes account of hold-out (where it occurs) is likely to balance the competing interests better than notions of additional, punitive or statutory damages. For these reasons it is suggested that remedies of lost profits and account of profits should generally be avoided for SEIP, and an award of a reasonable royalty preferred. Where the laws of a jurisdiction mandate the availability of disgorgement of profits and do not provide, or minimally provide, for reasonable royalty (e.g. under United States copyright law), particular scrutiny is likely to be required of methodologies for the apportionment of profits from the infringing activity as between the right holder and user. Such reconsideration will need to occur, not through the lens of discouraging infringements of standards-essential copyrights (which, in the wake of *Oracle* v. *Google,* may become commonplace, at least in the United States), but rather of finding an appropriate allocation of the profits associated with the exploitation of the standard as between the right holder and users of the standard.

Likewise, the large variability in damages depending on the degree of wilfulness on the part of the user will not necessarily result in damages awards that appropriately balance the competing rights of right holders and users of standards-essential copyrights. Where an account of profits is ordered, it may be difficult for a court to distinguish which profits are attributable to the infringement of the SEIP, and which to the user's own efforts. Of course, where there appears to be a situation of 'hold-out' occurring, there may be grounds for courts to award additional damages, depending on all the circumstances. Statutory damages, which are prevalent in copyright law, are likely to be applied in too rigid and inflexible a manner to successfully balance the competing rights of right holders and users.

6.4.2.2 Implications for Reasonable Royalty Awards

Scholarly Opinion on Reasonable Royalties for SEIP To date, scholarly opinion has focussed predominantly on the proper valuation of SEPs, particularly those subject to FRAND commitments. Lemley and Shapiro (2013) have suggested that the reasonable royalty for SEPs subject to a FRAND declaration 'should reflect the ex ante value of the patented technology, not the additional ex post value resulting from the standardization itself'.[93] Lemley and Shapiro consider: 'Under patent law, a reasonable royalty normally is based on a hypothetical, arms-length negotiation between a willing buyer and a willing seller that takes place at the time the infringement begins';[94] further: 'By construction, the reasonable royalty rate does not include the value attaching to the creation and adoption of the standard itself. To allow patentees to capture that value, which flows from the collective adoption decisions of the group rather than from the underlying value of the technology chosen, would undermine the goals of the FRAND commitment'.[95] Varian and Shapiro

---

[93] Mark A. Lemley and Carl Shapiro, 'A Simple Approach to Setting Reasonable Royalties for Standard-Essential Patents' (2013) 28 Berkeley Technology Law Journal 1135, 1139–40.
[94] Ibid. 1148.
[95] Ibid.

explain, similarly: 'Reasonable should mean the royalties that the patent holder could obtain in open, up-front competition with other technologies, not the royalties that the patent holder can extract once other participants are effectively locked in to use technology covered by the patent'.[96]

This 'ex ante' perspective is not universally shared. Siebrasse and Cotter suggest that it would also be appropriate for courts to incorporate some value to the patent that results from its incorporation in the standard, without enabling the patent holder to extract ex post rents that are not associated with the incorporation of the patent into the standard.[97] Sidak considers that an individual-rationality constraint provides an appropriate framework for the calculation of FRAND royalties. This would involve a bargaining range, with the lower bound set by the SEP holder's opportunity cost of becoming involved in the standard-setting process, and the upper bound set by the licensee's willingness to pay for the SEPs.[98] Baumol and Swanson suggest that an efficient component pricing rule (ECPR) would be appropriate,[99] while Layne-Farrar, Padilla and Schmalensee propose a valuation based on the Shapley value of the patents in question.[100]

The ECPR seeks to compensate a right holder not merely for the incremental cost of licensing, but also for the opportunity cost of licensing the technology, such that the right holder is indifferent as between licensing the technology and producing the product itself.[101] In other contexts, the ECPR has attracted considerable criticism: it is based on highly specific and detailed assumptions, for example constant returns to scale of the relevant production technology, and where these assumptions are relaxed, applying the ECPR will likely harm total utility.[102]

---

[96] Carl Shapiro and Hal Varian, *Information Rules* (Harvard Business Press 1998) 241.
[97] Norman V. Siebrasse and Thomas F. Cotter, 'Judicially Determined FRAND Royalties' (2016) 68 Florida Law Review 929, 964.
[98] J. GregorySidak, 'The Meaning of FRAND, Part I: Royalties' (2013) 9 Journal of Competition Law & Economics 931, 933.
[99] William J. Baumol and Daniel G. Swanson, 'Reasonable and Nondiscriminatory (RAND) Royalties, Standards Selection, And Control of Market Power' 73 Antitrust Law Journal 1.
[100] Anne Layne-Farrar, A. Jorge Padilla and Richard Schmalensee, 'Pricing Patents for Licensing in Standard-Setting Organizations: Making Sense of FRAND Commitments' (2007) 74 Antitrust Law Journal 671, 671.
[101] Ibid. 686–7.
[102] Nicholas Economides and Laurence J. White, 'Access and Interconnection Pricing: How Efficient Is the "Efficient Component Pricing Rule"?' (1995) 40 The Antitrust Bulletin 557, 559–60.

6.4 IMPLICATIONS FOR INJUNCTIONS AND COMPENSATION

Based on cooperative game theory, the Shapley value 'divides rents (or costs) among players belonging to a group according to their average marginal or incremental contribution to alternative combinations of the members of the cooperative group'.[103] This approach assumes that the total value created by the standard should be shared among all the various right holders;[104] this assumption needs to be questioned however: it may be preferable to divide that value between right holders and users of the standard (noting that some firms may be both right holders and users of the same standard).

Nevertheless, at a high level of abstraction, the Shapley value makes intuitive sense in the context of SEPs, given the observed skewed distribution of patent values: some patents are highly valuable while others are not.[105] In *Microsoft v. Motorola*, Judge Robart (without referring to the Shapley value by name), adopted an approach that appears to draw on the intuition of the Shapley value,[106] and a similar approach was taken by the Japanese courts in the *Samsung v. Apple* litigation, also.

Insights from Domestic Judicial Decisions Domestic courts have developed well-established principles governing reasonable royalty awards, such as the 'Georgia-Pacific factors' applied under United States patent law. Whilst these methodologies are broadly appropriate to the calculation of reasonable royalties in the context of SEIP, some modifications are likely to be required to take account of the particular context of interoperability standard-setting.

For example, in *Microsoft Corporation v. Motorola, Inc., et al.*,[107] the United States District Court of Western Washington estimated both a pinpoint FRAND royalty, and a permissible FRAND royalty, for sixteen Motorola patents claimed essential to the ITU H.264 standard, and twenty-four patents claimed essential to the IEEE 802.11 standard, in the immediate context of a breach of contract claim by Microsoft and the broader context of a variety of patent infringement claims brought by both parties in various jurisdictions. The District Court anchored its estimates of the permissible FRAND rates in the general US law framework for the calculation of reasonable royalties, namely the fifteen

---

[103] Layne-Farrar, Padilla and Schmalensee (n. 100) 693.
[104] Ibid. 694.
[105] Ibid. 676–7.
[106] *Microsoft Corporation v. Motorola, Inc, et al* [2013] 2013 WL 2111217 (United States District Court for the District of Western Washington) [113].
[107] Ibid.

'Georgia-Pacific' factors.[108] Nevertheless, the District Court modified the Georgia-Pacific factors to take particular account of the context provided by SEPs and by Motorola's binding FRAND commitments,[109] summarizing its approach as follows:

> With the aforementioned framework for determining a RAND royalty rate set forth, the court conducts a hypothetical negotiation for Motorola's 802.11 and H.264 SEPs. First, the court examines Motorola's H.264 and 802.11 patent portfolios to determine each portfolio's importance to its respective standard as well as the importance to Microsoft's products. Second, the court fashions a royalty rate and range for Motorola's H.264 and 802.11 patent portfolios based on certain Microsoft products. In determining a royalty rate and range, the court considers possible comparable licensing agreements and patent pools, which could provide indications of a reasonable royalty rate for Motorola's patent portfolios. The court also applies the principles behind the RAND commitment in finding the appropriate royalty rate and range.[110]

As outlined above, the Court assessed the contribution of each SEP both to the applicable standard in general, and to Microsoft's products in particular. In undertaking the former assessment, the Court took account of alternatives to the patented technology that were available to the relevant SSO at the time the standard was drafted.[111]

Before settling on its methodology, the court heard expert testimony from a number of economists. Several, including Dr Kevin Murphy and Dr Richard Schmalensee, proposed an approach that involved calculating the incremental value of each SEP to the standard, taking account of alternatives that were available to the SSO at the time the standard was adopted.[112] Whilst acknowledging the practical difficulties for the courts in adopting this approach, Judge Robart expressed in-principle support for an approach based on the Shapley value:

> Nevertheless, a reasonable royalty rate for an SEP committed to a RAND obligation must value the patented technology itself, which necessarily requires considering the importance and contribution of the patent to the standard. If alternatives available to the patented technology would have provided the same or similar technical contribution to the standard, the

---

[108] Ibid. 87–93.
[109] Ibid. 100–13.
[110] Ibid. 16.
[111] See, e.g., ibid. 27–8.
[112] Ibid. 80–2.

actual value provided by the patented technology is its incremental contribution.[113]

The Court rejected other licence agreements proffered by Motorola, on the grounds that they were reached under the shadow of litigation, and did not concern FRAND-encumbered patents.[114] The Court accepted the rates for similar SEPs set by patent pools, however.[115] It also accepted expert assessments of the RAND rate as probative.[116]

Notably, the District Court was able to undertake its calculation within the context of existing US law relating to patent reasonable royalties, namely the Georgia-Pacific framework, taking appropriate account of the particularities of the interoperability standard-setting context.

In the subsequent case of *In re Innovatio IP Ventures, LLC Patent Litigation*,[117] the principles expounded were affirmed, albeit modified somewhat in their application.[118] Unlike Motorola's patent portfolio as examined in *Motorola v. Microsoft*, Innovatio's twenty-three asserted patents were found to be relatively important to IEEE's 802.11 family of standards.[119] For a variety of reasons, however, the court found that none of the proffered comparator licence agreements was probative in establishing a RAND royalty: (i) Innovatio's licence to Broadcom was not comparable because the value of the patents licensed could not be isolated from the rest of the transaction; furthermore, the purchase price reflected a discount for the risk that the patents could not be successfully monetized;[120] (ii) the Motorola Mobility/VTech licence (also rejected by Judge Robart in *Microsoft v. Motorola*) was found to be not comparable because the licence was merely a small part of a larger licensing agreement that the parties entered into to settle significant litigation;[121] (iii) the Symbol Technologies Inc. Licences with Proxim and Terabeam were not comparable because they were adopted under the duress of litigation;[122] (iv) the Symbol Technologies licence with LXE was rejected because it could not be established what portion of the royalties

---

[113] Ibid. 80.
[114] Ibid. 48–53.
[115] Ibid. 55–69.
[116] Ibid. 70–3.
[117] *In re Innovatio, LLC Patent Litigation* 2013 WL 5593609 (United States District Court for the Northern District of Illinois, Eastern Division).
[118] Ibid. 5–6.
[119] Ibid. 15–24.
[120] Ibid. 39–40.
[121] Ibid. 41–2.
[122] Ibid. 42–4.

were attributable to Symbol's 802.11 patents;[123] and (v) the Qualcomm licence with Netgear was not comparable because the large number of Qualcomm's patents included in the licence agreement made it an inappropriate comparator for Innovatio's twenty-three patents.[124]

Likewise, the Via Licensing Patent Pool and four non-RAND licences were rejected as not comparable.[125] The court also considered two expert modelling approaches to valuing Innovatio's patents, a 'bottom-up approach' and a 'top-down' approach, rejecting the first but accepting the second. The 'bottom-up' approach involved determination of the cost of implementing reasonable alternatives to the Innovatio patents that could have been adopted into the standard, and dividing that cost by the total number of infringing units, to determine the maximum per unit royalty Innovatio's patents would have merited in the 1997 hypothetical negotiation.[126] This approach was rejected because: (i) the court had already found there were no alternatives to the Innovatio patents that would provide all the functionality of Innovatio's patents with respect to the 802.11 standard;[127] (ii) calculating the incremental value added by a patent for multipatent standards is a very complicated exercise;[128] and (iii) the model did not account for possible patent royalties applicable in respect of the alternatives to Innovatio's patents.[129]

The 'top-down' approach (which the court accepted) began with the average price of a Wi-Fi chip. The average profit earned on the sales of each chip was then estimated. This exercise isolated the portion of the income from the sale of the chip available to the chipmaker to pay royalties on intellectual property.[130] This 'available profit' was multiplied by a fraction reflecting the number of Innovatio's SEPs, divided by the total number of 802.11 SEPs.[131] This method resulted a RAND rate of 9.56 cents per Wi-Fi chips.[132] Finally, a 'reality check' was undertaken by comparing this FRAND calculation with other rates determined by litigation.[133]

---

[123] Ibid. 44.
[124] Ibid. 45.
[125] Ibid. 46–8.
[126] Ibid. 48.
[127] Ibid.
[128] Ibid. 49.
[129] Ibid.
[130] Ibid.
[131] Ibid.
[132] Ibid. 57.
[133] Ibid. 57–9.

6.4 IMPLICATIONS FOR INJUNCTIONS AND COMPENSATION

A further US court decision in *Commonwealth Scientific and Industrial Research Organization v. Cisco Systems, Inc.*[134] is highly significant because the bulk of the patents in dispute were SEPs but were not subject to any FRAND commitment. This case also involved patents essential to the 802.11 family of standards. The court held that, even though CSIRO's patents were not FRAND-encumbered, nevertheless CSIRO was not entitled to charge a royalty that captured the value of the standard, over and above the incremental technological contribution of its patents.[135]

Justice Birss of the UK High Court, Chancery Division has provided the first EU's decision on the calculation of the FRAND value of two patents found to be essential to ETSI standards,[136] in *Huawei v. Unwired Planet*. Justice Birss relied on comparable licensing agreements obtained by the right holder (Unwired) in respect of the patents in suit.[137] Justice Birss also 'cross-checked' his valuation using a 'top-down' calculation, in which he calculated the total royalty burden for all SEPs relating to the standard, and then allocated this among the various SEPs.[138]

Chinese courts have also ruled on these matters. In July 2008, China's Supreme People's Court issued a judicial reply to the Liaoning High People's Court concerning the infringement of standards-essential patents. As reported by Sokol and Zheng, the SPC opined:

> if a patent holder has participated in the making of a national, sector or local standard or has consented to including its patents in a national, sector or local standard, the patent holder will be deemed to have consented to allow others to use the patents for purposes of implementing the standard, and those uses will not constitute patent infringement. The patent holder may ask users to pay a royalty fee, but the amount of the fee should be significantly lower than the normal amount.[139]

More recently, a Chinese court established a FRAND licensing rate in *Huawei v. InterDigital*. In two interlinked cases, the Shenzhen Intermediate People's Court held that InterDigital had violated the Chinese Anti-Monopoly Law by (i) making proposals that the court

---

[134] *Commonwealth Scientific and Industrial Research Organisation v. CISCO Systems Inc* [2015] 809 F3d 1295 1295 (United States Court of Appeals for the Federal Circuit).
[135] Ibid. 14–16.
[136] Jorge L. Contreras, 'A New Perspective on FRAND Royalties: Unwired Planet v Huawei' (2017) 2 dc.law.utah.edu accessed 16 February 2018.
[137] *Unwired Planet International v. Huawei Technologies Co Ltd and Huawei Technologies (UK) Co Ltd* [2017] 2017 EWHC 711 (High Court) [179–80].
[138] Ibid. 476; Contreras (n. 136) 7–8.
[139] Daniel Sokol and Wentong Zheng, 'FRAND in China' (2013) 22 Texas Intellectual Property Law Journal 71, 86.

believed were excessive; (ii) tying the licensing of essential patents to the licensing of non-essential patents; (iii) requesting as part of its licensing proposals that Huawei provide a grant-back of certain patent rights to InterDigital and (iv) commencing a United States International Trade Commission (USITC) action against Huawei while still engaging in discussions over a licence with Huawei.[140]

In addition to ordering damages against InterDigital, the court ruled that the royalties paid by Huawei for InterDigital's SEPs (which were essential to 2G, 3G and 4G mobile telephony standards) should not exceed 0.019 per cent of the sales price of each Huawei product.[141] In reaching this ruling the court had regard to the following factors: (i) estimates of the fees proposed by InterDigital to Apple and Samsung for licensing the patents in suit;[142] (ii) Huawei's and InterDigital's respective contributions to telecommunications technologies, as measured by their respective patent portfolios and employment of research and development staff;[143] and (iii) InterDigital's lack of any production base.[144]

Japanese courts have also determined FRAND royalties. In *Samsung Electronics Co. Ltd. v. Apple Japan Godo Kaisha*,[145] Japan's Grand Court IP Panel established a FRAND royalty for a single patent (Samsung's patent no. 4642898), which was essential to ETSI's UMTS standard and subject to a FRAND declaration given to ETSI under French Law. The patented inventions sought the efficient use of radio resources through improved modalities for Voice over Internet Protocol (VOIP) communications, and were found not to have made a significantly high contribution to fulfilment of the UMTS standard.[146] Having determined that Samsung was entitled to claim no more in damages than a FRAND royalty[147], the court proceeded to calculate such royalty. It derived the following formula for a FRAND royalty:[148]

FRAND royalty = $C(S) \times ARC \times C(P)$

Where:

---

[140] Ibid. 89.
[141] Ibid.
[142] Ibid. 90.
[143] Ibid. 90–1.
[144] Ibid.
[145] *Samsung Electronics Co, Ltd v. Apple Japan Godo Kaisha* (Grand Panel of the Japanese Intellectual Property High Court).
[146] Ibid. 136.
[147] Ibid. 130.
[148] Ibid. 138.

C(S) = Contribution of compliance with the applicable standard to sales turnover of the products in question

ARC = Aggregate royalty cap (in this case, calculated at 5% of C(S))

C(P) = Contribution made by the patent to compliance with the applicable standard (expressed in this case as 1/total number of SEPs for the UMTS standard)

A number of observations may be made about this approach. First, by estimating (i) the contribution of the standard to the product; and (ii) the contribution of the patent to the standard, this approach acknowledges the intuitive appeal of the Shapley value methodology, and underscores the legitimacy of the approach taken by Judge Robart in *Microsoft v. Motorola*, whilst avoiding somewhat questionable propositions, such as the suggestion that patent holders should recoup no more than the ex ante (i.e. pre-standardization) value of the patent.[149] Second, the court assessed that Patent No. 4642898 contributed no more than an average amount to compliance with the UMTS standard, and hence that an appropriate value for C(P) was 1/529, there being an estimated 529 essential patent families for the UMTS standard.[150] Third, the court had regard to private licensing agreements and applicable patent pool royalties in determining the aggregate royalty cap.[151]

Analysis – Reasonable Royalties for Infringement of Standards-Essential Intellectual Property So far, domestic courts adjudicating on the value of FRAND-encumbered SEPs have used as their starting point the ordinary principles of applicable law governing reasonable royalty awards under that jurisdiction (e.g. the Georgia-Pacific factors in United States patent law). These ordinary principles of law have then been modified to take particular account of the standard-setting context. This approach is recommended, as it enables the courts to draw on their existing expertise to develop appropriate reasonable royalty awards.

One of the most common criticisms of court-ordered liability rules is that courts have imperfect information and are likely to fall into error (either setting the liability rule too high or too low), whereas an exclusive property rule permits the terms of licences to be established in negotiations between private parties. Yet one of the most compelling answers to this criticism is that in almost all cases of alleged infringement, the courts

---

[149] Siebrasse and Cotter (n. 97) 20.
[150] *Samsung Electronics Co., Ltd v. Apple Japan Godo Kaisha* (n. 145) 136–8.
[151] Ibid. 131.

will be asked to estimate damages, in respect of the infringement that has occurred up to the date of the court's ruling. Hence, the courts already have very significant capability in establishing liability rules. By using as the basis of calculation of court-ordered liability rules the ordinary principles of reasonable royalty calculation, the existing capability and understanding of the courts can be harnessed.

One threshold question is the extent to which reasonable royalties should include incremental value accruing to the patent associated with its inclusion in a standard. Following Cotter, we do consider it will be appropriate to include some measure of such 'ex post valuation'. This is recommended for a number of reasons. First, it will enable SEPs to continue to attract higher reasonable royalties than non-SEPs, thus providing incentives for technology companies to continue to devote research and development funding to developing new, standardized technologies. Furthermore, it reflects the obvious reality that a patented invention capable of being incorporated into a standardized solution should be accorded a greater value than an equivalent patented invention which does not have the potential for such incorporation.

Nevertheless, we do not consider that reasonable royalties should include any 'hold-up value', since this would reward strategic behaviour and encourage a few unscrupulous right holders to extract too much of the value associated with the standard. More generally, allowing SEIP holders to extract 'hold-up' value is unlikely to provide well-calibrated incentives for innovative activities giving rise to both the creation of new standards and greater uptake of existing standards.

Furthermore, in the presence of multiple rights reading on a particular standard (notably in the case of SEPs), it may be appropriate for the courts to estimate the marginal contribution of each right to the total value created by the standard, where such an approach is technically feasible. This approach is credible from a theoretical perspective and was applied (albeit in modified form) by the United States District Court in *Microsoft v. Motorola*,[152] demonstrating its practical utility; the Japanese courts in estimating FRAND royalties have also taken account of the contribution of the SEP in question to the value created by the standard.[153]

In contrast, some courts have adopted a 'top-down' approach rather than the 'bottom-up' approach implied by the Shapley value. This approach begins with the price of the end-consumer product. The profit on each

---

[152] *Microsoft Corporation v. Motorola, Inc., et al* (n. 106) para. 113.
[153] *Samsung Electronics Co., Ltd v. Apple Japan Godo Kaisha* (n. 145) para. 138.

6.4 IMPLICATIONS FOR INJUNCTIONS AND COMPENSATION

unit is estimated, which provides the total available pool of royalties to all SEP holders. This pool of profit is then allocated proportionally to each SEP.[154] This alternative methodology should be approached with some caution. First, it essentially involves imposing a numeric proportionality valuation on all SEPs to a given standard. As such, it raises risks of under-rewarding highly valuable SEPs, and over-rewarding less valuable SEPs. It therefore overlooks the observed skewed distribution of patent values. Furthermore, it gives no consideration to alternatives that were available to the SSO at the time the standard was drafted, thus squarely raising hold-up risks. Finally, it is based on an estimate of the total profit on the sale of end-consumer products available to pay royalties. Thus, it gives insufficient attention to the existence of other innovative features (patented or unpatented) in the final consumer product, which may also be drivers of sales and profitability. Therefore the 'top-down' methodology applied by the United States District Court in *In re Innovatio* is not recommended as a basis for valuing SEIP more generally.

Where application of the 'bottom-up' methodology is not practicable, domestic courts would be better advised to look to proxy values such as: (i) licensing agreements in respect of the SEIP in question; and (ii) valuation ascribed to the SEIP in question by collective rights organizations such as patent pools. As the domestic courts' competence in this field develops, other factors may also come to be considered. The existence of other SEIP in relation to the same standard, and the proper valuation to be ascribed to non-SEIP associated with final consumer products, are also likely to be of relevance.

There has not, to date, been significant scholarly consideration of the value that should be ascribed to standards-essential intellectual property, beyond the paradigm of FRAND-encumbered SEPs. Nevertheless, in circumstances where the courts consider it appropriate to substitute a liability rule for an exclusive property rule, in line with the economic principles elucidated above, the scholarship regarding FRAND valuation is likely to have significance beyond those SEPs which are FRAND-encumbered, and indeed to categories of rights other than patents.

The FRAND declaration is effectively a voluntary, ex ante commitment designed to carefully balance the competing interests of right holders and implementors of interoperability standards, in order to optimize incentives both for the creation of new standards and the implementation of existing standards. As such the concept is clearly

---

[154] *In re Innovatio, LLC Patent Litigation* (n. 117) 30.

capable of broader application, notably to those narrow classes of other intellectual property rights for which, in accordance with the principles outlined above, the imposition of a liability rule will be appropriate. This is confirmed by the articulation by US and EU courts of principles very similar to 'fair, reasonable and non-discriminatory' in the context of compulsory licensing of SEIP on findings of unilateral conduct abuses, notably in the *Microsoft* cases[155] and *IMS Health*.[156]

As in the case of FRAND-encumbered SEPs, the starting point for the domestic courts will be ordinary principles of law governing damages for infringement, adjusted as appropriate to take account of the standard-setting context. Our proposed principles for the award of liability rules are likely to affect narrow classes of intellectual property only. For these narrow classes of intellectual property, confining damages awards to an amount that is fair and reasonable is also likely to provide a valuation that balances the competing incentives of right holder and user.

Furthermore, a number of general principles, such as the Shapley value and the principle that damages should not include hold-up value, will clearly have a broader application beyond the paradigm of FRAND-encumbered SEPs. Consider, for example, the case of an SEP for which no FRAND undertaking has been given. Despite the lack of an undertaking to license, it would be hardly appropriate for the right holder to have the opportunity to extract a value that exceeds the contribution of the SEP to the standard in question. That is not to say that a FRAND undertaking should, in effect, be implied even where it has not been given. Clearly, the absence of such an undertaking will have a material bearing on a court's choice of methodology. Nevertheless, principles developed in the context of the valuation of FRAND-encumbered SEPs will clearly remain of relevance.

6.4.3 *Implications for Compulsory Licensing*

Application of the framework of liability rules and exclusive property rules suggests that, at least from an economic standpoint, there is no

---

[155] *State of New York, et al.* v. *Microsoft Corporation, Final Judgment* [2002] 224 FSupp2d 76 (United States District Court for the District of Columbia) 271–2; *Microsoft (Case COMP/C-3/37/792 – Microsoft)* (European Commission) 299; *Microsoft* v. *Commission of the European Communities (Case T-167/08)* [2012] ECLI:EU:T:2012:323 (European Court of First Instance); *Microsoft (Case COMP/C-3/37792)* [2009] OJ C 16520 (European Commission).
[156] *NDC Health/IMS Health: Interim Measures (Case COMP D3/38044)* [2001] OJ 59 (European Commission) L59/46.

6.4 IMPLICATIONS FOR INJUNCTIONS AND COMPENSATION

meaningful difference between: (i) a court declining to award injunction for an established infringement of an intellectual property right; and (ii) the court awarding a compulsory licence in respect of that intellectual property right: in both cases, an exclusive property rule is substituted for a liability rule. This suggests that harmonization of principles as between reasonable royalties and compulsory licences is to be encouraged.

Drawing from the scholarship of Merges, it is suggested that statutory compulsory licences which do not pay close attention to the precise valuation of the relevant rights, are not well-suited to SEIP, and will be prone to either over-reward or (most likely) under-reward SEIP holders, generating negative incentives for investment in future SEIP. Nevertheless, it cannot be precluded that an appropriate statutory compulsory licensing regime for SEIP could be designed, provided that it accorded appropriate flexibility to the courts to apply the topical methodology and provided for a careful valuation of the relevant rights.

Concerning judicial compulsory licences, in general courts appear to apply a less sophisticated approach to the calculation of compulsory licences, compared with the approach of the courts towards reasonable royalties in the context of damages. In the European Union, by way of example, courts and the Commission, when calculating compulsory licences, have: (i) required that supply continue on previously agreed terms (*Commercial Solvents*); (ii) required that a licence be granted on fair, reasonable and/or non-discriminatory terms (*Magill, IMS Health, Microsoft, Huawei*); (iii) proposed or required independent third-party arbitration in the event of the failure of negotiations (*IMS Health, Huawei*); and/or (iv) proposed other relevant measures (e.g. establishment of an evaluation mechanism in Microsoft).

It is recommended instead that jurisdictions seek to align the principles for calculation of compulsory licences with principles for the calculation of reasonable royalties, as outlined above. This merely reflects the basic understanding that a compulsory licence award and an award of reasonable royalties (absent injunction) are simply two sorts of liability rules; there does not appear to be any good reason for the principles for calculation to differ significantly from one to the other.

As such, it is recommended that where compulsory licences are applied by domestic courts and administrative authorities in cases of access to SEIP, the principles outlined above regarding the circumstances in which liability rules should be available, and principles regarding the calculation of liability rules, should also apply in relation to compulsory licences.

6.4.4 Broader Implications for Unilateral Competition Law Disciplines, Including the Essential Facilities Doctrine

Our analysis suggests a fairly narrow range of situations in which a liability rule should replace a property rule regarding access to interoperability standards and SEIP. At a high level of abstraction, this could take place either through the application of competition laws (e.g. via an essential facilities doctrine), or through application of the limiting doctrines in intellectual property law. Indeed, it could occur through other bodies of law, such as abuse of rights, as is currently seen under Japanese law. In some cases, competition laws may actually provide for the award of compulsory licences, whilst in other cases the application of competition law (e.g. abuse of a dominant market position) may preclude the courts from awarding injunction.

In practical terms, however, the differences between these approaches are unlikely to be material, particularly when viewed through the lens of the Calabresi and Melamed framework, since in the latter case, the primary remedy will be the availability of damages, most likely in the form of reasonable royalty. As outlined above, alignment is recommended as between principles for the calculation of reasonable royalties on the one hand, and compulsory licences on the other.

In cases where the primary focus is a refusal to supply interoperability information, rather than the refusal to licence SEIP as such (e.g. the EU *Microsoft* case), the same principles will equally apply. In particular it is recommended that a liability rule (in the form of a mandatory obligation to supply) replace a property rule (i.e. refusals to supply are per se legal) only in the narrow circumstances outlined above. Indeed, it may be preferable to address access to interoperability standards and SEIP (including, where necessary, the imposition of liability rules) through the application of the limiting doctrines in intellectual property law, rather than competition law, and allow refusals to supply or refusals to licence (including requests for injunction in respect of SEIP) to be per se legal.

7

Access to Interoperability Standards and Standards-Essential Intellectual Property

International Dimensions

7.1 Basis for an International Approach

Since concerns have arisen concerning access to standards, and to SEIP, a further question is whether the regulatory measures currently being undertaken at the domestic level within various jurisdictions should be complemented by international initiatives to achieve a more harmonized regulatory approach. These issues are now being addressed across numerous jurisdictions, including the United States, European Union, China, Korea and Japan. Therefore, it may be contended that some sort of international action would be in order to ensure a coordinated response, rather than each jurisdiction pursuing its own entirely separate approach. Such a harmonized approach is likely to facilitate cross-border commercial activity.

A further consideration is that essentially the same litigation matter often happens across multiple jurisdictions. Well-known litigation involving SEPs such as the *Qualcomm* cases, *Rambus* cases, and *Microsoft* v. *Motorola* involved parallel claims being brought simultaneously in multiple jurisdictions; quite similar cases against Microsoft were brought in the United States and the EU. Indeed, the impetus for the European Commission's investigation of Microsoft was an exchange of letters between Microsoft's Washington headquarters and Sun Microsystems' California headquarters. In the overwhelming majority of contested litigation matters involving SEPs, there is ultimately a settlement and a licence issued – the main points of contention being the terms upon which the SEPs are licensed. Moreover, worldwide licensing of SEPs now appears to have become the norm.[1] As such, the

---

[1] *Unwired Planet International* v. *Huawei Technologies Co Ltd and Huawei Technologies (UK) Co Ltd* [2017] 2017 EWHC 711 (High Court) [534].

outcomes of litigation across diverse jurisdictions are likely to affect the licensing terms eventually agreed.

Moreover, there is considerable scope for spillovers. Outcomes in one jurisdiction could affect licensing in other jurisdictions. If a single, important jurisdiction (e.g. Germany) issues an injunction in relation to SEPs, this could impact on licensing fees agreed to across other jurisdictions. In some cases, the inherent potential for cross-border spillovers arising from domestic enforcement of SEIP has explicitly been referenced in court and regulatory body decisions, for example: (i) the United States Federal Trade Commission Order and Decision of 23 July 2013 concerning Google's proposed acquisition of the patent portfolio of Motorola Mobility is expressed to apply to with respect to patent claims made anywhere in the world;[2] (ii) in *Huawei-InterDigital*, InterDigital was found in violation of China's Anti-Monopoly Law for seeking an exclusion order before the United States Court of International Trade;[3] and (iii) in *Huawei v. Unwired Planet*, Mr Justice Birss ruled that a worldwide licence, rather than a UK-specific licence, was more consistent with the FRAND determination given by Unwired.[4]

A further reason to pursue an international approach relates to the footloose nature of standard-setting and the dangers of either a 'race to the bottom' (in terms of legal obligations imposed on SEIP holders) or a 'race to the top' (in terms of the protection of SEIP). It will be very difficult to address SEIP issues by imposing more stringent obligations on SSOs, as this could risk the migration of SSOs to other, more permissive, jurisdictions, giving rise to a 'race to the bottom'. Likewise, absent international coordination, enforcement of SEIP, including attempts to secure injunctions, is likely to migrate to those jurisdictions most inclined to grant injunction. Indeed, this trend is already evident, with Germany in particular becoming the preferred jurisdiction owing to the perception that German courts are relatively more favourably disposed to granting injunctions. As the issue grows in scope, the danger may arise

---

[2] *Statement of the Federal Trade Commission, In the Matter of Motorola Mobility, LLC and Google Inc* [2013] Federal Trade Commission C–4410 2.

[3] Daniel Sokol and Wentong Zheng, 'FRAND in China' (2013) 22 Texas Intellectual Property Law Journal 71, 89.

[4] *Unwired Planet International v. Huawei Technologies Co. Ltd and Huawei Technologies (UK) Co Ltd* (n. 1) paras. 545–72; Jorge L. Contreras, 'A New Perspective on FRAND Royalties: Unwired Planet v Huawei' (2017) 4 dc.law.utah.edu accessed 16 February 2018.

for countries to adopt protectionist approaches, and either over-protect or under-protect SEIP in order to favour domestic producers.

As such, problems associated with access to interoperability standards, and to SEIP, may exhibit the features of a collective action problem. A collective action will occur in circumstances where each actor will be better off if every other actor performs a certain action, but even better off if every actor except themselves performs the action.[5] The term was coined by economist Mancur Olsen Jr in his classic 1965 work.[6] Olsen explained that collective action can itself be a public good; as such, collective action cannot be called upon to solve public goods problems or coordination problems.[7] As Olsen explained: '[U]nless the number of individuals in a group is quite small, or unless there is coercion or some other special device to make individuals act in their common interest, rational, self-interested individuals will not act to achieve their common or group interests'.[8] Olsen noted in particular the difficulties associated with collective action in large groups.[9] Free-riding may offer an attractive alternative to bearing some portion of the costs of collective action.[10] The question of collective action problems has been examined in the context of global public policy; Sandler, for example, has observed: 'Transnational collective action is closely tied to the presence of a pure public good or an externality, with benefit or cost 'spillovers' or consequences that affect two or more nations'.[11] Sandler defines an externality in this context as occurring 'when the action of one nation influences the well-being of one or more other nations and no compensation is paid or received'.[12]

Closely associated is the notion of a coordination problem, which may be defined as: 'A situation in which the interests of agents coincide, and the aim is to try to reach an outcome in which those interests are satisfied. Informally, this is a situation in which each person has an interest in

---

[5] Robert Goodin, 'The Collective Action Problem' in Marion Danis and others (eds.), *Fair Resource Allocation and Rationing at the Bedside* (Oxford University Press 2015).
[6] Mancur Olsen, *The Logic of Collective Action: Public Goods and the Theory of Groups* (Harvard University Press 1965).
[7] Roger D. Congleton, 'The Logic of Collective Action and Beyond' (2015) 164 Public Choice 217, 217.
[8] Olsen (n. 6) 2.
[9] Congleton (n. 7) 219.
[10] Ibid.
[11] Todd Sandler, 'Overcoming Global and Regional Collective Action Impediments' (2010) 1 Global Policy 40, 41.
[12] Ibid. 42.

doing something that chimes in with what the others do'.[13] In an increasingly globalized economy, characterized by an increasing degree of international independence, there is likely to be a greater need for international coordination; yet a number of obstacles to such coordination, including collective action problems, are likely to persist. Little scholarly attention has thus far been directed towards the question of whether concerns associated with interoperability standards and SEIP might exhibit either a collective action problem, or some broader species of coordination problem. Bradford considers that the difficulties of negotiating an international competition agreement constitute a collective action problem.[14]

As outlined above, there appear to be some indications of a collective action problem in this area, with attendant incentives for jurisdictions to either over-protect or under-protect SEIP, in accordance with their perceived national interests, resulting in negative externalities or spillovers. There appears to be the potential for such externalities or spillovers to impose negative consequences on global standards development and uptake, to the detriment of technological development. As Sykes has noted, countries exercising their suite of policy tools independently, without international coordination, will result in suboptimal outcomes where externalities exist.[15] As such, an international approach to addressing the issues associated with access to interoperability standards and SEIP is recommended.

7.2 Binding Treaty Action or International Soft Law?

The issues relating to access to SEIP do not appear to be amenable to binding treaty action at the present time. First, the solutions at the domestic level have not reached a sufficient level of maturity. For example, in US courts there is a growing body of jurisprudence to support the proposition that injunctions should not be available in relation to SEPs subject to a FRAND commitment. However, this

---

[13] Simon Blackburn, *The Oxford Dictionary of Philosophy* (3rd ed., Oxford University Press 2016).

[14] Anu Bradford, 'International Antitrust Cooperation and the Preference for Nonbinding Regimes' in Andrew T. Guzman (ed.), *Cooperation, Comity and Competition Policy* (Oxford University Press 2011) 322.

[15] William Sykes, 'International Law' in A. Mitchell Polinsky and Stephen Shavell (eds.), *Handbook of Law and Economics*, vol. 1 (Elsevier 2007) 767–8; see also Andrew T. Guzman and Timothy L. Meyer, 'International Soft Law' (2010) 2 Journal of Legal Analysis 171, 180–1.

7.2 TREATY ACTION OR INTERNATIONAL SOFT LAW? 283

approach is not consistently applied across all intellectual property at this point in time, with the US lower courts adopting notably divergent approaches in relation to copyright infringement; indeed the *eBay* precedent has not even been applied consistently across patent law, since exclusion orders under section 1337 of the United States Tariff Act are not currently subject to the principles outlined in *eBay* v. *MercExchange.*

Likewise, in the EU, the case law does not yet reflect a settled position on key issues pertaining to standards and SEIP. In particular, although the ECJ's judgment in *Huawei* v. *ZTE*,[16] together with the decisions of the European Commission in *Motorola*[17] and *Samsung*,[18] have confirmed the applicability of the European essential facilities doctrine to licensing negotiations in connection with SEPs, questions remain also in EU law, for example in relation to de facto standards where there is no FRAND commitment. The case law in *Magill*, *IMS Health* and *Microsoft* does not present a perfectly consistent picture: the *Microsoft* test for compulsory licensing or an essential facilities doctrine with respect to SEIP differs from the *IMS Health/Magill* test; this divide has not yet been resolved. Collectively, the EU case law in this area reveals fault lines both between the EU organs and the Member States, and between EU organs (consider the subtle differences in approach between the Commission and the Court of Justice in the *IMS Health* case).

In China the picture also remains somewhat blurred. There have been very few court decisions concerning SEIP, and no case law on this particular issue has yet emerged from the Supreme People's Court, China's highest court. It is reasonably clear at this point in time that Chinese law includes an essential facilities doctrine, and that the doctrine extends to SEIP in some circumstances. Yet many of the details are not yet filled in. The theoretical principles underpinning the Chinese essential facilities doctrine are far from clear; nor is the legal test for determining to which facilities access must be accorded, and upon what terms. Early cases such as the NDRC *Qualcomm* investigation and *Huawei* v. *InterDigital* appear to embrace an excessive pricing approach.

In many other jurisdictions around the world, domestic courts have not yet fully grappled with these issues. Therefore, in any international

---

[16] *Huawei Technologies Co Ltd v. ZTE Corp, ZTE Deutschland GmbH (Case C/170–13)* [2015] ECLI:EUC:2015:477 (European Court of Justice).
[17] *Motorola – Enforcement of GPRS Standard Essential Patents (Case AT39985)* (European Commission).
[18] *Samsung – Enforcement of UMTS Standard-Essential Patents (Case AT39939)* [2014] OJ C35008 (European Commission).

negotiation for a binding international treaty in connection with SEIP, many countries would simply be in 'listening mode', seeking to maintain maximum flexibility for future actions, rather than looking to lay down clear rules.

A second reason not to pursue an international treaty approach is more practical: there remain major differences, notably between the regulatory approaches in the United States and the European Union, but also involving other jurisdictions. There are fundamental differences between United States law and European Union law in terms of the applicability of unilateral competition law, including where intellectual property rights are concerned. In the EU, TFEU Article 102, which deals with abuse of a dominant market position, is well-accepted, and has been applied in the context of SEPs subject to FRAND commitments, as well as to SEIP more broadly, notably in the *Microsoft* case. By contrast, unilateral competition law disciplines, such as the essential facilities doctrine, monopoly leveraging and refusal to supply obligations, are generally not accepted within United States law (with the possible exception of the fact situation of the *Aspen Skiing* case[19] and with the better-established exception of tying offences). The intellectual heritage of the Chicago School of law and economics looms large over US competition law, as highlighted by the United States Supreme Court's prominent reference to Philip Areeda's work in its *Verizon* v. *Trinko* decision.[20]

The 'single monopoly profit' theorem, which takes such a dim view of any mandatory duty to deal pursuant to competition law – has been questioned by the post-Chicago School – but only in certain confined circumstances; for the most part, the doctrine remains undisturbed, and has on occasions been accepted directly into United States law.[21] Acceptance of the single monopoly profit theorem necessarily implies great reluctance for courts to intervene to address unilateral refusals to supply an input, even a monopoly input. The essential facilities doctrine, once regularly applied by United States courts, remains moribund.

Given that there are really only superficial differences between the essential facilities doctrine and TFEU Article 102, the death of the essential facilities doctrine implies a major transatlantic divide. Whereas EU

---

[19] *Aspen Skiing* v. *Aspen Highlands Skiing* [1985] 472 US 585 (United States Supreme Court); see *Verizon Communications, Inc* v. *Law Offices of Curtis V Trinko, LLP* [2004] 540 US 398 (United States Supreme Court) 409.

[20] See *Verizon Communications, Inc.* v. *Law Offices of Curtis V. Trinko, LLP* (n. 19) 410.

[21] See, e.g., *Schor* v. *Abbott Laboratories* [2006] 453 F3d 609 (United States Court of Appeals for the Seventh Circuit) 611–12.

regulators and courts will intervene to address unilateral refusals to license, United States regulators and courts will not, absent some other antitrust violation (e.g. deceptive or coordinated conduct). Thus, a binding treaty approach that either mandates or precludes the application of unilateral competition law approaches to SEPs would appear to be unachievable in the near future (if ever). At a more fundamental level, the transatlantic divide may be an economic one rather than a legal one, reflecting the differences between German ordoliberalism and the Chicago School. The EU's greater willingness to apply unilateral competition disciplines in the context of SEPs may also reflect the fact that EU jurisdiction is much more extensive with respect to competition laws than in relation to IP law.

A further issue that may assume greater prominence in the future involves the relatively greater willingness of some jurisdictions (notably China) to apply exploitative competition law disciplines, notably excessive or unfair pricing, including in the context of SEIP. This was evident in both the NDRC's *Qualcomm* investigation, and the *Huawei v. InterDigital* case. By contrast, no such discipline exists under US law (although there have been some attempts by the United States Federal Trade Commission to achieve a somewhat similar result through section 5 of the FTC Act); in the European Union an excessive pricing discipline is 'on the books' but is unlikely to be imposed in the context of intellectual property rights.

It is also important to point out that a number of attempts to agree to binding treaty obligations in this field have already failed. For example, a multilateral agreement in relation to substantive competition law disciplines has never succeeded (notable failed initiatives include the Havana Charter). Whilst competition policy chapters are frequently included in preferential trade agreements, such chapters tend to deal with procedural matters rather than substantive competition law obligations. Were such a treaty to be negotiated, the scope of unilateral disciplines, particularly in the context of intellectual property rights, would likely be one of the major points of contention, if not the most contentious question.

Similarly, negotiation of a substantive patent law treaty under the auspices of WIPO has languished, again due to significant differences concerning the proper scope of the substantive disciplines. Thus, there appears to be a manifest inability to reach international agreement in relation either to competition laws (notably unilateral disciplines) or substantive patent laws. Therefore, agreement concerning the possible application of unilateral competition laws in the context of SEIP would seem to be, in practical terms, impossible, at least for the moment.

Even in the unlikely event that a binding international agreement were attainable, it would take up much time and resources to negotiate, and the final outcome would probably be reduced to a lowest common denominator approach imposing such minimal obligation that little would have been achieved. As Bradford points out, countries may simply consider that the potential benefit from negotiating an international competition agreement will simply not be worth the time taken to negotiate such an instrument.[22]

In light of the extreme difficulties in reaching a binding hard law approach, adopting an 'international soft law' approach would seem to present numerous advantages. First, soft law can be negotiated by experts instead of diplomats, offering better quality results. In this instance, bringing together right holders, users, legal and economic experts, competition and intellectual property regulators, judges, and other interested parties in a non-contentious forum to negotiate non-binding statements of principle would seem to be both more feasible and offer substantial benefits. It will likely be easier to achieve consensus among various stakeholder groups if the result is not legally binding.

Also, it does not appear to be necessary for countries to amend their existing laws. If the principal way forward is to tailor the availability of the injunctive remedy in the context of SEIP (together with appropriate principles of compensation), then in many cases, substantive amendments to countries' domestic laws are unlikely to be necessary; the injunctive remedy is often an equitable remedy implying considerable discretion on the part of the courts, and as such, courts in many jurisdictions already have sufficient flexibility to award (or decline to award) injunctions depending on relevant facts and circumstances.

Rather, what courts and regulators need is guidance, not binding or prescriptive rules. Because domestic courts and regulators will not necessarily be entirely comfortable making rulings at the intersection of competition and intellectual property law, particularly given the highly technical characteristics of SEIP and the potential applicability of economic theory, the availability of authoritative yet non-binding guidance from acknowledged experts is likely to provide considerable assistance to

---

[22] Anu Bradford, 'International Antitrust Negotiations and the False Hope of the WTO' (2007) 48 Harvard International Law Journal 383, 401–5.

courts and regulatory bodies around the world. In addition, an international soft law document would probably be easier to amend – an important consideration given the fast-moving nature of standardized technologies, particularly in the information and communications technology fields. Therefore, an international soft law approach is recommended as the way forward. A soft law approach in the near term could well provide the basis for binding treaty initiatives in the future.[23] International soft law may be defined as: 'those nonbinding rules or instruments that interpret or inform our understanding of binding legal rules or represent promises that in turn create expectations about future conduct'.[24] The difference between hard law and soft law can be represented by a weakening through one or more of the dimensions of obligation (i.e. whether the norm is binding or non-binding), precision (whether the norm is tightly or loosely defined) and delegation (whether there is a delegation of authority to a third-party decision-maker).[25]

International soft law offers numerous benefits over international treaty-making. Whereas international agreements are generally negotiated by diplomats, international soft law can be developed by experts. Agreement can also be easier to reach in expert, non-state forums because entrenched differences over what are essentially political issues are much less likely to arise among private experts.[26] In addition, because the final product will not be legally binding, less concern is likely to arise about the precise contents of the document, and subsequent amendments, where required, are likely to be easier to effectuate.[27]

Even where international agreement is optimal, transaction costs may prevent this from occurring.[28] A soft law approach may be able to move international actors towards optimal coordination, without the attendant transaction costs associated with treaty negotiations. As Guzman and Meyer point out, hard law offers the prospect of greater 'compliance pull', but at the same time is likely to involve higher costs associated with violations,[29] which can act as a disincentive to States entering into

---

[23] See Gregory C. Schaffer and Mark A. Pollack, 'Hard versus Soft Law in International Security'; (2011) 52 Boston College Law Review 1147, 1157.
[24] Guzman and Meyer (n. 15) 174.
[25] Kenneth W. Abbott and Duncan Snidal, 'Hard and Soft Law in International Governance' (2000) 54 International Organization 421, 422; see also Schaffer and Pollack (n. 23).
[26] See Chris Brummer, 'Why Soft Law Dominates International Finance—and Not Trade' (2010) 13 Journal of International Economic Law 623, 631.
[27] Ibid.
[28] Sykes (n. 15) 768.
[29] Guzman and Meyer (n. 15) 177.

binding international treaties.[30] Moreover if, as hypothesized by Franck, international law obtains its 'compliance pull' as a result of the degree of legitimacy of the instrument in question, rather than through the application of coercive measures,[31] it follows that soft law instruments, depending prominently on the degree of legitimacy they are able to garner, could provide valuable in promoting optimal international coordination.

That is not to say that any exercise in non-state rulemaking by experts is always going to be easy; quite the contrary. Standard-setting bodies, for example in the area of drafting interoperability standards, have found over the years that the preparation of standards can be a very contentious matter and it is often difficult to get everybody to fully agree on a standard. Nevertheless, SSOs have developed over the years sophisticated notions of what 'consensus' means, which allows them to move forward, even where there is not complete agreement, but in a manner that preserves the legitimacy of the document which is to become the final product.

In terms of the appropriate process, there is much to be learned from the 'best practices' of leading SSOs. These organizations have become skilled in eliciting a workable consensus from groups of experts in relation to documents which are of a highly technical nature. These organizations have developed detailed processes relating to the drafting and promulgation of standards, including matters such as membership, notice-and-comment procedures, appeals mechanisms, publication and revision of standards. Such insights could prove useful in the current context.

7.3 Selecting the Appropriate Forum

The next question is: under the auspices of which permanently established international body should such a document be negotiated and drafted? Or should agreement be negotiated outside any permanently established body? Some general observations may be made. First, it is important context that several previous initiatives to establish international competition rules have failed. Differences of opinion between leading jurisdictions regarding the applicable legal tests, including in relation to unilateral conduct, would seem to have been prominent

---

[30] See Abbott and Snidal (n. 25) 434.
[31] See Thomas M. Franck, 'Legitimacy in the International System' (1988) 82 The American Journal of International Law 705.

reasons for the failure of those discussions. When a soft law instrument is negotiated, it needs to be borne in mind that the same inter-jurisdictional differences are likely to arise again, as long as governmental representatives are involved in the negotiations. Even if this does not preclude finalization of a soft law document, it may lead to compromise drafting that significantly reduces the value of any final document.

Another consideration relates to the nature of international instruments that generally emerge from state-state negotiations. Generally, each country comes to the negotiating table hoping that the document will reflect the laws of the home jurisdiction: that way the home jurisdiction will comply fully, and moreover the home jurisdiction's law will become influential internationally – the best-case outcome being that the final negotiated text replicates word for word the relevant provisions of domestic law. When multiple countries negotiate in this fashion, it can lead to a shallow compromise, which allows all countries to comply with the letter of the rules drafted, but without much deeper reflection as to the underlying policy merits of what is proposed.[32] However in the arena of interoperability standards and SEIP, underlying policy considerations – notably those based on the discipline of law and economics – should be considered with care. As such, the involvement of private participants, including academic experts, may yield more coherent results than a conventional state-state negotiation.

As such, it is recommended that expert private parties play a very significant role in the development of a soft law instrument – perhaps even the predominant role. Accordingly, the relative attractiveness of any particular negotiating forum will depend on its track record acting as host for the negotiating of soft law instruments with significant input from private participants. Of course, the development of a soft law instrument in the first instance may provide the basis for subsequent initiatives, including possible treaty-level documents, in the future. With these observations in mind, the relative merits of each of the most salient potential forums are considered.

7.3.1 *International Organization for Standardization*

ISO is primarily a standard-setting body. It does not have recognized competence in either intellectual property law or competition law.

---

[32] These observations come from the author's own experience in treaty negotiations in the field of international economic law.

Moreover, ISO's Code of Good Practice for Standardization[33] (which deals inter alia with questions of intellectual property and standards) has already been concluded under the ISO's auspices. It has not gained significant traction. Notably when a subsequent Code of Good Practice for the Preparation, Adoption and Application of Standards was annexed to the WTO TBT Agreement,[34] the provisions of the ISO Code dealing with intellectual property were omitted. A further reason for not pursuing an enterprise of this nature within the ISO is that ISO Members are national standard-setting bodies from countries around the world. While some of these bodies are private, others have significant links to government. As such, any standard negotiated under the auspices of ISO is likely to have significant governmental involvement, and perhaps inadequate involvement from private actors.

Other major SSOs such as IEEE, IEC, ETSI and IETF are also unlikely to present the right forum. IEC (which focuses on electrotechnical matters), ETSI (which has as its focus the telecommunications industry) and IETF (which deals primarily with Internet standards) each have a focus that is too narrow to encompass all the relevant issues arising in relation to SEIP. IEEE, perhaps the best qualified SSO, will not have the requisite expertise spanning across economics, intellectual property law, competition law and other applicable laws. Generally, there has been a drift of standard-setting away from the largest SSOs over the last couple of decades.[35] As such, a document drafted under the auspices of one of these SSOs is likely to be decreasingly reflective of the highly variegated standard-setting landscape. A further concern would be that a document drafted under the auspices of a recognized, formal SSO might give undue consideration to issues arising in the context of formal SSO-drafted standards, to the exclusion of parallel issues arising in the context of de facto standard-setting.

7.3.2 *International Telecommunication Union*

ITU's expertise is mainly confined to telecommunications and related computing issues. Like ISO it does not have recognized expertise in

---

[33] 'ISO/IEC Guide 59: 1994 Code of Good Practice for Standardization' www.iso.org/standard/23390.html accessed 20 May 2019.
[34] Agreement on Technical Barriers to Trade, April 15 1994, Marrakesh Agreement Establishing the World Trade Organization, Annex 1A 1994 (1868 UNTS 120) Annex 3.
[35] Han-Wei Liu, 'International Standards in Flux: A Balkanized ICT Standard-Setting Paradigm and Its Implications for the WTO' (2014) 17 Journal of International Economic Law 551, 559–65.

intellectual property law or competition law. ITU has also gained a reputation for being slow-moving and dominated by the interests of state-controlled telecommunications monopolies;[36] it is therefore not recommended as the forum in which to advance the issue.

7.3.3 World Intellectual Property Organization

WIPO has taken an active interest in the relationship between standards and intellectual property law, for example through its Standing Committee on the Law of Patents. This forum has provided some useful insights into the current state of play around the world in this field. For example, at the Fifteenth Session of the Standing Committee on the Law of Patents, participants discussed issues relating to standards and patents based on a paper presented by the WIPO Secretariat at the Thirteenth Session. WIPO also provides numerous resources on its website in relation to intellectual property rights and standard-setting.[37]

Since, fundamentally, this is an issue about the protection of intellectual property rights in the context of interoperability standards, WIPO would seem to be the best placed international organization to intervene. In addition, WIPO has experience in semi-private rulemaking exercises, having presided over the process for allocating international domain names.[38] This exercise involved the close collaboration of State and non-State actors, notably experts in various fields, coming together to develop a report on intellectual property issues in the context of domain name allocation. As such, this process may provide a model for the develop of an instrument concerning access to interoperability standards and to SEIP. Nevertheless, the process undertaken by WIPO did not escape criticism, for example it has been suggested that the role played by non-State experts was, in substance, quite minor. Froomkin has observed in this regard:

> My first introduction to the workings of the expert group was a two-day meeting in Geneva, in December 1998, to discuss the Interim Report that

---

[36] Rohan Samarajiva and Hosuk-Lee Makiyama, 'Whither Global Rules for the Internet? The Implications of the World Conference on International Telecommunication for International Trade' (ECIPE Policy Briefs 2012) 12/2012 1 www.econstor.eu accessed 20 May 2019; Liu (n. 35) 557.

[37] 'WIPO Website' www.wipo.int accessed 6 December 2017.

[38] A. Michael Froomkin, 'Semi-Private International Rulemaking: Lessons Learned from the WIPO Domain Name Process Regulating the Global Information Society' in Christopher T. Marsden (ed.), *Regulating the Global Information Society* (Routledge 2001).

was due to issue shortly thereafter. Unfortunately, we were provided with only minimal text in advance of our meeting–some by email shortly before we left, more under the door of our hotel rooms the night before our first meeting. While our debates are confidential, I think it breaks no confidence to say that our meeting in Geneva was not a drafting session. Rather, we were invited to comment on the issues, and discussed the rather limited texts we had been given. WIPO then revised the texts very extensively, and e-mailed us the revised versions.[39]

A further consideration is that the negotiation of an international soft law instrument concerning access to interoperability standards and SEIP is likely to involve significant discussion of matters falling outside the domain of intellectual property law, including the application of competition laws, the nature of the interoperability standards-setting landscape, the standard-setting process, and the technical and engineering characteristics of interoperability standards. Because of the complex and multidisciplinary nature of these discussions, WIPO may not possess the requisite expertise in all relevant fields.

7.3.4 World Trade Organization

Building on important international disciplines in this area, notably the TBT Agreement, the WTO's TBT Committee has taken some interest in the relationship between intellectual property and standards. The TBT Committee has also produced a document entitled Principles for the Development of International Standards, which sets out a number of recommendations for standard-setting that include transparency, openness, impartiality and consensus, effectiveness and relevance, and the development dimension.[40] This document, whilst insightful, is notably silent on issues concerning intellectual property, or abuses of rights by IP holders.

The WTO's Committee of Participants on the Expansion of Trade in Information Technology Products (ITA Committee) has been active in leading discussions about concerns in relation to standard-setting and trade, producing numerous reports and convening symposia. Indeed in 2000, the ITA Committee established a non-tariff measures work programme that included the following phases: (i) identify non-tariff

---

[39] Ibid. 223.
[40] 'Decisions and Recommendations Adopted by the WTO Committee on Technical Barriers to Trade since 1 January 1995' (World Trade Organization, Committee on Technical Barriers to Trade 2011) WTO Doc G/TBT/1/Rev.13 46 https://docs.wto.org.

measures (NTMs) which are impediments to trade in information technology products; (ii) examine the economic impact of such measures and consider the benefits from addressing the trade-distorting effects of such measures; and (iii) seek formal consideration by the ITA Committee of the work undertaken pursuant to the first two phases.[41] However little by way of concrete action has yet been forthcoming in this forum. In its 2017 report, the Committee noted that it has met twice in the previous year, and was continuing with its Non-Tariff Measures work programme, which still appears to be in its first phase.[42]

In principle the WTO, like WIPO, could address this issue. However, the WTO is an international organization, in which the interests of its Members (sovereign States or separate customs territories) take precedence. Given the entrenched differences among sovereign States concerning the issues discussed in this work, it is very unlikely that an international organization such as the WTO could sponsor the creation of an effective document in this area. The WTO's track record suggests that any document it produced would say little if anything about concerns arising in relation to SEIP.

Should the WTO membership be minded to pursue such a project, it could perhaps be pursued jointly through the WTO's Committees on Technical Barriers to Trade (TBT Committee) and its Council for TRIPS. Another possibility would be to hold discussions under the auspices of the ITA Committee, perhaps with a view to expanding the coverage of the WTO Information Technology Agreement to address non-tariff barriers in connection with interoperability standards.

7.3.5 International Competition Network

The ICN is a network of competition agencies from around the world, which interact closely with private actors concerned about international competition issues; it could he described as a 'virtual organization'.[43] ICN's members are national, regional and international competition

---

[41] 'WTO Committee of Participants on the Expansion of Trade in Information Technology Products – Non-Tariff Measures Work Programme' (World Trade Organization 2000) WTO Doc. G/IT/19.
[42] 'WTO Report (2017) of the Committee of Participants on the Expansion of Trade in Information Technology Products' (World Trade Organization 2017) WTO Doc. G/L/1200.
[43] Oliver Budzinski, 'The International Competition Network: Prospects and Limits on the Road towards International Competition Governance' (2004) 8 Competition and Change 223, 227.

regulatory organizations.[44] With 104 members,[45] ICN's membership is approaching universality. Since ICN is a virtual organization with no permanent secretariat, legal status, secretariat or budget, its principal organ is its steering committee, composed of fifteen representatives of member competition agencies, which sets the ICN's agenda and identifies priorities.[46] Although ICN is dominated by its governmental members, it nevertheless maintains significant links to non-governmental actors.[47]

ICN has produced practical recommendations on matters such as best practices, investigative techniques and analytical frameworks in the areas of merger review, unilateral conduct, anti-cartel enforcement and competition policy.[48] ICN currently has five working groups, including a Unilateral Conduct Working Group, established in May 2006. This working group is in the process of developing a workbook on the analysis of unilateral conduct. Draft chapters of the workbook are presently available from ICN's website. These chapters do not presently deal with specifically issues associated with access to interoperability standards, nor to SEIP.[49] Moreover in relation to unilateral conduct standards more generally, ICN's draft chapters tend to discuss broad concepts and underlaying considerations, rather than prescriptively recommending legal standards for intervention.[50]

Budzinski describes ICN's approach as involving two key approaches: (i) cognitive convergence through permanent interaction; and (ii) a combination of best practice proposals and peer pressure.[51] Regarding the first strategy, the idea is that the views and approaches of competition regulatory officials from various jurisdictions will become harmonized over time due to their constant interaction within the ICN forum. Over time this may help overcome observed differences in the

---

[44] Marie-Laure Djelic, 'International Competition Network' in Thomas Hale and David Held (eds.), *Handbook of Transnational Governance: Institutions and Innovations* (Polity Press 2011) 80.

[45] 'ICN Factsheet and Key Messages' (*International Competition Network*, April 2009) www.internationalcompetitionnetwork.org accessed 9 February 2018.

[46] Djelic (n. 44) 81.

[47] Ibid. 82.

[48] 'ICN Factsheet and Key Messages' (n. 45).

[49] 'Unilateral Conduct' www.internationalcompetitionnetwork.org accessed 9 February 2018.

[50] 'Unilateral Conduct Workbook Chapter 1: The Objectives and Principles of Unilateral Conduct Laws' (International Competition Network 2012) 9–15 www.internationalcompetitionnetwork.org accessed 14 February 2018.

[51] Budzinski (n. 43) 228.

regulatory approaches seen in various jurisdictions.[52] Regarding the second strategy, working groups are convened to develop best practice guidelines; once published, these guidelines will put pressure on competition regulators around the world to conform with these published best practices.[53]

The achievements of the ICN, which are to be contrasted with the various failed attempts to negotiate a binding international treaty in the field of competition law, highlight that soft law initiatives are much more likely to succeed than treaty negotiating initiatives. While there is no good reason why ICN should not address concerns associated with access to interoperability standards and SEIP, this virtual organization's focus on competition-related matters may mean that it is not be best-placed organization to pursue a holistic approach to such matters.

7.3.6 Organization for Economic Co-operation and Development

The OECD is an international organization with its headquarters in Paris, France. The OECD has thirty-seven members, mostly developed economies. The OECD's main role is the provision of information in the form of data collection and analysis, research reports and monitoring reports.[54] The OECD has solid expertise in both competition law and intellectual property law. It has also demonstrated the ability to host the negotiation of both binding hard law treaties and soft law instruments. Notable instruments negotiated under the auspices of the OECD include: the Convention on Bribery of Foreign Public Officials,[55] which was negotiated under the auspices of the OECD; the Multilateral Convention to Implement Tax Treaty Related Measures to Prevent Base Erosion and Profit Shifting,[56] a treaty recently negotiated under the auspices of the OECD; and the OECD Guidelines for Multinational Enterprises,[57] a non-binding instrument intended to assist multinational enterprises in their operations.

---

[52] Ibid.
[53] Ibid. 229–30.
[54] 'OECD' (*OECD*) www.oecd.org/ accessed 14 March 2018.
[55] Convention on Combating Bribery of Foreign Public Officials in International Business Transactions (adopted 21 November 1997, entered into force 15 February 1999) (37 ILM 1).
[56] Multilateral Convention to Implement Tax Treaty Related Measures to Prevent Base Erosion and Profit Shifting (opened for signature 31 December 2016, entered into force 1 July 2018).
[57] Organization for Economic Co-operation and Development, *OECD Guidelines for Multinational Enterprises* (OECD Publishing 2011).

The OECD Secretariat has strong capability and tends to take a leading role in the negotiation of such instruments. This makes OECD instruments more like expert-negotiated documents and less like traditional State-based treaty instruments. Nevertheless, the OECD has limited membership: it has mostly developed country members. Major developing countries like China, Russia, Brazil and India are not represented. The OECD's work is unlikely to be accepted as legitimate by non-Member jurisdictions, given its limited membership. Furthermore, while OECD unquestionably works closely with private sector entities, it is a traditional international organization and decisions are taken by its Member States. As such, any document negotiated under the auspices of the OECD is likely to suffer the same problems that are currently inhibiting the emergence of consensus in this area.

7.3.7 Standalone Forum

A further possibility is to pursue agreement through a dedicated, standalone forum. This could be undertaken, for example, through a multistakeholder approach, involving diverse groups of stakeholders, or even a private lawmaking approach, where governmental representatives are largely excluded and private stakeholders undertake the key roles. Raymond and DeNardis define multistakeholderism as follows: 'multistakeholderism entails two or more classes of actors engaged in a common governance enterprise concerning issues they regard as public in nature, and characterized by polyarchic authority relations constituted by procedural rules'.[58] These authors divide the various types of stakeholders into four broad classes: states, formal intergovernmental organizations, firms and civil society actors.[59] Polyarchy 'entails situations where authority is distributed among a number of actors'; such distribution could be heterogeneous (i.e. some actors or actor types hold much more authority than others) or homogeneous (where all actors hold essentially the same degree of authority).[60] Strickling and Hill define an 'authentic multistakeholder process' as one that is: (i) stakeholder driven; (ii) open (i.e. any stakeholder can participate); (iii) transparent (i.e. all stakeholders and the public have access to deliberations); and

---

[58] Mark Raymond and Laura DeNardis, 'Multistakeholderism: Anatomy of an Inchoate Global Institution' (2015) 7 International Theory 572, 574.
[59] Ibid. 576.
[60] Ibid. 580.

7.3 SELECTING THE APPROPRIATE FORUM

(iv) consensus-based.[61] Multistakeholder approaches can be seen in a variety of contexts including regulation of the Internet.

7.3.7.1 ICANN: A Multistakeholder Approach

One particularly apposite example of a multistakeholder approach is provided by the Internet Corporation for Assigned Names and Numbers (ICANN), a non-profit corporation established under Californian law in 1998, which plays an important role in Internet governance through its control of the Internet's domain name system.[62] ICANN's primary function is the maintenance of the Internet's Domain Name System (DNS), which provides unique domain name addresses for every user (similar to telephone directory services),[63] thus facilitating the stable and orderly functioning of the Internet. ICANN describes its governance function as follows:

> At the heart of ICANN's policy-making is what is called a 'multistakeholder model.' This decentralized governance model places individuals, industry, non-commercial interests and government on an equal level. Unlike more traditional, top-down governance models, where governments make policy decisions, the multistakeholder approach used by ICANN allows for community-based consensus-driven policy-making.[64]

ICANN has no members.[65] Decisions are made by its board of sixteen voting directors, with participation by four non-voting directors. The sixteen voting directors and four non-voting directors are appointed by the Empowered Community, a non-profit association established under California law. The Empowered Community draws its membership from five stakeholder organizations: the Address Supporting Organization (ASO), the Country Code Names Supporting Organization (ccNSO),

---

[61] Lawrence E. Strickling and Jonah Force Hill, 'Multi-Stakeholder Internet Governance: Successes and Opportunities' (2017) 2 Journal of Cyber Policy 296, 300.

[62] Hans Klein, 'ICANN and Internet Governance: Leveraging Technical Coordination to Realize Global Public Policy' (2002) 18 The Information Society 193, 193–4.

[63] Milton M. Mueller and Farzaneh Badiei, 'Governing Internet Territory: ICANN, Sovereignty Claims, Property Rights and Country Code Top-Level Domains' (2017) XVIII Columbia Science and Technology Journal 435, 437. 'The Domain Name System (DNS) provides a global standard for assigning unique character strings that function as Internet addresses anywhere in the world'.

[64] Internet Corporation for Assigned Names and Numbers, 'Beginner's Guide to Participating in ICANN' (*ICANN*) 2 www.icann.org accessed 24 February 2018.

[65] Internet Corporation for Assigned Names and Numbers, 'Amended and Restated Articles of Incorporation of Internet Corporation for Assigned Names and Numbers' (*ICANN*) www.icann.org/ accessed 24 February 2018 Art. 4.

the Generic Names Supporting Organization (GNSO), the At-Large Community (ALAC) and the Governmental Advisory Committee (GAC). In making board appointments, the Empowered Committee selects: eight voting directors nominated by the Nominating Committee (itself drawing its composition from a broad set of stakeholder committees); two directors nominated by each of ASO, ccNSO and GNSO, respectively; and one director nominated by ALAC.[66] In nominating its eight voting directors, the Nominating Committee must ensure that each of five geographic regions (Europe, Asia/Australia/Pacific, Latin America/Caribbean, Africa and North America) has at least one director and no more than five.[67]

Thus, the board's composition makes concrete the ambition of achieving a diverse, multistakeholder organizational structure. The board's decision-making is informed by recommendations provided by various stakeholder groups, such as: network operators; domain name registries; SSOs; Internet service providers; national governments; and business stakeholders.[68] For many years the United States maintained control over ICANN's functions through its contractual arrangements with ICANN,[69] but this arrangement ceased during 2017.[70]

The development of multistakeholder models, such as ICANN's, is seen as a highly significant development,[71] and it has been suggested that ICANN's multistakeholder approach could have broader relevance as a model of governance.[72]

7.3.7.2 Private Transnational Rulemaking Approach

Another option would be to adopt a private transnational rulemaking approach, giving the principal roles to private actors and either excluding

---

[66] Internet Corporation for Assigned Names and Numbers, 'Bylaws for Internet Corporation for Assigned Names and Numbers' (*ICANN*, 22 July 2017) www.icann.org/resources/pages/governance/bylaws-en accessed 25 February 2018.

[67] William Brown, Mark Engle and Greg Rafert, 'Independent Review of the ICANN Nominating Committee: Assessment Report' 25–6 www.analysisgroup accessed 24 February 2018.

[68] Lennard G. Kruger, 'The Future of Internet Governance: Should the United States Relinquish Its Authority over ICANN?' (Congressional Research Service 2016) 1 www.fas.org accessed 21 May 2020.

[69] Ibid. 1–3.

[70] Kal Raustiala, 'An Internet Whole and Free: Why Washington Was Right to Give up Control Essays' (2017) 96 Foreign Affairs 140, 140.

[71] Kal Raustiala, 'Governing the Internet' (2016) 110 American Journal of International Law 491, 503.

[72] See, e.g., Strickling and Hill (n. 61) 310.

state representatives entirely or relegating them to relatively minor roles. There may be some overlap between concepts of multistakeholderism and private transnational rulemaking: for example, a private rulemaking approach could satisfy Raymond and DeNardis' definition of multistakeholderism if representatives of firms and civil society were present.

The development of interoperability standards within private forums (e.g. IEEE) may be characterized as transnational rulemaking, whilst collective rights organizations such as patent pools are another example of private ordering solutions within the field of interoperability standards. Indeed, such regimes are becoming quite common in the modern, globalized economy:[73] diverse examples include international commercial arbitration regimes, professional self-regulatory arrangements and non-State product certification regimes.[74] Teubner characterizes such regimes as part of an emerging global order, which should not be measured against the standards of national legal systems, and which can be explained by differentiation observed within an emerging world-society.[75]

One useful example of private transnational rulemaking comes from the field of international security law, where there is a long history of experts coming together, sometimes under the auspices of an international organization or other body but more often without the backing of any particular body, to draft an international law 'expert manual'. Such manuals have included over the years the *Oxford Manual on the Laws of Naval War* (1913),[76] the *San Remo Manual on International Law Applicable to Armed Conflicts at Sea* (1994),[77] the *Harvard Manual on International Law Applicable to Air and Missile Warfare* (2009),[78] and the *Tallinn Manual on the International Law Applicable to Cyber Operations* (2013).[79]

---

[73] Gunther Teubner, 'Foreword: Legal Regimes of Global Non-State Actors' in Gunther Teubner (ed.), *Global Law without a State* (Dartmouth Publishing Company 1996) xiii.

[74] Benjamin Cashore, 'Legitimacy and the Privatization of Environmental Governance: How Non-State Market-Driven (NSMD) Governance Systems Gain Rule-Making Authority' (2002) 15 Governance 503.

[75] Gunther Teubner, '"Global Bukowina": Legal Pluralism in the World Society' in Gunther Teubner (ed.), *Global Law without a State* (Dartmouth Publishing Company 1996) 4.

[76] D. Schindler and J. Toman, *The Laws of Armed Conflicts* (Martinus Nihjoff 1988) 858–75.

[77] International Institute of Humanitarian Law, 'San Remo Manual on International Law Applicable to Armed Conflicts at Sea' (1995) November–December 1995 International Review of the Red Cross 595.

[78] *Harvard Manual on International Law Applicable to Air and Missile Warfare* (Cambridge University Press 2009).

[79] *Tallinn Manual on the International Law Applicable to Cyber Operations* (Cambridge University Press 2013).

The *Tallinn Manual*, the most recently completed expert manual in the field, was drafted by twenty experts under the auspices of the North Atlantic Treaty Organization (NATO). Its task was to elucidate the international law of armed conflict (both jus ad bellum and jus in bello)[80] in the context of cyberspace. The *Tallinn Manual* itself states: 'Like its predecessors, the Manual on the International Law Applicable to Cyber Warfare, or "Tallinn Manual", results from an expert-driven process to produce a non-binding document applying existing law to cyber warfare'.[81] The experts participating in the process include international lawyers, scholars and technical experts.[82] Participants were selected primarily on the basis of their expertise.[83] The Manual observes in this regard: 'This mix [of experts] is crucial to the credibility of the final product. So too is the inclusion of technical experts who provided input to the discussions and the text to ensure the Manual was practically grounded and addressed key issues raised by actual or possible cyber operations'.[84] Three observer organizations were permitted: NATO's Allied Command Transformation; the United States Cyber Command; and the International Committee of the Red Cross.[85] The Manual clarifies, however, that: 'Despite the invaluable active participation of the observers in the process, this Manual is not intended to reflect the legal positions or doctrine of any of these three organizations'.[86] In terms of the actual process followed by the Expert Group to develop the Manual, drafting was allocated among three teams of Experts, each lead by a Group Facilitator.[87] These drafts texts were then presented to plenary meetings of the full International Group of Experts. The intention was that consensus would be obtained regarding the Rules. Final drafts were then edited by an Editorial Committee, drawn from among the International Group of Experts, to ensure accuracy and clarity. The Rules were then approved by the International Group of Experts in plenary.[88]

An expert forum was selected instead of a traditional treaty forum primarily because of the complete inability of sovereign States to agree on the applicable international law in this particular context. The resulting

---

[80] Ibid. 4.
[81] *Tallinn Manual on the International Law Applicable to Cyber Operations* (n. 79).
[82] Ibid. 9.
[83] Ibid.
[84] Ibid.
[85] Ibid. 9–10.
[86] Ibid. 10.
[87] Ibid.
[88] Ibid.

product is not binding law as such – yet is enormously helpful to practitioners in the field, partly because there are so few other sources to turn to. Expert manuals in the field of international security law seek to clarify applicable law in specialized contexts in circumstances where codification appears highly difficult and precise customary rules remain unclear. These manuals have generally sought to explicate *lex lata* rather than *lex ferenda*. Nevertheless, they have at times shown creativity in 'filling gaps' in the applicable law. In the context of ensuring access to interoperability standards and SEIP there is no applicable customary international law to discover or delineate; what is proposed cannot be regarded in any sense as a codification exercise; nevertheless, the idea of bringing together a diverse array of highly reputable experts to provide guidance for domestic courts could draw extensively on these 'manuals' and the work they have generated.

7.3.8 Analysis and Conclusions as to the Appropriate Forum

Within the domain of international soft law, choices will need to be made about the appropriate forum, the stakeholders to be involved in deliberations, and the appropriate by-laws to govern the process of drafting the necessary document. Factors that will critically influence these choices are likely to be: (i) the relevant expertise and reputation held by the organization; (ii) the experience of the organization in dealing with the creation of soft law instruments that bring together stakeholders from diverse backgrounds to create credible soft law instruments; and (iii) in particular, the track record of the organization in encouraging significant, meaningful participation from non-State actors in formulating such soft law instruments.

There is really no currently existing, permanently established forum that would be perfectly suited to the development of an international soft law instrument dealing with access to interoperability standards and SEIP, pursuant to a comprehensive process of deliberation that takes cognizance of diverse fields of expertise, including intellectual property and competition laws, economics, engineering and interoperability standard-setting practices.

Furthermore, there have already been numerous unsuccessful attempts to reach international agreement in matters bearing upon access to interoperability standards and SEIP, within the field of international economic law, most prominently the numerous failed attempts to negotiate an international competition agreement. The difficulty in agreeing to an international competition treaty would appear to result, at least in part, from entrenched inter-jurisdictional differences which, as the surveys of applicable domestic law provided in this work indicate, are unlikely to be resolved in the immediate future. Such entrenched inter-jurisdictional difference might perhaps be further reflected by the relatively broad and high-level nature of best practice guidelines relating to unilateral conduct developed under the auspices of the International Competition Network.[89] Equally, inter-jurisdictional differences may be inferred from the lack of progress of WIPO Member States in taking forward negotiation for a Substantive Patent Law Treaty within WIPO.

Similarly, there appear to have been roadblocks to the pursuit of deliberations regarding these matters within the WTO forum. For example, although ISO's best-practice guide for standard-setting recommended that patented technologies should be excluded from standards, unless justified and subjected to agreements of licence on reasonable terms and conditions,[90] no similar provision was included in subsequent initiatives with respect to private standard-setting developed under the auspices of the WTO, notably the Code of Good Practice for the Preparation, Adoption and Application of Standards in the final texts of the Uruguay Round of negotiations, annexed to the Agreement on Technical Barriers to Trade,[91] developed by the WTO's Committee on Technical Barriers to Trade.[92] This suggests that WTO Members were reluctant to adopt the approach taken by the ISO guide regarding access to SEIP.

Likewise, there has been little progress with the WTO forum over many years to address non-tariff barriers impacting upon trade in information technology products. As such, it appears that entrenched differences between jurisdictions are preventing established, international organizations in the field of international economic law from pursuing development of meaningful international rules addressing access to interoperability standards.

Furthermore although WIPO, in particular, is experienced in hosting multi-stakeholder rulemaking exercises, for example the drafting of

---

[89] 'Unilateral Conduct Workbook Chapter 1: The Objectives and Principles of Unilateral Conduct Laws' (n. 50) 9–15.
[90] 'ISO/IEC Guide 59: 1994 Code of Good Practice for Standardization' (n. 33) Art. 5.8.
[91] Agreement on Technical Barriers to Trade, Annex 1A to the Marrakesh Agreement Establishing the World Trade Organization (adopted 15 April 1994, entry into force 1 January 1995) (1868 UNTS 120).
[92] 'Decisions and Recommendations Adopted by the WTO Committee on Technical Barriers to Trade since 1 January 1995' (n. 40) 46.

a report relating to domain names, this process has attracted criticism, on the grounds that the role undertaken by private participants was, in substance, a relatively minor one, with key decisions being reserved to state representatives.[93] Such problems may well afflict any attempt to negotiate an expert-led soft law instrument under the auspices of an established negotiating forum, such as WIPO or the WTO, since participating states would likely reserve for themselves the core decision-making functions, in exercise of their powers under the organization's constituent documents.

Therefore, initiating discussions outside the auspices of an established forum, by way of a standalone approach, is likely to be most attractive option, at least in the first instance. Furthermore, if the intention is to pursue a soft law approach that seeks to achieve the benefits of international coordination whilst minimizing the accompanying transaction costs, then it would likely be difficult to justify the establishment of a new, permanent forum in the immediate future. Rather, convening a negotiating group on an ad hoc basis may present a more streamlined and workable means of proceeding, at least in the first instance.

In terms of the participating negotiating group, it is suggested that, whilst a multistakeholder approach is clearly one that warrants consideration in the medium term, one difficulty that is likely to arise will be finding a way to reach agreement on an allocation of voting power, as well as other important applicable levels of controlling the final output of the negotiating group, as between governmental and non-governmental representatives.

Following the taxonomy of DeNardis and Raymond, a heterogeneous polyarchic model, in which state representatives hold the key decision-making powers, is unlikely to produce consensus, in view of the lack of progress in negotiating international agreements in this field. A homogeneous polyarchic approach, in which state representatives were allocated equal voting power along with other types of stakeholders (e.g. academic experts or firm representatives) would be more likely to deliver consensus: however, this approach is unlikely to be acceptable to states, who would likely be very reluctant to be associated publicly with the outcomes of a process of this nature.

Furthermore, these issues concerning access to interoperability standards and to SEIP could easily become politicized, and once this occurs it will likely be difficult to obtain any degree of consensus among

---

[93] Froomkin (n. 38) 13.

negotiating governmental representatives. It is instructive to recall the difficulties experienced by the OSI standard-setting initiative undertaken in the ISO forum during the 1970s and 1980s, where hundreds of industry, academic and governmental representatives convened to attempt the devise a universal Internet standard; committee chairman, Charles Bachman, recalled:

> The organizational problem alone is incredible. The technical problem is bigger than any one previously faced in information systems. And the political problems will challenge the most astute statesmen. Can you imagine trying to get the representatives from ten major and competing computer corporations, and ten telephone companies and PTTs [state-owned telecom monopolies], and the technical experts from ten different nations to come to any agreement within the foreseeable future?[94]

Therefore, the most appropriate approach, at least in the first instance, would seem to be an exercise in private rulemaking (perhaps with governmental representatives participating as observers only). Indeed, an approach where the key decision-making roles are reserved to experts without significant links to governments would seem to offer distinct benefits. It will likely avoid the inter-jurisdictional disagreements that have precluded international agreement in the field of competition law. It will facilitate deep engagement on the underlying public policy considerations which should underlie international rules in this area, rather than a shallow negotiating with a view to determining which jurisdiction's law provides the superior template. It will enable experts to be gathered from all relevant fields, including competition law, intellectual property law, other bodies of law, economics, standard-setting, engineering and other applicable disciplines. It will permit frequent revisions to its original output. Furthermore, governmental representatives could participate as observers, so as to ensure that any conclusions reached by the drafting group were both accurate and feasible.

Therefore, on balance, the development of an expert manual by private participants, within a non-permanent standalone forum appears to be the optimal starting point, and would appear to offer the largest, immediate gains, with the lowest accompanying transaction costs. Of course, without the credibility that might be lent by an existing international organization, care will need be taken to ensure that the potential for

---

[94] Andrew L. Russell, 'OSI: The Internet That Wasn't' [2013] *IEEE Spectrum* https://spectrum.ieee.org/tech-history/cyberspace/osi-the-internet-that-wasnt accessed 11 March 2018.

a document with a high degree of credibility and legitimacy is maximized, for example by ensuring that participants have recognized expertise, that there is appropriate representation from all significant stakeholder groups, and that the document is developed through a transparent and well-documented process.

In the medium to long term, the participation of state representatives, who are the ultimate rulegivers in this context, is likely to be essential. As Budzinski observes, the development of non-binding instruments within the ICN forum seeks to influence state practice through the operation of two key modalities: (i) cognitive convergence through permanent interaction; and (ii) a combination of best practice proposals and peer pressure.[95] An exclusively private transnational rulemaking approach, in which state representatives are excluded entirely or relegated to observer status only, could provide for 'best practices' and, at least over time, generate a degree of peer pressure (if it is followed), but it could not engender cognitive convergence through permanent interaction.

Therefore, in the longer term, it may be advisable to establish a more permanent forum, perhaps adopting a multistakeholder approach which draws on the experience of ICANN, to discuss issues concerning access to SEIP and produce best-practice guides and more comprehensive soft law instruments. If the soft law instruments emanating from such discussions receive widespread acceptance, this could energize discussions among jurisdictions within more established fora, such as the WTO's TBT Committee and Council for TRIPS. In the long term, there may even be prospects for the negotiation of binding international rules in this field, perhaps negotiated under the auspices of the WTO or WIPO.

7.4 The Appropriate Process to Be Followed in Developing an Expert Manual

Although an expert manual dealing with access to interoperability standards and SEIP would not be binding law as such, it could still carry considerable legitimacy, and therefore effectiveness, provided that three conditions are met: (i) the expertise of the group needs to be outstanding and widely acknowledged; (ii) the group needs to be adequately representative of all affected stakeholder groups; and (iii) the process through

---

[95] Budzinski (n. 43) 228.

which the expert manual is developed needs to be transparent, robust and comprehensive.[96]

At the same time, care needs to be taken to ensure that none of these factors impedes the attainment of the consensus that will be essential to the finalisation of an expert manual. Governmental participation in an observer status should be encouraged, but direct governmental participation in the drafting of the manual is not recommended, since this would take the process too far towards the negotiation of an international agreement.

7.4.1 Expertise

The expert group needs to include people whose expertise is widely acknowledged and recognized. The economic, legal and engineering fraternities each need to be well-represented. Participants should be familiar with issues involved in the creation and dissemination of interoperability standards, and in the creation, licensing, enforcement and use of SEIP; it would be preferable for participants to be renowned experts in their field. Industry and academic participation, in particular, should be encouraged.

7.4.2 Adequately Representative Composition of an Expert Group

Composition of the expert group should be composed of a broad spectrum of perspectives; neither the views of creators or of users of SEIP should be privileged. Careful attention should be given to participants' history of consulting for one 'side' of the issue or another, to ensure that the full spectrum of views is properly represented. Moreover, the perspectives of a wide array of jurisdictions should be taken account of, including lawyers, engineers and economists based in the United States, Europe, China, Japan and many other jurisdictions. No jurisdiction of significance that is currently grappling with concerns associated with access to interoperability standards, and to SEIP, should be overlooked.

7.4.3 Robust and Transparent Process

In terms of the recommended process to be followed, the expert group should have written procedures. Such procedures could draw on the

---

[96] See generally Franck (n. 31) Franck states at 711: 'The legitimacy of a rule, or of a rule-making or rule-applying institution, is a function of the perception of those in the community concerned that the rule, or the institution, has come into being endowed with legitimacy: that is, in accordance with the right process'.

7.4 FOLLOWED IN DEVELOPING AN EXPERT MANUAL

procedures followed in the development other expert manuals, such as the *Tallinn Manual*. A further source of inspiration will be the written procedures of SSOs, particularly those acknowledged as being in conformity with latest best practices. Standard-setting organizations can lend important guidance in relation to matters such as open participation, notice-and-comment, consensus, appeals and publication of the final product.

Formal modalities to guide discussion will likely be needed, as SSOs such as IEEE have discovered over the years.[97] The conception of 'consensus' followed by the expert group will likely be of the utmost importance. The expert group should include participation by those associated with all parts of the information industries, and familiar with the laws and practices of many different jurisdictions. They are not going to agree on everything. The group cannot proceed in the absence of a degree of consensus that is sufficient to lend the resulting document a high degree of credibility. Strongly held objections must be considered with great care. Nevertheless, no particular individual, organization or interest group should be permitted to 'hold-up' the proceedings to the detriment of all other participants.

SSOs have vast experience dealing with such issues, and the by-laws of the best of them should be scrutinized with care. For example, the IEEE Standards Association's Study Group Guidelines provide the following details about consensus in the standard-setting process: 'While it is desirable that the Study Group develop its output using a consensus-based process as defined by its Sponsor, there may be times when majority voting is needed to address a particular issue'.[98] Where voting occurs, it is recommended that 75 per cent approval be obtained among those present and voting either 'approve' or 'disapprove'.[99] Many other SSOs maintain similar policies, which nevertheless may vary in terms of prescriptiveness; IETF, for example, applies the concept of 'rough consensus':

> Working groups make decisions through a 'rough consensus' process. IETF consensus does not require that all participants agree although this is, of course, preferred. In general, the dominant view of the working group shall prevail. (However, 'dominance' is not to be determined on the

---

[97] See Kai Jakobs, Wolter Lemstra and Victor Hayes, 'Creating a Wireless Standard: IEEE 802.11' in Wolter Lemstra, Victor Hayes and John Groenewegen (eds.), *The Innovation Journey of Wi-Fi: The Road to Global Success* (Cambridge University Press 2010) ch. 3.
[98] 'IEEE Standards Association Study Group Guidelines' 3 http://standards.ieee.org accessed 6 December 2017.
[99] Ibid. 3–4.

basis of volume or persistence, but rather a more general sense of agreement). Consensus can be determined by a show of hands, humming, or any other means on which the WG agrees (by rough consensus, of course). Note that 51% of the working group does not qualify as 'rough consensus' and 99% is better than rough. It is up to the Chair to determine if rough consensus has been reached.[100]

Russell notes in relation to IETF's notion of 'rough consensus':

> IETF veterans place an acceptable level of agreement at around 80 to 90 percent: a level high enough to demonstrate strong support, but flexible enough to work in the absence of unanimity. In short, rough consensus was an apt description of this informal process in which a proposal must answer to criticisms, but need not be held up if supported by a vast majority of the group.[101]

Ultimately the guiding principle is that the rules should be appropriately tailored to the relevant context; a greater or lesser degree of prescriptiveness may be preferable on the basis of the nature of the group and also the nature of the final product. Generally, having comprehensive rules and publishing them in advance of the drafting project is likely to enhance both the quality and the credibility of the final product.

7.5 The Appropriate Purpose and Structure of an Expert Manual

7.5.1 General Observations

The purpose of an expert manual in relation to access to SEIP would be to provide normative guidance to domestic courts and to regulatory agencies (as well as to SSOs, consortia, private firms and other interested actors) about the appropriate approach to dealing with issues pertaining to access to interoperability standards and to SEIP, including discussion of issues arising under domestic intellectual property and competition laws. The expert manual would explain to courts and regulators the most policy-appropriate manner in which to exercise their existing level of discretion when dealing with SEIP.

Where the manual recommends an approach that falls outside the boundaries of the existing law of a particular jurisdiction, that country's courts and regulators would not be able to refer to it as such; nevertheless,

---

[100] Scott Bradner, 'IETF Working Group Guidelines and Procedures' https://tools.ietf.org accessed 6 December 2017.
[101] Andrew L. Russell, '"Rough Consensus and Running Code" and the Internet-OSI Standards War' (2006) 28 IEEE Annals of the History of Computing 48, 55.

even in that instance, the manual would provide a signal to legislators in that country that perhaps some revisions to the existing laws on the books are called for. As a non-binding, soft law document, a manual would be persuasive but would not hold binding legal force, although it could influence the direction of future legislative initiatives. In particular, it might, over time, encourage jurisdictions to resolve internal contradictions within their domestic approaches to SEIP.

An expert manual should be grounded in a deep understanding of the applicable provisions of existing law. Nevertheless, it should not simply restate existing law, for several reasons. First, different jurisdictions have different laws and it would not be practicable to develop a document that reflects all of them. Second, many countries' laws currently confer considerable discretion on courts and regulatory agencies, for example upon courts in the context of when to award an injunction, and on competition regulatory agencies in terms of when to initiate an investigation. Rather than synthesizing existing law, an expert manual would be of greater value if it explains to courts and regulators, from a policy perspective, how they ought to exercise the discretionary powers which they currently have.

The policy insights in an expert manual, whilst drawing closely on provisions of existing law, should also be firmly grounded in generally accepted principles of law and economics, including deep understanding of the law and economics of both intellectual property laws and competition laws. Its proposals should be valid and defensible from an economic standpoint. Moreover, an expert manual should be robust and workable from a technical and engineering perspective. It should reflect expertise in drafting interoperability standards across a wide variety of domains: mobile telephony; wireless LANs; computing and Internet standards; and perhaps also from standard-setting outside the information and communications technology industries.

7.5.2 *Proposed Substantive Contents*

First, an international instrument should describe the concept of a standard, distinguishing between formal and de facto standards, as well as a suitable definition of an interoperability standard. Next, the instrument would define the concept of standards-essential intellectual property. Care should be taken to distinguish between claimed essentiality and actual essentiality as established by a court. Particular attention should be given to standards-essential patents, copyrights and trade secrets. Some comments may be in order regarding the concept of SEIP in the specific context of each of these three types of rights.

In relation to copyrights, the distinction between ideas (which cannot be protected) and expressions of those ideas in works (which can be protected) should be emphasized. It should further be noted that it may be appropriate to provide exceptions to copyright in relation to: (i) situations where the idea and its expression are 'merged'; (ii) situations where the expression has become commonplace or standard; and (iii) use of the copyrighted work is essential to achieving interoperability. Regarding patents, the importance of the obligation to publish the patented information in sufficient detail as to enable one skilled in the art to practise the invention, should be emphasized; the importance of experimental exceptions should also be noted.

The role of formal SSOs should be noted, along with significant aspects of SSO rules, policies and by-laws (intellectual property policies in particular), such as (i) the duties to search for existing intellectual property rights; (ii) and FRAND obligations; (iii) competition law obligations; and (iv) basic procedural requirements. The status of FRAND declarations under applicable domestic law should be discussed.

Possible harms to competition arising from the market power (in some cases monopoly power) accruing to SEIP holders should be noted. Concerns relating to both 'hold-up' and 'hold-out' should be canvassed. The broader context of intellectual property rights (including patent rights) in high technology markets, such as component patents and 'patent thickets', should be discussed.

The possible applicability of competition laws should be discussed, noting flexibility, a number of potential approaches, and other approaches not recommended (e.g. reliance on excessive or unfair pricing).

General principles concerning the principal intellectual property remedies of injunctions and damages (including in particular the calculation of reasonable royalties) should be outlined. Significant international obligations (e.g. the requirements of the TRIPS Agreement) should be noted. Regarding court awards of injunctive relief, the following observations would be appropriate:

- the flexible and discretionary nature of the remedy in many jurisdictions;
- the equitable nature of the remedy in many jurisdictions;

7.5 PURPOSE AND STRUCTURE OF AN EXPERT MANUAL 311

- the general principle expressed most recently in *eBay v. MercExchange*[102] that injunctions in the context of the infringement of an intellectual property right should be made available pursuant to the same principles as under the general laws of the jurisdiction, that is, there should not be an automatic entitlement to an injunction for any infringement of intellectual property law;
- it should be emphasized that injunctions should be awarded on a case-by-case basis on the basis of all relevant facts and circumstances, including:
  - the risks of 'hold-up' and 'hold-out';
  - whether the intellectual property rights in questions have been established by a court of recognized competence to be, standards-essential, i.e. that it is technically impossible to implement the standard without infringing the relevant rights;
  - whether the intellectual property rights in question are subject undertakings to license, e.g. FRAND undertakings given to a formal SSO;
  - the record of negotiations between the right holder and the user;
  - whether there has been bad faith, dishonesty, fraud or deceptive conduct by either the rights holder or the user; and
  - the public interest, including the public interest in:
    - promoting technological progress, and
    - ensuring economic efficiency and competitive markets.

Subject to the foregoing, the expert manual could additionally note that, in general and subject to all the relevant facts and circumstances of the matter, courts should be reluctant to award injunctions in respect of SEIP where:

- the relevant market(s) exhibit(s) a Cournot complements problem; and
- the award of an injunction is likely to have the effect of prohibiting significant non-infringing conduct.

Furthermore an expert manual could outline a further situation in which it would be appropriate (albeit not necessarily recommended) that courts decline to make available the injunctive remedy, namely situations where: (i) access to the SEIP is indispensable to compete in a secondary market (i.e. the SEIP exhibits 'double essentiality');[103] (ii) failure to

---

[102] *eBay Inc. v. MercExchange, LLC* [2006] 547 US 388 (United States Supreme Court).
[103] As outlined above, 'double essentiality' exists where: (i) the intellectual property right is essential to the practice of an interoperability standard; and (ii) practice of that

license the SEIP would eliminate competition in that secondary market; (iii) the SEIP is needed to create a new product for which there is likely consumer demand; and (iv) there is no objective justification for the refusal to license the SEIP.

The contents could also address other matters, such as appropriate principles for compensation. These are likely to include the following:

- compensation should be based on ordinary principles of law, notably those laws pertaining to the calculation of reasonable royalties, adjusted as appropriate to take account of the standard-setting context;
- compensation should seek to adequately compensate the right holder for the value of the SEIP, excluding any 'hold-up value' associated with the SEIP, but not necessarily excluding all incremental value accruing to the SEIP holder as a result of the inclusion of the technology subject to the intellectual property right into the standard;
- compensation should take account of the value of other SEIP and other technologies (whether or not they are standardized and whether or not they are subject to intellectual property rights) which are incorporated into the relevant end-consumer products;
- compensation should be calculated on an economically sound basis;
- compensation should take account of the marginal contribution of the SEIP to the standard in question, having regard to alternative technologies that were available to the SSO when the standard was drafted; and
- courts may gain insights from: (i) the value at which the SEIP has been licensed to other users; (ii) the value attributed to the SEIP by any recognized collective rights organization, such as a patent pool; and (iii) expert testimony as to the value of the SEIP.

It would also be appropriate for an expert manual to include some comments about the potential applicability of competition laws in connection with interoperability standards and SEIP. It should be recommended that the ordinary principles of the competition laws of the relevant jurisdiction should apply equally in relation to interoperability standards and SEIP as they apply across the economy generally.

interoperability standard is essential to competition in a market other than the market for the licensing of the intellectual property right.

7.6 INTERNATIONAL LAW OF PROPOSED APPROACH   313

Having regard to the profound importance of standard-setting to the global information society, domestic competition regulators should be encouraged to look favourably upon standard-setting activities generally; nevertheless, standard-setting activities should not be used as a mere front for coordinate conduct (e.g. market-sharing or price-fixing). It would be appropriate (albeit not necessarily recommended) for unilateral competition law disciplines to apply in situations where: (i) access to the SEIP is indispensable to compete in a secondary market (i.e. the SEIP exhibits 'double essentiality'); (ii) failure to license the SEIP would eliminate competition in that secondary market; (iii) the SEIP is needed to create a new product for which there is likely consumer demand; and (iv) there is no objective justification for the refusal to license the SEIP. The application of competition law principles of excessive or unfair pricing should be discouraged.

7.6 Consistency with International Law of the Proposed Approach

Given that international soft law is not binding as such, the provisions of any soft law instrument should remain fully consistent with applicable international law. As outlined in Chapter 3, relevant international economic law, in particular international intellectual property law, is primarily focussed on minimum rights of protection and non-discrimination, and does not require States to actively take measures to address private abuses in connection with access to interoperability standards and SEIP. It now falls to be considered whether at the present time, the relevant provisions of international economic law are sufficiently flexible as to permit States (and indeed private parties) to implement the measures recommended in this treatise.

This question falls primarily within the domain of international intellectual property law, and in particular the TRIPS Agreement, which represents to date the most advanced degree of international harmonization in the field of international intellectual property law, has achieved near-universal membership, and moreover incorporates by reference the principal obligations from the WIPO treaties predating the provisions of TRIPS.

7.6.1 Patents

Article 28 (Rights Conferred) of the TRIPS Agreement outlines the exclusive rights associated with a patent. It is unclear whether Article

28 mandates that courts must award injunctions in respect of each and every infringement of a patent. As a starting point, it is to be recalled that domestic court decisions are 'measures' subject to the obligations of the WTO Agreement, including the provisions of the TRIPS Agreement. Article 28, by its terms, requires that patent holders must be able to prevent infringers from making use of the patent without consent. Where a court finds infringement but awards damages only, the infringer is effectively permitted to use the patented invention, notwithstanding the lack of consent by the right holder.

As such this result can be seen as inconsistent with the exclusive rights granted by the patent and therefore could give rise to an inconsistency with the requirements of Article 28; our analysis in this work suggests that from an economic standpoint, there is little difference in substance between the non-award of an injunction and the award of a compulsory licence. On both cases an exclusive property rule is substituted for a liability rule.

Article 44(2) of the TRIPS Agreement appears to address the issue squarely; it states:

> Notwithstanding the other provisions of this Part and provided that the provisions of Part II specifically addressing use by governments, or by third parties authorized by a government, without the authorization of the right holder are complied with, Members may limit the remedies available against such use to payment of remuneration in accordance with subparagraph (h) of Article 31. In other cases, the remedies under this Part shall apply or, where these remedies are inconsistent with a Member's law, declaratory judgments and adequate compensation shall be available.

In terms of commentary, Cotropia considers that the non-award of an injunction is tantamount to a compulsory licence and would need to be permitted under either Article 30 or Article 31 of TRIPS;[104] Taubman also takes this view.[105] Mace, however, considers that Article 44(2), read together with Article 44(1), requires only that injunctions be available.[106]

---

[104] Christopher A. Cotropia, 'Compulsory Licensing under TRIPS and the Supreme Court of the United States' Decision in EBay v. MercExchange' in Graeme Dinwoodie and Mark D. Janis (eds.), *Patent Law and Theory: A Handbook of Contemporary Research* (Edward Elgar 2009) 561.

[105] Antony Taubman, 'Rethinking TRIPS: "Adequate Remuneration" for Non-Voluntary Patent Licensing' (2008) 11 Journal of International Economic Law 927, n. 20.

[106] Andrew C Mace, 'TRIPS, EBay and Denials of Injunctive Relief: Is Article 31 Compliance Everything?' (2009) X Columbia Science and Technology Journal 233, 254.

7.6 INTERNATIONAL LAW OF PROPOSED APPROACH

A close reading of Article 44(2) suggests that it takes a sequential approach to three separate situations. The first situation, which is addressed by the first sentence of Article 44(2), involves governmental use or the issuance of compulsory licences; in this case, the courts may award remuneration only, in accordance with Article 31(h) of the TRIPS Agreement. The second situation is in 'other cases', in which the remedies available under Part III of the TRIPS Agreement (which include injunctions (Article 44(1)), damages (Article 45) and other remedies (Article 46)) shall apply. The third situation is where the remedies provided for in Part III are inconsistent with a Member's law; in this case, declaratory judgments and compensation must be available. If reliance is not to be placed on Article 31 of TRIPS in any particular, the first sentence of Article 44(2) is not applicable. While the third situation may be applicable for some WTO Members in some cases, our study of countries' laws pertaining to awards of injunctions indicated that in numerous jurisdictions, the power is a discretionary one that is left to the domestic courts to decide; in these jurisdictions it could not be said that the award of an injunction would be inconsistent with the Member's law. This leaves the second situation.

Meaning must be given to the phrase 'in other cases'. Based on the ordinary meaning of the provision, two readings are possible. First, since the first sentence makes particular reference to compulsory licensing under Article 31, 'other cases' may refer to forms of intellectual property other than patents. On this reading, any decision of a court not to award injunction upon a finding that a patent has been infringed would be considered tantamount to compulsory licensing and would need to be excused via Article 31 – or, implicitly, by recourse to Article 30; for rights other than patents, however, additional flexibility not to award injunctions may be implicit in Article 44(2). The second possible reading of 'in other cases' is that it refers to situations where the requirements of Article 31 are not satisfied, even for patents. Thus, on this reading, there would potentially be scope for Member courts not to award injunctions, even for patent infringement, without breaching the requirements of Article 28.

Which interpretation is to be preferred? There is no Panel or Appellate Body case law to provide guidance. Cottier and Veron prefer the first reading, but do not provide reasons.[107] Gervais, whilst not addressing the

---

[107] Thomas Cottier and Pierre Veron (eds.), *Concise International and European IP Law: TRIPS, Paris Convention, European Enforcement and Transfer of Technology* (3rd ed., Kluwer Law International 2015) 127.

question specifically, is inclined to read Article 44.2 restrictively.[108] Malbon et al., by contrast, see Article 44.2 as operating to 'prevent an absurdity', because otherwise Members would be obligated to make injunctions for infringement available even where compulsory licence has been issued pursuant to Article 31.

Clearly, in light of the lack of case law and the conflicting views of authorities, the phrase 'in other cases' should be construed by way of accepted principles of interpretation of customary international law. At the outset, it should be noted, that if the negotiators of TRIPS had intended 'in other cases' to mean 'for categories of intellectual property other than patents', they could have included words to this effect in Article 28. Perhaps some Members read the provision in this way, but there would appear to be a measure of constructive ambiguity in the provision. The ordinary meaning of the phase 'in other cases' would, in addition, seem sufficiently broad to encompass a meaning that is not limited to 'other categories of intellectual property'.

The *Oxford English Dictionary* defines 'case', relevantly, as: 'An instance of a particular situation; an example of something occurring; a particular circumstance or state of affairs'. Thus, the term is concerned less with categories or things, and more with particular situations, inviting precise consideration of 'facts on the ground' rather than rigid nomenclatures. Contextually, Article 44.2 is clearly intended to clarify and determine the relationship between the availability of the remedies specified in Part III of TRIPS and the compulsory licensing provisions outlined in Articles 31 and 37.2.

Less clear is whether the provision is also intended to refer to the 'three-step tests' provided for in Articles 13, 17, 26.2 and 30, together with Article 9.2 of the Berne Convention. Most likely it does not; although these provisions could well act to excuse the non-award of injunctions in particular cases, they do not deal specifically with use by governments or third parties without the authorization of the right holder. Therefore, the phrase 'in other cases' should be construed to refer to the situations provided for in the 'three-step tests', including Article 30.

---

[108] Daniel Gervais, *The TRIPS Agreement: Drafting History and Analysis* (2nd ed., Sweet & Maxwell 2003) 205. 'The Agreement provides strict conditions on measures to authorise use by governments or third parties authorised by government. If, and only if, those conditions are respected, then WTO Members may limit remedies available against governments to payment of a remuneration in the circumstances of each case, including the economic situation of the WTO Member concerned'.

7.6 INTERNATIONAL LAW OF PROPOSED APPROACH

Consequently, from a contextual standpoint, it seems unlikely that the phrase 'in other cases' was intended to mean 'for other classes of intellectual property rights', since it will need to operate broadly enough to encompass use pursuant to Article 30 of TRIPS. From the perspective of the objects and purposes of intellectual property protection – which, as clarified by Article 7, are also the objects and purposes of TRIPS – it does not make sense for patents to be subject to stricter requirements concerning injunctive relief than other categories of intellectual property. Furthermore, provided the classes of situations in which injunctive relief is not made available for patents, beyond the requirements of Article 31, is relatively confined and pursued in consonance with other provisions of TRIPS such as Articles 7 and 40, such an approach would not render the first sentence of Article 44(2) inutile.

Therefore, the second reading of 'in other cases' is to be preferred, namely that 'other cases' includes situations of patent infringement where the requirements of Article 31 are not met. However, in such cases, the decision not to award injunction would need to be in harmony with the underlying policy purposes underlying the protection of patents, as articulated in the Preamble, Articles 7 and 8, and as supplemented by other relevant TRIPS provisions such as Article 40 and Article 41. That will be the case in the present instance.

Non-award of injunctions for SEP infringement in the limited circumstances contemplated in Chapter 6 would be strongly consonant with the underlying rationale for patent protection, and in particular would provide for a balance of rights and obligations and have proper regard to the interests of producers and users of patents, thus properly balancing the twin goals of promoting initial and follow-on innovation through patent protection. Such measures would squarely be directed towards abusive practices in connection with SEPs, and therefore would be in harmony with Articles 8(2), 40 and 41(1) of TRIPS.

Such non-award would further amount to a fair and equitable approach, as required by Article 41(2), since our approach involves due consideration being given to all relevant factors and circumstances and properly balances the interests of all parties. The final sentence of Article 44(2) provides that 'in other cases', the remedies in Part II, including damages and other remedies, shall apply. Imposing a liability rule in limited classes of situation would satisfy this requirement, since the remedy of damages would still be available.

Thus, on balance, our proposed approach would likely be consistent with the requirements of Article 28 of TRIPS, in the light of the context supplied by Articles 40, 41 and 44 of TRIPS and also of the objects and purposes of TRIPS as articulated by the Preamble and Articles 7 and 8. It would therefore not need to be justified by way of either Article 30 or Article 31 of TRIPS.

Nevertheless, and out of an abundance of caution, we consider whether our proposed approach would also satisfy the requirements of Article 30 and/or Article 31. We proceed in this regard on the basis that any curtailment of Article 28 rights arising from the proposed action is likely to be small in scope, given that Article 28 does not explicitly require that an injunction must be awarded in every case of infringement, and because adequate compensate in the form predominantly of reasonable royalties would still be accorded to right holders.

7.6.1.1 Article 30 of TRIPS – the Three-Step Test for Patents

Our proposed approach is likely to impact much more on patents than other forms of intellectual property (such as copyrights), because so far only patents have to date been shown consistently to exhibit the combination of Cournot complements and the risk of injunctions prohibiting significant non-infringing conduct – therefore Article 30 of TRIPS will be of most relevance. As such, our interpretive approach takes the approach of the existing panel reports as its starting point, augmented as appropriate with reference to general interpretive principles and scholarly commentary.

7.6.1.2 'Limited' Exceptions

The first requirement of Article 30 is that an exception must be 'limited'. In *Canada – Pharmaceuticals*,[109] the panel found that Canada's regulatory review exception was limited because of its narrow scope of curtailment of Article 28.1 rights.[110] However the same panel, in its analysis of Canada's 'stockpiling' exception, undertook both a qualitative and a quantitative analysis to ascertain whether the exception was indeed 'limited' in nature. The measure was held to impact deeply on pharmaceutical manufacturers, by allowing a stockpile of unlimited size to be accumulated in the last six months of patent protection. This impacted deeply on the Article 28.1 rights of 'making' and 'using' a patented product.[111]

---

[109] WTO, *Canada – Patent Protection of Pharmaceutical Products – Report of the Panel* (17 March 2000) WT/DS114/R.

[110] Ibid. [7.45].

[111] Martin Senftleben, 'Towards a Horizontal Standard for Limiting Intellectual Property Rights? WTO Panel Reports Shed Light on the Three-Step Test in Copyright Law and

In the present instance, the curtailment of Article 28 rights arising from the proposed approach would seem to be very limited indeed. As discussed above, Article 28 refers to 'exclusive rights' but does not explicitly mandate that injunctions be granted in each case of violation; the specific requirements of the TRIPS Agreement relating to injunctions are set out in Article 44 and do not mandate injunction for every infringement.

Our proposed approach is narrow in a qualitative sense because holders of SEPs would retain the full panoply of rights, with the exception of an automatic right to injunction – most importantly, they would still receive adequate compensation for infringement. Moreover, our proposed approach is also narrow in a quantitative sense because it is limited only to a subset of all SEPs, namely those SEPs: (i) where both Cournot complements and the prohibition of significant non-infringing uses are present; or (ii) where the strict requirements established in the *Magill/ IMS* cases are satisfied. As such our proposed approach will likely be consistent with the first step of the Article 30 test.

7.6.1.3 Unreasonable Conflict with Normal Exploitation of a Patent

Regarding the term 'normal exploitation', the *Canada – Pharmaceuticals* panel observed:

> The Panel considered that 'exploitation' refers to the commercial activity by which patent owners employ their exclusive patent rights to extract economic value from their patent. The term 'normal' defines the kind of commercial activity Article 30 seeks to protect. The ordinary meaning of the word 'normal' is found in the dictionary definition: 'regular, usual, typical, ordinary, conventional'. As so defined, the term can be understood to refer either to an empirical conclusion about what is common within a relevant community, or to a normative standard of entitlement. The Panel concluded that the word 'normal' was being used in Article 30 in a sense that combined the two meanings.[112]

Indeed, both the patent and copyright panels, examining the meaning of 'normal', concurred that the term should be given both an empirical and a normative meaning.[113] Regarding the empirical meaning, the two

---

Related Tests in Patent and Trademark Law' (2006) 37 International Review of Intellectual Property and Competition Law 407, 417–18.
[112] WTO, *Canada – Patent Protection of Pharmaceutical Products – Report of the Panel* (17 March 2000) WT/DS114/R (n. 109) [7.54].
[113] Senftleben (n. 111) 428.

panels adopted a broadly similar approach. The patent panel considered that it was for the European Communities to demonstrate that most patent owners extracted value from their patents in the manner foreclosed by the regulatory review exemption.[114] The copyright panel held that the first sense of normal means 'of an empirical nature, i.e. what is regular, usual, typical or ordinary',[115] and accepted United States arguments that in practice this involved consideration of 'whether there are areas of the market in which the copyright owner would ordinarily expect to exploit the work, but which are not available for exploitation because of [the exemption at issue]'.[116]

In terms of the 'normative' meaning of 'normal', however, the two panels took significantly divergent approaches. The patent panel, addressing this question, considered that the European Communities should have adduced evidence to show that the means of patent exploitation prohibited by the Canadian measure was 'essential to the achievement of the goals of patent policy'.[117] The copyright panel, by contrast, held that in this second, more normative meaning, 'normal' meant:

> We believe that an exception or limitation to an exclusive right in domestic legislation rises to the level of a conflict with a normal exploitation of the work (i.e., the copyright or rather the whole bundle of exclusive rights conferred by the ownership of the copyright), if uses, that in principle are covered by that right but exempted under the exception or limitation, enter into economic competition with the ways that right holders normally extract economic value from that right to the work (i.e., the copyright) and thereby deprive them of significant or tangible commercial gains.[118]

Concerning the first, empirical meaning of the term 'normal', any future panel would presumably find it highly significant that FRAND declarations in respect of SEPs are extremely common in the context of the drafting of interoperability standards under the auspices of formal standard-setting bodies, and that even outside such forums, standards developers often seek to take credible steps convince would-be implementors that the exploitation of SEPs will be kept within reasonable bounds.

---

[114] WTO, *Canada – Patent Protection of Pharmaceutical Products – Report of the Panel* (17 March 2000) WT/DS114/R (n. 109) [7.58].
[115] WTO, *United States – Section 110(5) of US Copyright Act – Report of the Panel* (15 June 2000) WT/DS160/R [6.166].
[116] Ibid. [6.177]–[6.178].
[117] WTO, *Canada – Patent Protection of Pharmaceutical Products – Report of the Panel* (17 March 2000) WT/DS114/R (n. 109) [7.58].
[118] WTO, *United States – Section 110(5) of US Copyright Act – Report of the Panel* (15 June 2000) WT/DS160/R (n. 115) [6.183].

7.6 INTERNATIONAL LAW OF PROPOSED APPROACH   321

As such, it is commonplace for right holders negotiating standards to agree to limit their ability to recover licensing royalties for SEPs to some formulation of 'reasonable and non-discriminatory' royalties. Arguably this reflects an intention on the part of participants in interoperability standards drafting processes to constrain the ability of right holders to exploit ex-post the hold-up value associated with their SEPs. In addition, there are sound arguments to be made that the FRAND declaration is inconsistent with seeking court injunctions, since it reflects a view that damages will be an adequate remedy for infringement. As such, our proposed approach would not impact on the ability of SEPs holders to exploit their patent rights in ways that are typical, common or habitual.

The second meaning accorded to the term 'normal' by the Panel in *Canada – Pharmaceuticals* is that of a 'normative standard of entitlement'. Adopting this normative interpretation, it is strongly arguable that the 'normal exploitation' of a patent does not include patent hold-up, patent ambush or like conduct. The underlying goal of patent policy is to provide right holders with adequate incentives for future innovative activities; yet patent hold-up allows a small number of right holders to extract more than this, to the detriment of other right holders and users of the standard more generally; such conduct does not align with the underlying purposes of patent policy and is unnecessary to promote the policy purposes of patent laws.

Turning to the normative meaning given to the term 'normal' in *US – Copyright*, the panel placed emphasis upon the way in which exempted uses enter into competition with the normal ways that right holders extract value from their patents, and whether this deprives right holders of significant or tangible gains. As outlined above, it is normal on the context of interoperability standards for FRAND declarations to be given; as such it will not necessarily be the case that the extraction of 'hold-up' value associated with a SEP reflects its normal exploitation. Furthermore, if right holders are unable to extract such 'hold-up' value, this will not necessarily result in commercial losses to SEP holders generally; instead, it will simply prevent an opportunistic few SEP holders from extracting value from the commercialization of standards that would otherwise accrue to many other right holders, many of which are also users of the same technologies.

Thus, whether the interpretive approach of either the *Canada – Pharmaceuticals* panel or the *United States – Copyright* panel is adopted, our proposed approach is unlikely to result in conflict with the normal exploitation of a patent. Several additional factors buttress this conclusion: (i) even if such conflict did arise, there would be a further question as to whether such conflict was 'unreasonable'; presumably the legitimate policy intentions underlying our proposed approach would ensure that any such conflict was not considered 'unreasonable'; (ii) scholarly commentary has in any case generally favoured the more liberal approach of the patent panel over the more restrictive approach of the copyright panel; and (iii) the approach of the patent panel would seem to be better aligned with the objects and purposes of the TRIPS Agreement, notably those elaborated in Articles 7 and 8, and as such is to be preferred. Therefore, our proposed approach is highly likely to be consistent with the second step of the three-step test provided in Article 30.

7.6.1.4 Unreasonable Prejudice to the Legitimate Interests of the Patent Holder

Legitimate Interests Constructing the term 'legitimate interests', the patent panel stated:

> To make sense of the term 'legitimate interests' in this context, that term must be defined in the way that it is often used in legal discourse – as a normative claim calling for protection of interests that are 'justifiable' in the sense that they are supported by relevant public policies or other social norms. This is the sense of the word that often appears in statements such as 'X has no legitimate interest in being able to do Y'.[119]

This approach was adopted with approval by the panel in *EC – Trademarks*.[120] The jurisprudence of the patent panel will clearly be of most assistance in interpreting Article 30. It is reasonable to suggest that the ability of a patent holder to extract 'hold-up value' in association with its exploitation of a SEP cannot be considered a 'legitimate interest' when considered in light of the underlying public policy interests sought to be achieved by patent protection.

Such public policy interests can be gleaned inter alia from the provisions of the TRIPS Agreement itself. For example, the Preamble to the TRIPS Agreement refers to 'the underlying public policy objectives of national systems for the protection of intellectual property, including

---

[119] *WTO, Canada – Patent Protection of Pharmaceutical Products – Report of the Panel (17 March 2000) WT/DS114/R* (n. 109) [7.69].

[120] *WTO, European Communities – Protection of Trademarks and Geographical Indications for Agricultural Products and Foodstuffs – Report of the Panel (15 March 2005) WT/DS290/R* [7.663].

7.6 INTERNATIONAL LAW OF PROPOSED APPROACH

developmental and technological objectives', thus highlighting that the developmental and technological objectives underlying intellectual property protection are especially prominent. The purpose of intellectual property protection in stimulating technological innovation is further outlined in Article 7 of TRIPS; Article 8 highlights that measures to address abuses of intellectual property rights may be called for in some circumstances.

As outlined at length in the preceding chapters, our proposed approach is carefully calibrated to optimize the technological objective underlying intellectual property protection. This is achieved in particular by addressing certain well-recognized abuses of intellectual property rights, such as patent hold-up and royalty stacking. Furthermore, our approach finds clear support in Article 40, since it is directed towards anticompetitive licensing practices in connection with SEIP.

Likewise, our approach is in consonance with Articles 8(2) and 41(1), since it applies safeguards to the abuse of SEPs, and also Article 41(2), since an equitable approach is applied. As such, adopting the interpretive approach of the patent panel, the requirements of the third step will likely be met since the exploitation by right holders of the 'hold-up' value of the patents is unlikely to be considered a legitimate interest. In *United States – Section 110*, considering the third step of the test in Article 13, the panel began by observing that the term 'legitimate' was susceptible of two possible meanings: 'Thus, the term relates to lawfulness from a legal positivist perspective, but it has also the connotation of legitimacy from a more normative perspective, in the context of calling for the protection of interests that are justifiable in the light of the objectives that underlie the protection of exclusive rights'.[121] Developing this line of reasoning, the panel then stated:

> Given that the parties do not question the 'legitimacy' of the interest of right holders to exercise their rights for economic gain, the crucial question becomes which degree or level of 'prejudice' may be considered as 'unreasonable'. Before dealing with the question of what amount or which kind of prejudice reaches a level beyond reasonable, we need to find a way to measure or quantify legitimate interests.[122]

The panel then stated:

---

[121] *WTO, United States – Section 110(5) of US Copyright Act (15 June 2000)* (n. 115) para. 6.224.
[122] Ibid. 6.226.

> In our view, one – albeit incomplete and thus conservative – way of looking at legitimate interests is the economic value of the exclusive rights conferred by copyright on their holders. It is possible to estimate in economic terms the value of exercising, e.g., by licensing, such rights. That is not to say that legitimate interests are necessarily limited to this economic value.[123]

First, it is worth noting that Article 13 jurisprudence will be less useful in the interpretation of Article 30, because the third step is worded differently in these provisions; for example, Article 30 refers to 'third parties' whereas Article 13 does not. Second, whilst in *US – Section 110* the panel considered that all exploitation of copyrighted sound recordings in that context was 'legitimate', in the current context the exploitation of hold-up value by right holders is unlikely to be considered legitimate. Thus, the situations can be distinguished.

'Unreasonable' Prejudice to Legitimate Interests   Even if prejudice to the legitimate interests of SEP holders were found to occur, it would need to be considered whether such prejudice rises to a level that is considered 'unreasonable'. This element of the third step was not examined by the patent panel; in *US – Section 110*, the copyright panel explained: 'In our view, prejudice to the legitimate interests of right holders reaches an unreasonable level if an exception or limitation causes or has the potential to cause an unreasonable loss of income to the copyright owner'.[124] In the present instance, given that any income lost by SEP holders through their inability to obtain injunctions from the courts will most likely be categorized as 'hold-up value' we think it very unlikely that this would be characterized as an unreasonable income loss. As such, our proposed approach is highly likely also to satisfy the third step of the three-step test provided for in Article 30.

7.6.1.5 Compulsory Licensing under Article 31 of the TRIPS Agreement

Even if the requirements of Article 30 could not be satisfied, Article 31 of the TRIPS Agreement, addressing other uses without the authorization of the right holder, would also be available, although in practical terms Article 31 will be of most practical significance in respect of licences issued following an established contravention of competition law.

---

[123] Ibid, 6.227.
[124] Ibid. 6.229.

7.6 INTERNATIONAL LAW OF PROPOSED APPROACH

For such cases (noting in particular the impact of Article 31(k)), Article 31 requires that: (i) the authorization must be considered on its individual merits (paragraph (a)); (ii) the scope and duration of such use shall be limited to the purpose for which it was authorized (paragraph (c)); and (iii) such use shall be non-exclusive (paragraph (d)), non-assignable (paragraph (e)), and liable to be terminated if no longer required (paragraph (g)). Most pertinently, the right holder shall be paid adequate remuneration in the circumstances of each case, taking into account the economic value of the authorization (paragraph (h)). Taubman observes in this regard that the adequacy of such remuneration will depend on the nature of the intervention;[125] and considers that the 'economic value' of the patent will not necessarily reflect its full market value, nor the economic loss suffered by the right holder.[126] Indeed, in light of the objects and purposes of the TRIPS Agreement, an equitable balance that takes account of the interests of right holders and users may be appropriate.[127]

Our proposed approach is capable of satisfying each of these requirements; for example, the principles enumerated in connection with compensation will be well-suited to taking into account the economic value of the SEIP in question. In particular, our proposed approach takes account of a number of economic methodologies for calculating the appropriate remuneration. Moreover, it is reasonable to distinguish 'economic value' from 'commercial value'; the 'economic value' would seem capable of taking account of factors such as estimates of the likely 'hold-up value' associated with a SEP.

Therefore, to the extent our proposed approach could not be justified pursuant to Article 30 (in our view, it can be), there is also scope, at least in cases of established competition law contraventions, for it to be permissible under Article 31 of the TRIPS Agreement.

7.6.2 Copyrights

As is the case with Article 28 of the TRIPS Agreement, it falls to be considered whether each and every instance of the non-award of an injunction would potentially place the regulating Member in violation of the provisions of the Berne Convention and also of the TRIPS Agreement (aside from the flexibility accorded by the three-step test).

---

[125] Taubman (n. 105) 952.
[126] Ibid. 953.
[127] Ibid. 956.

Article 9(1) of the Berne Convention, like Article 28 of the TRIPS Agreement, makes no reference to injunctions, or indeed to any court order that would need to be made in any particular case. Nor was this the subject of discussion at the 1967 Stockholm Conference, where the right of reproduction was inserted for the first time, although earlier drafts of Article 9(1) were somewhat more explicit as to the imposition of an exclusive property rule: 'Serial novels, short stories and all other works, whether literary, scientific or artistic, whatever their purpose, and which are published in the newspapers or periodicals of one of the countries of the Union shall not be reproduced in the other countries without the consent of the authors'.[128] In one particularly illuminating intervention during the Stockholm Conference, the delegate of Monaco, Mr Straschnov, remarked (in relation to a French proposal) that:

> if the draft amendment submitted by the Delegation of France merely meant that an author could limit or determine in the contract dealing with reproduction rights, the purpose to which his work was to be put, the amendment was superfluous because it was obvious that when negotiating an agreement the author could attach any kind of restriction to the right of reproduction.[129]

By this excerpt it appears it was envisaged that an author holding the right of reproduction could effectively impose in licensing agreements whichever terms he or she wished, which would be consistent with the understanding of the right as implying an exclusive property rule, rather than a liability rule, that is, an automatic entitlement to injunction. It is, of course, the case that the non-award of an injunction following a court finding of infringement of copyright in effect permits the infringer to reproduce the copyrighted work without the right holder's permission.

Thus, the ordinary meaning of Article 9(1) would seem to imply that the right of reproduction implies an automatic entitlement to injunction. Finally, at least insofar as the provisions of the Berne Convention have been incorporated into the TRIPS Agreement, the impact of Article 44(2) also needs to be considered. As discussed above in relation to Article 28 of the TRIPS Agreement, Article 44(2) most probably gives domestic courts very little discretion not to award injunctions for established infringements of intellectual property rights, subject to applicable

---

[128] World Intellectual Property Organization, *Records of the Intellectual Property Conference of Stockholm (1967)*, vol. 1 (World Intellectual Property Organization 1971) 113.

[129] World Intellectual Property Organization, *Records of the Intellectual Property Conference of Stockholm (1967)*, vol. 2 (World Intellectual Property Organization 1971) 856.

exceptions, in this case those provided for in Article 9(2) of the Berne Convention and Article 13 of the TRIPS Agreement.

7.6.2.1 Assessment under Article 9(2) of the Berne Convention and Article 13 of TRIPS

First Step: 'Certain Special Cases'

'Certain' Regarding the term 'certain', the panel in *US – Section 110* stated:

> The ordinary meaning of 'certain' is 'known and particularised, but not explicitly identified', 'determined, fixed, not variable; definitive, precise, exact'. In other words, this term means that, under the first condition, an exception or limitation in national legislation must be clearly defined. However, there is no need to identify explicitly each and every possible situation to which the exception could apply, provided that the scope of the exception is known and particularised. This guarantees a sufficient degree of legal certainty.[130]

There are no concerns regarding the clarity or the certainty of our proposed approach.

'Special' Regarding 'special', the panel in *US – Section 110* stated:

> This term means that more is needed than a clear definition in order to meet the standard of the first condition. In addition, an exception or limitation must be limited in its field of application or exceptional in its scope. In other words, an exception or limitation should be narrow in quantitative as well as a qualitative sense. This suggests a narrow scope as well as an exceptional or distinctive objective.[131]

Our proposed approach as it applies to copyrights is likely to satisfy this test. The primary test to be applicable for the application of the liability rule is that there must be: (i) Cournot complements, and (ii) the prohibition of significant non-infringing conduct. These criteria to date have been rarely encountered in the realm of copyright, given the traditional assumption that interfaces were not copyrightable, or were amenable to reverse-engineering solely for interoperability purposes. In a post-*Oracle* v. *Google* world, this may change. However, it is important to keep in mind that our approach will apply only in the context of those elements of programs which are indispensable for interoperability purposes, notably standardized interfaces. This is likely to render our approach narrow in a qualitative and a

---

[130] WTO, *United States – Section 110(5) of US Copyright Act (15 June 2000)* (n. 115) [6.108].
[131] Ibid. [6.109].

quantitative sense, even should liability rules to standards-essential copyright apply beyond circumstances where Cournot complements are observed.

Regarding our secondary test, based on the *IMS Health/Magill* criteria, this test is likely to be met in rare circumstances, and only where under many jurisdictions' laws there would be considered to exist abuse of a dominant market position. As such, our proposal for liability rules is likely to apply to copyrights in a quantitatively and qualitatively narrow manner, consistently with the requirements of the first step of the copyright three-step test.

Second Step: No Conflict with the Normal Exploitation of the Work
The requirements of the second step of the copyright three-step test are outlined above in our analysis concerning Article 30 of the TRIPS Agreement. Given the relatively minimal application of our proposed approach in a copyright context to date, our approach is highly to satisfy the requirements of the second step as articulated in *US – Section 110*. It should further be noted that the panel's 'economic' approach to the second step of the test has attracted considerable academic criticism, and has been compared quite unfavourably to the *Canada – Pharmaceuticals* panel's more 'policy-based' approach.[132] Geiger, Griffiths and Hilty, for example, have proposed the following, alternative approach to the interpretation of this step:

> Limitations and exceptions do not conflict with a normal exploitation of protected subject matter, if they
> – are based on important competing considerations or
> – have the effect of countering unreasonable restraints on competition, notably on secondary markets, particularly where adequate compensation is ensured, whether or not by contractual means.[133]

Under this proposed interpretive approach, which aligns more closely with the panel's approach in *Canada – Pharmaceuticals*, and (more importantly) with the objects and purposes of the TRIPS Agreement as elaborated in the Preamble and in Articles 7 and 8, the proposed

---

[132] Christoph Geiger, Daniel J. Gervais and Martin Senftleben, 'The Three Step Test Revisited: How to Use the Test's Flexibility in National Copyright Law' (2014) 29 American University International Law Review 581, 598–600.
[133] Christoph Geiger and others, 'Declaration A Balanced Interpretation of the "Three-Step Test" in Copyright Law' (2010) 1 Journal of Intellectual Property, Information Technology and Electronic Commerce Law 119, 12 1.

approach regarding to access to SEIP is likely to be permissible, since it is based on well-founded policy considerations and seeks to address concerns associated with restraints on competition in secondary markets. Likewise, our approach will find considerable support in Article 40, and in paragraphs 1 and 2 of Article 41.

Third Step: No Unreasonable Prejudice to the Legitimate Interests of Right Holders Given the relatively narrow application of our proposals in a standards-essential copyright context, our proposed approach is highly likely to satisfy the third step of the copyright three-step test.

7.6.2.2 Compulsory Licenses

Where a copyright is subject to compulsory licensing (e.g. after an established contravention of applicable competition law), most likely this would need to be justified by reference to the three-step tests in Article 9(2) of the Berne Convention and Article 13 of the TRIPS Agreement, since TRIPS does not address compulsory licences for copyright explicitly, and the compulsory licensing provisions in the Berne Convention, which deal with the specific contexts of broadcasting and related rights (Article 11bis(2)) and musical works (Article 13(1)) will rarely if ever be applicable in the context of SEIP).

7.6.2.3 WIPO Copyright Treaty

The WIPO Copyright Treaty extends the right of reproduction into the digital domain, without amending its contents and preserving in full the applicable exceptions and limitations provided for in the Berne Convention.[134] As such we consider our proposed approach would likely be consistent with the requirements of the WIPO Copyright Treaty.

7.6.3 Layout Circuits

Article 6(1)(a) of the Washington Treaty merely requires that certain acts be 'considered unlawful' but does not mandate that any particular remedy be ordered in any particular case. Neither the Washington Treaty nor the TRIPS Agreement provides for a three-step test in relation to layout circuits, although significant exceptions are available for: (i) private use (Article 6(2)(a)(i) of the Washington Treaty); (ii) evaluation, analysis,

---

[134] WIPO Copyright Treaty (adopted 20 December 1996, entered into force 6 March 2002) (2186 UNTS 5) art. 1(4).

research or teaching (Article 6(2)(a)(i) of the Washington Treaty); reverse-engineering (Article 6(2)(b) of the Washington Treaty) and independent creation (Article 6(2)(c) of the Washington Treaty), as well as rights to issue compulsory licences, either on grounds of innocent infringement (Article 37(1) of the TRIPS Agreement) or in accordance with the requirements of TRIPS Article 31 (Article 37(2) of the TRIPS Agreement.

Given the significant exceptions and limitations to the exclusive right conferred pursuant to Articles 35 and 36 of the TRIPS Agreement, and the likely marginal relevance of the sui generis layout circuit protection to concerns associated with SEIP, on balance the provisions of Section 6 of the TRIPS Agreement are very unlikely to pose any obstacle to our proposed approach.

7.6.4 Trade Secrets

The proposed course of action is unlikely to result in the forcible disclosure of any trade secrets. In any case the reference in paragraph 1 of Article 39 to the protection of unfair competition under Article 10bis of the Paris Convention is likely to provide strong support to the proposed course of action, one of the underlying purposes of which is to address unfair competitive practices by holders of SEIP. As such our proposals are very unlikely to raise concerns under Article 39 of the TRIPS Agreement.

7.6.5 Enforcement of Intellectual Property Rights

Regarding Article 44 of the TRIPS Agreement, it is important to pay careful regard to the opening words of Article 44(1), 'The judicial authorities shall have the authority to order'. For a phrase of such importance, which appears throughout the TRIPS Agreement, there is surprisingly little case law. In *India – Pharmaceuticals*,[135] the panel did address the meaning of these words, albeit tangentially and only in response to arguments made by India that sought to shed light on the interpretation of Article 70.9 of TRIPS; the panel opined: 'the function of the words "shall have the authority" is to address the issue of judicial discretion, not that of general availability'.[136] Although brief, this statement is useful: these words are intended to require that judicial

---

[135] WTO, *India – Patent Protection for Pharmaceutical and Agricultural Chemical Products – Report of the Panel* (24 August 1998) WT/DS50/R.
[136] Ibid. [7.66].

7.6 INTERNATIONAL LAW OF PROPOSED APPROACH   331

authorities are to have discretion as to whether to award the applicable remedy; they are not required to award it in any particular case. Our proposed approach does not preclude the judicial authorities from ordering an injunction in any particular case. Rather, judicial authorities are encouraged to weigh all applicable factors in deciding whether an injunction is appropriate.

Article 41 provides important context to the interpretation of Article 44. It highlights that injunctions should be available under a Member's law so as to: permit effective action against any act of infringement; deter further infringement; avoid the creation of barriers to legitimate trade; and provide safeguards against abuses of intellectual property rights. Our proposed approach will quite clearly overcome barriers to legitimate trade and furthermore provides safeguards against abuses of SEIP. Moreover, the award of compensation in the form of reasonable royalties is likely to constitute effective action against infringement, presuming the valuation of the relevant rights is adequately carried out.

Furthermore, the imposition of appropriately tailored liability rules for infringements of SEIP is also expected to deter further acts of unwarranted infringement. In addition, our proposed approach is highly likely to be characterized as fair and equitable, having regard to all relevant circumstances. As such, the context lent to the interpretation of Article 44 by Article 41 strongly supports the view that our proposed approach is very unlikely to give rise to an inconsistency. In addition, Article 44 should be read in light of the objects and purposes of the TRIPS Agreement, as outlined above, which is likely to reinforce this conclusion. Therefore, the proposed approach would be fully consistent with the requirements of Article 44 of the TRIPS Agreement.

Our proposed approach would involve right holders being adequately remunerated for infringements and is very unlikely to give rise to any issues under Article 45. There can be little doubt that the proposed approach would compensate right holders for injuries suffered arising from infringement.

7.6.6   *Conclusion regarding Consistency of the Proposed Approach with Existing International Agreements*

For the reasons outlined above, the approach proposed in this work is likely to be fully in conformity with international agreements in the field of intellectual property. As such, it is not necessary for this work to propose any modifications to existing international obligations dealing with the protection of intellectual property. Indeed, our proposed approach would seem better aligned with the requirements of TRIPS, when properly read in light of the context and object and purpose of that agreement, than an alternative approach that would mandate a property rule automatically in respect of SEIP. Notably, such an approach would not align with the underlying policy purposes of both IP protection and of TRIPS, as enunciated in Article 7, nor would it give rise to a balance of rights and obligations.

Automatic entitlement to injunction could encourage abuses of intellectual property rights, condemned by paragraph 2 of Article 8 of TRIPS. Indeed, those jurisdictions persisting with automatic entitlement to injunction in all circumstances could risk acting inconsistently with the requirements of Article 41(1) of TRIPS, insofar as such an approach could create barriers to legitimate trade, and does not provide adequate safeguards against abuses of intellectual property rights. Such an approach would also ignore the fair and equitable methodology mandated by Article 41(2).[137]

Perhaps, then, the question should not be so much whether our approach is permitted by international intellectual property law, but rather whether our proposed approach, or a similarly proportionate and calibrated approach to SEIP protection is required by international intellectual property law. Irrespective of the answer to these questions, our conclusions underscore the value of a soft law approach that provides guidance to regulatory and judicial authorities, as distinct from a hard law approach that would seek to further constrain the existing discretion of those authorities.

---

[137] See Henning Grosse Ruse-Khan, *The Protection of Intellectual Property in International Law* (Oxford University Press 2016) ch. 5.

8

Concluding Observations

The creation and implementation of interoperability standards has generated highly significant benefits to society, and more are expected in the future; technologies such as 5G mobile, mobile payment services and the Internet of Things are still developing. By and large, interoperability standards are developed privately, by either formal SSOs or consortia. Formal SSOs are generally governed by bylaws, including intellectual property policies, which may lay down the terms upon which members will make available standards-essential intellectual property (generally SEPs) to implementors of a standard.

Many interoperability standards are characterized by the presence of network externalities, which can incline standardized markets to dominance or even monopoly. Moreover, intellectual property protection in the context of interoperability standards – in particular standards-essential patents, copyrights and trade secrets – can combine with network externalities to confer on certain right holders gatekeeper privileges in connection with standardized technologies, to the detriment of competitors. Concerns regarding access to SEPs in particular are significant and widespread.

The presence of large numbers of SEP holders gives rise to the well-known phenomenon of Cournot complements, under which each holder of an SEP can be characterized as a monopolist with the ability to restrict access to the underlying standardized technology. The presence of Cournot complements in the form of 'patent thickets' gives rise to attendant concerns of 'patent hold-up' and 'royalty stacking' in connection with SEPs.

Although standard-setting organizations have developed sophisticated patent policies to address precisely such concerns, these policies are unable to specify with sufficient precision and binding force the relevant rights and responsibilities of all relevant parties; as such, these policies can best be characterized as an 'incomplete contract' which is unable to mitigate the risks of patent hold-up. While greater specificity in SSO patent policies has been proposed and potentially represents one way forward, interoperability standard-setting is a footloose enterprise and participants can easily migrate their activities to another SSO in the face of policies which place undue burdens on technology contributors. In any case, to bring SSO policies to a level where a complete contract existed, not merely as between all members of the SSO but also all potential current and future implementors of standards would impose a significant regulatory burden on SSOs and require them to act more like quasi-regulatory bodies than as technology forums. As such, national courts with specialized competence in both intellectual property and competition law would seem best placed to address such concerns.

Standards-essential copyrights have traditionally attracted a lesser degree of scrutiny than SEPs, perhaps because of the traditional position under the laws of leading jurisdictions that interfaces were either uncopyrightable, or such to limiting doctrines that gave liberal scope for reverse-engineering for purposes of ensuring interoperability between programs, hardware and/or users. While this remains the case under EU and Chinese law, the 2014 and 2018 decisions of the United States Court of Appeals for the Federal Circuit in *Oracle* v. *Google* have raised the prospect – at least under American law – of much more extensive copyrightability of standardized interfaces. Should this decision be upheld by the United States Supreme Court, it could yield a new world where many implementations of well-established standards result in copyright infringements. Concerns have also occasionally arisen in connection with standards-essential trade secrets, for example in the EU *Microsoft* litigation, where Microsoft asserted a suite of intellectual property rights, including trade secrets, to justify its refusal to provide essential interface specifications to competitors.

Where a single firm has created a de facto interoperability standard and has been able to maintain proprietary control over the interfaces and protocols associated with the standard, it can use its 'gatekeeper' privileges to exclude competitors from supplying solutions compliant with the standard. This could manifest, for example, in a refusal to supply the specifications of key interfaces or protocols to competitors (such as occurred in the EU *Microsoft* and *IMS Health* cases, and in US cases such as *Sega* v. *Accolade* and *Donnelley* v. *BellSouth*).

In some instances, the interoperability information whose supply has been refused might already be in the public domain (as it was in *Donnelley* and *IMS Health*) or susceptible to reverse-engineering (as it was in *Sega*), in which case the refusal to disclose interfaces or protocols will not, in itself, have negative impacts on the marketplace, and the most important question will be the precise scope of relevant intellectual property rights over the interoperability information. Where the interoperability information is not public and is not amenable to reverse-engineering (e.g. because reverse-engineering is infeasible due to a combination of technical complexity, cost, time and frequent upgrades to the information), the supply of the information itself could assume critical importance.

In the case of interoperability standards developed by more than one firm or individual, similar problems can also arise, but they will manifest predominantly in the form of the power of SEIP holders to prevent access to the standard through the assertion of intellectual property rights, most prominently patents or copyrights, in connection with the standard.

Perhaps the most well-known problems are those of 'patent hold-up' and 'royalty stacking' which are associated with SEPs in the context of interoperability standards drafted under the auspices of formal standard-setting organizations (SSOs). Such SSOs will generally have intellectual property policies which require SEP holders to undertake to licence their SEPs on FRAND terms. As such, when courts are called upon to adjudicate upon an alleged infringement, they will often consider the precise terms of the relevant SSO's intellectual property policy, and of the particular FRAND undertaking, in rendering their judgment. There may be hundreds or even thousands of SEPs in relation to a single standard, especially for major standards like mobile telephony air interface standards (e.g. ETSI's 4G LTE standard) and wireless LAN standards (e.g. IEEE's 802.11 family of standards, colloquially known as 'Wi-Fi' standards).

When a firm holds even a single SEP, especially in connection with a standard which has become ubiquitous in the marketplace, it can undertake gatekeeper functions which are very similar to those exercised by single dominant firms in the context of de facto standards. The assertion of a single SEP against a would-be implementer of a standard could result in the imposition of an injunction over the entire product or service being supplied by the would-be implementer, effectively precluding it from practising the standard. Indeed, where the standard has, through network effects, become indispensable to competition in the marketplace, the assertion of a single patent could, in effect, exclude the would-be user from the market entirely.

For example, during 2011, Motorola asserted a single SEP against Apple before the German courts, and obtained an injunction from the Mannheim District Court against Apple products sold in Germany, including iPhones and iPads. Following an unsuccessful appeal by Apple and further negotiations, Apple and Motorola settled their patent licensing dispute, on terms highly favourable to Motorola. In the eyes of many (including the European Commission), Motorola's SEP had enabled Motorola to 'hold-up' Apple and extract from Apple an unjustifiable share of its profits associated with implementing the 2.5G GPRS technology.

The fact situation presented by patent hold-up and royalty stacking holds many similarities to the situations observed in cases of de facto standardization: a monopolistic firm, through the assertion of its patent rights, is effectively able to exclude other firms or individuals from practising the standard. Hence a more general concern can be discerned: the need for open access to interoperability standards, especially those that have become, through operation of network effects, essential to participation in a market. The refusal to supply interoperability information (e.g. in *Microsoft*) and the assertion of the SEP before domestic courts (e.g. in *Motorola*) can therefore be conceptualized as parallel cases of abuses of the dominance, market power or monopoly associated with interoperability standards, and in particular as a denial of access to the standard.

Where a dominant firm in control of an interoperability standard can exclude competitors from supplying compatible, standardized goods or services, this will likely impose costs on society by precluding the full network effects associated with the standard from being realised. There will be the usual static efficiency losses associated with monopoly pricing. There may also be dynamic efficiency losses resulting from suboptimal implementation of standards. Would-be innovators of standardized products may decide that, in view of the expected problems associated with access to SEPs, it is just too costly or difficult to produce the final consumer product.

Courts and regulatory agencies around the world are considering the most appropriate regulatory tools to address such concerns. Competition laws, such as an essential facilities doctrine, would seem to provide an obvious solution. This doctrine, which arose originally in US antitrust law, holds that in certain situations, notably where the 'facility' in question is a natural monopoly, a dominant firm should be required to share its facilities with competitors on reasonable and non-discriminatory terms. The doctrine is no longer part of United States law but remains on the books (whether called an essential facilities doctrine or something else) in many other jurisdictions including the EU, China and Japan.

Although some scholars consider the essential facilities doctrine to provide an obvious regulatory tool for dealing with abuses associated with access to interoperability standards,[1] the doctrine has been roundly criticized over the years. Criticisms include: that it lacks a theoretical basis; that the essential facilities cases (notably before United States lower courts) do not display any coherent logic explaining which facilities should be subject to open access obligations and which should not; that dominant firms have sufficient incentives to share their essential facilities anyway, and that any refusal to supply is likely to be economically efficient (e.g. in order to impose efficient price discrimination); that forced sharing is likely to harm dynamic efficiency; that courts and regulators make errors and have insufficient information to determine the proper terms of access; and that courts and tribunals are otherwise poorly placed to supervise access to the facility deemed to be essential on an ongoing basis. As such, more than sixty years after the famous 'single monopoly profit' theorem was first proposed, many economists remain of the view that refusals to supply by dominant firms should be per se legal (as is currently the case under American law).

Proponents of the essential facilities doctrine have sought to address many of these criticisms. Yet two key objections to the doctrine have stood the test of time: first, that it is difficult if not impossible to craft a doctrine that will encourage follow-on innovation more than it discourages initial creations; and second, that (as was prominently illustrated by the EU *Microsoft* case), courts will have great difficulty in effectively supervising any open access obligations they impose. Equally, in view of the controversy associated with the essential facilities doctrine, it cannot realistically or feasibly be proposed as a basis for an international instrument addressing access to essential interoperability standards and SEIP at this point in time. In all probability, leading

---

[1] Marina Lao, 'Networks, Access and "Essential Facilities": From Terminal Railroad to Microsoft' (2009) 62 Southern Methodist University Law Review 557; Teague I. Donahey, 'Terminal Railroad Revisited: Using the Essential Facilities Doctrine to Ensure Accessibility to Internet Software Standards' (1997) 25 AIPLA Quarterly Journal 277; Cristiano Antonelli, 'Technological Knowledge as an Essential Facility' (2007) 17 Journal of Evolutionary Economics 451; Brett Frischmann and Spencer Weber Waller, 'Revitalizing Essential Facilities' (2008) 74 Antitrust Law Journal 1.

jurisdictions such as the United States, the EU and China will be unable to reach any sort of consensus on these issues at this point in time.

In the United States, the doctrine is no longer good law following the *Trinko* case, and refusals to supply (including refusals to license intellectual property rights) are per se legal. In the EU, by contrast, TFEU Article 102 can be characterized as providing for an essential facilities doctrine, although the state of the law is complex, unsettled and evolving. There are (at least) four separate tests applicable: the *Bronner* test for refusals that do not involve the assertion of an intellectual property right; the *IMS Health/Magill* test for refusals to license an intellectual property right; the somewhat idiosyncratic *Microsoft* test; and the *Motorola/Huawei* approach to court injunctions for FRAND-encumbered SEPs (although it is unclear at this point in time whether the Motorola/Huawei approach really involves an essential facilities doctrine). There is currently no recognized EU approach dealing with injunctions in the context of non-FRAND encumbered SEPs. It is early days for the doctrine in China, but some cases so far appear to embrace the somewhat controversial doctrine of excessive pricing, including for SEPs. Given these observed differences between leading jurisdictions, and the controversy associated with the doctrine more broadly, an international approach with the essential facilities doctrine as its centrepiece is not recommended at this time.

Another possible approach to addressing concerns associated with access to interoperability standards and SEIP is to rely on limiting doctrines in intellectual property law. In patent law, traditional limiting doctrines include exceptions for experimental use, government use, non-commercial use and, in some cases, compulsory licences. In more recent times a further solution has appeared, and one that can be tailored to address concerns associated with SEPs. This involves tailoring the availability of injunctions for infringement, such that injunctions will not be awarded automatically by the courts, but rather on a case by case basis and in view of all relevant factors.

This approach harkens back to the equitable roots of the injunctive remedy, and is consistent with the topical methodology. In *eBay v. MercExchange*,[2] the United States Supreme Court overturned the long-held view that any infringement of a patent established by the courts should automatically be remedied by an injunction (whether interlocutory or final) removing the infringing product from sale in the marketplace. Instead, the Supreme Court held that courts should decide whether

---

[2] *eBay Inc. v. MercExchange, LLC* [2006] 547 US 388 (United States Supreme Court).

to award injunction for patent infringement pursuant to the four-factor test that holds in US law for injunctions more generally.[3] Concerns associated with non-practising patent entities were specifically mentioned in the concurrence of Justice Kennedy as one reason for the Court's approach.[4]

Since the *eBay* decision a number of United States lower courts, citing *eBay* and applying the four-factor test, have declined to award injunctions to redress infringements of FRAND-encumbered SEPs, instead awarding only damages in the form of reasonable royalties. The lower courts have displayed a nuanced approach, having regard to all relevant factors, and thus it cannot be said that there now exists a presumption against injunctions for FRAND-encumbered SEPs, since at least in some cases such injunctions have been awarded. Implementation of the *eBay* doctrine has not been universal, either: exclusion orders remain the default remedy under §1337 of the Tariff Act of 1930, and *eBay* has not been followed much outside of patent law.

The approach taken by the US courts in *eBay* and its progeny would seem to present certain advantages: it involves a careful tailoring of the relevant rights themselves to avoid overprotection or abuse. One notable advantage over applying competition rules (e.g. the essential facilities doctrine) is that, by first establishing validity, infringement and technical essentiality in relation to the relevant patent rights, the courts can ensure that access is mandated only in relation to those intellectual property rights that are genuinely essential to the practice of the standard in question.

Moreover, the rules of equity associated with assessing requests for injunction are well-suited to incorporating the full suite of relevant considerations, such as the nature of the standardized technology, the respective contributions to the standard of the right holder, other right holders and the user, the governing rules of the applicable SSO relating to intellectual property, the course of conduct of the right holder and the user, and the precise terms of any FRAND undertaking given; by contrast, the proper weight to be given to such matters in the context of competition law is a very difficult issue which to date has not been resolved.

Similarly, copyright laws already include numerous limiting principles, including: the distinction between unprotectable ideas and protectable expressions of those ideas; merger; *scènes à faire*; fair use; and for reverse-engineering of interface information solely for interoperability

---

[3] Ibid. 391.
[4] Ibid. 396–7.

purposes. The proper application of the limiting doctrines in copyright law may obviate the need for courts to adopt the *eBay* approach to awarding injunctions (this seems, however, less apparent in light of the United States Court of Appeals for the Federal Circuit's 2014 decision on copyrightability and its 2018 decision on fair use, in the *Oracle v. Google* litigation); nevertheless, the *eBay* approach could remain useful, as a fallback in circumstances where the limiting doctrines in copyright are insufficient to ensure appropriate access to standards-essential copyrights.

More generally, if the *Oracle v. Google* decisions give rise to a new paradigm,[5] under which widespread infringement of standards-essential copyrights becomes commonplace, careful consideration will need to be given to the current suite of remedies available to redress such violations; remedies such as disgorgement profits and statutory damages, to the extent they seek to discourage infringement rather than establish an appropriate access price, will need to be comprehensively re-examined.

Thus, surveying leading jurisdictions such as the United States, the EU and China, two key approaches are apparent. The first approach, grounded in competition law, treats refusals to supply interoperability information and refusals to licence SEIP as abuses of a dominant market position which may be remedied, privately negotiated solutions unavailing, by the award of a compulsory licence. The EU and China favour this approach. The second approach does not involve the application of competition law; instead, limiting doctrines in intellectual property law (including tailoring the availability of the injunctive remedy) are applied to avoid abuses associated with SEIP. American courts have traditionally favoured this approach.

One useful way of framing these issues, in order to appreciate these differences in approach and perhaps to offer a compromise solution in terms of international approaches, is the framework of liability rules and exclusive property rules first developed by Calabresi and Melamed.[6] This framework has been applied to many bodies of law, including extensive treatment in relation to intellectual property laws. The framework is sufficiently broad to encompass both intellectual property and competition law approaches. Adopting this framework, we can see that both the US approach (where injunctions are unavailable for certain

---

[5] This case will be heard by the United States Supreme Court during its 2020-1 term.
[6] Guido R. Calabresi and A. Douglas Melamed, 'Property Rules, Liability Rules, and Inalienability: One View of the Cathedral' (1972) 85 Harvard Law Review 1089.

infringements) and the EU/China approach (where competition law disciplines such as the essential facilities doctrine apply) both involve the substitution of an exclusive property rule (either patent injunction or per se legality for refusals to licence) with a liability rule (in the form of either no injunction plus reasonable royalties, or imposition of a compulsory licence for breach of the competition laws).

Viewed through the analytical lens of the Calabresi and Melamed framework, there exists considerable symmetry among the approaches followed by leading jurisdictions to ensuring adequate access to interoperability standards and the SEIP – and therefore, potentially, a basis for international consensus. Namely, one could broadly envisage an approach whereby abuses associated with SEIP are to be addressed (whether through competition law or the limiting doctrines in intellectual property law) by the substitution of an exclusive property rule for a liability rule.

Nevertheless, finding a potential basis for consensus among leading jurisdictions, whilst important in terms of practicality, should be viewed as a necessary but insufficient condition for an international solution. Rather, any proposed international solution to addressing concerns associated with access to interoperability standards and to SEIP must have a sound basis in public policy. Since the usual public policy basis given for both intellectual property and competition laws is predominantly economic, a law and economics foundation for any proposed future solution is therefore recommended.

In which situations should liability rules replace exclusive property rules for SEIP? Economic theory suggests that mandating access to goods, services, programmes, information or intellectual property requires decision-makers to ensure that their actions will encourage more innovative activity than they discourage. That is, the positive impact of the intervention on dynamic efficiency needs to outweigh the negative impact of the intervention.

Whilst the European courts, in their decisions on Microsoft's conduct, sought to address this problem by seeking to balance the relevant incentives, courts in general are poorly placed to undertake such an assessment – they have imperfect information and are prone to errors. Furthermore, in view of the imperfect information held by courts and the costs of error, any intervention on the basis of an essential facilities doctrine should probably involve a series of 'screens' that enable courts to exclude from liability those actions which are not obviously anticompetitive and detrimental to economic efficiency. The carefully calibrated approach of the European Court of Justice to imposing unilateral obligations to license intellectual property in the *Magill* and *IMS Health* cases has been characterized, and approved, as such.[7]

Doubtless jurisdictions will continue to regulate markets through the application of their own competition laws. Those jurisdictions which are just beginning to regulate their markets in this fashion, and which are inclined to intervene on the basis of an 'essential facilities doctrine', monopoly leveraging or some other cognate doctrine, would do well to look to the European Court of Justice's *IMS Health/Magill* test, which is the most narrowly confined approach taken by EU courts and regulatory authorities for mandating access to SEIP.

A sounder basis for the substitution of an exclusive property rule for a liability rule can be found where the phenomena of 'patent hold-up' and 'royalty stacking' are observed. Since each holder of SEIP can be characterized as a monopolist (one cannot legally practise a standard without rights to use each and every essential intellectual property right embedded in it), this dispersion of exclusive rights gives rise to a Cournot complements problem: each holder of SEIP is, in effect, a monopolistic gatekeeper to the practice of the standard. Uncoordinated pricing between gatekeepers leads to a Cournot complements problem (by contrast, coordinated pricing would involve a cartel). Moreover, an injunction awarded by a domestic court over the final consumer product which complies with the applicable standard may well have the practical effect of prohibiting very significant non-infringing activity, including the manufacturer of the product's own innovations based on the standard. Where these conditions hold, there is a good case for substituting an exclusive property for a liability rule.

The phenomena of thickets, royalty stacking and hold-up have been infrequently documented in the context of standards-essential copyrights. Should the *Oracle* v. *Google* litigation herald a new era for standards-essential copyrights, in which these phenomena begin to manifest more commonly, then the case for liability rules for standards-essential copyrights will apply with equal force. Indeed, given the breadth of protection conferred by copyright and the exceptionally long term of protection enjoyed by copyrighted works (which could far exceed the

---

[7] See Christian Ahlborn, David S. Evans and A. Jorge Padilla, 'The Logic & Limits of the Exceptional Circumstances Test in Magill and IMS Health' (2004) 28 Fordham International Law Journal 1109.

expected commercial life of a standardized interface), a case could be made for an even broader application of liability rules.

Turning to standards-essential trade secrets, the case for liability rules is significantly weaker. In particular, the forcible disclosure of a trade secret would in effect remove its secrecy, and thus deprive it of commercial value. Such remedies should be pursued sparingly, if at all. This is subject to an important qualification: given that adequate disclosure is an indispensable element of patent protection, no company should enjoy both patent and trade secret protection in respect of the same invention. If an invention is patented, it must be disclosed. If it is kept secret, it should not be patented.

What form should such liability rules take? Obviously one possibility, highlighted by the European Court of Justice's decision in Huawei[8] and buttressed by the much more rigorous analytical approach exhibited by the EC in its investigation of Samsung,[9] is to establish abuse of a dominant market position (namely, for the seeking of an injunction notwithstanding an undertaking to licence) and order compulsory licensing as the appropriate remedy.

This approach, while defensible, is not recommended. Competition regulators are rarely in a position to determine whether allegedly SEIP is valid, infringed and essential. Thus, applying the unilateral disciplines in competition law to redress refusals to license allegedly SEIP will probably give rise to the imposition of mandatory access obligations in respect of IP which is not truly essential to participation in a market. More fundamentally, it should be questioned whether the tools of competition law enforcement (which include investigations, prosecutions, heavy fines and other punitive measures) are sufficiently finely calibrated to resolve what is essentially a negotiating problem as between the creators and users of SEIP. Competition law is better for punishing flagrant economic wrongdoing (such as anticompetitive mergers, cartels and foreclosures) than facilitating efficient negotiating bargains between commercial market participants.

Rather than extending the reach of competition laws to address the apparent overprotection of SEIP, better to tailor the scope, application and remedies associated with that SEIP, to reflect the underlying purposes for the protection of intellectual property, namely to overcome the

---

[8] *Huawei Technologies Co Ltd v. ZTE Corp, ZTE Deutschland GmbH (Case C/170–13)* [2015] ECLI:EUC:2015:477 (European Court of Justice).
[9] *Samsung – Enforcement of UMTS Standard-Essential Patents (Case AT39939)* [2014] OJ C35008 (European Commission).

public goods problem associated with technological knowledge by supplying a time-limited legal monopoly in order to provide adequate incentives for the innovative endeavours that are apt to optimize the pace of technological advancement.

As such, the better approach may not involve competition law at all, but rather rely on limiting doctrines in intellectual property law, including judicious application of the *eBay* principle. In this way, mandatory obligations to license an intellectual property right can be confined only to those situations where the right in question truly is standards-essential: intellectual property courts and administrative bodies are best placed to make this assessment based on a granular assessment of the precise boundaries of the relevant right, and a proper understanding of the technical requirements of the standard in question.

Thus, a law and economics methodology supports the application of liability rules for SEIP in carefully confined circumstances, namely where: (i) Cournot complements are observed; and (ii) the imposition of an exclusive property rule would have the result of prohibiting significant non-infringing conduct.[10] In theory this result could be accomplished either through the application of competition law or through the application of intellectual property law, but in practice, competition law is seen as a 'blunt instrument' for addressing concerns arising from the assertion of SEIP; as such an approach grounded in the limiting doctrines in intellectual property is to be preferred. Furthermore, it would be acceptable, but not recommended, for access to SEIP to be addressed through a carefully circumscribed essential facilities doctrine, applying for example the *IMS Health/Magill* test articulated by the European Court of Justice. These conclusions could therefore provide the basis for an international instrument that is both: (i) potentially acceptable to leading jurisdictions; and (ii) carefully grounded in public policy, notably law and economics.

What form should such an international instrument take? It is probably overly ambitious to aspire to finalising a widely ratified multilateral treaty dealing with access to interoperability standards and SEIP, at this point in time. Courts and regulatory agencies around the world are just beginning to grapple with the problems, and entrenched differences between jurisdictions are already emerging. Given the highly technical,

---

[10] The pioneering scholarship of Carl Shapiro and Mark A. Lemley, 'Patent Holdup and Royalty Stacking' (2007) 85 Texas Law Review 1992 must be acknowledged in this regard.

economic and legal complexity of the issues, expert rulemaking is recommended.

Rather than a conventional negotiation between States (which has been tried and failed numerous times in relation to international competition law), an expert document is probably better placed not simply to find the necessary degree of consensus, but also to ensure that such consensus is properly grounded in law and economics, as well as other applicable disciplines (e.g. engineering). Furthermore, given the speed of technological change in this area, regular and ongoing revisions to any international instrument will be needed. For these reasons, a soft law instrument is recommended as the best way forward.

Whilst a variety of fora are available, a free-standing expert colloquium is perhaps the best approach, possibly with state representatives participating in an observer capacity only. Given the entrenched inter-jurisdictional differences observed in relation to SEIP, including the much-discussed transatlantic divide, discussions between governments on these issues are unlikely to bear fruit, at least in the short to medium term. Yet many experts have already written extensively about these issues and would doubtless be delighted to step up to the task. It is therefore recommended that a colloquium of experts, meeting outside the auspices of any existing international body, convene to draft an expert manual addressing issues associated with access to interoperability standards and to SEIP. The objective of developing such an expert manual would, in the first instance, be to provide guidance to domestic courts as to how they should exercise their judicial or regulatory discretion in adjudicating upon cases that involve access to interoperability standards and to SEIP.

If such a group of eminent experts could be assembled, to produce such a document using a transparent and robust process, perhaps drawing on best practices observed by international SSOs, such a document could garner a high degree of credibility, and could as such be attractive to domestic courts around the world as a useful reference point – even if not cited directly in judicial or administrative decisions. A draft expert manual is provided. This draft expert manual: (i) defines relevant concepts, including interoperability standards and SEIP; (ii) offers insights for SSOs; (iii) provides recommendations concerning the availability of injunctions in respect of SEIP; (iv) outlines principles for the calculation of compensation for established infringements of SEIP; and (v) suggests acceptable approaches regarding the application of competition laws to interoperability standards and SEIP.

Such an expert manual would thus be capable of providing guidance to domestic courts in making efficient and accurate decisions about access to interoperability standards and SEIP. The intention is to assist courts and regulatory agencies to make decisions that will provide optimal incentives for interoperability standard-setting, and for innovation in standardized markets, in future decades. In particular, an expert manual could explain the most policy-appropriate ways to apply the discretion such courts and regulatory agencies already possess. A document bearing a high degree of legitimacy (arising from its expertise, representativeness and robust process) could also send a signal to jurisdictions to address the internal contradictions currently existing in their laws in this area.

For jurisdictions approaching these questions for the first time, an expert manual could prove to be invaluable to both courts and legislators, and may in due course be referred to and relied on quite frequently. In the longer term, the successful development of an expert manual could pave the way for the establishment of a more permanent forum within which to continue deliberating on the relevant issues and prepare further best practice guides and other soft law instruments.

Initiatives already undertaken in the field of Internet governance, such as ICANN, could provide a useful template for a polyarchic multistakeholder forum (either heterogeneous or homogeneous in its decision-making structure) to develop the issues further, and to embed participating state representatives within a more permanent process. Ultimately, binding treaty law initiatives, pursued for example under the auspices of WIPO or the WTO, may become more feasible – although in an international climate of increasing economic nationalism, formal treaty-making approaches involving all the major jurisdictions appear decreasingly likely. But this merely serves to underscore the timeliness and value of an expert-led soft law initiative.

As such, in view of the vital importance of interoperability standards in the future, undertaking the development of an expert manual addressing issues associated with access to interoperability standards and to SEIP could prove to be both important and timely. Regulatory approaches developed within such a forum could retain a high degree of congruence with a carefully reasoned underlying policy basis (e.g. law and economics), at the same time remaining entirely consistent with existing requirements of international law, notably the requirements of the TRIPS Agreement.

9

Draft Expert Manual

[Location] Manual on Ensuring Appropriate Access to Interoperability Standards and Standards-Essential Intellectual Property

The drafters of this Expert Manual,

Considering that interoperability standards form part of the essential information infrastructure of the global economy

Acknowledging the indispensable contribution of private market actors to the development of the digital economy generally and to the ongoing development of interoperability standards in particular

Mindful of the vital importance of appropriately tailored intellectual property rights in preserving incentives for optimal innovation in networked markets, including follow-on innovation

Mindful also of the vital importance of standard-setting activities to the global digital economy

Concerned that the overprotection of intellectual property, notably in the presence of Cournot complements and multi-component assertion of rights, could give rise to the problems of 'hold-up' in relation to standards-essential intellectual property, having appropriate regard also to the competing concerns of 'hold-out' by users of technology

Desiring to give due weight to undertakings provided by intellectual property holders to licence their technology, in the context of standard-setting initiatives

Wishing to secure adequate access by all market actors to standards-essential intellectual property,

Consider as follows:

9.1 Interpretation

For the purposes of this Expert Manual, terms shall be understood to have the following meanings:

Interoperability refers to the ability of systems to exchange and make useful information in a straightforward and useful way, which is enhanced by the use of standards in communication and data format;

Interoperability standard refers to any standard that is prepared with the purpose of promoting interoperability between goods, services, programs or systems;

Standard refers to rules that seek to promote order with respect to products, services or processes by encapsulating expert knowledge in the form of written requirements; standards can either be formal (i.e. drafted or promulgated by a standard-setting organization) or de facto; in the latter case the document or specifications must obtain widespread marketplace acceptance in order to be considered a de facto standard;

Standard-essential intellectual property (SEIP) refers to any intellectual property right under applicable law the practice of which is technically essential to the implementation of an interoperability standard,[1] noting that the question of 'essentiality' should not be established merely on the basis of claims made by the right holder, but rather should be established as a matter of fact by a competent court or administrative body based on the interpretation of the relevant intellectual property right;

Standard-essential patent (SEP) means any patent under applicable law the practice of which is technically essential to the implementation of an interoperability standard; and

Standard-setting organization (SSO) refers to any organization involved in the preparation or the promulgation of formal interoperability standards.

9.2 Standards-Essential Intellectual Property

9.2.1 Standards-Essential Patents

1. SEIP most commonly will take the form of standards-essential patents (SEPs), standards-essential copyrights and standards-essential trade secrets.

---

[1] An intellectual property right will be considered essential to the practice of an interoperability standard in circumstances where it is technically impossible to implement the standard without infringing the intellectual property right.

9.3 STANDARD-SETTING ORGANIZATIONS

2. Concerning SEPs, jurisdictions should be mindful of the vital importance of disclosure requirements in connection with SEPs; in particular, SEPs should be disclosed publicly in sufficient detail to enable a person skilled in the relevant art to practice the SEP; these principles should apply equally in the particular contexts of computer software and databases.
3. Jurisdictions should also be mindful of the importance of experimental and research exceptions to patent rights. The question of whether or not a patent is standards-essential will turn critically upon the ability for users to 'invent around' the patent; it may be appropriate for experimental and research exceptions to apply in the context of such efforts to 'invent around' SEPs.

9.2.2 Standards-Essential Copyrights

4. Jurisdictions should be mindful of the distinction between ideas (which cannot be copyrighted) and the creative expression of those ideas in the form of works (which can be protected by copyright), including in the particular contexts of computer programs and databases.
5. Appropriate exceptions should be made available for standards-essential copyright in circumstances where: (i) an idea and its creative expression in the form of a work have 'merged' such that the idea can only be expressed in a single way, or in a limited number of ways; (ii) the creative expression of an idea has become commonplace or standardized; or (iii) the use of copyrighted information is indispensable for purposes of ensuring interoperability between a computer program and another program, between a computer program and computer hardware, or between a computer program and a user.

9.3 Standard-Setting Organizations

6. Having due regard to the fundamental importance of standard-setting activities to the global information society, jurisdictions should provide adequate regulatory space for standard-setting organizations (SSOs) to pursue their legitimate activities.
7. SSOs should comply with all applicable domestic laws, including competition laws, and should be mindful of relevant international

obligations, notably the obligations imposed under the WTO Agreement on Technical Barriers to Trade (TBT Agreement).[2]

8. SSOs should accept and comply with applicable codes of standard-setting best practice, including the WTO's Code of Good Practice for the Preparation, Adoption and Application of Standards,[3] the WTO TBT Committee's Principles for the Development of International Standards,[4] and ISO/IEC Guide 59: 1994, Code of Good Practice for Standardization.[5]

9. Jurisdictions should apply their competition laws in a manner that is sympathetic to the legitimate purposes served by the standard-setting activities of SSOs.

10. SSOs should not be used as a venue for coordinated anticompetitive activities such as price-fixing or market-sharing.

11. SSOs should maintain written policies or guidelines in relation to SEIP.

12. SSO intellectual property policies should obligate all members of the SSO to search their portfolios of intellectual property rights and pending intellectual property rights, and disclose to the SSO any and all intellectual property rights, existing or pending which, in the opinion of the concerned member, may be or may, in the future, become essential to the practice of an interoperability standard developed under the auspices of the SSO.

13. SSOs should require all members to provide undertakings to license, on fair, reasonable and non-discriminatory terms, any SEIP, or alternatively require members to renounce all rights to such SEIP.

14. It is understood and acknowledged that such bindings should be enforceable in law, either as binding contracts, or by way of principles of estoppel or other like doctrines of applicable law.

15. It should not be considered to be price-fixing for members to make binding undertakings to license at a given royalty rate at the time they provide the undertakings referred to in paragraph 13 above.

---

[2] Agreement on Technical Barriers to Trade, Annex 1A to the Marrakesh Agreement Establishing the World Trade Organization (adopted 15 April 1994, entry into force 1 January 1995) (1868 UNTS 120).

[3] Ibid. Annex 3.

[4] 'Decisions and Recommendations Adopted by the WTO Committee on Technical Barriers to Trade since 1 January 1995' (World Trade Organization, Committee on Technical Barriers to Trade 2011) WTO Doc G/TBT/1/Rev.13 https://docs.wto.org.

[5] 'ISO/IEC Guide 59: 1994 Code of Good Practice for Standardization' https://www.iso.org/standard/23390.html accessed 20 May 2019.

16. Undertakings referred to in paragraph 13 above should be considered to attach to the intellectual property right in question, such that they will retain legal currency in the event of assignment, licensing, merger or like event.
17. SSOs should make available copies of their standards to the public on reasonable and non-discriminatory terms.

9.4 Undertakings to License

18. Courts should consider undertakings to license given in the context of formal standard-setting procedures to be binding under applicable law, either as binding contracts or by way of estoppel or another like doctrine of law.

9.5 Injunctions

19. It is understood that the award of an injunction by a domestic court in respect of SEIP amounts to an exclusive property rule in respect of that SEIP, whereas the award of damages or reasonable royalties, in the absence of the award of an injunction, amounts to a liability rule in respect of that SEIP.
20. Courts should be mindful of the equitable nature of the injunctive remedy.
21. SEIP should not be subject to a presumption in favour of injunction which departs from the ordinary grounds for the grant of injunction under the laws of the applicable jurisdiction.
22. Jurisdictional practices regarding awards of injunctive relief for infringement of SEIP should seek to preserve adequate incentives for innovative activities in the creation, revision, upgrading and implementation of interoperability standards.
23. In considering whether to award an injunction in relation to SEIP, courts should take into account all relevant information, including most prominently:
    a. the nature of the standardized technology;
    b. the nature and scope of the SEIP in question;
    c. the forum within which the relevant standard has been developed, including any applicable intellectual property policies;
    d. any undertakings given by the right holder or another relevant person to license the SEIP;

e. the course of negotiations between the right holder and the user, including whether the evidence tends to indicate that the right holder has engaged in 'hold-up' or that the user or prospective user has engaged in 'hold-out';
f. the dispersion among diffuse organizations of other SEIP in relation to the applicable interoperability standard, and whether such dispersion could potentially lead to a situation of Cournot complements;
g. the inclusion in consumer products practicing the standard of other technologies, inventions or creative ideas, whether standardized or non-standardized and whether or not protected by intellectual property rights;
h. whether an injunction awarded in relation to SEIP would have the effect of prohibiting significant non-infringing conduct on the part of the implementor of an interoperability standard; and
i. applicable provisions of competition law.

24. Having regard to the factors and considerations outlined in above, courts and administrative bodies adjudicating upon an established breach of SEIP should generally favour the imposition of a liability rule over the imposition of an exclusive property rule in circumstances where (i) there appears to exist a 'Cournot complements' problem in relation to the SEIP as a result of numerous right holders being able to act effectively as monopolists in relation to the licensing of the SEIP; and (ii) an injunction would have the effect of prohibiting significant non-infringing conduct by the implementor of an interoperability standard.

25. While it is not necessarily recommended, jurisdictions may in addition consider it appropriate to favour a liability rule over an exclusive property rule in circumstances where: (i) access to the SEIP is indispensable to compete in a secondary market (i.e. the SEIP exhibits 'double essentiality');[6] (ii) failure to license the SEIP would eliminate competition in that secondary market; (iii) the SEIP is needed to create a new product for which there is likely consumer demand; and (iv) there is no objective justification for the refusal to license the SEIP.

---

[6] As outlined above, 'double essentiality' exists where: (i) the intellectual property right is essential to the practice of an interoperability standard; and (ii) practice of that interoperability standard is essential to competition in a market other than the market for the licensing of the intellectual property right.

9.6 Calculation of Compensation

26. Courts should award damages or compensation for infringement of SEIP, preferably in the form of reasonable royalties, with a view to providing adequate incentives for the creation and use of interoperability standards and of SEIP.
27. The calculation of such compensation should be based on ordinary principles of law, such as lost profits of the right holder, account of profits or reasonable royalties, adjusted as appropriate to take account of the particular context of the creation and implementation of interoperability standards, and of the protection and assertion of SEIP.
28. The calculation of such compensation should seek to adequately compensate the right holder for the value of the SEIP, excluding any 'hold-up value' associated with the SEIP, but not necessarily excluding all incremental value accruing to the SEIP holder as a result of the inclusion of the relevant technology into the interoperability standard.
29. The calculation of such compensation should be undertaken on the basis of a recognized and appropriate economic methodology.
30. The calculation of compensation should take account of the marginal contribution of the SEIP to the standard in question, having regard to alternative technologies that were available to the SSO when the standard was drafted.
31. In calculating such compensation, courts may consider it appropriate, in light of all the prevailing facts and circumstances, to have regard to the following factors:
    a. the cost to the right holder of developing the SEIP
    b. the commercial value of the SEIP in the marketplace, excluding any 'hold-up' value associated with the SEIP, but not necessarily excluding all incremental value accruing to the SEIP as a result of its incorporation into the standard
    c. the particular characteristics of the SEIP that have rendered it amenable to incorporation into the interoperability standard
    d. the terms of any applicable undertaking given by the right holder (or by a prior owner or licensor of the SEIP) to license the SEIP
    e. any prior agreements given by the right holder (or by a prior owner or licensor of the SEIP) to license the SEIP on arms-length, commercial terms

f. expert assessment as to the proper economic, technical and commercial valuation of the SEIP
   g. the value of comparable SEIP available for licensing from collective rights organizations such as patent pools
   h. the value of other SEIP and other technologies (whether or not they are standardized and whether or not they are subject to intellectual property rights) which are incorporated into the relevant end-consumer products which implement the interoperability standard
   i. the conduct of the right holder during the development of the standard, including whether the right holder has engaged in fraud, misconduct or bad faith, or has acted in any manner contrary to the bylaws of the relevant standard-setting organization, and
   j. The need to deter wilful infringement of SEIP.

9.7 The Application of Competition Law in the Context of Interoperability Standards and SEIP

32. Whilst matters pertaining to access to SEIP are, in the first instance, primarily the concern of intellectual property law, rather than of competition law, the applicable competition laws of jurisdictions should, nevertheless, apply equally in the context of interoperability standards as they apply in relation to commercial activities within the jurisdiction more generally.
33. Participants in standard-setting activities, and in particular holders and users of SEIP, should act at all times in conformity with the requirements of applicable competition in laws.
34. Competition laws should provide for adequate remedies to redress coordinated conduct in the context of the development and implementation of interoperability standards.
35. Competition laws relating to exploitative conduct, such as excessive or unfair pricing, should apply in relation to SEIP in very rare circumstances only, on the basis of a clearly reasoned approach with a sound basis in economic science, with due regard to the need to preserve adequate incentive for dynamic efficiency, and with the utmost circumspection and caution.
36. Competition laws dealing with refusals to provide access to an interoperability standard, or refusals to license SEIP, on the basis of an essential facilities doctrine or a cognate doctrine of law, are not

recommended and, if imposed, should apply with respect to SEIP in exceptional circumstances only, such as in situations where: (i) acquiring a license to use the SEIP is essential in order to supply goods or services to end-consumers; (ii) refusal to license is likely to result in the elimination of all competition in the supply of goods or services to end-consumers in the relevant market; (iii) the refusal is likely to prevent emergence of a new product for which there is end-consumer demand; and (iv) the refusal is not objectively justified.

9.8 Final Provisions

37. This Expert Manual is intended to be revised on a regular basis to take account of new developments in the fields of interoperability standards and SEIP, and new developments in domestic laws.
38. This Expert Manual is not a legally binding document.
39. Copies of this Expert Manual shall be made available to all interested parties on a reasonable and non-discriminatory basis.

Done this day, the [day] of [month], [year] in [place].

BIBLIOGRAPHY

Treaties, Laws, Regulations and Other Legislative Instruments

Treaties and Other International Instruments

Agreement on Technical Barriers to Trade (adopted 12 April 1979, entered into force 1 January 1980) 1186 UNTS 276 (Tokyo Round Standards Code)

Agreement on Technical Barriers to Trade, Annex 1A to the Marrakesh Agreement Establishing the World Trade Organization (adopted 15 April 1994, entered into force 1 January 1995) 1868 UNTS 120 (TBT Agreement)

Agreement on Trade-Related Aspects of Intellectual Property Rights, Annex 1C to the Marrakesh Agreement Establishing the World Trade Organization (adopted 15 April 1994, entered into force 1 January 1995) 1869 UNTS 299 (TRIPS Agreement)

Annex on Telecommunications to the General Agreement on Trade in Services, Annex 1B to the Marrakesh Agreement Establishing the World Trade Organization (adopted 15 April 1994, entered into force 1 January 1995) 1869 UNTS 214 (GATS Annex on Telecommunications)

Articles on the Responsibility of States for Internationally Wrongful Acts 2001 (Yearbook of the International Law Commission, A/CN4/SERA/2001/Add1 (Part 1))

Convention Establishing the World Intellectual Property Organization (adopted 14 July 1967, entered into force 26 April 1970) 828 UNTS 5 (WIPO Convention)

Convention on Combating Bribery of Foreign Public Officials in International Business Transactions (adopted 21 November 1997, entered into force 15 February 1999) 37 ILM 1 (OECD Anti-Bribery Convention)

'Decisions and Recommendations Adopted by the WTO Committee on Technical Barriers to Trade since 1 January 1995' (World Trade Organization, Committee on Technical Barriers to Trade 2011) WTO Doc G/TBT/1/Rev.13 <https://docs.wto.org>

Doha WTO Ministerial Declaration, 20 November 2001, WTO Doc WTMIN01DEC1 (Doha Ministerial Declaration)

General Agreement on Tariffs and Trade 1994, Annex 1A to the Marrakesh Agreement Establishing the World Trade Organization (adopted 15 April 1994, entered into force 1 January 1995) 1867 UNTS 190 (GATT 1994)

General Agreement on Trade in Services, Annex 1B to Marrakesh Agreement establishing the World Trade Organization (adopted 15 April 1994, entered into force 1 January 1995) 1869 UNTS 183 (GATS)

Geneva Ministerial Declaration on Global Electronic Commerce, 20 May 1998, WTO Doc WTMIN98DEC2 (Declaration of Global Electronic Commerce)

International Convention for the Protection of Performers, Producers of Phonograms and Broadcasting Organizations (adopted 26 October 1961, entered into force 18 May 1964) 496 UNTS 43 (Rome Convention)

Marrakesh Agreement Establishing the World Trade Organization (adopted 15 April 1994, entered into force 1 January 1995) 1867–1869 UNTS (WTO Agreement)

Ministerial Declaration on Trade in Technology Products (Information Technology Agreement) 1996 (WTO Doc WT/MIN (96)/16)

Multilateral Convention to Implement Tax Treaty Related Measures to Prevent Base Erosion and Profit Shifting (opened for signature 31 December 2016, entered into force 1 July 2018) <www.oecd.org> accessed 27 April 2019

Paris Act relating to the Berne Convention for the Protection of Literary and Artistic Works (adopted September 9, 1886, entered into force 5 December 1887, as revised at Paris, 24 July 1971, entered into force 15 December 1972) (331 UNTS 219) (Berne Convention)

Paris Convention for the Protection of Industrial Property (adopted 20 March 1883, entered into force 7 July 1884, as revised at Stockholm, 14 July 1967, entered into force 26 April 1970) (828 UNTS 305) (Paris Convention)

Patent Law Treaty (adopted 1 June 2000, entered into force 28 April 2005) 2340 UNTS 3 (Patent Law Treaty)

Treaty on Intellectual Property in Respect of Integrated Circuits (adopted 26 May 1989) (28 ILM 1484)(Washington Treaty on Integrated Circuits)

Vienna Convention on the Law of Treaties (adopted 23 May 1969, entered into force 27 January 1980) 1155 UNTS 331 (VCLT)

WIPO Copyright Treaty (adopted 20 December 1996, entered into force 6 March 2002) 2186 UNTS 5 (WCT)

WIPO Performances and Phonograms Treaty (adopted 20 December 1996, entered into force 20 May 2002) 2186 UNTS 203 (WPPT)

WIPO Standing Committee on the Law of Patents, 5th session, Draft Regulations and Practice Guidelines under the Draft Substantive Patent Law Treaty (2001)

WTO Decision of the Committee on Technical Barriers to Trade on Principles for the Development of International Standards, Guides and Recommendations with Relation to Articles 2, 5 and Annex 3 of the Agreement 2000 (G/TBT/9)

WTO, Doha WTO Ministerial, Declaration on the TRIPS Agreement and Public Health (20 November 2001), WTO Doc WT/MIN(01)/DEC/1

European Union Directives, Regulations and Other Instruments

Agreement on a Unified Patent Court (2013/C 175/01)
Agreement relating to Community Patents 1989 (OJ L 401)
Charter of Fundamental Rights of the European Union ([2016] OJ C 202)
Communication from the Commission: Guidelines on the Applicability of Article 101 of the Treaty on the Functioning of the European Union to Horizontal Cooperation Agreements ([2011] OJ C11/1)
Consolidated Version of the Treaty on the Functioning of the European Union ([2008] OJ C115/13) (TFEU)
Convention on the Grant of European Patents (adopted 5 October 1973, entry into force 7 October 1977) (1065 UNTS 199)
Council Directive of 16 December 1986 on the Legal Protection of Topographies of Semiconductor Products 1986 (OJ L 24)
Council Regulation (EC) No 1/2003 of 16 December 2002 on the Implementation of Rules of Competition laid down in Articles 81 and 82 of the Treaty 2002 (OJ L 1)
Directive 96/9 of the European Parliament and of the European Council of 11 March 1996 on the Legal Protection of Databases 1996 (OJ L 77)
Directive 2004/48/EC of the European Parliament and of the Council of 29 April 2004 on the Enforcement of Intellectual Property Rights 2004 (L 157)
Directive 2009/24/EC of the European Parliament and of the Council of 23 April 2009 on the Legal Protection of Computer Programs 2009 (OJ L 111)
Regulation No. 1257/2012 of the European Parliament and of the Council of 17 December 2012 Implementing Enhanced Cooperation in the Area of the Creation of Unitary Patent Protection 2012 (OJ L 361 1)
Treaty between the Federal Republic of Germany, the Kingdom of Belgium, the French Republic, the Italian Republic, the Grand Duchy of Luxembourg and the Kingdom of the Netherlands Instituting the European Coal and Steel Community 1951 (261 UNTS 140) (Treaty of Paris)
Treaty Establishing the European Economic Community (4300 UNTS 11) (Treaty of Rome)

National Laws, Regulations and other Legislative Instruments

Australia

Competition and Consumer Act (Cth) 2010
Patents Act (Cth) 1990

Federal Republic of Germany

Gesetz gegen den unlauteren Wettbewerb (Act against Unfair Competition) 2010 (Published 3 March 2010 (Federal Law Gazette I, p. 254), as amended by Article 4 of the Act of 17 February 2016 (Federal Law Gazette I, p. 233))

Gesetz uber Urheberrecht und verwandte Schutzrechte (Copyright Act) 1965 (Federal Law Gazette I, p. 1273, as last amended by the Act of 20 December 2016 (Federal Law Gazette I, p. 3037))

Patentgesetz (Patent Act) 1980 (Federal Law Gazette I, p 1, as last amended by the Act of 8 October 2017 (Federal Law Gazette I p. 3546))

France

Code de la Propriété Intellectuelle (Intellectual Property Code) 1992 (Act No. 92–597 of 1 July 1992 on the Code of Intellectual Property, as published in the Official Journal of 3 July 1992)

Hong Kong Special Administrative Region (China)

Patents Ordinance (HK), Chapter 514 1997

Japan

Shiteki-dokusen no Kinshi oyobi Kōseitorihiki no Kakuho ni Kansuru Hōritsu (Act on Prohibition of Private Monopolization and Maintenance of Fair Trade) 1947 (Act No. 54 of 1947 as amended)

Tokkyohō (Patent Act) 1959 (Act No. 121 of 13 April 1959 as amended up to Act No. 55 of 10 July 2015)

People's Republic of China

Anti-Monopoly Guidelines on the Abuse of Intellectual Property Rights (Draft for Comment) (23 March 2017) <http://fldj.mofcom.gov.cn/> accessed 18 May 2020, 公开征求《关于滥用知识产权的反垄断指南（征求意见稿）》的意见

Anti-Monopoly Law (Promulgated by Order No. 68 of 30 August, 2007) of the People's Republic of China, 中华人民共和国反垄断法

Copyright Law of the People's Republic of China (as amended up to the Decision of 26 February 2010, by the Standing Committee of the National People's Congress on Amending the Copyright Law of the Peoples' Republic of China), 中华人民共和国著作权法 1990

General Principles of Civil Law (1986, amended 2010), 中华人民共和国民法通则

Law of the People's Republic of China against Unfair Competition (as revised at the 30th Meeting of the Standing Committee of the 12th National People's Congress on 4 November 2017), 中华人民共和国反不正当竞争法 1993

Patent Law of the People's Republic of China (as amended up to the Decision of 27 December 2008, regarding the Revision of the Patent Law of the People's Republic of China), 中华人民共和国专利法 1985

Regulations on the Protection of Layout-Designs of Integrated Circuits (Decree No. 300 of the State Council of the People's Republic of China), 中华人民共和国集成电路布图设计保护条例 2001

Regulations on Computer Software Protection (as amended up to Decision of the State Council of the People's Republic of China of 30 January 2013), 2002 (计算机软件保护条例)

United States of America

Copyright Act 1976 (17 USC §§101–801)
Federal Trade Commission Act 1914 (15 USC §§ 41–58)
Patents Act 1952 (35 USC §§1–376)
Protection of Semiconductor Chip Products Act 1984 (17 USC §§ 901–914)
Protection of Trade Secrets Act 1996 (18 USC § 1836–1839)
Sherman Antitrust Act 1890 (15 USC §§1–38)
Standards Development Organization Act 2004 (15 USC §§ 4301–4306)
Tariff Act 1930 (19 USC §§1301–1683 g)

United Kingdom

Copyright, Designs and Patents Act 1988
Patents Act 1977

Cases

International Cases

International Court of Justice

Case Concerning Pulp Mills on the River Uruguay 2010 ICJ Rep 18

World Trade Organization Dispute Settlement Reports

WTO, Australia – Certain Measures Concerning Trademarks, Geographical Indications and Other Plain Packaging Requirements Applicable to Tobacco Products and Packaging – Report of the Panel (28 June 2018) WT/DS435/R, WT/DS441/R, WT/DS458/R, WT/DS467/R

WTO, Canada – Patent Protection of Pharmaceutical Products – Report of the Panel (17 March 2000) WT/DS114/R

WTO, China – Certain Measures Affecting Electronic Payment Services – Report of the Panel (16 July 2012) WT/DS413/R

WTO, European Communities – Protection of Trademarks and Geographical Indications for Agricultural Products and Foodstuffs – Report of the Panel (15 March 2005) WT/DS290/R

WTO, India – Patent Protection for Pharmaceutical and Agricultural Chemical Products – Report of the Panel (24 August 1998) WT/DS50/R

WTO, Mexico – Measures Affecting Telecommunications Services – Report of the Panel (2 April 2004) WT/DS204/R

WTO, United States – Measures Affecting the Production and Sale of Clove Cigarettes – Report of the Appellate Body (4 April 2012) WT/DS406/AB/R

WTO, United States – Measures Concerning the Importation, Marketing and Sale of Tuna and Tuna Products – Report of the Panel (15 September 2011) WT/DS381/R

WTO, United States – Measures Concerning the Importation, Marketing and Sale of Tuna and Tuna Products – Report of the Appellate Body (16 May 2012) WT/DS381/AB/R

WTO, United States – Section 110(5) of US Copyright Act – Report of the Panel (15 June 2000) WT/DS160/R

WTO, United States – Section 211 Omnibus Appropriations Act of 1998 – Report of the Appellate Body (6 August 2001) WT/DS176/R

European Cases and other Judicial and Administrative Reports

AB Volvo and Erik Veng (UK) Ltd (Case 238/87) [1988] ECR 06232 (European Court of Justice)

Asynchronous Resynchronization of a Commit Procedure/International Business Machines (T1173/97) [1998] OJ 1999/609 (Boards of Appeal of the European Patent Office)

Auction Method/Hitachi (T258/03) [2004] OJ 2004/575 (Boards of Appeal of the European Patent Office)

Autortiesību un komunicēšanās konsultāciju aģentūra/Latvijas Autoru apvienība (Case C-177/16) [2017] ECLI:EU:C:2017:698 (European Court of Justice)

Bezpečnostní softwarová asociace – Svaz softwarové ochrany v. Ministerstvo kultury (Case C-393/09) [2010] ECR -13971 (European Court of Justice)

Commercial Solvents (72/457/EC) [1972] 1972 OJ 299 (European Commission)

Controlling Pension Benefits System/PBS Partnership (T931/95) [2000] ECLI:EP:BA:2000:T093195.20000908 (Boards of Appeal of the European Patent Office)

Corinne Bodson v. SA Pompes funebres des regions liberees (Case 30/87) [1988] ECR 1988–02479 (European Court of Justice)

Data Transfer with Expanded Clipboard Formats/Microsoft (T424/03) [2006], accessed 23 October 2019 (Boards of Appeal of the European Patent Office)

Deutsche Post AG – Interception of Cross-Border Mail (COMP/C-1/36915) [2001] OJ 331 (European Commission)

Estimating Sales Activity/Duns Licensing Associates (T0154/04) [2006] OJ 2008/46 (Boards of Appeal of the European Patent Office)

Europemballage Corporation and Continental Can Company Inc v. Commission of the European Communities (Case 6/72) [1973] ECR 1973–00215 (European Court of Justice)

General Motors NV v. Commission of the European Communities (Case 26/75) [1975] ECR 1975 – 01367 (European Court of Justice)

Hoffman-La Roche & Co AG v. Commission of the European Communities (Case 85/76) [1979] ECR 461 (European Court of Justice)

Huawei Technologies Co Ltd v. ZTE Corp, ZTE Deutschland GmbH (Case C/170–13) [2015] ECLI: EUC:2015:477 (European Court of Justice)

IMS Health GMBH & Co and NDC Health GMBH & Co (Case C-418–01) [2004] ECR -05039 (European Court of Justice)

IMS Health Inc v. Commission of the European Communities (Case T-184/01 R) [2001] ECR II-03193 (European Court of First Instance)

Istituto Chemioterapico Italiano SpA and Commercial Solvents Corporation v. Commission of the European Communities (Cases 6 and 7/73) [1974] ECR 00223 (European Court of Justice)

Kanal 5 and TV 4 (Case C-52/07) [2008] EU:C:2008:703 (Court of Justice of the European Communities (Fourth Chamber))

Load Distribution/Club IT (T0318/10) (T038/10) [2014] ECLI:EP:BA:2014: T031810.20140902 (Boards of Appeal of the European Patent Office)

Magill TV Guide/ITP, BBC and RTE (89/205/EEC) [1988] OJ 78/43 (European Commission)

Method and Apparatus for Improved Digital Processing/Vicom Systems Inc. (T208/84) [1985] OJ 1987 14 (Board of Appeal of the European Patent Office)

Microsoft (Case COMP/C-3/37.792) [2009] OJ C 166/20 (European Commission)

Microsoft v. Commission of the European Communities (Case T-201/04) [2007] 2007 ECR II-03601 (European Court of First Instance)

Microsoft v. Commission of the European Communities (Case T167-08) [2012] ECLI:EU:T:2012:323 (European Court of First Instance)

Motorola – Enforcement of GPRS Standard Essential Patents (Case AT39985) [2014] http://ec.europa.eu accessed 19 December 2017 (European Commission)

NDC Health/IMS Health: Interim Measures (Case COMP D3/38044) [2001] OJ 59 (European Commission)

NDC Health/IMS Health: Interim Measures (Case COMP D3/38044) [2003] OJ 268 (European Commission)

Oscar Bronner GmbH & Co KG v. Mediaprint Zeitung (C-7/97) [1998] ECR -07791 (European Court of Justice)

Programs for Computers (G0003/08) [2010] OJ 2011 10 (Enlarged Board of Appeal of the European Patent Office)

Radio Telefis Eirann (RTE) and Independent Television Publications (ITP) v. Commission of the European Communities (C-241/91 and C-242/91 P) [1995] ECR -00743 (European Court of Justice)

Samsung – Enforcement of UMTS Standard-Essential Patents (Case AT39939) [2014] OJ C350/08 (European Commission)

SAS Institute Inc v. World Programming Limited [2012] ECLI:EC:C:2012:259 (European Court of Justice)

Scandlines Sverige AB v. Port of Helsingborg (Case COMP/A36568)/D3 [2004] <http://ec.europa.eu>, accessed 2 May 2019 (European Commission)

Sea Containers v. Stena Sealink (Case IV34/689) 1993 OJ L158 (European Commission)

Summary of Commission Decision of 9 December 2009 under Article 102 of the Treaty (Case COMP/38636 – RAMBUS) [2009] OJ C 30 (European Commission)

System and method for adding a skill aspect to games of chance/Gameaccount Limited (T1543/06) [2007] ECLI:EP:BA:2007:T154306.20070629 (Boards of Appeal for the European Patent Office)

United Brands Company and United Brands Continentaal BV v. Commission of the European Communities (Case 27/76) [1978] ECR 00207 (European Court of Justice)

Domestic Cases

Japan

Samsung Electronics Co, Ltd v. Apple Japan Godo Kaisha [2014] accessed 19 July 2017 (Grand Panel of the Japanese Intellectual Property High Court)

Federal Republic of Germany

BGH July 11, 1995, 1996 NJW 782 (785) (Clinical Trials I), translated in [1997] RPC 623 (642) (German Federal Court of Justice)

People's Republic of China

Interdigital Communications, Inc v. Huawei Investment & Holding Co, Ltd, Zongji Renmin Fayuan 2013 (Shenzhen Intermediate People's Court)

Notice of the Supreme People's Court on Issuing the Opinions on Several Issues concerning Intellectual Property Trials Serving the Overall Objective under the Current Economic Situation [2009] No 23 (Supreme People's Court)

United Kingdom

Aerotel and others in the Matter of the Patents Act 1977 2006 EWCA Civ 1371 (Court of Appeal)

Allnutt v. *Inglis* [1810] 104 Engl Rep 206 1810 12 East 527 (Court of King's Bench)

American Cyanamid Co v. *Ethicon Ltd* [1975] 1975 1 ER 504 (House of Lords)

Attheraces Ltd & Anor v. *The British Horseracing Board Ltd & Anor* 2007 EWCA Civ 38 (Court of Appeal)

Bolt v. *Stennett* [1800] 101 Engl Rep 1572 8 Term Rep 606 (Court of King's Bench)

Coflexip SA v. *Stolt Comtex Seaway MS Limited* 2000 EWCA Civ 242 (Court of Appeal)

Monsanto Co. v. *Stauffer Chemical Co. and Another* [1985] RPC 515 (Court of Appeal)

SAS Institute Inc v. *World Programming Limited* (2013) 69 EWHC (High Court)

Series 5 Software Ltd v. *Clarke* [1995] 1996 ER 853 (High Court)

Shelfer v. *City of London Electric Lighting Co* Civ 1895 (Court of Appeal)

Symbian Ltd v. *Comptroller-General of Patents* 2008 EWCA Civ 1066 (Court of Appeal)

Unwired Planet International Limited v. *Huawei Technologies Co Limited* 2016 EWHC 576 Pat (High Court)

Unwired Planet International Ltd and Unwired Planet LLC v. *Huawei Technologies Co Limited and Huawei Technologies (UK) Co Limited* [2018] 2018 EWCA Civ 2344 (Court of Appeal)

Unwired Planet International v. *Huawei Technologies Co Ltd and Huawei Technologies (UK) Co Ltd* [2017] 2017 EWHC 711 (High Court)

United States of America

Adobe System Inc v. *Feather* [2012] 895 FSupp2d 297 (United States District Court for the District of Connecticut)

Alaska Airlines, Inc. v. *United Airlines, Inc* [1991] 948 F2d 536 (United States Court of Appeals for the Ninth Circuit).

Alice Corporation Pty Ltd v. *CLS Bank International et al* [2014] 134 S. Ct 2347 (United States Supreme Court)

Amdocs (Israel) Limited v. *Openet Telecom Inc* [2016] 841 F3d 1288 (United States Court of Appeals for the Federal Circuit)

Apple Computer, Inc v. *Microsoft Corp* [1994] 35 F3d 1435 (United States Court of Appeals for the Ninth Circuit)

Apple Computer Inc v. *Microsoft Corporation* [1992] 799 FSupp 1006 (United States District Court for the Northern District of California)

Apple Inc v. *Motorola, Inc* [2014] 757 F3d 1286 (United States Court of Appeals for the Federal Circuit)

BIBLIOGRAPHY

Apple, Inc v. *Motorola Mobility, Inc* [2012] 886 F Supp 2d 1061 (United States District Court for the District of Western Washington)

Aspen Skiing v. *Aspen Highlands Skiing* [1985] 472 US 585 (United States Supreme Court)

Associated Press et al v. *United States* (1945) 65 S. Ct. 1416 (United States Supreme Court)

Baker v. *Selden* [1879] 101 US 99 (United States Supreme Court)

BellSouth Adv & Pub v. *Donnelley Inf Pub* [1988] 719 FSupp 1551 (United States District Court for the Southern District of Florida)

BellSouth Advertising & Pub Corp v. *Donnelley Information Pub Inc* [1993] 999 F2d 1436 (United States Court of Appeals for the Eleventh Circuit)

Broadcom Corp v. *Qualcomm Inc* [2006] 2006 WL 2528545 (United States District Court for the District of New Jersey)

Broadcom Corp v. *Qualcomm Inc* [2007] 501 F3d 297 (United States Court of Appeals for the Third Circuit)

Chase Jarvis Inc v. *K2 Inc* [2007] 486 F3d 526 (United States Court of Appeals for the Ninth Circuit)

Cohen v. *United States* 100 Fed Cl 461 (United States Court of Federal Claims)

Commonwealth Scientific and Industrial Research Organisation v. *CISCO Systems Inc* [2015] 809 F3d 1295 1295 (United States Court of Appeals for the Federal Circuit)

Commonwealth Scientific and Industrial Research Organisation v. *Buffalo Technology Inc* [2007] 492 FSupp2d 600 (United States District Court for the Eastern District of Texas)

Commonwealth of Massachusetts, ex rel v. *Microsoft Corporation* [2004] 373 F3d 1199 (United States Court of Appeals for the District of Columbia Circuit)

Computer Associates International, Inc v. *Altai, Inc* [1992] 982 F2d 693 (United States Court of Appeals for the Second Circuit)

Data General v. *Grumman Systems Support* [1994] 36 F3d 1147 (United States Court of Appeals for the First Circuit)

Deltak, Inc v. *Advanced Systems, Inc* [1985] 767 F2d 357 (United States Court of Appeals for the Seventh Circuit)

eBay Inc v. *MercExchange LLC* [2006] 547 US 388 (United States Supreme Court)

Ericsson, Inc v. *D-Link Systems Inc* [2014] 773 F3d 1201 (United States Court of Appeals for the Federal Circuit)

Feist Publications, Inc v. *Rural Telephone Service Company, Inc* [1991] 499 US 340 (United States Supreme Court)

Fonar Corp v. *General Electric Co* [1997] 107 F3d 1543 (United States Court of Appeals for the Federal Circuit)

Georgia Pacific Corp v. *United States Plywood Corp* [1971] 318 FSupp 1116 (United States District Court for the Southern District of New York)

German Alliance Insurance Co v. *Lewis* [1914] 233 US 389 (United States Supreme Court)

Golden Bridge Technology v. *Apple Inc* [2014] 2014 WL2194501 (United States District Court, Northern District of California)

Image Technical Services, Inc v. *Eastman Kodak Co* [1997] 125 F3d 1195 (United States Court of Appeals for the Ninth Circuit)

In re Independent Service Organizations v. *Xerox Corp* [2000] 203 F3d 1322 (United States Court of Appeals for the Federal Circuit)

In re Innovatio, LLC Patent Litigation 2013 WL 5593609 (United States District Court for the Northern District of Illinois, Eastern Division)

In the matter of Dell Computer Corporation, Consent Order in relation to Alleged Violation of Section 5 of the Federal Trade Commission Act (C–3658), 121 FTC Decisions 616 (Federal Trade Commission)

In the Matter of Rambus, Inc (2006-2 Trade Cases P 75464) [2006] 2006 WL 2330117 (Federal Trade Commission)

Intergraph Corporation v. *Intel Corporation* [1999] 195 F3d 1346 (United States Court of Appeals for the Federal Circuit)

John M. J. Madey v. *Duke University* [2002] 307 F3d 1351 (United States Court of Appeals for the Federal Circuit)

Lexmark Int'l Inc v. *Static Control Components* [2004] 387 F3d 522 (United States Court of Appeals for the Sixth Circuit)

Lotus Development Corporation v. *Borland International, Inc* [1995] 49 F3d 807 (United States Court of Appeals for the First Circuit)

Malibu Media LLC v. *Kurt Schelling* 31 FSuppD 910 (United States District Court for the Eastern District of Michigan)

MCI Communications Corporation and MCI Telecommunications Corporation v. *American Telephone and Telegraph Company* [1983] 708 F2d 1081 (United States Court of Appeals for the Seventh Circuit)

McRoberts Software, Inc v. *Media 100, Inc* [2003] 329 F3d 557 (United States Court of Appeals for the Seventh Circuit)

Mentor Graphics Corp v. *EVE-USA Inc* [2017] 851 F3d 1275 (United States Court of Appeals for the Federal Circuit)

Microsoft Corp v. *Motorola, Inc* [2012] 854 FSupp2d 993 (United States District Court for the District of Western Washington)

Microsoft Corporation v. *Motorola, Inc* [2012] 696 F3d 872 (United States Court of Appeals for the Ninth Circuit)

Microsoft Corporation v. *Motorola, Inc, et al* [2013] United States District Court for the District of Western Washington No. C10-1823JLR, 2013 WL 2111217

Munn v. *Illinois* [1876] 94 US 113 (United States Supreme Court)

Norman F. Hecht, Harry Kagan and Marc A. Miller v. *Pro-Football, Inc* [1977] 570 F2d 982 (United States Court of Appeals for the District of Columbia Circuit)

Oracle, America Inc v. *Google Inc* [2012] 872 FSupp2d 974 (United States District Court for the Northern District of California)

Oracle, America Inc v. *Google Inc* [2014] 750 F3d 1339 (United States Court of Appeals for the Federal Circuit)

Oracle America, Inc v. *Google Inc* [2016] WL 1743154 (United States District Court for the Northern District of California)

Otter Tail Power Company v. *United States* [1973] 410 US 366 (United States Supreme Court)

Qualcomm Incorporated v. *Broadcom Corporation* [2008] 548 F3d 1004 (United States Court of Appeals for the Federal Circuit)

Rambus Incorporated v. *Federal Trade Commission* [2008] 522 522 F3d 456 (United States Court of Appeal for the District of Columbia Circuit)

Research in Motion Limited, et al v. *Motorola, Inc* [2008] 644 FSupp 2d 788 (United States District Court for the Northern District of Texas)

Schor v. *Abbott Laboratories* [2006] 453 F3d 609 (United States Court of Appeals for the Seventh Circuit)

SCM v. *Xerox Corp* [1981] 645 F2d 1195 (United States Court of Appeals for the Second Circuit)

Sega Enterprises Ltd v. *Accolade, Inc* [1992] 977 F2d 1510 (United States Court of Appeals for the Ninth Circuit)

Sheldon v. *Metro-Goldwyn Pictures Corp* [1940] 309 US 390 (United States Supreme Court)

Sony BMG Music Entertainment v. *Tenenbaum* [2011] 719 F3d 487 (United States Court of Appeals for the First Circuit)

Sony Computer Entertainment, Inc v. *Connectix Corp* (United States Court of Appeals for the Ninth Circuit)

Spansion, Inc v. *International Trade Commission* [2010] 629 F3d 1331 (United States Court of Appeals for the Federal Circuit)

State Industries, Inc v. *Mor-Flo Industries* [1989] 883 F2d 1573 (United States Court of Appeal for the Federal Circuit)

State of New York et al v. *Microsoft Corporation* [2002] 224 FSupp2d 76 (United States Court of Appeals for the District of Columbia)

State of New York et al v. *Microsoft Corporation, Final Judgment* [2002] 224 FSupp2d 76 (United States District Court for the District of Columbia)

State of New York et al v. *Microsoft Corporation, Memorandum Opinion* [2002] 231 FSupp2d 203 (United States District Court for the District of Columbia)

Statement of the Federal Trade Commission, In the Matter of Google Inc [2013] C-4336 (Federal Trade Commission)

Statement of the Federal Trade Commission, In the Matter of Motorola Mobility, LLC and Google Inc [2013] C-4410 (Federal Trade Commission)

Statement of the Federal Trade Commission, In the Matter of Robert Bosch GMBH [2013] C-4377 (Federal Trade Commission)

United States of America v. *Microsoft Corporation* [2001] 253 F3d 34 (United States Court of Appeals for the District of Columbia Circuit)

United States of America v. *Microsoft Corporation* [2001] 253 F3d 34 (United States Court of Appeals for the District of Columbia Circuit)

United States v. *Terminal Railroad Association of St Louis* [1912] 224 US 383 (United States Supreme Court)

Verizon Communications, Inc v. *Law Offices of Curtis V Trinko, LLP* [2004] 540 US 398 (United States Supreme Court)

Books and Journal Articles

Books

Abbate J., *Inventing the Internet* (MIT Press 1999)

Akman P., *The Concept of Abuse in European Competition Law: Law and Economic Approaches* (Hart Publishing 2012)

Band J. and Katoh M., *Interfaces on Trial* (Westview Press, Boulder, Colorado 1995)

Interfaces on Trial 2.0 (MIT Press 2011)

Baumol W. J., *Free Market Innovation Machine* (Princeton University Press 2002)

Blind K., *The Economics of Standards: Theory, Evidence, Policy* (Edward Elgar 2004)

Bork R. H., *The Antitrust Paradox: A Policy at War with Itself* (The Free Press, 2nd ed., 1993)

Cottier T., *Equitable Principles of Maritime Boundary Delimitation: The Quest for Distributive Justice in International Law* (Cambridge University Press 2015)

Cottier T. and Veron P. (eds.), *Concise International and European IP Law: TRIPS, Paris Convention, European Enforcement and Transfer of Technology* (3rd ed., Kluwer Law International 2015)

Cournot A., *Researches into the Mathematical Principles of the Theory of Wealth, 1838* (Nathaniel T Bacon tr., MacMillan 1929)

Cox C., *An Introduction to LTE: LTE, LTE-Advanced, SAE and 4 G Mobile Communications* (1st ed., John Wiley & Sons 2012)

Crane R., *The Politics of International Standards: France and the Color TV War (Communication and Information Science)* (Ablex Publishing 1979)

Dahlmann E., Parkvall S. and Skold J., *4G: LTE/LTE-Advanced for Mobile Broadband* (2nd ed., Academic Press 2014)

Eijo O. and others, *Advanced Internet Protocols, Services and Innovations* (John Wiley & Sons 2012)

Epstein R., *Principles for a Free Society* (Perseus Publishing 1998)

Esser J., *Vorverständnis Und Methodenwahl* (Athenäum-Fischer-Taschenbuch-Verlag 1972)

Ezrachi A., *EU Competition Law Guide: An Analytical Guide to the Leading Cases* (Hart Publishing 2014)

Gasser U. and Palfrey J., *Interoperability: The Promise and Perils of Highly Connected Systems* (Basic Books 2012)
Gerber D. J., *Law and Competition in Twentieth Century Europe: Protecting Prometheus* (Oxford University Press 1998)
Gervais D., *The TRIPS Agreement: Drafting History and Analysis* (2nd ed., Sweet & Maxwell 2003)
Gibson J. D. (ed.), *Mobile Communications Handbook* (3rd ed., CRC Press 2013)
Harvard Manual on International Law Applicable to Air and Missile Warfare (Cambridge University Press 2009)
Hookway B., *Interface* (MIT Press 2014)
Hovenkamp H., *The Antitrust Enterprise* (Harvard University Press 2005)
Hovenkamp H., Janis M. D. and Lemley M. A., *IP and Antitrust: An Analysis of Antitrust Practices Applied to Intellectual Property Law* (1st ed., Wolters Kluwer 2002)
Jones A. and Sufrin B., *EU Competition Law* (5th ed., Oxford University Press 2014)
Landes W. M. and Posner R. A., *The Economic Structure of Intellectual Property Law* (Harvard University Press 2009)
Levinson M., *The Box: How the Shipping Container Made the World Smaller and the World Economy Bigger* (2nd ed., Princeton University Press 2016)
Neale A. D., *The Antitrust Laws of the United States of America: A Study of Competition Enforced by Law* (2nd ed., 1970)
Olsen M., *The Logic of Collective Action: Public Goods and the Theory of Groups* (Harvard University Press 1965)
Polinsky M., *An Introduction to Law and Economics* (4th ed., Wolters Kluwer 2011)
Posner R., *Antitrust Law* (2nd ed., University of Chicago Press 2001)
Ruse-Khan H. G., *The Protection of Intellectual Property in International Law* (Oxford University Press Oxford 2016)
Schindler D. and Toman J., *The Laws of Armed Conflicts* (Martinus Nihjoff 1988)
Shapiro C. and Varian H., *Information Rules* (Harvard Business Press 1998)
Shavell S., *Foundations of Economic Analysis of Law* (Belknap Press 2004)
Spurgeon C., *Ethernet: The Definitive Guide* (O'Reilly Media Inc 2000)
Tallinn Manual on the International Law Applicable to Cyber Operations (Cambridge University Press 2013)
Tirole J., *The Theory of Industrial Organization* (MIT Press 1988)
Viehweg T., *Topics and Law* (Peter Lang 1993)
Villarreal A. B., *International Standardization and the Agreement on Technical Barriers to Trade* (Cambridge University Press 2018)
World Intellectual Property Organization, *Guide to the Berne Convention for the Protection of Literary and Artistic Works (Paris Act, 1971)* (World Intellectual Property Organization 1978)

Implications of the TRIPS Agreement on Treaties Administered by WIPO (World Intellectual Property Organization 2002)

Records of the Intellectual Property Conference of Stockholm (1967), vol. 1 (World Intellectual Property Organization 1971)

Records of the Intellectual Property Conference of Stockholm (1967), vol. 2 (World Intellectual Property Organization 1971)

Contributions to Edited Books

Bakhoum M. and Gallego B. C., 'TRIPS and Competition Rules: From Transfer of Technology to Innovation Policy' in Hanns Ullrich and others (eds.), *TRIPS plus 20: From Trade Rules to Market Principles* (Springer 2016)

Baldwin C. Y. and Woodard C. J., 'The Architecture of Platforms: A Unified View' in Annabelle Gawer (ed.), *Platforms, Markets and Innovation* (Edward Elgar, 2009)

Behrens P., 'The Ordoliberal Concept of "Abuse" of a Dominant Position and Its Impact on Article 102 TFEU' in Fabiana di Porto and Rupprecht Podszun (eds.) (Edward Elgar 2018)

Blind K., 'From Standards to Quality Infrastructure' in Panagiotis Delimatsis (ed.), *The Law, Economics and Politics of International Standardisation* (Cambridge University Press 2015)

Bradford A., 'International Antitrust Cooperation and the Preference for Nonbinding Regimes' in Andrew T. Guzman (ed.), *Cooperation, Comity and Competition Policy* (Oxford University Press 2011)

Burk D. L. and Lemley M. A., 'Designing Optimal Software Patents' in Robert W. Hahn (ed.), *Intellectual Property Rights in Frontier Industries: Software and Biotechnology* (AEI Press 2005)

Codding Jr. G. A., 'Three Times Forty: The ITU in a Time of Change' in Lawrence S. Finkelstein (ed.), *Politics in the International System* (Duke University Press 1988)

Contreras J. L., 'Essentiality and Standards-Essential Patents' in Jorge L. Contreras (ed.), *The Cambridge Handbook of Technical Standardization Law: Competition, Antitrust, and Patents* (Cambridge University Press 2017)

'Injunctive Relief in US Patent Cases' in Rafal Sikorski (ed.), *Patent Law Injunctions* (Wolters Kluwer 2018)

Cotropia C. A., 'Compulsory Licensing under TRIPS and the Supreme Court of the United States' Decision in EBay v. MercExchange in Graeme Dinwoodie and Mark D. Janis (eds.), *Patent Law and Theory: A Handbook of Contemporary Research* (Edward Elgar 2009)

Cottier T., 'Embedding Intellectual Property in International Law' in Pedro Roffe and Xavier Seuba (eds.), *Current Alliances in International Intellectual Property Law Rulemaking: The Emergence and Impact of Mega-Regionals*, vol. 4 (ICTSD/SEPI 2017)

Cottier T. and Germann C., 'Agreement on Trade-Related Aspects of Intellectual Property Rights' in Pierre Veron and Thomas Cottier (eds.), *Concise International and European IP Law: TRIPS, Paris Convention, European Enforcement and Transfer of Technology* (3rd ed., Kluwer Law International 2015)

David P. A., 'Some New Standards for the Economics of Standardization in the Information Age' in Partha Dasgupta and Paul Stoneman (eds.), *Economic Policy and Technological Performance* (Cambridge University Press 1987)

de Vries H. J., 'Standardisation' in Panagiotis Delimatsis (ed.), *The Law, Economics and Politics of International Standardisation* (Cambridge University Press 2015)

Djelic M.-L., 'International Competition Network' in Thomas Hale and David Held (eds.), *Handbook of Transnational Governance: Institutions and Innovations* (Polity Press 2011)

Farrell J. and Klemperer P., 'Chapter 31 Coordination and Lock-In: Competition with Switching Costs and Network Effects' in M. Armstrong and R. Porter (eds.), *Handbook of Industrial Organization*, vol. 3 (Elsevier 2007)

Froomkin A. M., 'Semi-Private International Rulemaking: Lessons Learned from the WIPO Domain Name Process Regulating the Global Information Society' in Christopher T. Marsden (ed.), *Regulating the Global Information Society* (Routledge 2001)

Gandal N. and Régibeau P., 'Standard-Setting Organisations' in Panagiotis Delimatsis (ed.), *The Law, Economics and Politics of International Standardisation* (Cambridge University Press 2015)

Gao H., 'Annex on Telecommunications' in Rüdiger Wolfrum, Peter-Tobias Stoll and Clemens Feinäugle (eds.), *WTO-Trade in Services* (Brill Nijhoff 2008)

Goodin R., 'The Collective Action Problem' in Marion Danis and others (eds.), *Fair Resource Allocation and Rationing at the Bedside* (Oxford University Press 2015)

Hale C. J. L. M., 'A Treatise in Three Parts. Pars Prima. De Jure Maris et Brachiorum Ejusdem. Pars Secunda. De Portibus Maris. Pars Tertia. Concerning the Customs of Goods Imported and Exported', *Collection of Tracts Relative to the Law of England* (E. Lynch 1787)

Hesse R. B. and Marshall F., 'U.S. Antitrust Aspects of FRAND Disputes' in Jorge L. Contreras (ed.), The Cambridge Handbook of Technical Standardization Law: Competition, Antitrust and Patents (Cambridge University Press 2017)

Hilty R. M., 'The Role of Enforcement in Delineating the Scope of Intellectual Property Rights' in Hans-W. Micklitz and Andrea Wechsler (eds.), *The Transformation of Enforcement: European Economic Law in Global Perspective* (Hart Publishing 2016)

'Ways Out of the Trap of Article 1(1) TRIPS' in Hanns Ullrich and others (eds.), *TRIPS plus 20: From Trade Rules to Market Principles* (Springer 2016)

Höpperger M. and Senftleben M., 'Protection against Unfair Competition at the International Level – The Paris Convention, the 1996 Model Provisions and the Current Work of the World Intellectual Property Organisation' in Reto M. Hilty and Frauke Henning-Bodewig (eds.), *Law against Unfair Competition: Towards a New Paradigm in Europe?* (Springer 2007)

Hovenkamp H., 'The Legal Periphery of Dominant Firm Conduct' in Abel M. Mateus and Teresa Moreira (eds.), *Competition Law and Economics: Advances in Competition Policy Enforcement in the EU and North America* (Edward Elgar 2010)

Jakobs K., Lemstra W. and Hayes V., 'Creating a Wireless Standard: IEEE 802.11' in Wolter Lemstra, Victor Hayes and John Groenewegen (eds.), *The Innovation Journey of Wi-Fi: The Road to Global Success* (Cambridge University Press 2010)

Johnson A., 'Directive 2004/48/EC of the European Parliament and of the Council of 29 April 2004 on the Enforcement of Intellectual Property Rights', *Concise International and European IP Law: TRIPS, Paris Convention, European Enforcement and Transfer of Technology* (Wolters Kluwer 2014)

Joskow P. L., 'Regulation of Natural Monopoly' in A. Mitchell Polinsky and Stephen Shavell (eds.), *Handbook of Law and Economics*, vol. 2 (North Holland 2007)

Koppell J., 'International Organization for Standardization' in Thomas Hale and David Held (eds.), *Handbook of Transnational Governance: Institutions & Innovation* (Polity Press 2011)

Kur A., 'From Minimum Standards to Maximum Rules' in Hanns Ullrich and others (eds.), *TRIPS plus 20: From Trade Rules to Market Principles* (Springer 2016)

Langlois R. N., 'Technological Standards, Innovation and Essential Facilities: Toward a Schumpeterian Post-Chicago Approach' in Jerry Ellig (ed.), Dynamic Competition and Public Policy: Technology, Innovation and Antitrust Issues (Cambridge University Press 2001)

Larouche P. and others, 'Continental Drift in the Treatment of Dominant Firms: Article 102 TFEU in Contrast to Section 2 Sherman Act', *The Oxford Handbook of International Antitrust Economics*, vol. 2 (Oxford University Press 2014)

Mann C. and Liu X., 'The Information Technology Agreement: Sui Generis or Model Stepping Stone' in Richard Baldwin and Patrick Low (eds.), *Multilateralizing Regionalism: Challenges for the Global Trading System* (Cambridge University Press 2009)

Menell P. S. and Scotchmer S., 'Intellectual Property Law' in A. Mitchell Polinsky and Stephen Shavell (eds.), *Handbook of Law and Economics*, vol. 2 (North-Holland 2007)

Nagaoka S., Tsukada N. and Shimbo T., 'The Structure and the Emergence of Essential Patents for Standards: Lessons from Three IT Standards' in Uwe Cantner, Jean-Luc Gaffard and Lionel Nesta (eds.), *Schumpeterian Perspectives on Innovation, Competition and Growth* (Springer 2009)

Neef A. and Reyes-Knoche S., 'Article 27. Patentable Subject Matter' in Peter-Tobias Stoll, Jan Busche and Katrin Arend (eds.), *WTO-Trade-Related Aspects of Intellectual Property Rights* (Brill Nijhoff 2009)

Reyes-Knoche, S., 'Article 29. Conditions On Patent Applicants' in Peter-Tobias Stoll, Jan Busche and Katrin Arend (eds.), *WTO-Trade-Related Aspects of Intellectual Property Rights* (Brill Nijhoff 2009)

Risse A., 'Injunctions in Germany' in Rafal Sikorski (ed.), *Patent Law Injunctions* (Wolters Kluwer 2018)

Sachs J. D. and McArthur J. W., 'Technological Advancement and Long-Term Economic Growth in Asia' in Chong-En Bai and Chi-Wa Yuen (eds.), *Technology and the New Economy* (MIT Press 2002)

Seaman C. B. and others, 'Lost Profits and Disgorgement' in C. Bradford Biddle and others (eds.), *Patent Remedies and Complex Products: Towards a Global Consensus* (Cambridge University Press 2019)

Shapiro C., 'Navigating the Patent Thicket: Cross Licenses, Patent Pools, and Standard Setting' in Adam B. Laffe, Josh Lerner and Scott Stern (eds.), *Innovation Policy and the Economy*, vol. 1 (MIT Press 2001)

Sikorski R., 'Patent Law Injunctions in the European Union Law' in Rafal Sikorski (ed.), *Patent Law Injunctions* (Wolters Kluwer 2018)

Suzuki M., 'Enforcement of FRAND-Encumbered SEPs' in Kung-Chung Liu (ed.), *Annotated Leading Patent Cases in Major Asian Jurisdictions* (City University of Hong Kong Press 2017)

Sykes W., 'International Law' in A. Mitchell Polinsky and Stephen Shavell (eds.), *Handbook of Law and Economics*, vol. 1 (Elsevier 2007)

Taubman A., Wager H. and Watal J. (eds.), *A Handbook on the WTO TRIPS Agreement* (Cambridge University Press 2012)

Teubner G., 'Foreword: Legal Regimes of Global Non-State Actors' in Gunther Teubner (ed.), *Global Law without a State* (Dartmouth Publishing Company 1996)

—— '"Global Bukowina": Legal Pluralism in the World Society' in Gunther Teubner (ed.), *Global Law without a State* (Dartmouth Publishing Company 1996)

Zhang L., 'Injunctive Relief in China's Patent Law' in Rafal Sikorski (ed.), *Patent Law Injunctions* (Wolters Kluwer 2018)

Journal Articles

Abbott K. W. and Snidal D., 'Hard and Soft Law in International Governance' (2000) 54 International Organization 421

Afori O. F., 'Flexible Remedies as a Means to Counteract Failures in Copyright Law' (2011) 29 Cardozo Arts & Entertainment Law Review 1

Ahlborn C. and Evans D. S., 'The Microsoft Judgement and Its Implications for Competition Policy Towards Dominant Firms in Europe' (2008) 75 Antitrust Law Journal 887

Ahlborn C., Evans D. S. and Padilla A. J., 'The Antitrust Economics of Tying: A Farewell to Per Se Illegality Antitrust in the U.S. and EU: Converging or Diverging Paths' (2004) 49 Antitrust Bulletin 287

'The Logic & Limits of the Exceptional Circumstances Test in Magill and IMS Health' (2004) 28 Fordham International Law Journal 1109

Alban D., 'Rambus v Infineon: Patent Disclosures in Standard-Setting Organizations' (2004) 19 Berkeley Technology Law Journal 309

Ali A. N. A., 'Comparison Study between IPV4 & IPV6' (2012) 9 International Journal of Computer Science Issues 314

Almeling D.S., 'Four Reasons to Enact a Federal Trade Secrets Act' (2009) 19 Fordham Intellectual Property, Media and Entertainment Law Journal 770

'Altera v. Clear Logic: 424 F.3d 1079 (9th Circuit, 2005)' (2007) 22(1) Berkeley Technology Law Journal 391

Anderson P. and Tushman M. L., 'Technological Discontinuities and Dominant Designs: A Cyclical Model of Technological Change' (1990) 35 Administrative Science Quarterly 604

Andrews J. G. and others, 'What Will 5 G Be?' (2014) 32 IEEE Journal on Selected Areas in Communications 1065

Angelov M., 'The "Exceptional Circumstances" Test: Implications for Frand Commitments from the Essential Facilities Doctrine Under Article 102 TFEU' (2014) 10 European Competition Journal 37

Antonelli C., 'Technological Knowledge as an Essential Facility' (2007) 17 Journal of Evolutionary Economics 451

Ard B., 'More Property Rules than Property? The Right to Exclude in Patent and Copyright' (2019) 68 Emory Law Journal 685

Areeda P., 'Essential Facilities: An Epithet in Need of Limiting Principles' (1989) 58 Antitrust Law Journal 841

Asay C. D., 'Software's Copyright Anticommons' (2016) 66 Emory Law Journal 265

Atzori L., Iera A. and Morabito G., 'The Internet of Things: A Survey' (2010) 54 Computer Networks 2787

Ballardini R. M., 'Software Patents in Europe: The Technical Requirement Dilemma' (2008) 3 Journal of Intellectual Property Law & Practice 563

Baron J. and Spulber D., 'Technology Standards and Standard Setting Organizations: Introduction to the Searle Center Database' (2018) 27 Journal of Economics & Management Strategy 462

'The Software Patent Thicket: A Matter of Disclosure' (2009) 6 SCRIPTed 207

Baumol W. J. and Swanson D. G., 'Reasonable and Nondiscriminatory (RAND) Royalties, Standards Selection, And Control of Market Power' (2005) 73 Antitrust Law Journal 1

Beebe B., 'An Empirical Study of US Copyright Fair Use Opinions, 1978–2005' (2008) 156 University of Pennsylvania Law Review 549

Bekkers R., Bongard R. and Nuvolari A., 'An Empirical Study on the Determinants of Essential Patent Claims in Compatibility Standards' (2011) 40 Research Policy 1001

Bell A. and Parchomovsky G., 'Restructuring Copyright Infringement' (2020) 98 Texas Law Review 689

Bender G.A., 'Clash of the Titans: The Territoriality of Patent Law vs. The European Union' (2000) 40 Idea 49

Bendix K., 'Copyright Damages: Incorporating Reasonable Royalty from Patent Law' (2012) 27 Berkeley Technology Law Journal 527

Besen S. and Farrell J., 'The Role of the ITU in Standardization: Pre-Eminence, Impotence or Rubber Stamp?' (1991) 15 Telecommunications Policy 311

Bharadwaj A. and Verma D., 'China's First Injunction in Standard Essential Patent Litigation' (2017) 12 Journal of Intellectual Property Law & Practice 717

Bi Q., Zysman G. I. and Menkes H., 'Wireless Mobile Communications at the Start of the 21st Century' [2001] IEEE Communications Magazine 110

Biddle B. and others, 'The Expanding Role and Importance of Standards in the Information and Communications Technology Industry' (2012) 52 Jurimetrics 177

Blair R. D. and Esquibel A. K., 'The Microsoft Muddle: A Caveat Symposium: Microsoft and the United States Department of Justice' (1995) 40 Antitrust Bulletin 257

Blind K., 'An Economic Analysis of Standards Competition: The Example of ISO ODF and OOXML Standards' (2011) 35 Telecommunications Policy 373

Bowman W. S., 'Tying Arrangements and the Leverage Problem' (1957) 67 Yale Law Journal 19

Bradford A., 'International Antitrust Negotiations and the False Hope of the WTO' (2007) 48 Harvard International Law Journal 383

Brummer C., 'Why Soft Law Dominates International Finance—and Not Trade' (2010) 13 Journal of International Economic Law 623

Budzinski O., 'The International Competition Network: Prospects and Limits on the Road towards International Competition Governance' (2004) 8 Competition and Change 223

Calabresi G. R. and Melamed A. D., 'Property Rules, Liability Rules, and Inalienability: One View of the Cathedral' (1972) 85 Harvard Law Review 1089

Carlton D. W. and Waldman M., 'The Strategic Use of Tying to Preserve and Create Market Power in Evolving Industries' (2002) 33 The RAND Journal of Economics 194

Cashore B., 'Legitimacy and the Privatization of Environmental Governance: How Non-State Market-Driven (NSMD) Governance Systems Gain Rule-Making Authority' (2002) 15 Governance 503

Chang E. K., 'Expanding Definition of Monopoly Leveraging' (2009) 17 University of Miami Business Law Review 325

Chao B., 'Lost Profits in a Multicomponent World' (2018) 59 Boston College Law Review 1321

Chiao B., Lerner J. and Tirole J., 'The Rules of Standard-setting Organizations: An Empirical Analysis' (2007) 38 The RAND Journal of Economics 905

Church J. and Gandal N., 'Network Effects, Software Provision, and Standardization' (1992) 40 The Journal of Industrial Economics 85

Coase R., 'The Problem of Social Cost' (1960) 3 Journal of Law and Economics 1

Codding G. A., 'The International Telecommunication Union: 130 Years of Telecommunications Regulation' (1994) 23 Denver Journal of International Law and Policy 501

Congleton R. D., 'The Logic of Collective Action and Beyond' (2015) 164 Public Choice 217

Contreras J. L., 'Fixing FRAND: A Pseudo-Pool Approach to Standards-Based Patent Licensing' (2013) 79 Antitrust Law Journal 47

'A Market Reliance Theory for FRAND Commitments and Other Patent Pledges' (2015) 2 Utah Law Review 479

Cotropia C. A. and Lemley M. A., 'Copying in Patent Law' (2008) 87 North Carolina Law Review 1421

Cotter T. F., 'Intellectual Property and the Essential Facilities Doctrine' (1999) 44 Antitrust Bulletin 211

'Patent Holdup, Patent Remedies and Antitrust Responses' (2009) 34 Journal of Corporation Law 1151

'Comparative Law and Economics of Standard-Essential Patents and FRAND Royalties' (2013) 22 Texas Intellectual Property Law Journal 311

Craig J. A., 'Deconstructing Wonderland: Making Sense of Software Patents in a Post-Alice World' (2017) 32 Berkeley Technology Law Journal 359

Cremers K. and others, 'Patent Litigation in Europe' (2017) 44 European Journal of Law and Economics 1

Dai J., Deng Z. and Jung S. K., 'Antitrust Enforcement against Standard Essential Patents in China' (2017) 62 The Antitrust Bulletin 453

David P. A., 'Clio and the Economics of QWERTY' (1985) 75 American Economic Review 332

DeBriyn J., 'Shedding Light on Copyright Trolls: An Analysis of Mass Copyright Litigation in the Age of Statutory Damages' (2012) 19 UCLA Entertainment Law Review 79

Demestichas P. and others, 'Emerging Air Interfaces and Management Technologies for the 5 G Era' (2017) 2017 EURASIP Journal on Wireless Communications and Networking 184

Demsetz H., 'When Does the Rule of Liability Matter?' (1972) 1 The Journal of Legal Studies 13

Depoorter B., 'Property Rules, Liability Rules and Patent Market Failure' (2008) 01 Erasmus Law Review 59

'Copyright Enforcement in the Digital Age: When the Remedy Is the Wrong' (2019) 66 UCLA Law Review 400

Doherty B., 'Just What Are Essential Facilities?' (2001) 38 Common Market Law Review 397

Dolmans M., 'Standards for Standards European Union Law' (2002) 26 Fordham International Law Journal 163, 181

Donahey T. I., 'Terminal Railroad Revisited: Using the Essential Facilities Doctrine to Ensure Accessibility to Internet Software Standards' (1997) 25 AIPLA Quarterly Journal 277

Drexl J., 'International Competition Policy after Cancun: Placing a Singapore Issue on the WTO Development Agenda' (2004) 27 World Competition 419

Duan C., 'Internet of Infringing Things: The Effect of Computer Interface Copyrights on Technology Standards' (2019) 45 Rutgers Computer & Technology Law Journal 1

Dufaux F., Sullivan G. J. and Ebrahimi T., 'The JPEG XR Image Coding Standard [Standards in a Nutshell]' (2009) 26 IEEE Signal Processing Magazine 195

Economides N., 'The Microsoft Antitrust Case' (2001) 1 Journal of Industry, Competition and Trade 7

Economides N. and Lianos I., 'Elusive Antitrust Standard on Bundling in Europe and in the United States in the Aftermath of the Microsoft Cases' (2009) 76 Antitrust Law Journal 483

Economides N. and Salop S. C., 'Competition and Integration Among Complements, and Network Market Structure' (1992) 40 The Journal of Industrial Economics 105

Economides N. and White L. J., 'Access and Interconnection Pricing: How Efficient Is the "Efficient Component Pricing Rule"?' (1995) 40 The Antitrust Bulletin 557

Eilmansberger T., 'The Essential Facilities Doctrine Under Art. 82: What Is the State of Affairs after IMS Health and Microsoft?' (2005) 16 King's Law Journal 329

Elhauge E., 'Defining Better Monopolization Standards' (2003) 56 Stanford Law Review 253

Evans D. S. and Padilla A. G., 'Designing Antitrust Rules for Assessing Unilateral Practices: A Neo-Chicago Approach' (2005) 72 University of Chicago Law Review 73

Evans D. S. and Padilla A. J., 'Excessive Prices: Using Economics to Define Administrable Legal Rules' (2005) 1 Journal of Competition Law & Economics 97

Evrard S. J., 'Essential Facilities in the European Union: Bronner and Beyond' (2004) 10 Columbia Journal of European Law 491

Farrell J. and others, 'Standard-Setting, Patents and Hold-Up' (2007) 74 Antitrust Law Journal 603

Farrell J. and Saloner G., 'Standardization, Compatibility and Innovation' (1985) 16 The RAND Journal of Economics 70

First H., 'Microsoft and the Evolution of the Intellectual Property Concept' [2006] Wisconsin Law Review 1369

Fox E., 'Competition Law and the Millennium Round' (1999) 2 Journal of International Economic Law 665

Franck T. M., 'Legitimacy in the International System' (1988) 82 The American Journal of International Law 705

Frischmann B. and Waller S. W., 'Revitalizing Essential Facilities' (2008) 74 Antitrust Law Journal 1

Funk J. L., 'The Co-Evolution of Technology and Methods of Standard Setting: The Case of the Mobile Phone Industry' (2008) 19 Journal of Evolutionary Economics 73

Galetovic A. and Haber S., 'Innovation Under Threat? An Assessment of the Evidence for Patent Hold-Up and Royalty Stacking in SEP-Intensive, IT Industries' (2016) 3 Competition Policy International Journal

 'The Fallacies of Patent Holdup Theory' (2017) 13(1) Journal of Competition Law & Economics 1

Gandal N., 'Compatibility, Standardization and Network Effects: Some Policy Implications' (2002) 18 Oxford Review of Economic Policy 80

Gandal N. and Shy O., 'Standardization Policy and International Trade' (2001) 53 Journal of International Economics 363

Geiger C. and others, 'Declaration A Balanced Interpretation of the "Three-Step Test" in Copyright Law' (2010) 1 Journal of Intellectual Property, Information Technology and Electronic Commerce Law 119

Geiger C., Gervais D. J. and Senftleben M., 'The Three Step Test Revisited: How to Use the Test's Flexibility in National Copyright Law' (2014) 29 American University International Law Review 581

Genschel P., 'How Fragmentation Can Improve Co-Ordination: Setting Standards in International Telecommunications' (1997) 18 Organization Studies 603

Gerardin D., 'Limiting the Scope of Article 82 EC: What Can the EU Learn from the U.S. Supreme Court's Judgment in Trinko in the Wake of Microsoft, IMS and Deutsche Telekom?' (2004) 41 Common Market Law Review 1519

Gerardin D., Layne-Farrar A. and Padilla A. J., 'The Complements Problem within Standard Setting: Assessing the Evidence on Royalty Stacking' (2008) 14 Boston University Journal of Science, Technology and Law 144

Gerber D.J., 'Rethinking the Monopolist's Duty to Deal: A Legal and Economic Critique of the Doctrine of "Essential Facilities"' (1988) 74 Virginia Law Review 1069

Gervais D. J., 'Towards a New Core International Copyright Norm: The Reverse Three-Step Test' (2005) 9 Marquette Intellectual Property Law Review 1

Gilbert R. J. and Katz M. L., 'Should Good Patents Come in Small Packages? A Welfare Analysis of Intellectual Property Bundling' (2006) 24 International Journal of Industrial Organization 931

Ginsburg D. H. and others, 'The Troubling Use of Antitrust to Regulate FRAND Licensing' (2015) 10 CPI Antitrust Chronicle 2

Ginsburg J. C., 'Copyright, Common Law and Sui Generis Protection of Databases in the United States and Abroad' (1997) 66 University of Cincinnati Law Review 151

'Towards Supranational Copyright Law? The WTO Panel Decision and the "Three-Step Test" for Copyright Exceptions' (2001) 3 Revue Internationale du Droit d'Auteur 7

Giocoli N., 'Competition versus Property Rights: American Antitrust Law, the Freiburg School, and the Early Years of European Competition Policy' (2009) 5 Journal of Competition Law & Economics 747

Glazer K., 'The IMS Health Case: A US Perspective' (2006) 13 George Mason Law Review 1197

Goold P. R., 'The Interpretive Argument for a Balanced Three-Step Test?' (2017) 33 American University International Law Review 187

Grasso R., 'The ECJ Ruling in Huawei and the Right to Seek Injunctions Based on FRAND-Encumbered SEPs under EU Competition Law: One Step Forward' (2016) 39 World Competition 213

Gratz J. A. and Lemley M. A., 'Platforms and Interoperability in Oracle v Google' (2018) 31 Harvard Journal of Law & Technology 603

Guan W., 'Diversified FRAND Enforcement and TRIPS Integrity' (2018) 17 World Trade Review 91

Guzman A. T. and Meyer T. L., 'International Soft Law' (2010) 2 Journal of Legal Analysis 171

Hancock P., 'From State Street Bank to CLS Bank and Back: Reforming Software Patents to Promote Innovation' (2013) 16 Vanderbilt Journal of Entertainment and Technology Law 425

Harz M. H., 'Dominance and Duty in the European Union: A Look through Microsoft Windows at the Essential Facilities Doctrine Comment' (1997) 11 Emory International Law Review 189

Hay G. A., 'A Monopolist's "Duty to Deal": The Briar Patch Revisited' (2002) 3 Sedona Conference Journal 1

Hayek F., 'The Use of Knowledge in Society' (1945) 35 American Economic Review 519

Hiertz G. R. and others, 'The IEEE 802.11 Universe' (2010) IEEE Communications Magazine 62

Holzapfel H. and Sarnoff J. D., 'A Cross-Atlantic Dialog on Experimental Use and Research Tools' (2008) 48 IDEA Intellectual Property Law Review 123

Hou L., 'Qualcomm: How China Has Invalidated Traditional Business Models on Standard Essential Patents' (2016) 7 Journal of European Competition Law & Practice 686

Hovenkamp H., 'Symposium: Intellectual Property Rights and Federal Antitrust Policy – Introduction Symposium: Intellectual Property Rights and Federal Antitrust Policy: Introduction' (1999) 24 Journal of Corporation Law 477

'Standards Ownership and Competition Policy' (2007) 48 Boston College Law Review 87

Huang Y., Wang E. X.-R. and Zhang R. X., 'Essential Facilities Doctrine and Its Application in Intellectual Property Space under China's Anti-Monopoly Law' (2015) 22 George Mason Law Review 1103

Hylton K. N., 'Economic Rents and Essential Facilities' (1991) Brigham Young University Law Review 1243

International Institute of Humanitarian Law, 'San Remo Manual on International Law Applicable to Armed Conflicts at Sea' (1995) November–December 1995 International Review of the Red Cross 595

Jacobs K., Procter R. N. and Williams R. A., 'The Making of Standards: Looking inside the Work Groups' (2001) 39 IEEE Communications Magazine 102

Ji H. H., 'District Courts versus the USITC: Considering Exclusionary Relief for F/Rand-Encumbered Standard-Essential Patents Note' (2014) 21 Michigan Telecommunications and Technology Law Review 169

Jin L. and Ying Y., 'Why Copyright Protection Falls Behind the Requirement for Protecting Graphic User Interfaces: Case Studies on Limitations of Protection for GUIs in China' (2012) 3 IP Theory 6

Kaplow L., 'The Patent-Antitrust Intersection: A Reappraisal' (1984) 97 Harvard Law Review 1813

Kaplow L. and Shavell S., 'Property Rules Versus Liability Rules: An Economic Analysis' (1996) 109 Harvard Law Review 713

Katz M. L. and Shapiro C., 'Systems Competition and Network Effects' (1994) 8 The Journal of Economic Perspectives 93

Keil T., 'De Facto Standardization through Alliances – Lessons from Bluetooth' (2002) 26 Telecommunications Policy 205

Kens P., 'Property, Liberty and the Rights of the Community: Lessons from Munn v Illinois' (2011) 30 Buffalo Public International Law Journal 157

Keszbom A. and Goldman A. V., 'No Shortcut to Antitrust Analysis: The Twisted Journey of the "Essential Facilities" Doctrine' (1996) 1996 Columbia Business Law Review 1

Kim J. and Lee I., '802.11 WLAN: History and New Enabling MIMO Techniques for next Generation Standards' (2015) 53 IEEE Communications Magazine 134

Klein H., 'ICANN and Internet Governance: Leveraging Technical Coordination to Realize Global Public Policy' (2002) 18 The Information Society 193

Koelman K. J., 'Fixing the Three-Step Test' (2006) 28 European Intellectual Property Review 407

Kolasky W. J., 'Network Effects: A Contrarian View' (1999) 7 George Mason Law Review 577

Krechmer K., 'The Fundamental Nature of Standards: Technical Perspective' (2000) 38 IEEE Communications Magazine 70

Kreiss R. A., 'Patent Protection for Computer Programs and Mathematical Algorithms: The Constitutional Limitations on Patentable Subject Matter' (1999) 29 New Mexico Law Review 31

Kreuzbauer G., 'Topics in Contemporary Legal Argumentation: Some Remarks on the Topical Nature of Legal Argumentation in the Continental Law Tradition' (2008) 28 Informal Logic 71

Krier J. E. and Schwab S. J., 'Property Rules and Liability Rules: The Cathedral in Another Light' (1995) 70 New York University Law Review 440

Lang J. T., 'Defining Legitimate Competition: Companies' Duties to Supply Competitors and Access to Essential Facilities' (1994) 18 Fordham International Law Journal 437

Lao M., 'Networks, Access and "Essential Facilities": From Terminal Railroad to Microsoft' (2009) 62 Southern Methodist University Law Review 557

Layne-Farrar A., 'Moving Past the SEP Rand Obsession: Some Thoughts on the Economic Implications of Unilateral Commitments and the Complexities of Patent Licensing' (2013) 21 George Mason Law Review 1093

Layne-Farrar A., Padilla A. J. and Schmalensee R., 'Pricing Patents for Licensing in Standard-Setting Organizations: Making Sense of Frand Commitments' (2007) 74 Antitrust Law Journal 671

   'Pricing Patents for Licensing in Standard-Setting Organizations: Making Sense of FRAND Commitments' (2007) 74 Antitrust Law Journal 671

Layne-Farrar A. and Salinger M. A., 'Bundling of RAND-Committed Patents' (2016) 45 Research Policy 1155

Layne-Farrar A. and Wong-Ervin K. W., 'Methodologies for Calculating FRAND Damages: An Economic and Comparative Analysis of the Case Law from China, the European Union, India, and the United States' (2017) 8 Jindal Global Law Review 127

Leal-Arcas R., 'China's Attitude to Multilateralism in International Economic Law and Governance: Challenges for the World Trading System' (2010) 11 The Journal of World Investment & Trade 259

Leiner B. M. and others, 'A Brief History of the Internet' (2009) 39 Computer Communication Review 22

Lemley M., 'Intellectual Property Rights and Standards-Setting Organizations' (2002) 90 California Law Review 1889

 'Ten Things to Do about Patent Holdup of Standards (and One Not To)' (2007) 48 Boston College Law Review 148

 'The Surprising Virtues of Treating Trade Secrets as IP Rights' (2008) 61 Stanford Law Review 311

 'Distinguishing Lost Profits from Reasonable Royalties' (2009) 51 William and Mary Law Review 655

 'Contracting Around Liability Rules' (2012) 100 California Law Review 463

Lemley M. A. and Shapiro C., 'A Simple Approach to Setting Reasonable Royalties for Standard-Essential Patents' (2013) 28 Berkeley Technology Law Journal 1135

Lemley M. A. and Weiser P. J., 'Should Property or Liability Rules Govern Information?' (2006) 85 Texas Law Review 783

Lerner J. and Tirole J., 'A Model of Forum Shopping' (2006) 96 American Economic Review 1091

 'Standard-Essential Patents' (2015) 123 Journal of Political Economy 547

Levanen T. and others, 'Radio Interface Evolution towards 5 G and Enhanced Local Area Communications' (2014) 2 IEEE Access 1005

Leveque F., 'Innovation, Leveraging and Essential Facilities: Interoperability Licensing in the EU Microsoft Case' (2005) 28 World Competition 71

Levi E. H., 'The Antitrust Laws and Monopoly' (1947) 14 The University of Chicago Law Review 153

Li B. C., 'The Global Convergence of FRAND Licensing Practices: Towards Interoperable Legal Standards Patent Law' (2016) 31 Berkeley Technology Law Journal 429

Li Y., 'The Current Dilemma and Future of Software Patenting' (2019) 50 International Review of Intellectual Property and Competition Law 823

Li Y. B., 'Antitrust Correction for Qualcomm's SEPs Package Licensing and Its Flexibility in China' (2016) 47 International Review of Intellectual Property and Competition Law 336

Liebowitz S. J. and Margolis S. E., 'The Fable of the Keys' (1990) 33 Journal of Law & Economics 1

 'Path Dependence, Lock-In and History' (1995) 11 Journal of Law, Economics & Organization 205

Lim A. S., 'Inter-Consortia Battles in Mobile Payments Standardisation' (2008) 7 Electronic Commerce Research and Applications 202

Lim D., 'Beyond Microsoft: Intellectual Property, Peer Production and the Law's Concern with Market Dominance' (2008) 18 Fordham Intellectual Property, Media & Entertainment Law Journal 291

Lipsky A. B. and Sidak J. G., 'Essential Facilities' (1998) 51 Stanford Law Review 1187

Liu H.-W., 'International Standards in Flux: A Balkanized ICT Standard-Setting Paradigm and Its Implications for the WTO' (2014) 17 Journal of International Economic Law 551

Liu J., 'Copyright Injunctions after EBay: An Empirical Study' (2012) 16 Lewis & Clark Law Review 215

Longhofer F. K., 'Patentability of Computer Programs Comment' (1982) 34 Baylor Law Review 125

Lucas A., 'For a Reasonable Interpretation of the Three-Step Test' (2010) 32 European Intellectual Property Review 277

MacCord A., 'Infringing a Standard-Essential Patent, or Not [Patent Reviews]' (2015) 2 IEEE Power Electronics Magazine 14

Mace A. C., 'TRIPS, EBay and Denials of Injunctive Relief: Is Article 31 Compliance Everything?' (2009) X Columbia Science and Technology Journal 233

Marsden P. and Bishop S., 'Intellectual Leaders Still Need Ground to Stand On' (2007) 3 European Competition Journal 315

Marshall J., 'Aggravated or Exemplary Damages for Copyright Infringement' (2017) 39 European Intellectual Property Review 565

Marsnik S. J. and Thomas R., 'Drawing a Line in the Patent Subject Matter Sands: Does Europe Provide a Solution to the Software & Business Method Patent Problem?' (2011) 34 Boston College International & Comparative Law Review 227

McAllister B. P., 'Lord Hale and Business Affected with a Public Interest' (1930) 43 Harvard Law Review 759

McIntyre S., 'Trying to Agree on Three Articles of Law: The Idea/Expression Dichotomy in Chinese Copyright Law' (2010) 1 Cybaris 62

Meddeb A., 'Internet of Things Standards: Who Stands out from the Crowd?' (2016) 54 IEEE Communications Magazine 40

Menell P. S., 'API Copyrightability Bleak House: Unraveling and Repairing the Oracle v. Google Jurisdictional Mess' (2016) 31 Berkeley Technology Law Journal 1515

 'Rise of the API Copyright Dead: An Updated Epitaph for Copyright Protection of Network and Functional Features of Computer Software' (2017) 31 Harvard Journal of Law & Technology 305

Merges R. P., 'Of Property Rights, Coase and Intellectual Property' (1994) 94 Columbia Law Review 2655

 'Contracting into Liability Rules: Intellectual Property Rights and Collective Rights Organizations' (1996) 84 California Law Review 1293

Miao M. and Jayakar K., 'Mobile Payments in Japan, South Korea and China: Cross-Border Convergence or Divergence of Business Models?' (2016) 40 Telecommunications Policy 182

Miyashita Y., 'International Protection of Computer Software' (1991) 11 The John Marshall Journal of Information Technology & Privacy Law 41

Möschel W., 'The Proper Scope of Government Viewed from an Ordoliberal Perspective: The Example of Competition Policy' (2001) 157 Journal of Institutional and Theoretical Economics (JITE)/Zeitschrift für die gesamte Staatswissenschaft 3

Mowery D. C. and Simcoe T., 'Is the Internet a US Invention?—An Economic and Technological History of Computer Networking' (2002) 31 NELSON + WINTER + 20 1369

Mueller M. M. and Badiei F., 'Governing Internet Territory: ICANN, Sovereignty Claims, Property Rights and Country Code Top-Level Domains' (2017) XVIII Columbia Science and Technology Journal 435

National Commission on New Technological Uses of Copyrighted Works (CONTU), 'Final Report on the National Commission on New Technological Uses of Copyrighted Works' (1981) 3 The John Marshall of Information Technology & Privacy Law 53

Nimmer D., 'Investigating the Hypothetical Reasonable Royalty for Copyright Infringement' (2019) 99 Boston University Law Review 1

Ohta M., 'IETF and Internet Standards' (1998) IEEE Communications Magazine 126

O'Rourke M., 'Toward a Doctrine of Fair Use in Patent Law' (2000) 100 Columbia Law Review 1177

Ozcan P. and Santos F. M., 'The Market That Never Was: Turf Wars and Failed Alliances in Mobile Payments' (2015) 36 Strategic Management Journal 1486

Pelkmans J., 'Making EU Network Markets Competitive' (2001) 17 Oxford Review of Economic Policy 432

Phillips J., 'EBay's Effect on Copyright Injunctions: When Property Rules Give Way to Liability Rules II. Copyright – Note' – Berkeley Technology Law Journal 405

Pitofsky R., Patterson D. and Hooks J., 'The Essential Facilities Doctrine Under United States Antitrust Law' (2002) 70 Antitrust Law Journal 443

Polinsky A. M., 'On the Choice between Liability Rules and Property Rules' (1980) XVIII Economic Inquiry 233

Portugal-Perez A., Reyes J.-D. and Wilson J. S., 'Beyond the Information Technology Agreement: Harmonisation of Standards and Trade in Electronics' (2010) 33 The World Economy 1870

Posner R. A., 'Natural Monopoly and Its Regulation' (1968) 21 Stanford Law Review 548

Puffert D. J., 'Path Dependence in Spatial Networks: The Standardization of Railway Track Gauge' (2002) 39 Explorations in Economic History 282

Radomsky L., 'Sixteen Years after the Passage of the US Semiconductor Chip Protection Act: Is International Protection Working' (2000) 15 Berkeley Technology Law Journal 1050

Ratner J. R., 'Should There Be an Essential Facility Doctrine' (1988) 21 U.C. Davis Law Review 327

Raustiala K., 'Governing the Internet' (2016) 110 American Journal of International Law 491

Raymond M. and DeNardis L., 'Multistakeholderism: Anatomy of an Inchoate Global Institution' (2015) 7 International Theory 572

Reiffen D. and Kleit A. N., 'Terminal Railroad Revisited: Foreclosure of an Essential Facility or Simple Horizontal Monopoly?' (1990) 33 The Journal of Law and Economics 419

Risberg R. L. Jr, 'Five Years without Infringement Litigation under the Semiconductor Chip Protection Act: Unmasking the Spectre of Chip Piracy in an Era of Diverse and Incompatible Process Technologies Comment' Wisconsin Law Review 241

Ritter C., 'Refusal to Deal and "Essential Facilities": Does Intellectual Property Require Special Deference Compared to Tangible Property?' (2005) 28 World Competition 281

Rochet J.-C. and Tirole J. (2003) 1 Journal of the European Economic Association 990

Rose I. and Nqwe C., 'The Ordoliberal Tradition in the European Union, Its Influence on Article 82 EC and the IBA's Comments on the Article 82 EC Discussion Paper Papers from the Chicago Conference' (2007) 3 Competition Law International 8

Russell A. L., '"Rough Consensus and Running Code" and the Internet-OSI Standards War' (2006) 28 IEEE Annals of the History of Computing 48

Rysman M., 'Competition between Networks: A Study of the Market for Yellow Pages' (2004) 71 The Review of Economic Studies 483

Rysman M. and Simcoe T., 'Patents and the Performance of Voluntary Standard-Setting Organizations' (2008) 54 Management Science 1920

Saint-Antoine P. H. and Trego G. D., 'Solutions to Patent Hold-up beyond FRAND: An SOS to SSOs' (2014) 59 The Antitrust Bulletin 183

Saltzman J., Chatterjee S. and Raman M., 'A Framework for ICT Standards Creation: The Case of ITU-T Standard H.350' (2008) 33 Information Systems 285

Samuelson P., 'Are Patents on Interfaces Impeding Interoperability?' (2009) 93 Minnesota Law Review 1943

   'The Past, Present and Future of Software Copyright Interoperability Rules in the European Union and United States' (2012) 34 European Intellectual Property Review 229

'Unbundling Fair Uses' (2009) 77 Fordham Law Review 2537

'The Uneasy Case for Software Copyrights Revisited' (2010) 79 George Washington Law Review 1746

Samuelson P. and Wheatland T., 'Statutory Damages in Copyright Law: A Remedy in Need of Reform' (2009) 51 William and Mary Law Review 439

Sandler T., 'Overcoming Global and Regional Collective Action Impediments' (2010) 1 Global Policy 40

Schaffer G. C. and Pollack M. A., 'Hard versus Soft Law in International Security' (2011) 52 Boston College Law Review 1147

Senftleben M., 'Towards a Horizontal Standard for Limiting Intellectual Property Rights? WTO Panel Reports Shed Light on the Three-Step Test in Copyright Law and Related Tests in Patent and Trademark Law' (2006) 37 International Review of Intellectual Property and Competition Law 407

Siebrasse N. V. and Cotter T. F., 'Judicially Determined FRAND Royalties' (2016) 68 Florida Law Review 929

Shapiro C. and Lemley M. A., 'Patent Holdup and Royalty Stacking' (2007) 85 Texas Law Review 1992

Sheremata W., 'Barriers to Innovation: A Monopoly, Network Externalities, and the Speed of Innovation' (1997) 42 The Antitrust Bulletin 937

Sherlock I., 'Wi-Fi Alliance: Connecting Everyone and Everything, Everywhere' (2017) 1 IEEE Communications Standards Magazine 6

Sidak J. G., 'The Meaning of FRAND, Part I: Royalties' (2013) 9 Journal of Competition Law & Economics 931

'What Aggregate Royalty Do Manufacturers of Mobile Phones Pay to License Standard-Essential Patents?' (2016) 1 The Criterion Journal on Innovation 701

Skitol R. A., 'Concerted Buying Power: Its Potential for Addressing the Patent Holdup Problem in Standard Setting Symposium: Buyer Power and Antitrust' (2005) 72(2) Antitrust Law Journal 727

Smith H. E., 'Intellectual Property as Property: Delineating Entitlements in Information' (2007) 116 Yale Law Journal 1742

Sokol D. and Zheng W., 'FRAND in China' (2013) 22 Texas Intellectual Property Law Journal 71

Stasik E., 'Royalty Rates and Licensing Strategies for Essential Patents on LTE (4 G) Telecommunication Standards' (2010) 3 les Nouvelles 114

Stoeckli W., 'Topic and Argumentation: The Contribution of Viehweg and Perelman in the Field of Methodology as Applied to Law' (1968) 54 Archives for Philosophy of Law and Social Philosophy 581

Strandburg K. J., 'Patent Fair Use 2.0' (2011) 1 University of California Irvine Law Review 265

Strickling L. E. and Hill J. F., 'Multi-Stakeholder Internet Governance: Successes and Opportunities' (2017) 2 Journal of Cyber Policy 296

Takigawa T., 'Standard-Essential Patents and the Japanese Competition Law in Comparison with China, the U.S. and the EU' (2017) 62 The Antitrust Bulletin 483

Tassey G., 'Standardization in Technology-Based Markets' (2000) 29 Research Policy 587

Taubman A., 'Rethinking TRIPS: "Adequate Remuneration" for Non-Voluntary Patent Licensing' (2008) 11 Journal of International Economic Law 927

Techatassanasoontorn A. A. and Suo S., 'Influences on Standards Adoption in de Facto Standardization' (2011) 12 Information Technology Management 357

Torremans P., 'Compensation for Intellectual Property Infringement: Admissibility of Punitive Damages and Compensation for Moral Prejudice' (2018) 40 European Intellectual Property Review 797

Trappey A. J. C. and others, 'A Review of Essential Standards and Patent Landscapes for the Internet of Things: A Key Enabler for Industry 4.0' (2017) 33 Advanced Engineering Informatics 208

Troy D. E., 'Unclogging the Bottleneck: A New Essential Facility Doctrine' (1983) 83 Columbia Law Review 441

Turney J., 'Defining the Limits of the EU Essential Facilities Doctrine on Intellectual Property Rights: The Primacy of Securing Optimal Innovation' (2005) 3 Northwestern Journal of Technology and Intellectual Property 179

von Lohmann F., 'The New Wave: Copyright and Software Interfaces in the Wake of Oracle v. Google' (2018) 31 Harvard Journal of Law & Technology (Special Issue) 517

Waller S. W., 'National Laws and International Markets: Strategies of Cooperation and Harmonization in the Enforcement of Competition Law' (1996) 18 Cardozo Law Review 1111

'Areeda, Epithets and Essential Facilities' [2008] Wisconsin Law Review 359

Waller S. W. and Tasch W., 'Harmonizing Essential Facilities' (2010) 76 Antitrust Law Journal 741

Walsh M. J., 'Disclosure Requirements of 35 USC 112 and Software-Related Patent Applications: Debugging the System' (1985) 18 Connecticut Law Review 855

Wan Y., 'Copyright Damages in China' (2013) Journal of the Copyright Society of the USA 517

Warlouzet L., 'The EEC/EU as an Evolving Compromise between French Dirigism and German Ordoliberalism (1957–1995)' (2019) 57 JCMS: Journal of Common Market Studies 77

Webb W., 'The Role of Networking Standards in Building the Internet of Things' (2012) 1 Communications & Strategies 57

Werden G. J., 'The Law and Economics of the Essential Facility Doctrine' (1987) 32 St Louis University Law Journal 433

Whinston M. D., 'Tying, Foreclosure, and Exclusion' (1990) 80 The American Economic Review 837

Wiegand T. and Sullivan G. J., 'The H.264/AVC Video Coding Standard [Standards in a Nutshell]' (2007) 24 IEEE Signal Processing Magazine 148

Williamson O. E., 'Symposium on Antitrust Law and Economics: Introduction' (1979) 127 University of Pennsylvania Law Review 918

  'Transactions-Cost Economics: The Governance of Contractual Relations' (1979) 22 Journal of Law and Economics 233

Wilson J., 'The IETF: Laying the Net's Asphalt' (1998) 31 Computer 116

Wong-Ervin K. W., 'An Update on the Most Recent Version of China's Anti-Monopoly Guidelines on the Abuse of Intellectual Property Rights' [2017] Competition Policy International 1

Yarsky J., 'Hastening Harmonization in European Union Patent Law through a Preliminary Reference Power' (2017) 40 Boston College International & Comparative Law Review 167

Wu Y. and Xiong Y., 'Comparison of the Bolar Exception in China and the United States' (2008) 3 China Patents & Trademarks 13

Zhang G., 'Rules for Denying Copyright Permanent Injunctions in China: Fog Needs to Be Cleared Part I' (2015) Journal of the Copyright Society of the USA 341

Zingales N. and Kanevskaia O., 'The IEEE-SA Patent Policy Update under the Lens of EU Competition Law' (2016) 12 European Competition Journal 195, 201–205

Conference Papers

Gilbert R. J. and Shapiro C., 'An Economic Analysis of Unilateral Refusals to Licence Intellectual Property' (1996) 93 Proceedings of the National Academy of Sciences of the United States of America 12749

Goodman D. J. and Myers R. A., '3 G Cellular Standards and Patents', *2005 International Conference on Wireless Networks, Communications and Mobile Computing* (2005)

Laporte C. Y., April A. and Renault A., 'Applying ISO/IEC Software Engineering Standards in Small Settings: Historical Perspectives and Initial Achievements', *Proceedings of the SPICE 2006 Conference, May 4–5, 2006, Luxembourg* (Curran Associates, Inc)

Maathuis I. and Smit W. A., 'The Battle between Standards: TCP/IP vs OSI Victory through Path Dependency or by Quality?', Proceedings of the Third IEEE Conference on Standardization and Innovation in Information Technology (IEEE 2003)

Tan L. and Wang N., 'Future Internet: The Internet of Things', *2010 3rd International Conference on Advanced Computer Theory and Engineering (ICACTE)* (2010)

Tilson D., Lyytinen K. and Sorensen C., 'Desperately Seeking the Infrastructure in IS Research: Conceptualization of "Digital Convergence" As Co-Evolution of Social and Technical Infrastructures', *2010 43rd Hawaii International Conference on System Sciences* (2010)

Waffenschmidt E., 'Wireless Power for Mobile Devices', *2011 IEEE 33rd International Telecommunications Energy Conference (INTELEC)* (2011)

Weitzel T., Wendt O. and Westarp F. V., 'Reconsidering Network Effect Theory', *European Conference on Information Systems Proceedings* (2000)

Encyclopaedia and Dictionary Entries

Blackburn S., *The Oxford Dictionary of Philosophy* (3rd ed., Oxford University Press 2016)

Brinsmead S., 'Delegated Regulation: Normalisation', *Elgar Encyclopaedia of International Economic Law* (Elgar 2017)

Hall B., 'Patents', *The New Palgrave Dictionary of Economics* (2nd ed., Palgrave Macmillan 2008)

'Mobile Air Interface', *Telecommunications Illustrated Dictionary* (2nd ed., CRC Press 2002)

'Modularity', *McGraw-Hill Dictionary of Scientific and Technical Terms* (6th ed., McGraw-Hill 2003)

Parisi F., 'Coase Theorem', *The New Palgrave Dictionary of Economics* (2nd ed., Palgrave Macmillan 2008)

Riffel C., 'Unfair Competition, International Protection', *Max Planck Encyclopaedia of Public International Law* (Oxford University Press)

Oxford English Dictionary (2nd ed., Oxford University Press 1989)

Unpublished Works

Reports

Biddle B., White A. and Woods S., 'How Many Standards in a Laptop? (And Other Empirical Questions)', *2010 ITU-T Kaleidoscope: Beyond the Internet? – Innovations for Future Networks and Services* (2010)

Bornkamm J., 'WIPO Advisory Committee on Enforcement: Intellectual Property Litigation under the Civil Law Legal System; Experience in Germany' (2004) WIPO/ACE/2/3 <www.wipo.int> accessed 24 May 2019

Brown W., Engle M. and Rafert G., 'Independent Review of the ICANN Nominating Committee: Assessment Report' <www.analysisgroup.com> accessed 24 February 2018

'DG Competition Discussion Paper on the Application of Article 82 to Exclusionary Abuses' (European Commission, DG Competition 2005) <http://ec.europa.eu > accessed 8 October 2017

'Exceptions and Limitations to Patent Rights: Compulsory Licences and/or Government Use (Part I)' (World Intellectual Property Organization 2014) SCP/21/4 Rev. <www.wipo.int> accessed 5 August 2017

'Exceptions and Limitations to Patent Rights: Prior Use' (World Intellectual Property Organization 2013) SCP/20/6 <www.wipo.int> accessed 19 September 2017

Japan Fair Trade Commission, 'Guidelines for the Use of Intellectual Property under the Antimonopoly Act (Unofficial Translation)' (Japan Fair Trade Commission 2007, revised 2016) accessed 21 May 2020

'The Guidelines for Exclusionary Private Monopolization under the Antimonopoly Act (Tentative Translation)' (Japan Fair Trade Commission 2009) <www.jftc.go.jp> accessed 24 May 2019

Kruger L. G., 'The Future of Internet Governance: Should the United States Relinquish Its Authority over ICANN?' (Congressional Research Service 2016) accessed 21 May 2020

Motta M. and de Streel A., 'Excessive Pricing in Competition Law: Never Say Never?', *The Pros and Cons of High Prices* (Swedish Competition Authority 2007)

Organization for Economic Co-operation and Development, 'OECD Guidelines for Multinational Enterprises' (OECD Publishing 2011)

'Report on the International Patent System' (World Intellectual Property Organization, Standing Committee on the Law of Patents 2008) SCP/12/3 Rev. <www.wipo.int> accessed 30 June 2019

Schultz M. F. and Lippoldt D. C., 'Approaches to Protection of Undisclosed Information (Trade Secrets): Background Paper' (OECD Publishing 2014) 62

'Standing Committee on the Law of Patents: Exceptions and Limitations to Patent Rights: Experimental Use and/or Scientific Research' (World Intellectual Property Organization 2013) SCP/20/4 <www.wipo.int> accessed 19 January 2018

'Study on Trade Secrets and Confidential Business Information in the Internal Market, Final Study' (European Commission 2013) <http://ec.europa.eu> accessed 26 August 2017

'Survey on Compulsory Licences Granted by WIPO Member States to Address Anti-Competitive Uses of Intellectual Property Right' (World Intellectual Property Organization 2011) CDIP/4/4 Rev./Study/Inf/5 <www.wipo.int> accessed 4 August 2017

'Unilateral Conduct Workbook Chapter 1: The Objectives and Principles of Unilateral Conduct Laws' (International Competition Network 2012) <www.internationalcompetitionnetwork.org> accessed 14 February 2018

United States Department of Justice and the Federal Trade Commission, 'Antitrust Enforcement and Intellectual Property Rights: Promoting Innovation and Competition' (United States Department of Justice and the Federal Trade Commission 2007) <www.ftc.gov> accessed 24 May 2019

World Trade Organization, 'World Trade Report 2005: Exploring the Links between Trade, Standards and the WTO' (World Trade Organization 2005) <www.wto.org> accessed 16 January 2018

'WTO Committee of Participants on the Expansion of Trade in Information Technology Products – Non-Tariff Measures Work Programme' (World Trade Organization 2000) WTO Doc. G/IT/19

'WTO Report (2017) of the Committee of Participants on the Expansion of Trade in Information Technology Products' (World Trade Organization 2017) WTO Doc. G/L/1200

Research Papers

Baron J. and others, 'Making the Rules: The Governance of Standard Development Organizations and Their Policies on Intellectual Property Rights' (2019) JRC 115004 <https://ec.europa.eu/jrc> accessed 16 May 2020

Bekkers R. and Updegrove A., 'IPR Policies and Practices of a Representative Group of Standards Setting Organizations Worldwide' (2013) <nap.edu> accessed 25 May 2020

Contreras J. L., 'A New Perspective on FRAND Royalties: Unwired Planet v Huawei' (2017) <https://dc.law.utah.edu> accessed 16 February 2018

Evans D. S., Zhang V. Y. and Zhang X., 'Assessing Unfair Pricing under China's Anti-Monopoly Law for Innovation-Intensive Industries' (University of Chicago 2014) 687 <https://chicagounbound.uchicago.edu> accessed 21 May 2019

Fliess B. A. and Sauve P., 'Of Chips, Floppy Disks and Great Timing: Assessing the Information Technology Agreement', *Paper Prepared for the Institute Francais des Relations Internationales (IFRI) and the Tokyo Club Foundation for Global Studies* (1997)

Larouche P. and Zingales N., 'Injunctive Relief in FRAND Disputes in the EU? Intellectual Property and Competition Law at the Remedies Stage' (Tilburg Law School 2017) No. 1 of 2017 <https://papers.ssrn.com> accessed 9 February 2018

Makiyama R. S. and H.-L., 'Whither Global Rules for the Internet? The Implications of the World Conference on International Telecommunication for International Trade' (ECIPE Policy Briefs 2012) 12/2012 <www.econstor.eu> accessed 20 May 2019

McGowan D., 'The Apportionment Problem in Copyright Law' (University of San Diego School of Law 2017) 17–307 <www.ssrn.com> accessed 2 May 2020

Siebrasse N. V. and others, 'Injunctive Relief' <https://scholar.smu.edu> accessed 10 May 2019

Magazine Articles

'A Brief History of Wi-Fi' [2004] *The Economist* <www.economist.com> accessed 10 March 2018

Raustiala K., 'An Internet Whole and Free: Why Washington Was Right to Give up Control Essays' (2017) 96 Foreign Affairs 14

Briefs to Courts

Microsoft Corporation, 'Supreme Court, Google v. Oracle: Brief of Microsoft Corporation as Amicus Curiae in Support of Petitioner' (2019) <https://supremecourt.gov> accessed 22 June 2020.

Theses

Aarnio T., 'Near Field Communication: Using NFC to Unlock Doors' (Master's Thesis, Aalto University 2013)

Media Releases

European Commission, 'Antitrust: Commission Closes Formal Proceedings against Qualcomm' (24 November 2009) <http://europa.eu/rapid/press-release> accessed 29 November 2017

'Partial Amendment of Guidelines for the Use of Intellectual Property under the Antimonopoly Act (Tentative Translation)' <www.jftc.go.jp> accessed 21 January 2018

Letters

Hesse, Renata B., Response to Electrical and Electronics Engineers Request for Business Review, 2 February 2015 <www.justice.gov> accessed 20 June 2020

Websites and Other Internet Materials

'About ETSI' (*ETSI*) <www.etsi.org/about> accessed 9 March 2018

'About JEDEC' (*JEDEC*) <www.jedec.org/about-jedec> accessed 9 March 2018

'About Mobile Technology and IMT-2000' (*International Telecommunication Union*) <www.itu.int> accessed 8 March 2018

BIBLIOGRAPHY

Alvestrand H., 'A Mission Statement for the IETF' (29 April 2004) <https://tools.ietf.org> accessed 30 November 2017

Band J., 'Interfaces on Trial 3.0' (2019) <www.policybandwidth.com/interfaces-2-0> accessed 4 March 2020F

Bradner S., 'IETF Working Group Guidelines and Procedures' <https://tools.ietf.org> accessed 6 December 2017

'Developing ISO Standards' (*International Organization for Standardization*) <www.iso.org> accessed 22 July 2016

'General Info' (*Blu-ray Disc*) <www.blu-raydisc.com> accessed 10 March 2018

'History of IEEE' (*IEEE*) <www.ieee.org> accessed 9 March 2018

'ICN Factsheet and Key Messages' (*International Competition Network*, April 2009) <www.internationalcompetitionnetwork.org> accessed 9 February 2018

'IEEE at a Glance' (*IEEE*) <www.ieee.org> accessed 8 March 2018

'IEEE Standards Association Study Group Guidelines' <http://standards.ieee.org> accessed 6 December 2017

'International Organization for Standardization Website' <www.iso.org/standards.html> accessed 30 November 2017

Internet Corporation for Assigned Names and Numbers, 'Bylaws for Internet Corporation for Assigned Names and Numbers' (*ICANN*, 22 July 2017) <www.icann.org/resources/pages/governance/bylaws-en> accessed 25 February 2018

   'Amended and Restated Articles of Incorporation of Internet Corporation for Assigned Names and Numbers' (*ICANN*) <www.icann.org/> accessed 24 February 2018

   'Beginner's Guide to Participating in ICANN' (*ICANN*) <www.icann.org> accessed 24 February 2018

'ISO Membership Manual' (International Organization for Standardization 2015) <www.iso.org> accessed 8 March 2018

'ISO/IEC Directives Part 1: Procedures for the Technical Work' (2016) <www.iec.ch> accessed 30 November 2017

'ISO/IEC Guide 2:2004 Standardization and Related Activities – General Vocabulary' <www.iso.org/standard/39976.html> accessed 30 November 2017

'ISO/IEC Guide 59: 1994 Code of Good Practice for Standardization' <www.iso.org/standard/23390.html> accessed 20 May 2019

'ITU-T Study Groups (Study Period 2017–2020)' (*International Telecommunication Union*) <www.itu.int> accessed 12 March 2018

Kerr S., 'IETF Support for IPv6 Deployment' (*IETF Journal*, 7 October 2007) <www.ietfjournal.org/ietf-support-for-ipv6-deployment/> accessed 8 March 2018

'Membership Categories' (*International Telecommunication Union*) <www.itu> accessed 8 March 2018

'OECD' (*OECD*) <www.oecd.org/> accessed 14 March 2018

'Our History' (*Bluetooth*) <www.bluetooth.com/about-us/our-history> accessed 9 March 2018

'Popular Standards' (*International Organization for Standardization*) <www.iso.org/popular-standards.html> accessed 8 March 2018

'Specifications' (*Bluetooth*) <www.bluetooth.com/specifications> accessed 25 January 2018

'Submitting a Project Request' (*IEEE Standards Association – Developing Standards*) <https://standards.ieee.org/develop/par.html> accessed 21 July 2016

'The Framework of ITU-T' (*International Telecommunication Union*) <www.itu.int/en/ITU-T/about/Pages/framework.aspx> accessed 8 March 2018

'The Tao of the IETF: A Novice's Guide to the Internet Engineering Task Force' <www.ietf.org/tao.html> accessed 30 November 2017

'Unilateral Conduct' <www.internationalcompetitionnetwork.org> accessed 9 February 2018

INDEX

3GPP. *See* Third Generation Partnership Project
802.11. *See* Wireless Local Area Network standards

Advanced Mobile Phone System, 32
air interface. *See* mobile wireless standards
Alice v. CLS Bank International case, 112–13
Allnut v. Inglis case, 159
AMPS. *See* Advanced Mobile Phone System
Apple, 9, 131–3, 202, 203, 206–8, 336
Apple v. Microsoft case, 81, 131–3
Apple v. Motorola case, 9, 206–9, 210, 211, 283, 336, 338
Areeda, Phillip, 170–1, 173, 179, 284
ARPANET, 31
Associated Press case, 164–5

Baran, Paul, 30
BellSouth v. Donnelley case, 6, 81, 136–7, 334
Berne Convention for the Protection of Literary and Artistic Works, 55, 57, 65, 66, 67, 316, 325–7, 329
Betamax, 27–8
Bluetooth Alliance, 43, 46
Blu-Ray Disc Association, 43
Bolt v. Stennett case, 159
Broadcom v. Qualcomm case, 218–19
Bronner case, 192, 338

Calabresi and Melamed framework, 258–9, 278, 340–1
Calabresi, Guido, 13, 233, 234–7, 240, 244, 245, 259, 278, 340, 341

Canada – Pharmaceuticals case, 66–7, 318, 319–20
CDMA. *See* Code Division Multiple Access
Cerf, Vinton, 30
Chicago school, 193, 195–6, 253–4, 284, 285
Coase theorem, 233–4
Code Division Multiple Access, 33
collective action problem, 10, 281–2
collective rights organizations, 85, 93, 155, 223, 239–40, 252, 275, 299, 354
Commercial Solvents case, 152, 153, 178–9, 277
compatibility, 22, 23
compulsory licensing, 100, 106, 150–4, 241, 283
  European law, 152–4
  liability rules, 276–7
  other countries' laws, 154
  TRIPS Agreement, 69, 315, 324–5, 329
  United States law, 151–2
Computer Associates v. Altai case, 81, 123–4, 126, 128, 130, 131, 133, 135
computer programmes, copyrightability, 57
computer programmes, patentability, 56
Consultative Committee for International Telephony and Telegraphy, 31
copyright
  compilations of data, 135–40
  compulsory licensing, 329
  computer programmes, 57, 121–35
  fair use, 124–5, 130, 339

395

copyright (cont.)
    idea/expression dichotomy, 6, 61, 121, 123, 126, 127–8, 129, 132–3, 310, 339, 349
    merger doctrine, 123, 137, 310, 339, 349
    originality, 6, 61, 120, 133, 134, 135, 136–7
    remedies, 140–7
    reverse engineering, 124–5
    right of reproduction, 325–7
    scènes à faire, 123, 339
    standards essential, 118–21, 349
    three step test, 66–8, 327–9
Cotter, Thomas, 243–4, 253
Cournot complements, 91, 95, 236, 243, 257, 261, 263, 311, 318, 319, 333, 342, 344, 347, 352
CRO. *See* collective rights organization

DARPA. *See* Defence Advanced Research Projects Agency
David, Paul A., 19, 21, 25, 26–7
de facto standards, 19
De Portibus Maris, 158–9
Declaration on a Balanced Interpretation of the Three-Step Test, 68
Defence Advanced Research Projects Agency, 30
defences, patent infringement
    fair use, 100
    prior use, 97–8
    scientific research and experiment, 98–9
dominant market position, abuse of, 5, 65, 95, 173, 174, 177–90, 203–12, 213–14, 219–20, 284, 338
double essentiality, 94–6, 311, 313, 352
DRAM. *See* Dynamic Random Access Memory
Dynamic Random Access Memory, 43, 217, 219–20

eBay v. MercExchange case, 9, 96, 101–4, 141, 283, 311, 338–9, 340

EC *Rambus* case, 219–20
ECPR. *See* efficient component pricing rule
efficient component pricing rule, 266
essential facilities doctrine, 336–8
    arguments for revival American law, 172–3
    Chinese law, 190–1
    criticisms, 337
    criticisms in American law, 169–71
    demise in American law, 171–2
    development in American law, 159–69
    development in European law, 178–82
    European law, intellectual property and interoperability standards, 182–90
    interoperability standards and intellectual property, 191–3
    origins in English law, 158–9
    origins in European law, 174–8
essential facilities doctrine, law and economics, 193–201
    court supervision of supply, 197–8
    dynamic efficiency, 198–201
    efficient investment in new facilities, 196–7
    incentives to supply, 195–6
    limitations on right to refuse supply, 194–5
    monopoly and consumer welfare, 194
    SEIP as an essential facility, 193–4
ETSI. *See* European Telecommunications Standards Institute
EU Database Directive, 137–8
EU Enforcement Directive, 104–5, 109, 141, 146, 205
EU *Microsoft* case, 5–6, 53, 149–50, 153, 156, 178, 182–3, 185–90, 198, 199–201, 222, 277, 283, 334, 337, 338
EU Software Directive, 125–6, 134, 146
European Coal and Steel Community, 174, 176

INDEX 397

European Economic Community,
  176, 178
European Telecommunications
  Standards Institute, 32, 33, 35,
  42, 85, 87, 91, 102, 204, 206, 209,
  271, 272, 290
excessive pricing, 212–15
  Chinese law, 214–15
  European law, 213–14
exclusive property rules and liability
  rules. *See* liability rules
expert manual, 10, 299–301, 345–6
  expertise, 306
  proposed contents, 309–13
  purpose and structure, 308–9
  representative group, 306
  robust and transparent process,
  306–8
expert manual, draft
  calculation of compensation, 353–4
  competition law, 354–5
  injunctions, 351–2
  interpretation, 348
  standard setting organizations,
  349–51
  standards essential copyright, 349
  standards essential patents, 348–9

fair, reasonable and non-
  discriminatory. *See* FRAND
  undertaking
Federal Trade Commission Act,
  202, 216
Feist v. Rural Telephone Service
  case, 135
FRAND. *See* FRAND undertaking
FRAND undertaking, 9, 65, 93, 95–6,
  101, 155, 192, 202, 229, 282, 284,
  310, 311, 320, 321, 335, 339
  and competition law, 203–12,
  213–14, 338
  and contract law, 88–9
  and fraud or misconduct, 223
  and injunctions, 101–4, 106,
  339
  and liability rules, 251–2, 262–3
  and reasonable royalties, 110–11,
  265–76

legal nature, 87–8
Frischmann, Brett, 172–3

Gerardin, Damien, 255
Global System for Mobile
  Communications, 32
Google, 44, 128–31, 134, 143–5, 280
Granger cases, 160–1
GSM. *See* Global System for Mobile
  Communications

Hale, Lord Matthew, 158–9
Havana Charter, 76, 285
hold-up, 9, 90, 122, 142, 156, 243,
  248–50, 252, 258, 274, 275, 310,
  311, 321, 325, 336, 352
horizontal conduct, 223–8
  Chinese law, 225
  European law, 225–7
  United States law, 223–4
Huawei, 106, 204–6, 213–14, 271–2
Huawei v. Unwired Planet case, 213–14,
  271, 280
Huawei v. ZTE case, 153, 182, 192,
  203–6, 210, 211, 277, 283, 343

ICN. *See* International Competition
  Network
idea/expression dichotomy
  TRIPS Agreement, 61
IEC. *See* International Electronic
  Commission
IEEE. *See* Institute for Electrical and
  Electronics Engineers
IEEE Standards Association, 307
IETF. *See* Internet Engineering Task
  Force
IMS Health case, 7, 81, 138–40, 153,
  182, 184–5, 189, 192, 199–201,
  260, 277, 283, 328, 334, 338
IMT-2000. *See* International Mobile
  Telecommunications for
  the Year 2000
information infrastructure, 16
injunction
  Chinese law, 105–7, 141–2
  competition law, 201–12
  copyright, 140–2

injunction (cont.)
  draft expert manual, 351–2
  European law, 9, 104–5, 141
  expert manual, 310–12
  German law, 9, 105, 138, 206–7
  law and economics, 261–3
  patent, 101–7
  TRIPS Agreement, 201–12, 325–32
  United States law, 8–9, 101–4, 140–1
Innovatio case, 269–70
Institute of Electrical and Electronics Engineers, 29, 31, 35, 36–7, 41, 45, 49, 224, 267, 269, 290, 307
intellectual property
  law and economics, 4, 81–3
intellectual property, standards essential
  circuit layouts, 148
  compulsory licensing, 150–4
  concept, 81
  copyright, 118–47
  patents, 84–118
  trade secrets, 148–50
interface, 20, 22, 23, 119–20
  application programming, 186
  copyright protection, 140, 142, 147, 251, 327–8, 334
  mobile air, 32
interface, mobile air, 32
interfaces
  copyright protection, 175–96
international competition law, 75–7, 345
International Competition Network, 77, 293–5, 305
International Electrotechnical Commission, 17, 29, 35, 40
International Mobile Telecommunications for the Year 2000, 33
International Organization for Standardization, 17, 18, 29, 35, 39–40, 45, 46–7, 119, 289–90, 302, 303–4
International Packet Network Working Group, 30

international soft law, 286–8, 313
International Telecommunication Union, 31, 33, 35, 36, 37–9, 40, 45, 290–1
Internet Corporation for Assigned Names and Numbers, 297–8, 305, 346
Internet Engineering Task Force, 35, 41–2, 46, 290, 307–8, *See* IETF
Internet of Things, 17, 35–6, 333
interoperability, 23
interoperability standard
  definition, 21–5
  importance, 16–17
  language as, 25–6
interoperability standards
  economic characteristics, 4, 48–53
  importance, 3
  methods of creation, 44–8
  typologies, 19–21
INWG. *See* International Packet Network Working Group
ISO. *See* International Organization for Standardization
ISO/IEC Guide 59/1994, Code of Good Practice for Standardization, 39–40, 290, 302, 350
ITU. *See* International Telecommunication Union

Japan *Samsung v. Apple* case, 272–3
JEDEC. *See* Joint Electron Device Engineering Council
JEDEC Solid State Technology Association, 43
Joint Electron Device Engineering Council, 217
Joint Technical Committee 1, 40
JTC 1. *See* Joint Technical Committee 1

Kahn, Robert, 30
keyboard configuration, QWERTY, 27

law and economics, 9–10, 157–8, 289, 309, 341, 344
  Coase theorem, 233–4

essential facilities doctrine, 169–71, 193–201, 228–9
excessive pricing, 212
intellectual property, 81–3
liability rules, 234–44
　compulsory licensing, 258–61
　essential facilities doctrine, 278
　injunctions, 261–3
　reasonable royalty, 265–76
　refusal to supply, 258–61
　standards essential intellectual property, 244–58
　tying, 222–3
layout circuit designs, 148
Lemley, 90
Lemley, Mark, 91, 93–4, 118, 240, 241–3, 253, 256, 258, 259, 265
liability rules, 3, 9, 13, 142, 148
　Calabresi and Melamed framework, 234–9
　competition law, 278
　damages, 263–5
　injunctions, 261–3
　reasonable royalties, 265–76
　refusal to supply, 258–61
　standards essential intellectual property, 239–58, 341–4
Long-Term Evolution, 33
Lotus v. Borland Software case, 131, 133–4
LTE. *See* Long-Term Evolution

Magill case, 6, 153, 182, 183–4, 186, 188, 189, 192, 199–201, 260, 277, 283, 328, 338
markets, two-sided, 52–3
MCI Communications case, 167–9
Melamed, A. Douglas, 13, 233, 234–7, 240, 244, 245, 259, 278, 340, 341
Mentor Graphics v. EVE-USA case, 108–9
Merges, Robert, 239–40, 277
methodology, 10–14, 59
methodology, topical, 10–14, 104, 110, 143, 147, 257, 261, 338, 344

Microsoft, 5–6, 23, 44, 52, 53, 81, 110, 115, 131–3, 149–50, 151–2, 153, 154, 156, 178, 182–3, 185–90, 198, 201, 221–2, 260, 267–9, 334, 341
Microsoft v. Motorola case, 110, 267–9
Mobile Payment Forum, 43
mobile payment standards, 34–5
mobile wireless standards, 32–3, 49, 85, 87, 91–2, 94–5, 204, 206–8, 272–3
modularity, 24, 240
Motorola, 94–5, 102, 110, 202, 203, 206–8, 209, 267–9, 280, 336
multistakeholderism, 296–8, 299, 302, 303, 305, 346
Munn v. Illinois case, 159–60

National Institute of Standards and Technology, 31
Neale, A.D., 167
near field communications, 33
Neo-Chicago school, 190
network effects, 20–1, 25, 28, 32, 44, 50–2, 72, 94, 132, 134, 135, 140, 145, 155, 186, 201, 222, 247–8, 256, 264, 333, 335, 336
　direct, 50–1
　indirect, 50–1
NFC. *See* near field communications
NIST. *See* National Institute of Standards and Technology
Noerr-Pennington doctrine, 202–3, 210

OECD. *See* Organization for Economic Co-operation and Development
Open Systems Interconnection, 32, 303–4
Oracle, 134, 143–5
Oracle v. Google case, 123, 128–31, 143–5, 147, 263, 334, 340, 342
ordoliberalism, 175–8, 193, 285
Organization for Economic Co-operation and Development, 77, 295–6
Oscar Bronner case, 180–2
OSI. *See* Open Systems Interconnection
Otter Tail case, 166–7

INDEX

Paris Convention for the Protection of Industrial Property, 55, 56, 69, 330
  Article 10*bis*, 59–61
patent assertion entities, 96–7, 253–4
patent holdup, 333, 336, 342
patents
  compulsory licensing, 69
  disclosure requirements, 58
patents, standards essential
  and computer programmes, 111–18
  and standard setting organizations, 86–9
  concept, 84–6
  defences to infringement, 97–100
  disclosure requirements, 125,
  double essentiality, 94–6
  hold up, 90
  patent assertion entities, 96–7
  patent pools, 92–3
  remedies, 100–11
  royalty stacking, 91–2
  undertakings to license, 87–9
  voluntary price commitments, 93
path dependence, 27, 32, 140
platform, 24–5, 51–3, 129, 145, 221
platform, Java, 128–9, 145
positive feedback, 4, 44, 247
Post-Chicago school, 195–6, 253–4, 284
price commitments, voluntary, 93
private transnational rulemaking, 298–301, 304, 305
protocol, 22, 23, 149, 150, 152, 155, 156, 260, 298–301, 334
  Transmission Control Protocol/Internet Protocol, 29–32
  Wireless Local Area Network, 28

Qualcomm, 191, 214–15, 218–19, 220, 222, 270
Qualcomm case, 191, 214–15, 222
QWERTY. *See* keyboard configuration, QWERTY

Rambus, 216–18, 219–20
Rambus v. FTC case, 216–18
RAND. *See* FRAND undertaking

reasonable and non-discriminatory. *See* FRAND undertaking
remedies, copyright infringement
  account of profits, 143–5, 146
  injunction, 140–2
  lost profits, 143, 146, 147
remedies, patent infringement
  account of profits, 109
  injunction, 101–7
  lost profits, 107–9
  reasonable royalties, 109–11
request for injunction in competition law, 201–12
  Chinese law, 209
  European law, 203–9
  law and economics, 209–12
  United States law, 202–3
Rome Convention for the Protection of Performers, Producers of Phonograms and Broadcasting Organizations, 55
rough consensus, 448–49,
royalty stacking, 333, 336, 342

SAS Institute v. World Programming Limited case, 126–8
Sea Containers v. Stena Sealink case, 179–80
Sega v. Accolade case, 81, 124–5, 128, 129, 130, 131, 260, 334, 335
SEIP. *See* intellectual property, standards essential
SEIP, liability rules
  calculation of damages, 263–5
  collective rights organizations, 252
  component patents, 250–1
  compulsory licensing, 276–7
  conclusions, 257–8
  Cournot complements, 246–8
  cross-licensing, 253–4
  dynamic efficiency, 254–5
  existing scholarship, 239–44
  holdup, 248–50
  incentives to license, 253–4
  injunctions, 261–3
  patent assertion entities, 253–4
  reasonable royalties, 265–76

transaction and assessment costs, 255–7
undertakings to license, 251–2
unilateral disciplines, 278
SEIP, liability rules, 244–5
SEP. *See* patents, standard essential
Shapiro, Carl, 90, 91, 93–4, 241–2, 253, 256, 265–6
Shapley value, 267, 268, 274, 276
Sherman Act, 165, 166, 167, 168, 202, 217, 221, 223, 224
single monopoly profit theorem, 170, 192, 196, 284, 337
SSO. *See* standard setting organization
standalone forum, 296–301, 303–5
standard
 definition, 17–19
standards essential copyright
 calculation of damages, 142–7
 compilations of data, 135–40
 computer user interfaces, 131–5
 concept, 118–21
 injunctions, 140–2
 software-software interfaces, 122–31
standards, de facto, 44, 119–20, 143, 309
standards, formal, 19, 119, 263
standards, misconduct in the creation of, 215–21
 American law, 216–19
 European law, 219–20
standards, quality, 19–20
standards, reference, 19–20
standards, variety reduction, 19–20

Tallinn Manual on the International Law Applicable to Cyber Operations, 300–1, 307
Tariff Act 1930, 103, 339
TBT Agreement. *See* Agreement on Trade-Related Aspects of Intellectual Property Rights
TBT Code of Good Practice, 47, 69, 70–1, 290, 302, 350
TBT Committee. *See* WTO Technical Barriers to Trade Committee
TCP/IP. *See* Transmission Control Protocol/Internet Protocol

TDMA. *See* Time Division Multiple Access
Terminal Railroad case, 161–4
Third Generation Partnership Project, 33
three-step test, 65–8, 318–24, 327–9
 certain special cases, 327–8
 limited exceptions, 318–19
 no conflict with normal exploitation, 328–9
 no unreasonable prejudice to legitimate interests, 329
 unreasonable conflict with normal exploitation, 319–22
 unreasonable prejudice to legitimate interests, 322–4
Time Division Multiple Access, 32
tipping, 4, 32, 44, 247
topoi, 11, 12, 14
trade secrets, 148–50
transaction costs, 233–4, 235, 236, 237–8, 239–40, 241, 245, 252, 255, 256, 287
Transmission Control Protocol/Internet Protocol, 32, 42
Trinko case, 338
TRIPS. *See* Agreement on Trade-Related Aspects of Intellectual Property Rights
TRIPS Agreement. *See* Agreement on Trade-Related Aspects of Intellectual Property Rights
tying, 221–3

UMTS. *See* Universal Mobile Telecommunications System
unfair competition, protection against, 59–61, 136, 154, 330
United States – Section 110 of the Copyright Act case, 67, 323–4, 327
United States International Trade Commission, 103, 272
Universal Mobile Telecommunications System, 33, 272

US *Microsoft* case, 149, 151–2, 221–2
USITC. *See* United States International Trade Commission

VHS, 27–8
Viehweg, Theodor, 10

Waller, Spencer Webber, 172–3
Washington Treaty on Intellectual Property in Respect of Integrated Circuits, 55, 329–30
W-CDMA. *See* Wideband Code Division Multiple Access
Wideband Code Division Multiple Access, 33, 85
Wi-Fi. *See* Wireless Local Area Network standards
Wi-Fi Alliance, 28
WIPO. *See* World Intellectual Property Organization
WIPO Copyright Treaty, 57, 329
Wireless Local Area Network standards, 85, 110, 134–5, 267–71, 335
WLAN. *See* Wireless Local Area Network standards
World Intellectual Property Organization, 57, 120, 285, 291–2, 302, 305, 346
World Trade Organization, 47, 76–7, 292–3, 302, 305, 346
WTO. *See* World Trade Organization

WTO Agreement on Technical Barriers to Trade, 18, 69–72, 290, 292, 350
WTO Agreement on Trade-Related Aspects of Intellectual Property Rights, 54–69, 313–32
  compulsory licensing, 69, 329
  copyrights, 325–9
  enforcement, 331
  flexibilities, 62–9
  layout circuits, 329–30
  maximum standards, 57–61
  minimum standards, 54–7
  objectives and principles, 62–4
  three step tests, 65–8, 318–24, 327–9
  trade secrets, 330
WTO Committee of Participants on the Expansion of Trade in Information Technology Products, 292–3
WTO Doha Ministerial Declaration of 20 November 2001, 76
WTO Information Technology Agreement, 74–5, 293
WTO Technical Barriers to Trade Committee, 47–8
WTO Telecommunications Agreement, 72–4
  GATS Annex on Telecommunications, 73
  Telecommunications Reference Paper, 73–4

For EU product safety concerns, contact us at Calle de José Abascal, 56–1º,
28003 Madrid, Spain or eugpsr@cambridge.org.

www.ingramcontent.com/pod-product-compliance
Lightning Source LLC
LaVergne TN
LVHW011754060526
838200LV00053B/3600